Game Theory for Political Scientists

Game Theory for Political Scientists

James D. Morrow

Princeton University Press Princeton, New Jersey

Published by Princeton University Press, 41 William Street,
Princeton, New Jersey 08540
In the United Kingdom: Princeton University Press, Chichester, West Sussex

Library of Congress Cataloging-in-Publication Data

Morrow, James D., 1957–
Game theory for political scientists / James D. Morrow.
p. cm.
Includes bibliographical references and index.
ISBN: 0-691-03430-3 (cl)
1. Political science—Methodology. 2. Game theory. I. Title.
JA73.M67 1994 320′.01′5193—dc20 94-9256 CIP

This book has been composed in Times Roman

Princeton University Press books are printed on acid-free paper and meet the guidelines for permanence and durability of the Committee on Production Guidelines for Book Longevity of the Council on Library Resources

Printed in the United States of America

4 5 6 7 8 9 10

To the memory of William H. Riker

CONTENTS

LIST OF FIGURES AND TABLES

Figures

Tables

PREFACE AND ACKNOWLEDGMENTS

This book strives to give the political scientist a thorough and careful introduction to the essential ideas of game theory without requiring an extensive mathematical background. The objective is for readers to be able to solve their own models. I hope that readers will achieve an understanding of the basic concepts of game theory, the ability to solve games, and some knowledge of the basic models used in political science.

A broad and noble objective having been set, reality now impinges in a series of qualifications. First, game theory is now an immense subject that cannot be covered in one book. I cover in detail noncooperative analysis of games in the extensive form. This type of analysis now dominates the application of game theory in political science. I also cover the basics of strategic-form analysis of games, as well as utility theory. I have chosen to emphasize extensive-form analysis for three reasons. First, the sources on noncooperative game theory are written primarily for economists and consequently demand a stronger background in mathematics than most political scientists possess, whereas good, accessible treatments of classical game theory exist. Second, extensive-form analysis is becoming the essential tool of formal analysis in political science. Third, extensive-form analysis is, at its heart, more intuitive than classical analysis and thus often easier to grasp. For those who wish more detail about classical game theory, I have provided citations in the Further Reading section of each chapter.

This book was developed from a course on game theory for social scientists that I have taught since 1986 in the Inter-University Consortium for Political and Social Research (ICPSR) Summer Program at the University of Michigan. I wrote a set of notes for that course because there was no acceptable text then. I revised those notes over time on the basis of what worked and did not work in the classroom. The reader is the beneficiary of the work of many other students.

I would like to thank the many people I am indebted to for help in the development of this book. Hank Heitowit of the ICPSR Summer Program repeatedly gave me the opportunity to teach game theory. Without that teaching experience and Hank's encouragement, this book would not exist. Bill Zimmerman and Ken Organski of the Center for Political Studies at the University of Michigan provided me with office space during my visits to Ann Arbor to teach. Peter Barsoom, Bruce Bueno de Mesquita, David Dessler, David Epstein, Jim Fearon, Hein Goemans, David LeBlang, Bob Powell,

Albert Yoon, and Frank Zagare read and commented on the manuscript as it developed. The reviewers for Princeton University Press, Jeff Banks, Tom Gilligan, Mark Hansen, Bob Keohane, and Howard Rosenthal, provided detailed and perceptive comments on the draft manuscript. Without their careful assistance, I would have stumbled into many errors. My wife, Karen, provided love and encouragement even after bad days of writing and rewriting.

This book has been shaped by two groups of people, my teachers and my students. My teachers exposed me to formal theory in political science and gave me the discipline and knowledge needed to apply game theory to understand politics. My students impressed on me the importance of making game theory accessible to all those who were interested and pushed me to write a book that would open up the field to them. I thank them all.

This book is dedicated to an extraordinary teacher and man, the late William H. Riker. Bill transformed political science; without his work and vision, this book could not be imagined. He inspired his students to seek the truth and possessed the uncommon humanity to see the intellectual value within each and every one of his students. He nurtured our abilities so that we could achieve the scientific contribution of which each was capable. I hope this book helps others understand some of his vision of a science of politics.

Game Theory for Political Scientists

Chapter One
Overview

Strategy is the essence of politics; a nonstrategic politician cannot achieve his or her aims. The political scientist who has neither the time, the training, nor the inclination for strategic thought will be poorly equipped to understand the strategic twists and turns of politics. Candidates compete to win office in elections. After electoral campaigns in multiparty democracies, political parties strive to form governments. Legislators contend to advance their own legislation and block bills they oppose. Legislatures oversee executive agencies to verify that the bureaucrats carry out the intent of the laws they pass. National leaders vie to prevail in international crises, while also trying to avoid war. Nations raise and lower barriers to trade in order to influence other nations to lower their own trade barriers. All of these situations, and many others in politics, are strategic. Actions are taken to influence other actors' choices; no one actor alone can determine the outcome of the situation. All actors must think about what the other actors will do when choosing their own actions.

What Is Game Theory?

Strategic situations are a subgroup of social situations. Social situations involve the interaction of individuals; to study and understand social situations, we need a theory that explains how individuals' decisions are interrelated and how those decisions result in outcomes. Game theory is one such theory. It is a theory of interdependent decisions—when the decisions of two or more individuals jointly determine the outcome of a situation. The "individuals" can be persons or collective entities that make consistent choices.

Individuals' choices are also shaped by their social settings, which social scientists often call "structure." "Structure" ranges from the factors that produce the consequences of decisions, such as military capabilities in international politics, to whether people even believe that they have choices. Game theory provides a way to formalize social structures and examine the effects of structure on individual decisions. To specify the structure of a game, we must specify what choices the players face, how those choices lead to outcomes, and how the actors evaluate those outcomes. Those choices of game structure capture different social theories. If one of the themes of this book is that individual choices depend upon the choices of others, how the choice of game structure captures competing social theories is the second theme. Game theory cannot tell us whether certain theories are accurate descriptions of the world, but it can tell us what behavior we should expect as a consequence of those theories.

Game theory can model economic, political, or more general social situations. Economic situations include markets where the choices of many affect prices for all, oligopolistic competition where the marketing decisions of a few firms affect prices, and bargaining between two or more buyers and sellers. Political situations could be electoral competition among candidates, legislative voting in committees, and international bargaining in world politics. Social situations cover the range of group interactions in different settings. This book focuses on political settings as illustrations because it is written for political scientists. However, the techniques described are relevant for a broad range of social interactions.

What Can You Do with Game Theory?

Game theory began in the 1920s with the Minmax Theorem, the first statement of the basic solution of a situation of pure conflict, a two-person, zero-sum game. The early developments were collected into a coherent body of mathematical theory and published in 1943 by Von Neumann and Morgenstern in *Theory of Games and Economic Behavior*. That book became an instant classic and triggered an explosion of interest in game theory among mathematicians and economists. Von Neumann and Morgenstern produced the basics of classical game theory—how to solve two-person, zero-sum games and the classical approach to n-person games (i.e., games with more than two players).

With the explosion of government funding for the social sciences after World War II in the United States, game theory flowered as a field. In the decade between 1945 and 1955, game theory matured both in its basic mathematics and in its application to social and military situations. Many of the basic mathematical tools of game theory were developed during this period, and the applications of game theory to social situations helped to feed these developments. In a sense, this period was a golden age of game theory; after the mid-1950s, the field divided into mathematicians and social scientists as the mathematics became more technical and the applications less cutting-edge.

After the division of the field, the application of game theory to social situations became common. In economics, much of the basic theory has been recast in game-theoretic terms. For example, general equilibrium theory, which examines the properties of whole economies in equilibrium, relies on n-person game theory. This spread of application occurred during the 1960s and 1970s. At the same time, the performance of game theory lagged behind its promise. Many became convinced the theory could not produce what it had promised in its early days and that game theory was inadequate to answer most central questions in the social sciences. Outside of economics, game theory became more of a curio than a central methodology in the social sciences.

Game theory has changed fundamentally to address some of its weaknesses. It now has answers to many questions of interest to all social scientists. Formal developments in the concept of equilibrium have pushed game theory in ways not anticipated during its first flowering. These developments, known as noncooperative game theory, have been driven by substantive problems in the social sciences. The purpose of this book is to introduce the political scientist both to the traditional basis of game theory and to recent developments in noncooperative game theory with an eye to acquiring a competency to work with both.

Now more than ever, the tools exist to address formally many questions that are central to political science. Noncooperative game theory has been applied to both two-party and multiparty elections, legislative decisions, bureaucratic politics, international crises, and international organizations. General questions of how political institutions work and why they exist and change have been addressed with game-theoretic models. Communication in a variety of settings has been examined in these models.

This book also attempts to introduce the reader to many of the basic models in political science. Many journal articles are difficult to read without the proper training and an extensive background in the field. Nevertheless, the ideas in those articles can often be expressed in simpler models that are accessible to a wider audience. Several of the basic models used in political science are interwoven throughout this book. The reader can see how those models develop as different techniques are applied to them.

Four Problems in Political Science

This book pays special attention to four problems in political science: the role of legislative rules, deterrence in international crises, voting in mass elections, and bargaining. What is the strategic logic of each of these situations? There is no single correct model of any of these problems; instead, theory advances through sequences of models. Some models strive to answer questions presented by earlier models; other subsequent models address different aspects of problems. This book presents several models of each of these problems in separate chapters. You, the reader, can see how work on these four problems has developed. I discuss these four problems in general terms here to lay the groundwork for the models that follow. The book also presents models from areas other than these four, but these four recur in the book.

Legislatures adopt rules to regulate how bills are proposed and considered. In the U.S. Congress, the committee system regulates how bills are proposed, revised, and finally voted on. The common empirical observation is that committees and the chairs of committees have disproportionate influence on the shaping and adoption of legislation. Particular voting rules help protect the influence of committees. Why would a legislature adopt rules that appear to give some members disproportionate influence in an area of policy?

I present three different models of congressional rules that capture different arguments about why rules are adopted and what the consequences of those rules are. The first argument claims that the committee system is a way to enforce deals that support pork-barrel legislation across members of Congress. Members seek positions on committees that address issues of particular interest to their constituencies. On the floor, they defer to committees to support implicit bargains that protect legislation that addresses their particular interests. Legislative rules are adopted to help protect bills proposed by committees from amendments. The sections on structure-induced equilibria in Chapter Five develop this argument.

I also discuss a second approach to legislative rules in Chapter Five. Pork-barrel projects have distributive consequences. The benefits are concentrated in some districts, while the costs are spread across all districts. Members of Congress have an incentive to exclude some members from pork-barrel deals to increase the net benefits to their own constituents. But the excluded members can try to split the coalition behind any deal by offering a better deal to some members of the coalition. The result can be an endless chain of bargaining among legislators. In this view, legislative rules provide a way to discipline such deals. The voting rules have consequences for what deals are possible and how easily such deals can be upset by excluded legislators.

Chapter Eight presents a third view of legislative rules. Members of Congress cannot be certain about the consequences of legislation. They share an interest in having some members develop expertise in different policy areas. Specialized members serve on committees that propose legislation in their area of expertise. Rules protect legislation proposed by committees to motivate members to specialize.

Each of these three views leads to different models of congressional rules and committees. They all capture some part of the logic of legislative rules. The models help us understand the consequences of these different views.

Deterrence in international crises is the second problem. When two nations are embroiled in a crisis, each makes threats against the other to try to influence the other's actions. What makes such threats successful? Carrying out threats is costly to the threatener as well as the threatened. Nations receiving threats may not believe that the threat will be carried out if they do not comply. The credibility of a threat depends on both the magnitude of the costs to be imposed and the willingness of the threatener to carry it out.

Chapter Two presents the logic of deterrence from the perspective of decision theory. What probability of carrying out a threat is sufficient to deter a nation? The credibility of threats, as captured in the probability that the threat will be carried out, is given in this model. But deterrence is not the decision of an isolated nation; each nation must consider the other's reaction when it chooses to make a threat. Chapter Three uses deterrence to introduce the basic elements of a game. The resulting game is solved in Chapter Seven. This model considers how threats can be used to signal intentions in a crisis. If there is a cost to making a threat and then backing down from it, actors who are willing to carry out threats are more likely to make them than actors unwilling to carry them out. The probability of a threat's being carried out is determined within the model, rather than being fixed outside the model as in the decision-theoretic model.

Chapters Six and Eight present other models of deterrence. Nuclear deterrence is a special case of deterrence. If nuclear war is worse than any peaceful outcome, how can actors make nuclear threats credible? The model in Chapter Six considers one possible answer, the reciprocal fear of surprise attack. If there is an advantage to striking first, each actor may consider attacking if it fears that the other is planning to attack first. The model in Chapter Eight considers what inferences can be drawn from events that did not occur. Does the failure to make a costly threat signal weakness or strength? This model begins to consider some critical problems about how a reputation for resolve can be created.

The third problem is voting in mass elections. How do voters choose between candidates, and how can candidates influence voters' choices? Chapter Two includes the classic decision-theoretic model of why people vote (or more correctly, why they should not vote). Candidate strategy in a two-candidate race is addressed in Chapter Four. That section presents the Median Voter Theorem in a two-person, zero-sum game. But each of these models separates the voters' decisions from the candidates' strategies. Chapter Seven presents a simplified version of a model that combines the two problems. This model considers the decision to vote as a strategic problem among voters. If everyone else votes, then I do not want to bear the costs of voting. If no one else votes, I want to vote so that I can determine the outcome. Chapter Nine includes a model of retrospective voting. The other models of voting are prospective: voters choose candidates based on what the latter do once in office. In a retrospective voting model, voters use the record of the incumbent to judge what his or her future performance is likely to be.

Bargaining, the fourth problem, is common to many political settings. Bargaining occurs when two or more actors are willing to reach any one of several agreements, but they disagree about which agreement is best. They resolve their differences by bargaining. Chapter Four describes the Nash bargaining solution, the basic concept in two-person, cooperative game theory. This solution postulates four conditions that bargains should satisfy and then characterizes what bargain should occur. Chapter Five presents a different approach to bargaining, the Rubenstein bargaining model. That model treats offers within a bargaining session as strategic moves and solves for what offers are made and which accepted. This approach is extended in Chapter Eight by a model of bargaining where the sides do not know what bargains the other side will accept. These three examples provide an introduction to game-theoretic work on bargaining.

Why Model?

All four of the problems discussed above have been addressed by formal models. Formal modeling is a research strategy that is unfamiliar to many political scientists. The social and political world is immensely complex; how can the brute simplifications of formal models provide any insight into that world?

The primary advantage of formal modeling is the rigor and precision of argument that it requires. Writing down an argument formally forces the modeler to decide precisely what the assumptions of the argument are. Many verbal arguments in political science can be formalized in a number of different ways. Those verbal arguments fail to specify their assumptions and assertions completely. When we formalize those arguments, we may expose unstated assumptions. The conclusions of those arguments may not hold for all cases because they depend upon those unstated assumptions. Without the rigor of a formal model, we would fail to see the lack of generalizability of an informal argument.

Similarly, formal models allow us to see exactly why the conclusions of a model follow from its assumptions. Other supporting arguments that do not follow from the assumptions are ruled out. Some verbal arguments pile up supporting arguments that conflict with one another in an attempt to overawe the reader with argumentative bulk. Derivations of conclusions from assumptions can also suggest new avenues of argument that may lead to additional conclusions. Such avenues can lead to conclusions beyond the initial intuition underlying the model.

Formal modeling also creates a logical structure for the accumulation of a series of models about increasingly general questions. Many formal models produce some conclusions at variance with observations. The logical structure of a model allows modelers to add to it in order to derive new conclusions that may explain those observations at odds with existing models. Successful formal models generate streams of research that lead to areas never anticipated by the original work. Any particular model should be seen as one link in a chain of research. Still, each link must carry its own weight. Individual models within a chain of research must each lead to new insights or the clarification of problems in existing models.

Conceptual clarity and rigorous argument are obviously desirable, but do we sacrifice too much "realism" when we model? Models are by their very nature abstractions. Modeling aspires to lay bare social interactions in simplest terms.

Simplification is a virtue. Modeling tries to capture the essence of a social situation. Any argument, even the thickest of descriptions, is a simplification of an immensely complex world. More historical evidence has been lost by the failure of the participants to collect it at the time than has ever been published.

The proper criterion to judge the "realism" of an argument is the accuracy of its conclusions. Formal models help us determine the observable consequences of our arguments. We can then test those hypotheses against the real world. It is often difficult to determine what conclusions actually follow from informal arguments that invoke a more complex world. The purported conclusions usually follow from such arguments for most but not all cases. Testing such arguments is difficult at best; what counts as disconfirming evidence? In contrast, formal models often show that commonly used tests of theories are not appropriate. There are well-known formal models in which almost any behavior can result. Such models and the arguments they reflect cannot be tested by examining specific behavior; any evidence is consistent with the argument.

Fruitful models carefully combine intuition about political problems, skill in modeling, and common sense. Formal models have contributed to my understanding of politics by disciplining my intuition. Working with models forces you to refine your initial understandings of an argument. Solving the mathematics of a model leads you to see why some arguments are logically sound and others are not. Over time, your intuition changes to reflect the discipline of a model. The model has added rigor to the initial intuition, and now the refined intuition may lead to new models and additional insights.

The Rational Choice Approach to Social Modeling

There are models in political science that do not invoke the concept of rationality. Game theory, however, requires the assumption of rationality, an assumption quite familiar to economists, somewhat familiar to political scientists and psychologists, and probably alien to most sociologists and others. We assume that people have goals and that they attempt to realize those goals through their actions. The focus here is on how individuals' attempts to achieve their goals are constrained (or assisted) by one another's actions and the structure of the game.

The distinctive elements of the rational choice approach are as follows. First, rational choice theorists assume people have goals which they attempt to achieve; the moral value of actors' goals is not judged. Of course, those goals may be difficult to achieve, or the consequences of actions undertaken to achieve them may be unclear. Second, rational choice theorists assume that people have some freedom of choice. Although structure, as represented in a game tree, does constrain choices, actors believe they have some choices. The choices may be unpleasant for an actor, and how actors evaluate their choices may be colored by their beliefs, but some choice exists. Third, rational choice theorists assume that individuals choose actions that they believe will achieve their goals. The concept of goals seems worthless if we do not assume that actors strive to achieve their goals. Fourth, rational choice theorists deliberately simplify and abstract reality in their models. Game models do not even attempt to address all the complexity of the social world. Instead, they focus on certain elements of social situations to lay bare how motivations and actions are interrelated. At times, then, game-theoretic analyses seem simplistic, but such simplifications can help clarify complex interactions.

The idea of equilibrium accompanies a rational choice approach to understanding social phenomena. In equilibrium, no actor wishes to change its behavior on its own. Behavior at an equilibrium is stable in the sense that no actor, given its current position and knowledge, can improve its own position on its own. Equilibria are not assumed to be fair or balanced to the actors or desirable according to any ethical criteria. Often the equilibria of a model are grossly unfair to one actor or reflect a socially suboptimal outcome. Nor do we assume that an equilibrium must persist for eternity in society; very few models claim to address global change over long periods of time. Instead, a designation of equilibrium is just the statement that no actor, within the confines of the current model, wishes to change its choices.

This book strives to explain what the idea of equilibrium means in all its complexity. The idea that predictions of a model should require that no actor wishes to change its behavior is more subtle than its simple appearance. Equilibria serve as the predictions of a model. As the conditions we wish to model grow more complex, so must the concept of equilibrium. Although the general idea of equilibrium is straightforward, the conditions that equilibria must satisfy are not. This book begins with the cleanest definition of equilibrium and advances to the more elaborate definitions. But the idea of equilibrium underlying all those definitions is the same. They differ in how we understand that idea.

How to Use This Book

This book strives to achieve three ends. First, it introduces the reader to game theory at a level accessible to a general audience in political science. Second, it tries to teach the reader not only the concepts of game theory, but also how to solve simple models. Third, it introduces the reader to basic versions of the models commonly used in political science. I am convinced that political scientists need not only the ability to read, understand, and critique formal literature in the field, but also the ability to set up and solve their own models. Modeling imposes discipline upon one's arguments; one must model to gain the benefits of this discipline. Many arguments in political science would profit from even the great simplification of basic models. Great technical proficiency is not needed to solve such models.

However, some mathematics is necessary to solve game theory models. The first appendix provides a review of the basic mathematics that the book uses. It begins with algebra, progresses through set theory and probability theory, and on to both differential and integral calculus. It ends with a brief discussion of the idea of a mathematical proof. I recommend that you review this appendix unless you are very comfortable with all these topics. Most of the book requires only algebra and probability theory. For the sections that require more than just algebra, I note what mathematics is required for them at their beginning.

In choosing between accessibility and precision, I hope I have reached a happy medium. I have striven to be both careful and clear in my exposition. Where I have been forced to choose between the two, I have chosen to use minimal technical notation. Because of this choice, there are areas where I fail to reach the technical standards demanded of much formal work. This book is an introduction to the field and is not meant to be a definitive source.

As an aid to the reader, I have included a glossary of terms in game theory at the end of the book. The glossary gives informal statements of important terms that recur throughout the book. The reader should refer to the text for formal definitions of these terms.

As a guide to further reading, I provide annotated references at the end of each chapter. These "Further Reading" sections also include bibliographic essays on different substantive areas of political science. These essays survey work that uses game-theoretic models in a given area. They do not attempt to provide a complete survey of game theory models in these areas. Instead, they provide an entry into these literatures through work I have found useful and interesting. I have tried to draw on books and surveys of the literature in these essays because I feel those works are more helpful for the reader entering the formal literature. The table of contents lists these bibliographic essays to help readers find their area of particular interest. I encourage readers interested in a deeper treatment of these topics to seek out these additional sources. The bibliography provides ratings of the mathematical complexity of each cited work. Works with no asterisks are relatively simple and demand at most algebra to be understood. Those followed by one asterisk require either higher mathematics or else greater attention to the formal argument. Those followed by two asterisks are highly formal and require careful reading.

Because I want the reader to gain the ability to solve simple models, I have embedded problems in the text. The reader should solve these problems when he or she reaches them. Most of the embedded problems are not difficult, and they generally follow directly from the material in the text. Answers for many of the problems are provided in an appendix. I remind the reader that problems do you little good if you look up the answers in the back of the book before giving the problems a good try on your own. As some would say, no pain, no gain.

The Plan of This Book

The book falls into two main parts. The first half, Chapters Two through Four, presents utility theory, the formal specification of games, and a quick survey of classical game theory. The second half, Chapters Five through Nine, covers recent developments in noncooperative game theory. The development of the book parallels the historical development of game theory. I provide the survey of classical game theory for two reasons. First, it helps the reader understand the logic of equilibrium. The idea of equilibrium is easier to explain in classical game theory. I elaborate the idea of equilibrium in the second half of the book. Second, there appears to be much confusion in the field about the basic concepts of classical game theory. Many problems can be analyzed by using these tools. The best-known games come from classical game theory, but the application of those games to political science often fails to use the equilibrium concepts from classical game theory.

As mentioned above, Chapter Two covers utility theory, the theory of individual decision upon which game theory is built. Two examples, deterrence and why people vote, illustrate the application of utility theory. Chapter Three defines games in the extensive and strategic forms, using deterrence as an example of how to model a situation as a game. Chapter Four presents classical game theory. Equilibrium in the setting of pure conflict (two-person, zero-sum games) is compared to equilibrium in the setting of mixed motivations (two-person, non–zero-sum games). These games are analyzed in the strategic form. Chapter Four concludes with a brief discussion of cooperative games.

Chapter Five begins the discussion of noncooperative game theory. Here the extensive form, rather than the strategic form, is analyzed. Backwards induction is the focus of Chapter Five. This simple means of solving some extensive-form games is used widely in political science. Examples in legislative politics and bargaining illustrate backwards induction. Chapter Six adds the concepts of beliefs and perfect Bayesian equilibrium. It starts with Bayes's Theorem from probability theory. An example of the preference for biased information shows the use of Bayes's Theorem in decision theory. Beliefs are probabilities that model players' beliefs about uncertainties in the game. They help specify players' anticipations of future moves in the face of uncertainty. Perfect Bayesian equilibrium connects moves in a game with the players' beliefs about the game. Both moves and beliefs must be in equilibrium with each other. An example from nuclear deterrence theory illustrates perfect Bayesian equilibrium. Chapter Seven presents two related concepts, perfect and sequential equilibrium. Examples on deterrence and mass voting are given in that chapter. Chapter Eight discusses games of limited information where the players are uncertain about some aspect of the game. Perfect Bayesian equilibrium is used to solve sample models of congressional rules, bargaining, deterrence, and communication. An additional elaboration on perfect Bayesian equilibrium, restrictions on beliefs, is briefly discussed. Chapter Nine discusses repeated games. The central result for repeated games, the folk theorem, is presented in four different versions. The repeated Prisoner's Dilemma is the central example in this chapter. This chapter ends with the concept of stationarity, a different way to solve repeated games, and a model of retrospective voting.

Chapter Ten concludes the book by returning to the points made in this introductory chapter. The strengths and weaknesses of game theory models are assessed. The models that address the four problems discussed earlier in this chapter are used to illuminate this discussion. The conclusion also briefly discusses some of the frontiers of game theory.

Several different courses could be taught using this book, either in the classroom or through self-study. This book has been developed through a course I have taught at the ICPSR Summer Program at the University of Michigan over eight years. My course proceeds through the book in order. Chapter Four, on classical game theory, could be dropped to create a course that focused solely on noncooperative game theory. Chapter Two, on utility theory, can be dropped if the class or reader already knows rigorous utility theory. However, I recommend reading Chapter Two because many political scientists are unfamiliar with the rigorous basis of utility theory. I also suggest reading some current research papers using game theory while you read the book. Reading literature of interest to you will help you see how the material is used in current research.

Each chapter ends with a brief review of the main points of the chapter. These review sections reiterate the central concepts of the chapter. They should help the reader understand the fundamental points each chapter tries to make.

Further Reading

At the end of each chapter, I provide a discussion of sources for further reading. These sources are not comprehensive; instead they provide a guide to further reading. Here, I give a quick review of other textbooks in game theory. I also discuss some supplementary readings, esoteric books, and journals that publish work using game theory.

Textbooks

I begin with books that cover classical game theory. The most useful text for the beginning serious student is Luce and Raiffa 1957, recently rereleased by

Dover in paperback. Davis 1983 lives up to its subtitle; it is a nontechnical introduction. Owen 1982 is for those interested in a mathematical introduction to game theory. Shubik 1983 is a two-volume set using game theory to examine issues in political economy, primarily for economists. The first volume thoroughly presents classical game theory; the second, examples of its application.

Two textbooks that use utility and game theory to analyze politics are Riker and Ordeshook 1973 and Ordeshook 1986. The former is out of print and now dated. Both books present some game theory, but the presentation of formal political theory is their main objective. Both are recommended for students who wish to see how decision theory and classical game theory have been used to analyze politics.

There are now several textbooks in noncooperative game theory that I can recommend. They generally provide excellent presentations of the theory of noncooperative games. However, their examples are drawn from economics and are written for graduate students in economics. These books demand a higher level of mathematical sophistication than most political scientists possess.

The two textbooks I recommend most strongly are Kreps 1990a and Fudenberg and Tirole 1991. Kreps's book is a text on microeconomic theory; Chapters Eleven and Twelve address the theory of noncooperative games, and Chapters Fourteen through Eighteen cover models using noncooperative game theory. Chapter Three on utility theory is also quite good. The other chapters cover microeconomics. Fudenberg and Tirole's book is a text that provides material for more than one course on game theory. Its greatest strength is its breadth and depth of coverage of topics.

Binmore 1992 is a text for both undergraduates and graduate students. Binmore's presentation is not difficult, but it does demand a willingness to do mathematics. The order of his presentation differs from my historical approach. Friedman 1990 is a good text on game theory and its application to economics; the author's specialty is oligopoly theory. Myerson 1991 demands a very high level of mathematics but delivers a high quality of presentation for the reader capable of a more technical presentation. Myerson has been the central figure in the mechanism design literature. Not surprisingly, his coverage of this literature is excellent. Rasmusen (1989) walks the economist through noncooperative game theory, using a variety of models. He assumes that the reader knows utility theory and a fair amount of economics.

Ordeshook (1992) strives to present game theory and formal theory in political science at an accessible level. He emphasizes noncooperative game theory and lays out many of the important insights in formal theory. You may find Ordeshook's book to be a useful source in addition to mine.

Supplementary Readings

Two supplementary readings that are completely nontechnical are Schelling 1960 and Dixit and Nalebuff 1991. Schelling (1960) has been immensely influential in political science. *The Strategy of Conflict* is a great read and contains some very important and powerful insights in game theory. On the other hand, it does not even try to prepare the reader to solve games, and some of its points have been dated by noncooperative game theory. Dixit and Nalebuff (1991) attempt to present the ideas of noncooperative game theory to a general audience. This book is very accessible; it was a selection of the Book of the Month Club. It covers the central logic of strategic interaction and many of the important applications. This book is a good place to go to understand the intuition behind economic models.

The books by Kreps (1990b) and Gibbons (1992) are nontechnical introductions to game theory for economists. Kreps 1990b is based on a series of lectures on game theory that Kreps gave in 1990. His discussion of the limitations and frontiers of game theory is excellent. Gibbons 1992 is more technical than this book but less so than the textbooks above. Its examples are drawn from economics.

The New Palgrave (Eatwell, Milgate, and Newman 1989, 1990) is a dictionary of economics; it consists of essays on many topics in economics written by experts. Its two volumes, *Game Theory* and *Utility and Probability*, are useful places to begin further reading. The essays are typically less than ten pages. Historical essays as well as discussions of concepts can be found in *The New Palgrave*; Robert Aumann's essay on "Game Theory" in the volume of the same name is an excellent survey of the field and its historical development.

Esoteric Books on Game Theory

The following books are interesting, but off what is now the beaten track of game theory. Some present alternative ideas as to what constitutes the solutions of games. All are technically demanding and require very close attention to their technical arguments. Von Neumann and Morgenstern [1943] 1953, the book that started the field, is dated. I have great sentiment for this book because I read it as an undergraduate. It is packed with a ton of ideas, and I am still amazed to see how far the authors went in the first book on the subject. It is also a marvelous lesson on how to formalize something that at first sight appears impossible to formalize. But now other books make better first books on game theory.

Harsanyi 1977 is an intriguing introduction to decision and game theory, which advances Harsanyi's views on decision theory. It ranges from the basics of game theory to advancements in the concept of equilibrium to the relevance of decision theory to ethics. It is not meant as a thorough text of the field. Developments since the mid-1970s have dated some of the arguments in this book.

Harsanyi and Selten (1988) develop their approach to equilibrium, which is not commonly accepted. They seek to define a unique solution for each game. The book is worth reading because Harsanyi and Selten are two of the giants in the field of game theory. The reader is warned that this book assumes a very high level of mathematical competence.

Greenberg (1989) presents a different approach to game theory. His premise is that the equilibrium concept used to solve a game is part of the description of the situation, much like the rules of the game itself. His book is very demanding.

Journals

Research using game theory is most common in studies of U.S. politics, especially legislative studies, and international politics. The *American Political Science Review* publishes much of the best work in formal theory in all fields. The *American Journal of Political Science* is also a central journal for formal theorists. Although the substantive focus of the *American Journal of Political Science* is U.S. politics, it also publishes important pieces on international and comparative politics that use formal models. The *Journal of Politics* also publishes some work in formal theory. *Public Choice* is an interdisciplinary journal for political scientists and economists. It has played a central role in the development of formal theory in political science. Because formal theory has had a significant effect on the study of legislatures, the *Legislative Studies Quarterly* publishes work influenced by game theory models. The *Journal of Theoretical Politics* covers formal theory in addition to other theoretical approaches; it seeks to provide more accessible articles. In international relations, the *Journal of Conflict Resolution* publishes the most game-theoretic work. *World Politics*, *International Studies Quarterly*, and *International Interactions* also publish some work using game theory. In comparative politics, occasional pieces using game theory appear in *Comparative Politics* and *Comparative Political Studies*.

In economics, *Econometrica* and the *Journal of Economic Theory* are the primary outlets for game theory. Both of these journals are written by and for technically trained economists. Articles in these journals demand close reading at a high level of mathematical sophistication. *Games and Economic Behavior* is devoted to publishing game theory and is more accessible than *Econometrica* and the *Journal of Economic Theory*. The *American Economic Review*, the *Review of Economic Studies*, and the *Quarterly Journal of Economics* are leading journals in economics. As game theory has become central to the study of economics, these journals have published more articles that use game theory. The *Journal of Economic Literature*, the *Journal of Economic Perspectives*, and the *Journal of Economic Surveys* all provide survey essays on economics. Although articles on game theory are rare in them, these journals are a good source of accessible reviews. *Theory and Decision* publishes articles on and using decision and game theory that are generally less technically demanding. The *International Journal of Game Theory* is for mathematicians and mathematical economists.

Chapter Two
Utility Theory

Game theory is based on utility theory, a simple mathematical theory for representing decisions. In utility theory, we assume that actors are faced with choices from a set of available actions. Each action provides a probability of producing each possible outcome. Utility is a measure of an actor's preferences over the outcomes that reflects his or her willingness to take risks to achieve desired outcomes and avoid undesirable outcomes. The probabilities of obtaining each outcome after taking an action represent uncertainty about the exact consequences of that action.

We calculate an expected utility for an action by multiplying the utility of each possible outcome by the probability that it will occur if the action is chosen, and then summing across all possible outcomes. Utilities for outcomes are chosen so that the magnitude of expected utilities concur with preferences over actions. Actions with larger expected utilities are preferred. Given the probabilities that actions produce outcomes and preferences over actions, we can calculate utilities over outcomes so that actions with larger expected utilities are preferred.

Utility theory is closely tied to probability theory and is almost as old. As in the case of probability theory, the rigorous analysis of gambling problems drove the early development of utility theory. Daniel Bernoulli[1] first worked on utility theory to explain why the attractiveness of gambles did not necessarily equal the gambler's monetary expectation. After this initial observation, utility theory lay dormant until Jeremy Bentham advanced utilitarianism as a philosophy in the 1800s. Bentham's utility theory was, mathematically speaking, quite sloppy and is not useful for developing a rigorous theory of decision. Consequently, utility was rejected as a useful concept until the middle of the twentieth century.

Von Neumann and Morgenstern revived utility theory by providing a firm mathematical foundation for the concept in an appendix to their *Theory of Games and Economic Behavior* ([1943] 1953). Several rigorous versions of utility theory were produced after the publication of that book. Since then, economists have reformulated economic theory using utility theory and game theory as the description of individual behavior.

This chapter begins with the concept of rationality. The characteristics of rational preferences are presented, followed by a discussion of some common misconceptions about rationality. The elements of a formal decision problem are described, and the idea of expected utility is introduced. Two examples, one frivolous and one historical, illustrate these ideas. I then present the formal basis of utility theory, the Expected Utility Theorem. That theorem shows that a utility function can be found to represent preferences over actions when those preferences observe six conditions. Some common misconceptions about utility theory are rebutted. I next consider how utility functions represent different reactions to risk and preferences over time. I apply utility theory in two simple examples, one concerning deterrence and the other concerning when people should vote. I end the chapter with a discussion of the limitations of utility theory.

The Concept of Rationality

Game theory assumes rational behavior. But what is meant by rationality? In everyday parlance, rational behavior can mean anything from reasonable, thoughtful, or reflective behavior to wise, just, or sane actions. We generally do not think that someone who drives eighty miles per hour on narrow side streets is rational. But rational behavior for our purposes means much less than the common meaning of the term. Put simply, rational behavior means choosing the best means to gain a predetermined set of ends. It is an evaluation of the consistency of choices and not of the thought process, of implementation of fixed goals and not of the morality of those goals.

In utility theory, rational actors have specified goals and a set of actions they can choose. They then choose the action that will best attain those goals (at this point, I will be vague about what "best" and "attain" mean precisely). Rational behavior is goal directed; actors are trying to create more desired outcomes rather than less desired outcomes.

But how do we know what an actor's goals are? In general, we deduce actors' goals from observing their prior behavior or by experimentation. We then assume that actors will continue to pursue the goals we have deduced they pursued in the past. We fix actors' preferences and allow the information they have and the situation they face to change, creating variation in their actions.

To specify these goals formally, we begin with **consequences**, or **outcomes** (I use these two words interchangeably). A consequence is a possible final result of the actor's decision. It includes all relevant effects for the decider. The set of outcomes is exhaustive and mutually exclusive; one and only one outcome occurs. The definition of the consequences is the choice of the modeler. It can be as simple or complex as you choose. For example, the outcomes of a presidential election could be described as simply whether the Republican or Democratic candidate won. The consequences of the election could be the policies that the winning candidate enacts once in office. We could also consider the margin of victory or whether a particular individual voted as a relevant facet of an election in the eyes of an actor.

Actors have preferences over the set of outcomes. Let C be the set of all consequences, with specific consequences indicated by subscripts. Preferences are given by a relation, R, between pairs of consequences, with C_iRC_j read as "Consequence i is at least as good as consequence j."[2] R is called the **weak preference relation** because the actor weakly prefers the first outcome to the second. In other words, the first is at least as good as and maybe better than the second. **Indifference,** I, occurs when both C_iRC_j and C_jRC_i, and is written C_iIC_j. Because both outcomes are at least as good as each other, they are equally desirable in the actor's eyes. The **strong preference relation,** P, means the first outcome is better than the second. In other words, C_iPC_j is equivalent to (C_iRC_j and not C_jRC_i).

We assume each actor has a set of complete and transitive preferences over the set of outcomes. Completeness means that actors can make comparisons across all pairs of consequences.

> **Definition**: An ordering is **complete** iff (read if and only if) for all pairs of outcomes C_i and C_j, either C_iRC_j or C_jRC_i or both.

An actor can say that it prefers one outcome to the other or that it is indifferent between the two. Completeness implies that the preference order is **reflexive:** for all C_i, C_iRC_i. In other words, all consequences are at least as good as themselves. Preferences are also transitive.

> **Definition**: An ordering is **transitive** iff (C_iRC_j and C_jRC_k) implies C_iRC_k.

Transitivity means that if one outcome (C_i) is at least as good as a second (C_j), and the second is at least as good as a third (C_k), then the first must be at least as good as the third.

Completeness and transitivity are the basic elements of a preference ordering. Each actor can rank the outcomes from best to worst, allowing for indifference between outcomes. Because complete and transitive preferences order the outcomes, they are called **ordinal preferences**. These two assumptions are necessary for rationality. Without complete preferences, actors are unable to choose between noncomparable outcomes. But situations with noncomparable preferences are odd. For example, many of us would be hard pressed to state whether we prefer eating a bushel of pears or seeing Senator Kennedy elected president.[3] We do not think of those outcomes as comparable. But neither is it a plausible choice. Typically, we exclude situations with noncomparable consequences and restrict the set of consequences so that the actors have complete preferences over the whole set. Because we can choose the set of outcomes to fit the problem we are modeling, we can define the outcomes to avoid incomplete preferences.

Transitive preferences eliminate cycles among strong preferences, for example, C_iPC_j and C_jPC_k and C_kPC_i. Strong preference cycles prevent consistent choices. What outcome does the actor prefer among the three in this cycle? We cannot say even though it prefers one outcome in each pair of outcomes. The choice between the outcomes in the cycle depends on the order in which the outcomes are presented. If we compare C_i and C_j first, and then compare the result to C_k, we find that C_k is preferred. Comparing C_j and C_k first, and then comparing the result to C_i, we find that C_i is preferred, and so on. Can we say that these preferences are well-defined?

The classic example of preferences that violate transitivity concerns the sweetness of coffee. One grain of sugar in my coffee is at least as good as no grains of sugar, two grains is at least as good as one grain, and so on. In each case, I am indifferent because I cannot tell the difference that one grain of sugar makes to the sweetness of my coffee. If my preferences over the sweetness of coffee are transitive, then I should be indifferent about the amount of sugar in my coffee. But I am not indifferent between no sugar, the amount of sugar I like best, and several pounds of sugar per cup. I like about two teaspoons per cup. Less sugar than that and I prefer adding another grain; more than that, and I prefer not adding one more grain of sugar. So I am not really indifferent about the addition of one grain of sugar to my coffee. The paradox occurs because I cannot distinguish which cup has the additional grain of sugar in each comparison. We can avoid these situations by choosing outcomes that the actors can distinguish, eliminating this paradox of indifference.

Preferences over outcomes are assumed to be fixed. They do not change during the course of the decision being examined. Some argue that shifts in preference occur. We do not allow preference shifts because they rob the theory of its explanatory power. Preferences are unobservable; we infer preferences by observing actions. But shifts in preferences cannot be confirmed then. It is tempting to say that preferences have changed whenever we observe behavior at variance with a model. The model cannot be tested if we claim preferences shift when behavior changes because any disconfirming evidence can be ignored by claiming that preferences have changed. Instead, we assume that preferences are fixed and that changes in behavior are caused by changes in the situation and the information available to the actors.

The assumption of fixed preferences restricts the situations we can model. But it is not as restrictive as it seems because we can select the outcomes to suit our purposes. We distinguish between preferences over outcomes and preferences over actions (or strategies). Outcomes are the final results; actions are choices that could produce one of several outcomes. Preferences over outcomes are assumed to be fixed. Preferences over actions can change as the actors gain new information about the efficacy of different actions. By choosing the outcomes carefully, "shifts in preferences" are shifts in preferences among actions, rather than outcomes. For example, the outcomes of an election could be modeled as which candidate is elected, say, Bush or Dukakis for the 1988 presidential election. But then voters who change their minds about which candidate to vote for during the campaign appear to shift their preference over the outcomes. Instead, let the outcomes of the election be the policies that the winning candidate will adopt. Then voters could change their preference between the candidates as they learn what policies each candidate is likely to adopt if he or she is elected. A shift in preference between the candidates is now seen as a shift in preference over the actions of voting for Bush and voting for Dukakis.

Ordinal preferences can be represented by a descending sequence of numbers. The largest number is assigned to the most preferred outcome, the second-largest number to the next outcome in the preference order, and so on down to the least preferred outcome. Indifference between two outcomes requires equal numbers. Any sequence where the order of the numbers assigned to consequences mirrors the preference ordering is a representation of that ordering. We call these numbers **utilities**, u, and the function that maps from consequences to numbers that represent an individual's preferences over those outcomes is a **utility function**. With ordinal preferences, the larger the number the better the outcome, but the difference between the numbers assigned to two outcomes is meaningless. For example, both the function $u(C_1) = 1, u(C_2) = 2$, and $u(C_3) = 0$ and the function $u(C_1) = 1, u(C_2) = 104$, and $u(C_3) = -4$ are acceptable utility functions for the preference ordering, $C_2PC_1PC_3$. Only the order of the numbers in the representation reflects the preferences; hence the name *ordinal preferences.* If the intervals between these numbers were meaningful, we would have a cardinal preference order. Later, I show that cardinal utilities can be calculated that represent not only ordinal preferences over outcomes, but also the risks that an actor is willing to take to obtain preferred outcomes.

Some Misconceptions about the Notion of Rationality

Because the game-theoretic definition of rationality is narrower than the intuitive one, it is frequently misunderstood. Some of the common misinterpretations and the proper responses follow. First, we do not assume the decision process is a series of literal calculations. Instead, people make choices that reflect both their underlying goals and the constraints of the situation, and we can create a utility function that represents their actions given those constraints. Utility theory is not an attempt to explain the cognitive processes of individuals. It is an attempt to capture the important considerations underlying decisions in a general framework that can be manipulated mathematically while allowing for variation across the choices of individuals. Our purpose is not to explain cognition, but rather to understand political acts. We use the abstract model of choice here to represent individuals' choices in political settings. Strategic logic is quite complex even with this simple model of cognition. Rational choice models attempt to capture key facets of a situation and examine actors' decisions as a consequence of their preferences in conjunction with the constraints of a situation. To do so, we use the rational choice model to simplify away from the complexity of actual cognition.

Second, rationality tells us nothing about an actor's preferences over outcomes—only about its choices given those preferences and the situation that confronts it. The classic example here is Adolf Hitler; according to the common idea of rationality, he was crazy. He pursued abhorrent goals and took immense political risks that eventually led to his own destruction and that of Nazi Germany. But from the perspective of utility theory, his behavior can be explained rationally. He consistently pursued German nationalist expansion and responded to the environment he faced and the opportunities it presented him. In many ways, Hitler understood the international climate of the 1930s better than any other leader did.

Third, rational actors may not and probably will not all reach the same decision when faced with the same situation. Rational actors can differ in their preferences over the outcomes. A chess master playing with his or her child is unlikely to play purely to win the game. Instead, he or she strives to make the game enjoyable for the child to play. Moves that would appear irrational if the master were playing against a competitive opponent may be quite rational when playing against the child because the master's objective in playing the game is different. Moreover, even if two actors have the same ordinal preferences, they can have different reactions to risk and uncertainty that lead them to evaluate the available actions differently. Different reactions to risk are captured in the utility functions, and different reactions to uncertainty are captured in the actors' subjective probability distributions of outcomes that follow from each action. Everyone prefers winning at the roulette wheel to losing there. But some are willing to run the risk of the game while others are not. Both types prefer winning to losing, but nonplayers avoid the risks of the game, and this preference is captured in their utility functions over the outcomes. Later, I discuss attitudes to risks and how they are captured in utility functions. Finally, different actors could have different information that leads them to believe that different courses of action lead to preferred outcomes. Even risk-averse individuals might bet on a horse race if they knew which horse would win a fixed race.

Fourth, rational actors can make errors, that is, achieve undesirable outcomes, for three reasons. Rationality does not mean error-free decisions. First, situations are risky. When one takes a chancy course of action, bad outcomes may occur because one is unlucky. Second, the information available to actors is limited. Actors cannot determine the consequences of their actions and must make judgments that may be incorrect. Third, actors may hold incorrect beliefs about the consequences of their actions. They may believe that ineffective means of achieving their goals are effective. The critical point here is that hindsight is always correct, but actors do not know what the consequences of their actions will be when they must choose. Decisions can be judged properly only in the light of the conditions under which they are made. Bad decisions are obvious after their consequences are known. But actors cannot know the future; they make judgments about the likely future and act on those judgments. Utility theory attempts to capture this problem.

The difference between **ex ante facto** (before the fact) and **ex post facto** (after the fact) reasoning leads to a final observation. When we can choose the goals of an actor to fit its actions, it is very easy to produce circular explanations. For example, the statement "He jumped off the building because he wanted to" is not a very satisfying explanation of a suicide. To avoid this type of circular reasoning, we either make assumptions about preferences or base them on sufficient prior information. Frequently, both approaches are used together. Certain general assumptions are made about actors' preferences, allowing for terms that vary across actors that can be fit by examining the actors' prior behavior. Economists generally assume that "more is better" when it comes to consumer goods, but how much more of which good is an empirical question for specific individuals out to make purchases.

How Do Utility Functions Predict Actions?

Any decision problem can be described formally as follows:

1) A set of **acts**, A, one of which will be chosen as the decision.

2) A set of **states of the world**, S. The states are mutually exclusive and exhaustive—only one can occur, and one of them must occur. The "world" is defined to encompass all matters relevant to the problem beyond the control of the decider. An **event** is a subset of the states.

3) A set of **consequences** or **outcomes**, C, with one consequence for each pair of acts and states.

4) A **preference ordering** over the consequences, P. These preferences are assumed to be complete, transitive, and fixed.

Outcomes are produced by the decider's chosen action and other factors outside the decider's control. We summarize the latter factors as the **state of the world**. The state of the world consists of all those factors that influence the outcome but lie beyond the control of the decider. Generally, actors do not know the state of the world. Instead, they face several possible states of the world. If they knew the state of the world, actors could determine the consequences of their actions and choose the action that produces the most preferred outcome. But because they do not know the state of the world, deciders cannot determine the consequences of their actions. They must assess which action is most likely to produce the best final outcome, considering that each action could produce desirable or undesirable outcomes depending upon the state of the world. This assessment requires some judgment of the likelihood of each state and a more detailed scale of the actor's preferences than just ordinal preferences over the outcomes.

This more detailed scale is a **Von Neumann–Morgenstern utility function**. Such utility functions measure the attractiveness of outcomes to an actor by its willingness to take risks to obtain preferred outcomes. A probability distribution over the states capture an actor's assessment of the likelihood of each state. We calculate the expected utility for an action by multiplying the probability of each state's occurring by the utility of the outcome that results from that state and the action, and then summing these products over all the possible states. The available action with the highest expected utility is the choice. In mathematics, we have the following:

$$\mathrm{EU(A)} = \sum_{\mathrm{all\,S}} \mathrm{p(S)u[C(S, A)]} \text{ and}$$

Choose A such that EU(A) is maximized

where EU is expected utility, A is an available action, p is probability, S is a state, u is utility, and C(S,A) is the consequence that results when S is the state and A the action. Each action is evaluated both for the likelihood of the consequences it could produce and for the attractiveness of those outcomes. The action with the highest expected utility among the set of available actions is the choice.

A simple example may help clarify these ideas.[4] After working hard studying decision theory, you need a break to revive yourself. You head down to the soft-drink machine, which offers Classic Coke, Diet Coke, and Sprite (all registered trademarks of the Coca-Cola Company). You need caffeine and sugar to restore your alertness. If you cannot have both caffeine and sugar, you prefer caffeine to sugar. Your ordinal preferences are Classic Coke P Diet Coke P Sprite. You deposit your money, and as you are about to press the Classic Coke button, a friend of yours walks by and says, "Do you know that the man who services the machine got the Cokes and Sprites mixed up together? He dropped a case of each, and they broke open, spilling cans of both all over the place. He was in a hurry, so he just stuffed cans in the Coke and Sprite slots without looking to see what each can was. Mary got a Sprite when she pressed the Coke button." Now your choice is not so simple. The Classic Coke button might produce a Sprite. You know the Diet Coke button will produce a Diet Coke, so you are choosing between a Diet Coke for certain and a chance at either a Classic Coke or a Sprite.

The outcome is the drink you get after pushing a button, Classic Coke, Diet Coke, or Sprite. The actions available are the three buttons on the machine.[5]

You choose an action, and the combination of your choice and other factors outside of your control produce the outcome. These other factors are called the state of the world. Here, the state of the world is which drinks are next in each slot. Classic Coke in the Classic Coke slot, Diet Coke in the Diet Coke slot, and Classic Coke in the Sprite slot is one possible state of the world.

To decide which button to push, you need to judge how likely each state of the world is and what risk of getting a Sprite you are willing to accept to try to get a Classic Coke versus taking a Diet Coke for certain. The former is summarized in a probability distribution over the states, and the latter in a utility function over the outcomes. We use these two together to calculate an expected utility for each action. The action with the highest expected utility is the choice. Assume the following utility function and probability distribution where the states are read as drink in the Classic Coke slot, drink in the Diet Coke slot, and drink in the Sprite slot; all other possible states have probability 0:

u(Classic Coke) = 1 u(Diet Coke) = .4 u(Sprite) = 0

p(Classic Coke, Diet Coke, Classic Coke) = .15

p(Classic Coke, Diet Coke, Sprite) = .3

p(Sprite, Diet Coke, Classic Coke) = .2

p(Sprite, Diet Coke, Sprite) = .35

We calculate the expected utility of each action. If you press the Classic Coke button, you get a Classic Coke if either of the first two states is the state of the world and a Sprite if either of the latter two states is the state of the world. Thus the probability of getting a Classic Coke if you press the Classic Coke button is the sum of the probabilities of the first two states, p(Classic Coke, Diet Coke, Classic Coke) + p(Classic Coke, Diet Coke, Sprite) = .15 + .3 = .45, and the probability of getting a Sprite is the sum of the probabilities of the last two states, p(Sprite, Diet Coke, Classic Coke) + p(Sprite, Diet Coke, Sprite) = .2 + .35 = .55. The probability of getting a Diet Coke if you press the Classic Coke button is 0 because no state produces a Diet Coke when you press the Classic Coke button. Such probabilities are conditional probabilities; what is the chance of an outcome given that you take an action. Conditional probabilities are written as p(outcome| action). The expected utility of pressing the Classic Coke button is the sum of the utility of each outcome times the conditional probability of that outcome's occurring if you press the Classic Coke button. The calculation is as follows:

$$
\begin{aligned}
&\text{EU(Press Classic Coke)}\\
&\quad = \text{p(Classic Coke|Press Classic Coke)u(Classic Coke)}\\
&\qquad + \text{p(Diet Coke|Press Classic Coke)u(Diet Coke)}\\
&\qquad + \text{p(Sprite|Press Classic Coke)u(Sprite)}\\
&\quad = (.45)(1) + (0)(.4) + (.55)(0) = .45.
\end{aligned}
$$

Similarly, the expected utility of pressing the Diet Coke button is .4, and the expected utility of pressing the Sprite button is .35. Your choice is the action with the highest expected utility, pressing the Classic Coke button in this case.

An Example: Nixon's Christmas Bombing

Consider a simple example abstracted from an actual decision, Nixon's Christmas bombing of North Vietnam in December of 1972. After an initial agreement to end U.S. intervention in the Vietnam War, a disagreement over the exact nature of the settlement between the United States and North Vietnam emerged. From the point of view of the Nixon administration, the North Vietnamese government was trying to extract additional concessions by holding up the signing of the accord. However, it was also possible that an honest misunderstanding over the interpretation of the original agreement had arisen. We refer to each of these possibilities as a **state of the world**. When the Nixon administration had to decide what to do, it did not know what the actual state of the world was. It had to make a judgment about which state was more likely. We call the first state "Vietnamese Bluff," or S_1, and the second "No Bluff," or S_2. The states are mutually exclusive and exhaustive; the North Vietnamese could not be both bluffing and not bluffing at the same time, but one of the two had to occur.

We consider two available **actions**: (1) a demonstration of military power through aerial bombing and (2) agreeing to the additional concessions requested by the North Vietnamese government. Obviously, there were more options available than just these two, but I have chosen to simplify the situation this way for illustrative purposes. Call the first action "Bomb," or A_1, and the second "Do Not Bomb," or A_2. The states and the actions together create the **outcomes** or **consequences**. If the Nixon administration selects A_2, we assume that it will grant additional concessions and a revised settlement will be reached regardless of whether or not the North Vietnamese were bluffing. Call this consequence C_2. If the Nixon administration chooses A_1, the outcome will depend upon how the North Vietnamese respond to the bombing. If they were bluffing (i.e., if S_1 is the state of the world), we assume that the original agreement will be reaffirmed. Call this consequence C_1. If a simple misunderstanding had occurred, however, we assume that the bombing will

Table 2.1

		States	
		Bluff (S_1)	No Bluff (S_2)
Acts	Bomb (A_1)	North Vietnam returns to the table; quick agreement reached (C_1)	Talks break down; the war continues (C_3)
	Do Not Bomb (A_2)	Agreement reached with additional concessions (C_2)	Agreement reached with additional concessions (C_2)

Acts, States, and Consequences in the Christmas Bombing of North Vietnam

provoke the North Vietnamese to break off the talks and resume the ground war (we assume for simplicity that the renewed ground war will not involve U.S. ground troops). Call this consequence C_3. Table 2.1 arrays the choices, states, and consequences.

In the eyes of the Nixon administration (we assume), the consequences rank in the order of their subscripts: $C_1PC_2PC_3$. The Nixon administration preferred not making additional concessions to granting those concessions, but a continued war was worse than making the additional concessions. This order gives a set of ordinal preferences over the outcomes. But a utility function over the outcomes also specifies what degree of risk an actor will accept to gain preferred outcomes. The Nixon administration viewed the additional concessions as highly undesirable and was willing to take a chance to avoid making them. Let us assume that $u(C_1) = 1, u(C_2) = .3$, and $u(C_3) = 0$. The probability distribution over the states summarizes the beliefs about what the Nixon administration thought the North Vietnamese would do in response to its own action. It believed that the North Vietnamese government was bluffing. Assume that $p(S_1) = .7$ and $p(S_2) = .3$ (these two probabilities must sum to one because the two states are exhaustive). Calculating expected utilities, we can show that the Nixon administration preferred A_1 to A_2:

$$EU(A_1) = p(S_1)u(C_1) + p(S_2)u(C_3) = (.7)(1) + (.3)(0) = .7,$$

$$EU(A_2) = p(S_1)u(C_2) + p(S_2)u(C_2) = (.7)(.3) + (.3)(.3)$$

$$= .21 + .09 = .3,$$

and

$$EU(A_1) > EU(A_2), \text{ so } A_1PA_2.$$

The decision to bomb Hanoi and Haiphong was quite controversial in the United States. *The New York Times* heavily criticized the Nixon administration for the bombing. Although it shared the assumed ordinal preferences of the Nixon administration for the three outcomes, it did not share either the administration's willingness to take the risk of restarting the war or Nixon's estimation that the North Vietnamese were bluffing.

> Exercise 2.1: Show that either of the following changes is sufficient to reverse the decider's preference over the actions in the above example: (1) $u(C_2) = .8$ or (2) $p(S_1) = .2$ and $p(S_2) = .8$.

The final result of an expected utility comparison depends on both the utility attached to each outcome and the probability of each state. When we vary either, the choice may change, as in the exercise above.

The definition of the outcomes, actions, and states is a modeling decision. How you choose to represent the choices available to an actor and the consequences of those choices is the most important step in modeling. I have deliberately made the above example simple. One could add more actions, states, and outcomes to it. Of course, these additions will complicate this simple model. Decision problems can be structured at many levels of complexity. The choice of the appropriate level of complexity is a critical question in the design of any model. Set the level of complexity too high, and the problem becomes intractable. Set the level of complexity too low, and the results are trivial. The essential question here is what you want to say with your model and how you want to make your points. The level of complexity of a model is a choice between the additional complexity of a more detailed model and the clear exposition of a simple model. Simple models are adequate to establish many substantively important points; greater complexity and mathematical sophistication may not lead to greater political insight.

> Exercise 2.2: Recast the above decision problem by adding another action, A_3, reintervening with U.S. ground troops. The resulting consequences if A_3 is chosen are C_1 if S_1 is the state of the world and C_4, a renewed ground war involving U.S. as well as North and South Vietnamese troops (a new consequence) if S_2 is the state of the world. C_3PC_4. Continue to use the values in the example above for $u(C_1)$, $u(C_2)$, $u(C_3)$, $p(S_1)$, and $p(S_2)$.
>
> **a)** Solve for the expected utility of A_3. Let $u(C_4) = x$.
>
> **b)** Find a value for $u(C_4)$ such that A_2PA_3.

As a final note on this example, it should seem odd to you that we treat the actions of the North Vietnamese as fixed and determined by the state of the world. It is odd. The North Vietnamese government should be treated as a separate actor in its own right. To do so creates a game between the Nixon administration and the government in Hanoi. There is a natural parallel between decision theory and game theory that I want to suggest through this example. In game theory, the other players' actions parallel the states of the world in decision theory. But because other players also choose their actions to maximize their expected utility, each side's decision in a game must depend upon its anticipations about the other side's chosen action. This is a more complicated problem than the choice of an action in decision theory. But both types of decisions begin with the concept of utility presented in this chapter.

Certainty, Risk, and Uncertainty

The probability distributions reflect the decider's beliefs about which actions will lead to what consequences. These beliefs arise from the actor's knowledge about the situation. Decisions can be made under three different conditions reflecting the decider's knowledge about the states of the world:

1) Certainty—the state of the world is known prior to choosing an act. Then the act whose consequence is most preferred will be chosen. From the perspective of decision theory, decisions under certainty are trivial. The actual calculations that determine the outcome that results from each act may be so complicated that decisions under certainty may be quite computationally complex.

2) Risk—each state has a known probability of occurring, which obeys all the laws of probability. These probabilities can be assumed to be based on known frequencies over many repetitions. The condition of risk occurs in most gambling games, craps or roulette, for example, where the probabilities of different outcomes can be calculated and are well known.

3) Uncertainty—the probabilities of each state's occurring are either unknown or meaningless in the sense of reflecting any long-run frequency of occurrence.

Most decisions are made under the condition of uncertainty. Although some prior information about the likely state of the world is available, no long-run frequency of outcomes can be used to determine the chance of future outcomes. For example, people generally understand that flipping a fair coin generates a 50-50 probability of heads or tails. Thus decisions about how to bet on coin flips are made under risk. Other games of chance that people bet on, such as football games and horse races, do not have well-established, long-run frequencies.

Still, people do have prior information about those games that allows them to form beliefs about what outcomes are likely. Decisions on bets on these future outcomes are made under uncertainty. Under uncertainty, actors form subjective probability estimates that reflect their degree of belief about the underlying state of the world. The difference between the condition of risk and that of uncertainty lies in the probability distributions the deciders hold over the states. Under risk, all deciders must hold the same probability distribution because that distribution is known; under uncertainty, different deciders may hold different probability distributions because they hold different beliefs about the underlying state of the world.

The choice of the condition of information in a model is a matter of what you wish to capture in your model. Although most decisions of interest to political scientists are made under uncertainty because no long-run frequencies exist for the events, a model of decision under risk may be sufficient to demonstrate your point. For example, elections present decisions under uncertainty for both voters and candidates. Although long-run tendencies can be calculated and polls collected and analyzed, the actual outcome is a unique event, about which different actors may hold divergent beliefs. Still, modeling an election as a problem under risk may be sufficient to establish some points about electoral competition and behavior. The assumption of risk can be loosened later to reflect the effects of uncertainty.

Utility Theory under the Condition of Risk

I have not yet explained the logical basis of utility functions. Given a utility function over the outcomes and probability distributions from the actions to the outcomes, we can determine preferred actions. Where does the utility function come from? Utility functions capture the risks of less preferred outcomes that an actor will accept to gain more preferred outcomes. Ordinal preferences over outcomes are insufficient to create a Von Neumann–Morgenstern utility function. We need preferences over all possible risky choices. Abstractly, we represent risky choices over the outcomes as **lotteries**, where one outcome is selected from a fixed set of consequences with known probabilities of selecting each outcome. If an individual can rank all possible lotteries over the consequences and those preferences over the lotteries observe certain regularity conditions, then a utility function can be calculated to reflect those preferences.

Definition: A **lottery** (or **gamble**) is a matched pair of a set of probabilities $(p_1, p_2, \ldots, p_n)$ with

$$\sum_{i=1}^{n} p_i = 1$$

and a set of prizes $(Q_1, Q_2, \ldots, Q_n)$ (these prizes could be either consequences or other lotteries), where p_i gives the probability of obtaining prize Q_i. A lottery with only consequences as prizes is a **simple lottery**; one with other lotteries as prizes is a **compound lottery**. A lottery is written $(p_1Q_1, p_2Q_2, \ldots, p_nQ_n)$.

Actions are represented as lotteries, with the probability of each consequence's being the prize representing the probability that that consequence will occur given that action. Compound lotteries provide a way to consider decision problems where some risks lead to further risks. If we have an actor's preferences over all lotteries over the consequences, we can summarize those preferences in a utility function. The Expected Utility Theorem gives the consistency conditions that individuals' preferences over lotteries must observe for us to calculate a utility function to represent those preferences.

Theorem (the Expected Utility Theorem): If

1) the preference ordering over consequences is transitive and complete (for convenience, the subscripts on consequences give the preference ordering: $C_1PC_2PC_3 \ldots PC_n$),

2) compound lotteries can be reduced to simple lotteries (assuming each lottery is independent),

3) for each consequence C_i, there exists a lottery $\hat{C}_i$ involving just C_1 and C_n (the most and least preferred consequences) such that the actor is indifferent between C_i and $\hat{C}_i$,

4) $\hat{C}_i$ can be substituted for C_i in any lottery,

5) preference among lotteries is complete and transitive, and

6) (the Sure Thing Principle) $[pC_1, (1-p)C_n]$ is preferred to $[p'C_1, (1-p')C_n]$ iff $p > p'$,

then there exists a set of numbers $(u_1, u_2, \ldots, u_n)$ associated with a set of consequences $(C_1, C_2, \ldots, C_n)$ such that for any two lotteries L and L′, the magnitudes of the expected values $(p_1u_1 + p_2u_2 + \ldots + p_nu_n)$ and $(p'_1u_1 + p'_2u_2 + \ldots + p'_nu_n)$ reflect the preference between the lotteries.

If the six conditions above are satisfied and we have an actor's preferences over lotteries, we can calculate a utility function such that the magnitude of expected utilities gives the actor's preferences among lotteries.

But what do these six conditions commit us to accept? The first condition says that actors have preference orders over the consequences. I discussed this assumption earlier. The second condition allows us to use the laws of probability to reduce compound lotteries to simple lotteries, those with just outcomes as prizes. Some actions lead to multiple risks and can be thought of as a compound lottery. Reducing compound lotteries to simple lotteries gives us preferences over them because the other conditions provide preferences over simple lotteries. Reduction of compound lotteries is done according to the laws of probability, under the assumption that the probabilities in each lottery are independent. For example, let $L_1 = (.4C_1, .6C_2)$ and $L_2 = (.5C_1, .5C_3)$. Then $L_3 = (.6L_1, .4L_2)$ is equivalent to $L_3' = [.6(.4C_1, .6C_2), .4(.5C_1, .5C_3)] = [(.24 + .2)C_1, .36C_2, .2C_3] = (.44C_1, .36C_2, .2C_3)$.

> Exercise 2.3: Reduce the compound lottery $(.3L_1, .4L_2, .3L_3)$ to a simple lottery among C_1, C_2, and C_3 where each of the lotteries is defined as in the example directly above.

The third condition allows us to create a lottery between the best and the worst outcome that makes the decider indifferent between this lottery and the consequence for certain. The fourth condition states that the equivalent lottery can be substituted for the consequence. Together, these two assumptions allow us to take any lottery, compound or simple, and reduce it to a simple lottery between the best and the worst outcome. First, reduce any compound lottery to a simple lottery in all the consequences. Second, substitute the equivalent lottery for each outcome in the simple lottery other than the best and worst outcomes. Finally, reduce that new compound lottery to a simple lottery between just the best and worst outcomes.

But the third condition also contains a very important pair of assumptions—the best outcome is not so desirable that the decider will accept any lottery with a nonzero chance of the best outcome over any other outcome for certain, and the worst outcome is not so undesirable that the decider will accept any other outcome for certain over any lottery with a nonzero chance of the worst outcome. Put another way, the third condition excludes infinite utilities for outcomes. Infinite utilities produce very bizarre behavior.[6] For example, some argue that nuclear war has a negative infinite utility. If one accepts this position, then you must prefer any outcome without nuclear war—imagine your own personal nonnuclear nightmare here—for certain to any lottery that gives any nonzero probability of nuclear war. The nonnuclear nightmare is preferred to a lottery in which everyone on earth flips a coin simultaneously and if all five billion–plus coins come up heads, a nuclear war results, while if even one coin comes up tails, world peace (or your own personal idea of bliss) is realized.[7] I find it hard to believe that you would choose the nonnuclear nightmare for certain over the lottery. My point here is not that infinite utilities do not "exist," but, rather, that infinite utilities have some bizarre consequences for the choices predicted.

In the fifth condition, we assume transitivity in preferences among lotteries. The sixth condition is the Sure Thing Principle. If we compare two simple lotteries between the best and the worst outcomes, the lottery that gives the larger chance of the best outcome (and thus the lower probability of the worst outcome) should be preferred. It is a "sure thing." The Sure Thing Principle allows us to compare any lotteries. We reduce them to a simple lottery of the best and the worst outcomes, using the equivalent lotteries for each outcome. The lottery that produces the greater chance of the most preferred outcome is preferred according to the Sure Thing Principle.

These six conditions together allow us to estimate utilities as follows. First, we find a lottery equivalent to each consequence, using the third condition. Using the second and fourth conditions, we can substitute these lotteries for the consequences in any lottery and reduce the resulting compound lottery to a simple lottery between the best and worst outcomes, C_1 and C_n. Then the rank of all lotteries is given by the probability of obtaining the best outcome in these reduced lotteries by the Sure Thing Principle. Set the utility of the best consequence at 1, $u(C_1) = 1$, and the utility of the worst consequence at 0, $u(C_n) = 0$. The utility of each consequence is just the probability of obtaining C_1 in its equivalent lottery from the third condition.

The Expected Utility Theorem provides us with a way to represent deciders' preferences on a cardinal scale. The differences in utility among outcomes allow us to judge what risks deciders will accept. Because utilities are calculated from deciders' willingness to take risks, they measure relative preference among outcomes by the probabilities of obtaining different outcomes. Such utility functions are called **Von Neumann–Morgenstern utility functions** in honor of the two men who originally proved the Expected Utility Theorem.

Exercise 2.4:

a) Calculate a Von Neumann–Morgenstern utility function consistent with the following preferences: $C_1PC_2PC_3PC_4$ with equivalent lotteries $\hat{C}_2 = (.65C_1, .35C_4)$ and $\hat{C}_3 = (.4C_1, .6C_4)$ for C_2 and C_3.

b) Using this utility function, determine which of the following two lotteries is preferred: $L_1 = (.3C_1, .2C_2, .2C_3, .3C_4)$ or $L_2 = (.03C_1, .4C_2, .5C_3, .07C_4)$.

Utility functions reflect an individual's preferences for lotteries over the possible consequences. We can predict an individual's decisions if we have a utility function representing the decider's preferences and the probability of each possible consequence for each action. We calculate the expected utility for each action—the action with the greatest expected utility is the choice.

Some Common Misconceptions about Utility Theory

The concept of utility may seem simple, but it is frequently misunderstood. This section covers some simple misunderstandings of utility. I state each misconception, and then explain why it is incorrect.

> *Misconception 1:* L *is preferred to* L′ *because the expected utility of L is greater than the expected utility of* L′.

This fallacy has the causation backwards—the expected utility of L is greater because L is preferred to L′. Utilities are constructed to represent preferences; preferences do not arise from utilities. Almost everyone who works with utility theory slips into this fallacy at some point because of the close identification between utility calculations and decisions in utility models. Nevertheless, utilities are constructs to represent preferences over actions, not a simulacrum of the decision process. Criticisms of rational choice approaches that contend that actors do not perform the calculations in the theory are incorrect on their face. There is no claim that utilities reflect cognitive process within individuals. Rather, utility functions can be constructed that are consistent with observed behavior.

> *Misconception 2: Let* A, B, C, *and* D *be outcomes with* APBPCPD. *Suppose that* u(A) + u(D) = u(B) + u(C). *Then* L = ($\frac{1}{2}$B, $\frac{1}{2}$C) *should be preferred to* L′ = ($\frac{1}{2}$A, $\frac{1}{2}$D), *even though they have the same expected utility because the former has less utility variance.*

If two lotteries have identical expected utilities, then the decider must be indifferent between them. Otherwise the behavior is inconsistent. The expected utility of L is $\frac{1}{2}$u(B) + $\frac{1}{2}$u(C). The expected utility of L′ is $\frac{1}{2}$u(A) + $\frac{1}{2}$u(D), which equals the expected utility of L by assumption. Then the decider must be indifferent between these two lotteries. Utility functions are calculated to represent reactions to risky situations in the expected utilities. Recall that we chose the utility of an outcome based on the risk the decider was willing to accept in the lottery between the best and worst outcome that was equivalent to that outcome. The other assumptions of the expected utility theorem showed that these values represented all preferences of the lotteries if those preferences are consistent. Then all reactions to risk in lotteries are included in the expected utilities. The variance of the expected utilities has no meaning in utility theory.

Misconception 3: Let A, B, C, *and* D *be outcomes with* APBPCPD. *Suppose that* u(A) − u(B) > u(C) − u(D). *Then the change from* B *to* A *is more preferred than the change from* D *to* C.

Utility functions only represent preferences between gambles. They cannot be used to draw conclusions about the net desirability of moving from one outcome to another. If we could express this change in terms of lotteries, then we could judge which lottery would be preferred. But utilities do not give the net desirability of changes between outcomes. Rather, they specify what risks a decider prefers among a set of available actions.

Misconception 4: If A *and* B *are outcomes,* i *and* j *are actors, and* $u_i(A) - u_i(B) > u_j(A) - u_j(B)$, *then* i *prefers the change from* B *to* A *more than* j *does.*

Utility theory does not allow interpersonal comparisons of utilities. A utility function simply represents an individual's preferences over gambles, not his or her "true" intensity of preference. For example, let $u_i(A) = 1, u_i(B) = 0, u_j(A) = \frac{1}{2}$, and $u_j(B) = 0$. At first glance, it may appear that i prefers the shift from B to A more than j does. But if you recall the construction of the utilities from the equivalent lotteries, the utility of the best and worst outcomes were chosen arbitrarily to be 1 and 0, respectively. If we chose the endpoints of j's utility scale to be 10 and 0 instead, then all of j's utilities would be multiplied by a factor of 10, yielding $u_j(A) = 5$ and $u_j(B) = 0$. But then j appears to prefer the change from B to A more strongly than i does.

Interpersonal comparisons are more difficult than they appear from this simple illustration. Even if we give all actors identical utility for their best and worst outcomes, we cannot know that each actor's best outcome produces the same amount of "bliss" for him or her. Imagine a set of outcomes where all agree the best outcome is receiving a shot of heroin. A heroin addict would find this outcome far more desirable than would those of us with no curiosity about the effects of heroin and a substantial fear of addiction. Assigning the same utility to this outcome for all actors does not imply that all see the outcome as equally desirable.

Utility Functions and Types of Preferences*

Having covered the technical details of how utility is calculated and some common misunderstandings of the concept, I will now demonstrate the use of utility functions. Often we treat outcomes as a continuous set and define a

*This section requires differential calculus.

utility function across them. Although outcomes are rarely continuous (even money cannot be divided into smaller units than pennies for practical purposes), it is often easier to treat a large set of outcomes as a continuous set. For example, there are many, but probably only a finite number of, positions that a candidate can adopt on an issue. If the number of positions is large, say a hundred or more, it is easier to represent the set of positions on the issue as a continuum from the furthest left to the furthest right position possible on the issue. A function allows us to specify the utility of each position easily. The utility of a position is the value of the utility function for that position.

For example, let x be a number between -10 and 10. Let $u(x) = ax + b$, with $a > 0$, so more x is better—utility increases with x. Is $x = 2$ for certain preferable to $L = (.5, x = 1; .5, x = 3)$?

$$u(2) = a(2) + b = 2a + b,$$

and

$$u(L) = .5[a(1) + b] + .5[a(3) + b] = .5a + .5b + 1.5a + .5b$$
$$= 2a + b.$$

This decider is indifferent between an outcome of 2 for certain and the lottery L; $u(2) = u(L)$.

Now let $L' = (.5, x = -1; .5, x = 5)$ and $L^* = (.3, x = -10; .7, x = 8)$. Which is preferred?

$$u(L') = .5[a(-1) + b] + .5[a(5) + b] = 2a + b,$$

and

$$u(L*) = .3[a(-10) + b] + .7[a(8) + b] = 2.6a + b,$$

so L^*PL'.

Neither of these answers depends upon the values of a or b (given $a > 0$). Utility functions are determined only up to a linear transformation. You can add any number to a utility function or multiply it by any positive number, and the resulting function represents the same preferences over lotteries. This property determines in part why interpersonal comparisons of utilities are not permitted. If I can always multiply my utility function by any positive number and retain its ability to represent my preferences, the magnitude of utility differences between any two outcomes is meaningless. I can make that difference as large as I desire simply by multiplying my utility function by a large number.

But then how do utility functions capture different willingness to take risks? In their shapes. The utility function above, $ax + b$, evaluates gambles according to their mathematical expectation (see Appendix One for a definition of a mathematical expectation). The first pair of gambles had an identical expected value, 2. The first gamble in the second pair had an expected value of 2; the second, 2.6. We can show that the expected utility of any gamble using this utility function is a(expectation of the gamble) +b. **Risk-neutral** actors have no premium for or against risky gambles; they evaluate gambles solely on the basis of the expectation of those gambles. Risk-neutral utility functions are linear.

> Exercise 2.5: Show that the expected utility of a gamble, G, with $G = (p_1x_1, p_2x_2, \ldots p_nx_n)$, is $aE(G) + b$ for $u(x) = ax + b$, where $E(G) = \sum_{i=1}^{n} p_ix_i$ is the expectation of G.

Preferences for and against risks are represented in the shape of utility functions. Deciders unwilling to take risks have utility functions that bow upwards from a line, like an upside-down bowl. The mathematical term is *concave downward;* the second derivative of the utility function is less than zero, $u''(x) < 0$. Such actors are called **risk averse**. Among gambles with an equal expectation, risk-averse actors prefer the gamble with a smaller variance in outcome. Further, risk-averse actors prefer some gambles that have both less risk and a lower expectation than other gambles. **Risk-acceptant** preferences are represented by utility functions that bow below a line. The mathematical term is *concave upward;* the second derivative of the utility function is greater than zero, $u''(x) > 0$. Risk-acceptant actors prefer risky gambles among a set with the same expectation. They also prefer some gambles with both greater risk and lower expectation than other gambles. Neither risk acceptance nor risk aversion implies that such actors always prefer gambles with greater or lower risks, respectively. An actor that is more risk acceptant than another accepts all the gambles that the latter will and some that the latter will not.

Figure 2.1 shows three utility functions: one risk neutral, u_{rn}; one risk averse, u_{rav}; and one risk acceptant, u_{rac}. The outcomes are graphed on the horizontal axis, and utility on the vertical axis. Consider a choice between a median outcome, M, for certain and a gamble that will result in either the best outcome, B, with a probability of p, or the worst outcome, W, with a probability of $1 - p$. All three deciders have the same utility for the best and for the worst outcome. Let M be such that the risk-neutral decider is indifferent between the lottery and the median outcome for certain, $u_{rn}(M) = pu(B) + (1 - p)u(W) = EU$. The risk-neutral utility function is linear as noted above. The risk-averse utility function arches above the risk-neutral function. The risk-averse utility function prefers the median

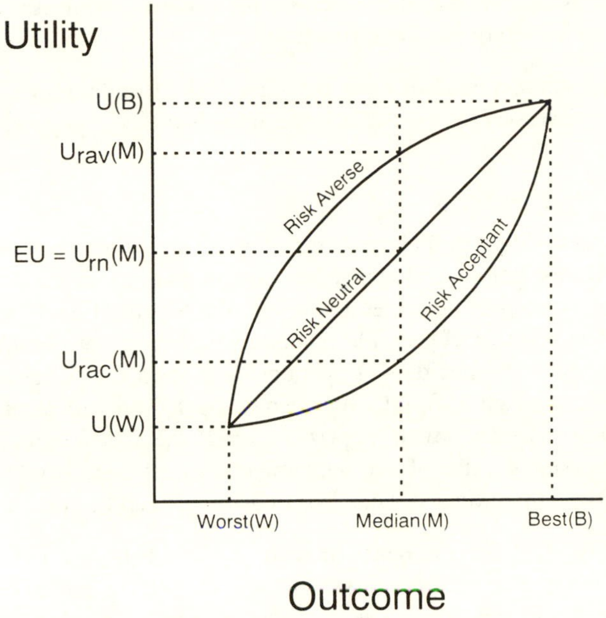

Figure 2.1 Three Utility Functions with Different Risk Attitudes

outcome for certain over the lottery because the utility of the median outcome is greater than the expected utility of the lottery, $u_{rav}(M) > EU$. The risk-acceptant utility function curves below the risk-neutral utility function. It prefers the lottery to the median for certain; its expected utility for the lottery exceeds its utility for the median outcome for certain, $u_{rac}(M) < EU$.

Exercise 2.6: Calculate the expected utility of each of the following gambles for each of the following utility functions (a total of nine calculations):

Gamble	Utility Function
$L_1 = (.5, x = 0; .5, x = 2)$	$u_1(x) = x$
$L_2 = (1, x = 1)$	$u_2(x) = x^2$
$L_3 = (.8, x = 0; .2, x = 4)$	$u_3(x) = \sqrt{x}$

For each utility function, rank the three gambles from most attractive to least attractive. Which of the three is risk acceptant, which is risk averse, and which is risk neutral? (Hint: it may help to sketch each of the three functions.)

Utility functions need not have the same risk attitude across all ranges of values. They can be risk averse in some areas and risk acceptant or neutral in others.

Preferences over Time

Actors can also differ in their preference over time when they receive prizes over several time periods. Models often assume that actors make choices over several time periods of equal length, where the length of each period is fixed and known in advance. Desirable outcomes earlier are preferable. **Discount factors** represent the deciders' impatience for rewards. An actor's discount factor, usually written as δ, falls between 0 and 1. The smaller it is, the more the actor prefers prizes now over prizes later. If the utility of an outcome is x now, the discounted value of that outcome one time period from now is δx, its discounted value two time periods from now is $\delta^2 x$, and so on.

Exercise 2.7: Governments in early modern Europe, particularly the Dutch government, raised money by selling annuities. The buyer would pay a lump sum of money, say, a hundred guilders, and then once a year from then on, would receive a payment of G guilders. Assume buyers are risk neutral for money; $u(x) = x$.

a) If a decider's discount factor is .9 per year, calculate the annual payment that makes it indifferent between paying the lump sum and the annuity. (Hint: it helps to know that

$$\sum_{i=1}^{+\infty} x^i = x + x^2 + x^3 \ldots = \frac{x}{1-x};$$

see Appendix One.)

b) If a decider's discount factor is δ per year, calculate the annual payment that makes it indifferent between paying the lump sum and the annuity.

A Simple Example: The Calculus of Deterrence

The above examples are calculations detached from substantive interest. I turn to a simple example of the application of utility theory, the logic of deterrence in international relations. Deterrence, in the broadest sense, is the attempt by one nation, called the defender, to forestall anticipated actions by another nation, called the challenger, by a threat to impose costs on the second nation. For the purposes of this discussion, I will not consider the many variations in international relations on this basic logic. I present a simple utility theory model that reflects the logic of deterrence in this broadest sense. The exercises in this section lead you through some alternatives. All of the mathematics here is very simple; as Barry Nalebuff has quipped, "[I]n truth, the calculus of deterrence might have better been called [the] algebra [of deterrence]" (1991, 313).

The general logic of deterrence covers many situations in politics. The threat of economic sanctions, the use of force to defend allies, and general deterrence of nuclear war are a few of the forms of deterrence in international relations. Deterrence also occurs in domestic politics. In the United States, for example, Congress uses its power of oversight as a threat against some executive agencies to try to control their policies. One justification for the punishment of criminals is the assumed deterrence of other crimes.

In this model, I assume that the situation is not purely a misunderstanding of the challenger's intentions by the defender; in other words, I assume that absent the deterrent threat, the challenger would take the anticipated action. I also assume that each side treats the other's response as a lottery with known probabilities.

Consider the challenger's decision after the defender has made a deterrent threat. It faces two options: it can press ahead with its intended action or back down. If the challenger backs down, the outcome is the existing situation, and the challenger may suffer some damage to its reputation in the eyes of its audience, either other nations or domestic constituencies. Call this outcome BD for Back Down; the challenger has utility $u_{CH}(BD)$ for it. (The subscript CH tells us that it is the challenger's utility for the back down outcome.) If the challenger presses ahead with its intended action, there is a chance, p, that the defender will carry out its deterrent threat. The challenger will suffer the costs of that retaliation. Call this outcome TC for Threat Carried out; the challenger has utility $u_{CH}(TC)$ for it. There is then a probability, $1 - p$, that the defender will not carry out its threat, in which case the challenger will take its intended action. Call this outcome CS for Challenger Succeeds (from the challenger's point of view, it is a success); the challenger has utility $u_{CH}(CS)$ for it. Assume that the challenger prefers success to backing down and prefers backing down to having the defender carry out its threat. Then $u_{CH}(CS) > u_{CH}(BD) > u_{CH}(TC)$.

Deterrence works when the challenger prefers backing down to pressing ahead with its intended action. The challenger is deterred when

$$u_{CH}(BD) > p[u_{CH}(TC)] + (1 - p)[u_{CH}(CS)].$$

Solving for p, we obtain

$$p > \frac{u_{CH}(CS) - u_{CH}(BD)}{u_{CH}(CS) - u_{CH}(TC)}.$$

We can think of p as the credibility of the defender's intention to carry out its threat. The greater p is, the stronger the challenger's belief that the defender will carry out its threat. The right-hand side of the inequality above is the challenger's critical risk. The challenger presses ahead if p, the credibility of the defender's intention, is less than its critical risk and is deterred when p is greater than that. The numerator of the challenger's critical risk gives the difference between success and backing down, the possible gain if the challenger takes its desired action. The denominator gives the difference between success and the threat's being carried out, the loss to the challenger if it presses ahead and then the defender carries out its threat.

We could determine when the challenger would press ahead with its threat if we knew the values of all the terms in the above inequality. However, these terms are difficult to measure because we cannot ask historical figures to give us their complete preferences over all possible lotteries. Instead, I derive hypotheses about when deterrence is more likely to work. If p is held constant, increases in the critical risk make deterrence less likely to succeed, and decreases make it more likely to succeed. If the challenger's critical risk is held constant, the greater the credibility of the defender's intention to carry out its threat (i.e., the larger p is), the more likely deterrence is to succeed.

How do changes in the challenger's utilities for the outcomes affect the probability that deterrence will succeed? The method of comparative statics can answer this question. Comparative statics analysis examines the effect of one variable on behavior by holding all other variables constant.[8] The greater the costs that the defender can impose on the challenger, the more likely deterrence is to succeed. As $u_{CH}(TC)$ decreases, the denominator grows, which lowers the critical risk. The greater $u_{CH}(BD)$ is, the more likely deterrence is to succeed. There are at least two ways the defender can influence $u_{CH}(BD)$. The more attractive the status quo is for the challenger, the greater is $u_{CH}(BD)$. The lower the audience costs of backing down, the more likely it is that the challenger will back down. Thus the prospects for deterrence can be improved by offering some concessions to the challenger if it backs down. Such concessions can reduce the audience costs of backing down, thereby raising the attractiveness of the resulting situation. The greater is $u_{CH}(CS)$, the less likely it is that deterrence will succeed. Increases in $u_{CH}(CS)$ raise both the numerator and denominator of the critical risk; the total effect causes the critical risk to rise. The greater the value of taking the desired action unopposed, the less likely it is that deterrence will succeed.

These results have two caveats. First, all three of the relevant terms are the challenger's utilities for the outcomes, not the outcomes themselves. The success of deterrence depends not on the objective damage that the defender can impose on the challenger, but on how the challenger reacts to the possibility of that damage. Concessions that the defender offers to encourage the challenger to back down may not be successful if the challenger does not see those concessions as valuable. Second, assuming that infinite utilities do not exist, deterrence will fail if the challenger's estimate of the defender's intention to carry out its threat is sufficiently low. Deterrence cannot work if the challenger does not believe the defender may carry out the threat, even if the threatened costs are high and the benefits of carrying out the action are small.

> Exercise 2.8: Some argue that deterrence involves not only a threat to prevent action by the challenger, but also a promise by the defender not to attack the challenger if the latter backs down. In some cases, the challenger wants to take the action because it fears that the defender's will attack if it backs down. Recast the decision problem above so there is a probability, q, that the defender will impose costs on the challenger if it backs down. What hypotheses can you derive from this revised model? Can deterrence ever work if $q > p$?

The defender faces a prior choice of whether to make a deterrent threat. If that threat always works, every defender wishes to make such a threat. If it never works, only defenders who gain by imposing costs on the challenger will make such a threat. But what should the defender do when it is uncertain how the challenger will respond to a threat? Assume that the defender believes that the challenger will take some action if it does not threaten the challenger with punishment. Call the resulting outcome NT for No Threat. The No Threat outcome entails the challenger's proceeding with its action, and the defender has utility $u_D(NT)$ for this outcome. If the defender makes a deterrent threat, the challenger could back down or press ahead with its intended action. Let there be a probability of r that the challenger presses ahead. We can think of this probability as the defender's perception of the challenger's intentions. The greater r is, the more convinced the defender is that the challenger intends to proceed regardless of a deterrent threat. There is a probability of $1 - r$ that the challenger backs down in the face of the threat. Call this outcome BD, as before, for Back Down. The status quo is preserved if the challenger backs down, and the defender has utility $u_D(BD)$ for this outcome. If the challenger presses ahead, the defender either carries out its threat or not. If it fails to carry out its threat, we have outcome CS, as before. If it does carry out its threat, outcome TC results. For now, I ignore the question of what the defender does if the challenger presses ahead and call the resulting outcome CP for Challenger Presses ahead. The defender has utility $u_D(CP)$ for the resulting outcome, where $u_D(CP)$ is the greater of $u_D(CS)$ or $u_D(TC)$. We assume that the defender prefers BD to NT and prefers NT to CP; $u_D(BD) > u_D(NT) > u_D(CP)$.

The defender makes a deterrent threat when

$$u_D(NT) < r[u_D(CP)] + (1 - r)[u_D(BD)].$$

Solving for r, we obtain

$$r < \frac{u_D(BD) - u_D(NT)}{u_D(BD) - u_D(CP)}.$$

As with the challenger's decision whether to press ahead, we can use comparative statics to determine when the defender is more likely to make a deterrent threat. The defender's critical risk is given by the right-hand side of the inequality above. If the defender's critical risk is held constant, deterrence is more likely to be tried as r decreases—as the defender becomes more convinced that the challenger can be deterred.

Increasing values of the defender's critical risk increase the chance that the defender will make a deterrent threat. Increases in the defender's utility for the No Threat outcome make it less likely that the defender will try deterrence. The less threatening the challenger's intended action if unchecked, that is, as $u_D(NT)$ increases, the less likely it is that the defender will run the risk of trying to deter it. The less attractive the outcome if the challenger presses forward, the less likely it is that the defender will attempt deterrence. As $u_D(CP)$ decreases, the denominator grows, and deterrence is less likely to be tried. Whether $u_D(CP)$ decreases with changes in $u_D(CS)$ and $u_D(TC)$ depends upon what the defender will do if deterrence is challenged. If the defender will not carry out the threat, that is, if $u_D(CP) = u_D(CS)$, then increases in the costs of carrying out the threat, that is, in $u_D(TC)$, have no effect on whether or not the defender tries deterrence. Similarly, changes in the audience costs of not carrying out a deterrent threat, that is, changes in $u_D(CS)$, do not matter if the defender intends to carry it out, that is, if $u_D(CP) = u_D(TC)$. Finally, increases in the defender's utility for the challenger's backing down increase the chance that deterrence will be tried. The critical risk rises.

> Exercise 2.9: Some argue that the challenger has no real intention of proceeding with the action in many situations where deterrent threats are made. Recast the model to capture this possibility. If no threat is made, there is a probability, s, that the challenger does not take the feared action, and consider this outcome the same as BD. When are deterrent threats made in this model? Discuss.

> Exercise 2.10: The assumed preferences play a large role in the analysis above. Discuss when deterrence is tried if $u_D(CP) > u_D(NT)$ and when deterrence succeeds if $u_{CH}(TC) > u_{CH}(BD)$. What situations do these alternate assumptions model?

It may seem odd to you that the two decisions appear unrelated. Deterrence is commonly thought of as an interaction between the two sides. Deterrence theorists often recommend increasing the credibility of the threat. But p, which measures the credibility of the defender's intention to carry out its threat, is fixed in this model. Actions to try to raise p are not available to the defender. This limitation of the calculus of deterrence is a consequence of modeling deterrence with decision theory. Deterrence theorists believe that the sides change their perceptions of each other's intentions through their interaction. The credibility of threats can be influenced by actions. The challenger may change its judgment of how likely the defender is to carry out the threat. The defender should choose its acts in part for their effect on the challenger's judgments about the defender's intentions. The challenger may imply that it intends to take actions that it has no interest in pursuing, simply to probe the intentions of the defender. If the defender offers no resistance, the challenger may expand its challenge to other, more valuable areas of conflict. Modeling these interactive decisions requires a game theory model, the subject of the following chapters.

Another Simple Example: The Decision to Vote

Consider an individual deciding whether to vote in an election, and if so, for which candidate. We assume that there are two candidates, with the colorful names of Candidate 1 and Candidate 2. Assume that the voter prefers Candidate 1, C1, to Candidate 2, C2, and that the voter's net benefit if Candidate 1 is elected over Candidate 2 is B. Let u(C1 elected) = B and u(C2 elected) = 0. The net benefit could include the policies that the voter believes that Candidate 1 will enact, judgments of the candidates' competence to hold office, or material benefits that Candidate 1 has promised to the voter. I simplify away from the questions of how the voter reaches the judgment that Candidate 1 will produce preferable outcomes for the voter. There are many interesting questions in decision theory in the evaluation of candidates, but I choose to focus on the question of when the voter should vote.

The act of voting imposes some costs, C, with $C > 0$, which are subtracted from the possible benefits of voting. These costs include time spent going to the polls and registering to vote. Let p(Ci wins|A) be the probability that Candidate i will win given that the voter takes action A, the action of voting for Candidate i, voting for Candidate j, or abstaining. Voting for a candidate increases his or her chance of winning, so

$$p(\text{Ci wins}|\text{vote Ci}) > p(\text{Ci wins}|\text{abstain}) > p(\text{Ci wins}|\text{vote Cj})$$

Calculate expected utilities for all three possible actions (voting for candidate 1, voting for Candidate 2, not voting):

$$\begin{aligned}
u(\text{vote C1}) &= p(\text{C1 wins}|\text{vote C1})B + p(\text{C2 wins}|\text{vote C1})0 - C,\\
u(\text{vote C2}) &= p(\text{C1 wins}|\text{vote C2})B + p(\text{C2 wins}|\text{vote C2})0 - C,\\
u(\text{abstain}) &= p(\text{C1 wins}|\text{abstain})B + p(\text{C2 wins}|\text{abstain})0.
\end{aligned}$$

Voting for Candidate 1 is always better than voting for Candidate 2 because $B > 0$. When will voters bother to vote for their preferred candidate? Compare the expected utilities of the two actions. Voting is preferred when

$$u(\text{vote C1}) > u(\text{abstain}),$$

that is, when

$$[p(\text{C1 wins}|\text{vote C1}) - p(\text{C1 wins}|\text{abstain})]B > C.$$

Although the costs of voting are small, they are not zero. The difference between the two probabilities is the marginal effect of a vote on a candidate's chance of winning. The magnitude of this difference depends on the number of other voters in the election and very roughly equals 1/[2(number of other voters)]. In a presidential election in the United States, p is vanishingly small (in the neighborhood of .00000002). Even if B is relatively large, it seems very likely that the costs of voting are greater than the expected benefits. Hence the question, Why does anyone bother to vote?

This paradox of voting produces significant problems for the application of utility theory to politics; large numbers of people vote in every election, even for such officials as dog catcher and commissioner of the Mosquito Abatement District. I will discuss several solutions to this paradox. The first involves the observation that utility functions reflect behavior, as opposed to the other way around. The costs may not be as great as we think. For example, many individuals may derive benefits from the act of voting itself (referred to as the D term), independent of how they cast their vote. A sense of civic obligation may drive them to feel they must vote, or a desire to express support for their government in general, or simply a fascination with voting machines and an appreciation for the entertainment value of voting (I fall into the last category). Then, if $D > C$ (i.e., if the benefits for the act of voting in and of itself are greater than the costs of voting), voting is rational.

But does this explanation provide us with any empirical handle on why people vote? Both C and D, the costs and benefits of voting apart from its value in electing candidates, are unobservable. Any turnout is consistent with this explanation, then. Anyone who votes has $D > C$, and anyone who does not vote has $C > D$, and there is no obvious way to check these values. Later, I discuss another possible solution to the paradox of voting.

Why Might Utility Theory Not Work?

Although utility theory is very flexible and allows us to represent consistency in behavior, psychological experiments demonstrate violations of utility theory in people's behavior. I begin with the best-known example, the Allais paradox.

Example: Choose one of the two gambles in each of the following two pairs of gambles (I suggest you note which gambles you would choose in each case):

Choice 1:

L_1 = \$500,000 for certain, or

L_2 = \$2,500,000 with probability .1;
\$500,000 with probability .89; and
\$0 with probability .01

Choice 2:

L_3 = \$500,000 with probability .11 and
\$0 with probability .89 or

L_4 = \$2,500,000 with probability .1 and
\$0 with probability .9

If you chose one even-numbered gamble and one odd-numbered gamble, your choices are inconsistent with utility theory because they violate the Sure Thing Principle. To see the inconsistency, calculate expected utilities for each of the four gambles:

$$u(L_1) = u(\$500{,}000);$$
$$u(L_2) = .1[u(\$2{,}500{,}000)] + .89[u(\$500{,}000)] + .01[u(\$0)];$$
$$u(L_3) = .11[u(\$500{,}000)] + .89[u(\$0)];$$
$$u(L_4) = .1[u(\$2{,}500{,}000)] + .9[u(\$0)].$$

If L_1 is preferred to L_2, then

$$.11[u(\$500{,}000)] > .1[u(\$2{,}500{,}000)] + .01[u(\$0)].$$

Add .89[u(\$0)] to each side and we have the following:

$$.11[u(\$500{,}000)] + .89[u(\$0)] > .1[u(\$2{,}500{,}000)] + .9[u(\$0)].$$

Substituting back gives us $u(L_3) > u(L_4)$, which implies that L_3 is preferred to L_4.

Choices of one even and one odd gamble in the pairs of choices are quite common in psychological experiments based on this paradox. In the Allais paradox, people often prefer certainties over chances in the first pair of gambles; in the second pair, they go for the big bucks. Another example, the Ellsberg paradox, uses subjective probabilities.[9] In experiments based on this paradox, people tend to shy away from an unknown probability in favor of an known probability. However, these are tendencies in behavior, not ironclad regularities. Many people do make consistent choices in these paradoxes.

What does this mean for utility theory? First of all, people do not always react to probabilities as the theory demands. When faced with very high-probablity or very low-probability events (i.e., p close to 1 or 0, respectively) some people respond in strange ways. They inflate the probabilities of very low-probability events or else ignore the probability of those events. When faced with very probable but not certain events, people tend to subjectively lower those probabilities. Consequently, they are willing to pay excessively to obtain a certain outcome.

These observations may explain why people vote. The probability of determining the outcome of an election is vanishingly small, but it may not be so in the minds of voters. If people treat this probability as, say, .01 instead of .00000002, voting could be rational for reasonable values of the costs and benefits of voting. However, such an explanation is no more satisfying than the addition of the benefits of voting argument was. Like the evocation of the D term, this argument cannot distinguish voters from nonvoters except by the observation that they voted. Hypotheses that address something other than patterns of turnout are needed to determine which hypotheses is supported by the evidence. It is possible that no evidence could separate the two explanations.

The use of reference points in decisions also violates utility theory. Preferences should not be influenced by the description of outcomes. Unfortunately, preferences can be shaped by the reference points people use to judge the outcomes. The following example, taken from Quattrone and Tversky 1988, demonstrates the idea of reference points:

> Example: There are two candidates in an election, Brown and Green, who both propose economic policies. Two highly regarded economists then make projections about the standard of living in the country over the next two years if each candidate's set of policies is adopted. The economists are both impartial and equally skilled. Both economists also provide a prediction for the standard of living in comparable nations in the next two years. Table 2.2 gives their predictions of living standards converted to dollars. Which candidate's policy do you prefer?

Table 2.2

	Other Nations	Brown's Policy	Green's Policy
Economist 1	$43,000	$65,000	$51,000
Economist 2	$45,000	$43,000	$53,000

Economic Forecasts for
Brown's and Green's Policies

In another election, Brown and Green again face each other. Their proposed policies are again evaluated by two eminent economists, who also provide predictions for a comparable set of other nations. Table 2.3 presents the new predictions. Which candidate's policy do you prefer?

It is not unusual to find that people prefer Green in the first race and Brown in the second. But the only changes from the first to the second comparison are the estimates of the other nations' standard of living. The outcomes remain the same in both comparisons. What is going on here? Of the two candidates, Brown's policy offers a higher expectation than does Green's policy, assuming each economist's prediction is equally likely to be true. But Green's policies are less risky in the economists' eyes. How people evaluate risks depends whether they see those risks as gains or losses. In the first election, Green is preferred because he offers a certain gain over the reference point of the other nations, while Brown offers a riskier gain. In the second election, Brown is preferred because she offers a chance of avoiding a loss relative to the now-higher reference point of the other nations, while Green offers the certainty of a loss. The generality lurking here is that people are risk averse when choosing among gambles that offer increases from the reference point and risk acceptant when choosing among gambles that offer losses from the reference point.

Table 2.3

	Other Nations	Brown's Policy	Green's Policy
Economist 1	$63,000	$65,000	$51,000
Economist 2	$65,000	$43,000	$53,000

More Economic Forecasts for
Brown's and Green's Policies

Utility functions can be risk acceptant over some outcomes and risk averse over other ranges. But here those ranges are defined by a reference point that can change. If the reference point changes, then the evaluation of outcomes is inconsistent. Reference points can be altered by how the gambles are offered—by what is called the framing of the question.

The observation of framing effects is important, but it begs the question of how reference points are defined and when they change. Psychologists can choose reference points in their experiments through the wording of their questions, altering those points when they choose. It is more difficult to see what reference points should be in political situations. For example, one can argue that the status quo in international politics is the reference point. Do all actors see the status quo as the reference point, or do some actors see their reference point elsewhere? When does the reference point change during a crisis—at at every intermediate step, or only at the end? These questions are not insurmountable, but they will require answers before prospect theory increases our understanding of politics.

These questions bring up the critical consideration that leads me to use utility and game theory even in the face of these problems. Is there a better alternative? Prospect theory, the psychologists' alternative to utility theory, is substantially more complicated than utility theory. It requires information about individuals' reference points and reactions to probabilities as well as their preferences over gambles. Although a substantial proportion of experimental subjects exhibit these inconsistencies, there are no results to my knowledge that tell us which individuals exhibit which inconsistencies. There are also theories of rational choice that do not use expected utilities (Machina 1987, 1989).

Selection pressures could explain why political leaders maximize expected utility. Inconsistent choices are common but not predominant in these experiments. Typically, one-quarter to one-third of the subjects exhibit inconsistent behavior. But inconsistent behavior is inefficient. Political leaders are selected as a consequence of their own decisions, through a competitive process. Inefficient choosers are less likely to be selected and advance than efficient choosers. Even if these inconsistencies are common in a population, they may be rare in that population's leaders. A model that demonstrated that inefficient choosers were denied advancement would strengthen this argument.

Further, the experimental results all address isolated decisions, rather than interactive decisions. Social and political settings involve interactive decisions; we need a theory that allows us to predict decisions in those settings. Strategic logic is quite complicated, even given the simplified representation of choices in utility theory. Game theory is built on utility theory. Someday, it may be replaced by a theory of strategic interaction based on some theory of individual choice other than utility theory. But for now, game theory is the tool we have to think about strategic interaction.

If these inconsistencies occur often in many phenomena of interest, then utility theory will not be a useful foundation on which to develop political science theory. However, if such violations are rare, then utility theory may be an acceptable framework. The test of whether utility theory is an acceptable foundation lies in how it can explicate useful theories of politics. Do such theories lead to novel hypotheses that can be tested? Do we gain insight into politics by using game theory to formalize our intuition? That test requires examining actual political decisions. The inconsistencies discussed here are experimental phenomena, not the choices of political actors. Establishing the case for the alternatives requires showing actual political choices that utility theory fails to predict and the alternative predicts successfully.

Although such approaches are quite interesting and may prove to be quite powerful, their proponents have not yet demonstrated their general importance to the construction of social theory based on individual choice. If you find these problems compelling, I encourage you to read further and try to apply them to explain political phenomena. You should also have an appreciation of what you abandon when you choose the alternative to game theory. Choice theory has led to a block of coherent and sophisticated theories of politics. Its application has led to testable hypotheses that are supported by the evidence of actual political decisions. Explicating political theory by using choice theory is difficult as it stands; strategic logic is complex. We should know what we can learn about politics with game theory before discarding it for an uncertain alternative.

Review

This chapter presents utility theory. The essential idea is that preferences over actions can be represented by a utility function. The expected utility for an action is the product of the utility of each outcome times the probability of that outcome given the action summed across all outcomes. Between a pair of actions, the one with greater expected utility is preferred.

Rational preferences are assumed to be connected and transitive. If preferences over consequences and lotteries are connected and transitive, compound lotteries can be reduced to simple lotteries, equivalent lotteries exist for all outcomes and are substitutable for them, and the Sure Thing Principle holds, then there exists a utility function that represents those preferences over lotteries. A utility function captures the willingness to take risks in its values. Differences in time preferences are captured in discount factors.

Further Reading

All of the textbooks on classical game theory discussed in the Further Reading section of Chapter One have chapters on utility theory at different levels of technical difficulty. I recommend Chapter Three of Kreps 1991 as the best source for further reading. Chapters Two and Thirteen in Luce and Raiffa 1957 are also a good source, although they include material that is quite dated. I learned from Savage 1972, one of the original sources. Savage 1972 presents the mathematics demonstrating the recovery of both a utility function and a subjective probability distribution from a set of preferences over actions. Savage also provides a good discussion of the motivation of utility theory and of many misinterpretations of the theory. *The New Palgrave: Utility and Probability* (Eatwell, Milgate, and Newman 1990) is a useful place to begin further reading.

Jackman 1993, Riker 1990, and Zagare 1990 are recent justifications of the assumption of rational choice in political science. The deterrence example traces originally back to Ellsberg 1960; my presentation here is different and more general. The voting example is quite well known in political science. Original sources are Downs 1957 and Riker and Ordeshook 1968. Aldrich 1993 is a recent survey on why people vote.

The work on violations of utility theory is found in psychology. Three initial sources are Quattrone and Tversky 1988, Kahneman and Tversky 1979, and Tversky and Kahneman 1981. The first uses political science examples, the second is the most technical and detailed, and the third is the shortest. Machina 1987 and Machina 1989 are accessible introductions to non–expected utility theories of rational choice.

Chapter Three
Specifying a Game

Game theory examines decisionmaking in situations where the decisions of several actors produce the final outcome. Consequently, each actor's decision depends upon the other actors' decisions. There is a very strong parallel between game theory and utility theory. The other actors' decisions in game theory correspond to the states of the world in decision theory. Actors attempt to establish the likely moves of the other actors and use their best available responses. Before we can analyze games, we need a formal structure to specify the players' interrelated decisions.

This chapter presents three different ways to specify a game. How do we go from an informal understanding of a situation to the formal statement of a game? The first section discusses deterrence in international crises and presents a game that captures some important aspects of such crises. This example introduces the basic elements of a game in the extensive form. The extensive form of a game details the players' choices, the order and consequences of their choices, how they evaluate those consequences, and what they know when they choose. Extensive forms can be reduced to the strategic form of a game through the use of strategies. A player's strategy for a game is a complete plan to play the game. In the strategic form, all players simultaneously select a strategy for the game. The interaction of their strategies determines the outcome.

Formalizing a Situation: Deterrence in the Cuban Missile Crisis

Political situations can present actors with many decisions under a variety of conditions. Before we can analyze those situations formally, we need to specify what choices the players have. Consider the Cuban missile crisis. Almost every analysis of the Crisis focuses on the three central decisions that Allison (1971, 39) identifies: "Why did the Soviet Union attempt to place offensive missiles in Cuba? Why did the United States choose to respond to the Soviet missile emplacement with a blockade of Cuba? Why did the Soviet Union decide to withdraw the missiles?"

But these questions are just the specific realizations of three general questions that arise in an explanation of any international crisis. We treat a crisis as a contest between two actors, a challenger and a defender. Why did the challenger attempt to change the status quo? Why did the other side respond to the

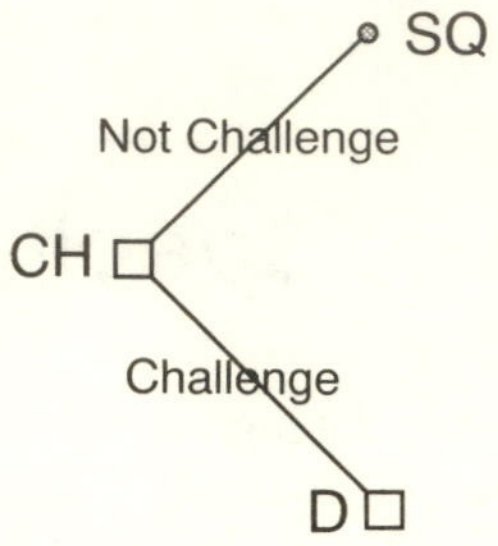

Figure 3.1 Challenger's First
Decision in Deterrence Game

challenge with a threat? Finally, why did one side or the other back down short of war, or if the crisis ended in war, why did both sides choose war instead of backing down? The choices of challenging the status quo and of resisting the challenger are necessary for a crisis. If the challenger does not attempt to change the status quo or if that attempt is not resisted, there is no crisis. Allison's three questions are just the specific examples in the Cuban missile crisis of these three general questions.

Models should strive to capture the general characteristics of a situation, as opposed to the specific decisions of a particular event. After the fact, one can always construct a model that reflects what happened. Game theory models are more illuminating when they address the general characteristics of recurrent situations in politics. For example, we study models of deterrence, rather than models of the Cuban missile crisis. The Cuban missile crisis will never occur again, but unfortunately military threats and deterrence may be with us forever.

The crisis began with the Soviet decision to place offensive missiles in Cuba. When this decision was made is not clear yet, but it certainly occurred before Kennedy's decision to blockade Cuba. It preceded the decision of the United States, and the decision of the Soviet Union was known to the United States when it decided on its response. We can model the initial decision in many ways. The simplest way is a simple binary choice between challenging or not challenging the status quo. We could create several types of challenges. In the Cuban missile crisis, these other challenges could include the deployment of Soviet ground troops in Cuba or a direct move against West Berlin. But those options are specific to the Cuban missile crisis; if we are constructing a model of international crises in general, we characterize the options simply as a provocative challenge or a nonprovocative challenge. For now, we keep our model simple and just examine two options, challenging or not challenging the status quo. Figure 3.1 represents this choice as a box called a **node,** labeled CH for the challenger, with two **branches** representing the two choices coming out of the box. The Not Challenge action ends the model with no crisis, an **outcome** labeled SQ, for status quo. The Challenge option leads to a decision

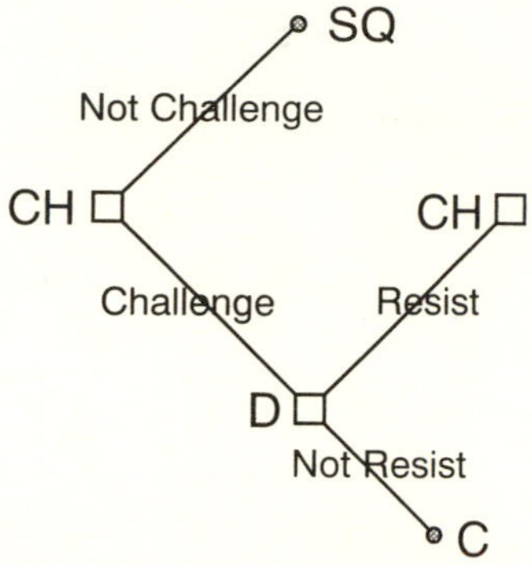

Figure 3.2 Challenger's First Decision and Defender's Decisions in Deterrence Game

by the defender, labeled D. This figure gives the model for the challenger's opening move.

The second decision in the crisis is up to the defender. It can resist the challenge, or it can make concessions to satisfy the challenger. Resistance could take one of many forms. In the Cuban missile crisis, for example, the United States could have resisted the challenge of the Soviet Union in a number of ways. It could have launched an air strike on the missile sites, invaded Cuba with ground troops, or applied diplomatic pressure through the United Nations. There were advocates of each of these options on the ExCom (short for Executive Committee) that discussed U.S. options. If the defender decides not to resist, concessions could take many possible forms. All of the challenger's demands could be granted, or negotiations could be opened after some initial concessions. But for simplicity, I allow the defender only two options, either resisting the challenge by making a threat or not resisting the challenge and granting sufficient concessions to the challenger to satisfy its demands. In the latter case, the crisis ends with an outcome I call C, for concessions. The defender makes this new move only after learning what the challenger did in its initial move. Adding the new move, we have Figure 3.2 of the first two decisions.

The decision by the United States to blockade Cuba parallels the defender's decision in the calculus of deterrence in Chapter Two. There, the challenger's response was treated as a lottery, in which the probability q gave the defender's confidence that the challenger would press its threat. But the challenger decided whether to press the threat in its own decision. The defender's confidence about the challenger's willingness to press its threat should reflect what the defender knows about the challenger's motivation to press the threat. That being the case, we need to include the challenger's final decision in the model.

The last choice in our model rests with the challenger, who must decide whether it will press the threat if the defender resists. We simplify this choice

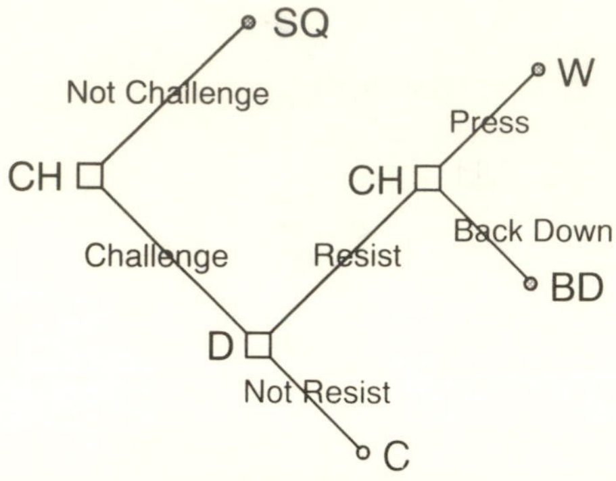

Figure 3.3 All Three Choices in Deterrence Game

into one between pressing the threat, which will cause a war, or backing down, which will end the crisis with no change in the status quo other than its effect on the players' reputations. Again, this choice in the real world is more complex than the choice in the model. The challenger could reduce its demands or make new threats, perhaps including third parties in the crisis. Like the defender in the second move, the challenger knows the prior decisions in the game when it must choose if it must make this final move. I label the last outcomes W, for war, and BD, for the challenger's backing down.

Figure 3.3 gives the complete sequence of decisions in this simple model of deterrence. It has four possible outcomes: the status quo (SQ), concessions by the defender to the challenger (C), the challenger's backing down (BD), and war, (W). As a next step, we need the actors' preferences over these outcomes. In this case, we can make some assumptions about which outcomes each actor prefers. All challengers should prefer concessions to the status quo and prefer the status quo to backing down. Having its demands granted changes the status quo in ways the challenger prefers—otherwise, it would not make those demands. And the deterrence literature generally sees backing down from a threat as more costly than not making the threat in the first place—the challenger may have to make concessions in the face of the defender's counterthreat; moreover, the credibility of its threats in the future is reduced (or at least many scholars think so). However, we cannot say how the challenger ranks war in its preference ordering. It could prefer war to concessions—that is, the challenger's demands could be simply an excuse to start a war—or it could prefer backing down to war, a true bluff.

Similarly, we can make some assumptions about the defender's preferences. It prefers the backing down outcome to the status quo and prefers the latter to making concessions itself. If the challenger backs down, future demands are unlikely either because the credibility of such threats has been reduced and or because the defender demanded concessions from the challenger to guarantee against future threats. Again, we cannot necessarily say where war falls in the defender's preference ordering. The defender could prefer war to any other outcome or prefer making concessions to war.

Finally, we need more than just a preference order over the outcomes; we need utilities for both players for each outcome. We call the players' utilities for particular outcomes their **payoffs**. Payoffs can be expected utilities. For instance, the war outcome is actually a lottery over all the possible outcomes of a war. Neither player knows in advance which side will win if war breaks out. Thus each player's payoff for the war outcome is an expected utility over that lottery. We could include the lottery in the game itself as a move by **Chance**, or **Nature**. Moves from one of Chance's, or Nature's, nodes are given by fixed and known probabilities of selecting each action. If the players choose the war outcome, they then play the war lottery. Instead, we generally do not include this lottery in the game because there are no other moves after it. We just give each side's expected utility for the war lottery as its payoff for the war outcome.

Because the players may face risks in their choices, we need the utilities they hold for the outcomes in order to judge what risks they will accept. The risks in the game arise from the other player's future actions. If the challenger threatens the status quo, will the defender give in or resist? Any challenger is happy to challenge if it knows that the defender will always grant its demands. All challengers prefer concessions to the status quo by assumption. Similarly, the defender probably does not know whether or not the challenger will go to war if the defender resists the initial threat. How can we represent these uncertainties in a game? In the calculus of deterrence, the probabilities in the lotteries represented these uncertainties. Typically, we assume that all players know the other players' payoffs, all players know that everyone else knows that information, and so on. Any information that all players know, that all players know that all players know, and so on, is **common knowledge**.

There is a clever way to represent uncertainty about payoffs. What if there were two types of defenders, one type that preferred war to making concessions (resolute) and one that preferred making concessions to war (irresolute)? If the challenger did not know what type of defender it was facing, it would have to judge whether it was worth the risk of encountering the resolute defender to gain the benefit of challenging the irresolute defender. Formally, we represent the challenger's uncertainty by beginning the game with a chance move that determines whether or not the defender is resolute. The defender is informed of the outcome of this chance move, but the challenger is not. As shown in Figure 3.4, Chance's opening move (labeled C) produces a tree with two main branches, the top one for resolute defenders and the bottom one for irresolute defenders. Payoffs in the bottom branch of Figure 3.4 are marked with an asterisk to remind us that they involve the irresolute defender so we

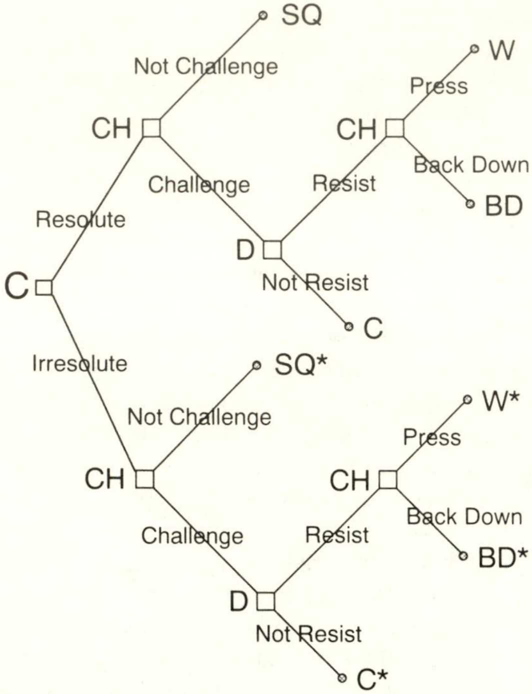

Figure 3.4 Deterrence Game with Two Types

cannot assume the defender's payoffs are the same as the parallel outcomes in the upper branch.

How can we represent the challenger's uncertainty then? We link together the corresponding nodes for the challenger in the two branches, as shown in Figure 3.5. Using a broken line, we link the challenger's two initial nodes and its two final nodes to show that the challenger cannot tell which of these two nodes it is at when it must choose. We call these sets of choice nodes **information sets** because they detail what information the moving player has about prior moves when he or she must choose. Here, the challenger does not know the result of the chance move that determines the defender's payoffs. We do not link the defender's two nodes into an information set because the defender does know the result of the chance move, that is, it does know its own payoffs.

Much of what actually occurs in a crisis is excluded in the model in Figure 3.5. The complex interaction of threats and offers is omitted. Instead, I have focused on the bare essentials of a crisis: a challenge, a response, and a final decision. Where there are many options in an actual crisis, I have simplified the decisions to binary choices. I have created a final choice for the challenger between war and backing down that may not exist in an actual crisis. But these simplifications establish a central point about modeling—every argument is

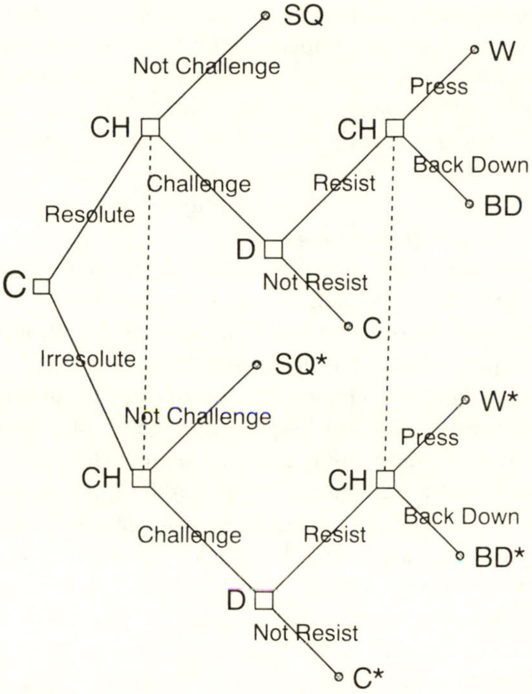

Figure 3.5 Deterrence Game with Uncertainty about Two Types of Defenders

a simplification of actual events. A formal model forces us to choose our assumptions and makes us aware that other reasonable alternative models exist. *The single most important decision in modeling is the design of the game.* The game states what choices we believe the actors see in the situation, what they understand about their choices, what consequences they believe can follow from their decisions, and how they evaluate those consequences. Careful thought is needed about what assumptions characterize a situation when developing a model. There are no correct models floating around out there; there are always many possible models. Formal theory alerts us to the plethora of possible models, allows us to capture the differences between them, and permits us to see if those differences have important consequences for the behavior those models predict.

For example, the deterrence model above contains several assumptions that many scholars would find objectionable. The final choice between war and backing down is artificial. The restriction to binary choices unrealistically limits the actors' range of options. The challenger is uncertain about the defender's resolve, but the defender knows the challenger's willingness to go to war. Some would find the very characterization of the actors as a "challenger" and "defender" inaccurate and morally loaded. But these objections are questions in social science theory, not game theory. Game theory can help us understand what evidence separates these different views of crises. After formalizing the different views, we can solve the models and see if the competing views lead to different predictions of behavior. In this fashion, we may be able to resolve differences about social science theory that may not be easily resolved by verbal descriptions of the competing views.

Because we must make simplifying assumptions when we model, truth rarely lies within a single model. A series of related models is needed to understand political situations. We must begin with a simple model, and then add complications. In the deterrence model above, we could add uncertainty for the defender about the challenger's resolve to go to war, add more options for both sides, or allow a longer interchange of threats. Any of these additions would make the model "more realistic." But the test of an individual model is whether it adds to our understanding, not whether it appeals to some abstract ideal of "reality." Deterrence in international crises is a very complicated problem; any particular model of deterrence cannot make us "feel" deterrence, nor can it exactly describe any one case of deterrence. Instead, a model helps us understand the strategic motivations underlying one aspect of that complexity. As great buildings are built one brick at a time, so do individual models slowly contribute to our growing understanding of politics.

Games in Extensive Form

How do we formally define a game? Extensive-form games are the basic formalization of game theory. To state a game in the extensive form, we must specify the actors, or players, and specify what decisions they face, in what order, by which player, under what conditions, and with what result.

> **Definition**: An **n-person game in extensive form** is
>
> **1.** a finite **game tree** composed of **nodes** and **branches** where each node of the tree is one move of the game or an endpoint of the game and the branches connect the nodes;
>
> **2.** a division of the nodes over the players, Chance, and the endpoints of the game, with one and only one player, Chance, or an endpoint assigned to each node (this division is called a **partition** of the nodes);
>
> **3.** a probability distribution for each chance move;

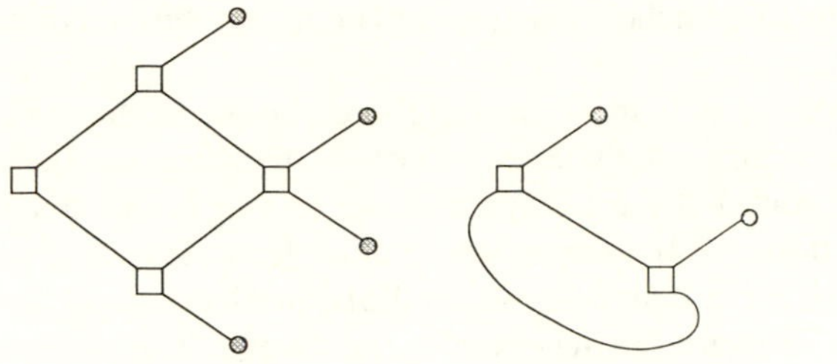
More than one path to the last choice node
Branch leads to a node prior to its start

Figure 3.6 Two Things Not Allowed in Game Trees

4. a refinement of the partition of the nodes into the player sets into **information sets** for each player;

5. a set of outcomes and an assignment of those outcomes to each endpoint of the tree so that each endpoint has one and only one outcome; and

6. a set of utility functions such that each player i has a utility function, u_i, over the outcomes.

All of the above is **common knowledge** to all of the players—all players are aware of it, all players are aware that all other players know it, and so on ad infinitum.

A **game tree** consists of a series of **nodes** linked in sequence. Each node has a number of **branches**, which lead to other nodes. The nodes represent decisions and the branches the actions that could be chosen at each decision. Some nodes have no branches because they give an endpoint of the game; we call them **terminal nodes**. The other nodes are called **choice nodes** or **choice points** because a player has a choice at that point in the game (including chance moves, as choices by Chance, or Nature). In Figure 3.5, there are a total of fifteen nodes. Eight are terminal nodes, four each in the top and bottom parts of the game. There are seven choice nodes, four assigned to the challenger, two to the defender, and one to Chance (the initial move). The branches give the players' choices from each choice node and the possible results of the chance move at the beginning of the game. I labeled each of the branches to help us see what actions they correspond to. The branches cannot "grow" back on themselves. No branch can lead to a node prior to the node it starts at. There is one and only one path through the tree to each node in the game. Figure 3.6 shows two examples of nodes and branches that are not allowed. The entire specification of what choices are available from each node and when the game ends is called a game tree because it resembles a tree. Each node spreads additional choices along its branches. The terminal nodes are the endpoints of each branch system.

Some nodes occur before others. If there is a path of choices or chance moves that leads from one node to a second node, the latter is called a **successor** (or **succeeding node**) of the former, and the former is called a **predecessor** (or **preceding node**) of the latter. If an action leads from one node to a second node, the former is called the **immediate predecessor** of the latter, and the latter is the **immediate successor** of the former. The defender's decision to resist the challenge is (immediately) preceded by the challenger's decision to challenge the status quo and (immediately) succeeded by the challenger's decision to press the threat within each part of the game. But the challenger's decision to challenge when the defender is resolute does not precede the defender's decision to resist when it is not resolute because there is no path of choices from the former node to the latter node. The complete sequence of moves that precedes a node is called the **history** of the game up to that point. Every node has a unique history, which summarizes all prior moves because there is one and only one path of actions and chance moves to each node in the game. The history of the deterrence game up to the point where a resolute defender must choose to resist a challenge is "Resolute, Challenge". We specify both the chance move and the challenger's decision to challenge in the history.

The nonterminal nodes are divided among the players, with one and only one player assigned to each node. To allow for chance moves, we consider Chance, sometimes referred to as Nature, to be a player. Chance moves are nodes where Chance moves instead of a player. At each node assigned to Chance, there is a separate probability distribution that selects its move. The probabilities attached to a chance move are known to all the players at the start of the game. Chance moves allow us to include random elements in a game. The deterrence game included a chance move to determine whether the defender was resolute. I earlier discussed including another chance move to represent the lottery that the war outcome represents. Chance moves can be placed at any point in the game.

Each player's nodes are further divided into **information sets**. Information sets express a player's knowledge of prior moves when it must decide. When a player reaches an information set with more than one node (for an example, see the sets designated by broken lines in Figure 3.5), it knows only that it must make a decision and that it is at one of the nodes in that information set. Information sets with multiple nodes reflect the player's ignorance of prior moves in the game tree. It cannot confirm which of several prior moves were made. Identical moves must follow from each node in an information set. Otherwise, the player could distinguish the nodes in an information set by examining its available choices. Information sets form the actual choice points in the game because they summarize when a player chooses and what it knows at that point in the game. Information sets containing only one node are referred to as **singletons**.

Information sets specify what information the players can verify about prior moves in the game. Imagine that each of the players is in a separate room and the game is played by having a referee who goes from room to room to tell each player which information set it is at when it must make a choice. If the referee tells a player that it is at a singleton information set, that player knows which node it is at and can reconstruct all prior moves from the history of the game that leads to that node. But if the referee tells the player that it is at an information set with multiple nodes, the player cannot reconstruct the history of the game as different histories lead to different nodes in that information set. Of course, the player may make inferences about the history of the game, but it cannot confirm that those inferences are correct. The term *information sets*, then, is odd name for the element of a game that summarizes the players' ignorance about the play of the game.

The terminal nodes indicate the end of the game, and an **outcome** is assigned to each terminal node. Each player has a utility function over all the outcomes. A player's utility function evaluates the desirability of the outcomes for that player. Often, we just give the players' utility evaluation of the outcome for each terminal node, rather than describing the outcome itself. If so, we call those utilities **payoffs**.

Finally, we assume that players know the game they are playing. An aspect of the game is **common knowledge** if all players know it, all players know the other players know it, and so on. We assume that the extensive form of the game is common knowledge. The players can use their knowledge of the game to anticipate other players' moves and form expectations about the future of the game when they face decisions. The assumption that the game is common knowledge eliminates the infinite-regress problem of "They think that we think that they know that, etc." Any piece of information known to a player that is not common knowledge is that player's **private information**.

The assumption that the game is common knowledge appears quite restrictive. One might think it prevents us from analyzing situations where the players face fundamental uncertainties about their situation. But the deterrence game shows us that we can represent such uncertainties in a game. The defender's payoffs are its private information; the challenger does not know the defender's payoffs. By setting up chance moves and information sets carefully, we can model uncertainty about a game without violating the assumption that the game is common knowledge.

At this point, a simple example may help clarify the definition of an extensive form. Consider the game of Matching Pennies. Two players each have a penny. Secretly, each player chooses to place the penny either heads up or tails up. The pennies are then revealed. If the pennies match, the first player receives both; if they do not match, the second player receives both. Figure 3.7

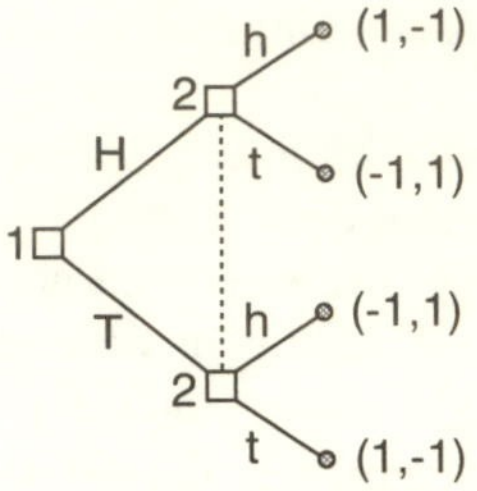

Figure 3.7 Extensive Form of Matching Pennies

gives the extensive form of Matching Pennies. This figure allows me to introduce the conventions I use in this book for extensive-form games. The boxes denote choice nodes with the moving player listed before each node. The game begins with Player 1 choosing between heads and tails, abbreviated as H and T in the diagram. Player 2 also chooses between heads and tails, denoted as h and t. For convenience, I write Player 2's move as succeeding Player 1's move. Because their moves are simultaneous, I could write Player 2's move first. There are two possible nodes for Player 2, one for Player 1's selecting heads and the other for Player 1's selecting tails. The actions are listed next to each branch. Terminal nodes are indicated by the filled-in circles and are followed by the players' payoffs for that outcome, given as (Player 1's payoff, Player 2's payoff). Although Player 2 has two choice nodes, she cannot confirm Player 1's move when she must choose; the players' moves are simultaneous. We represent the simultaneous moves by linking Player 2's two moves in one information set, represented by the broken line connecting her two nodes. This information set denotes that Player 2 does not know Player 1's move when Player 2 must choose her move. This is how simultaneous moves are represented in extensive-form games. Note that both of Player 2's nodes must have the same actions available. Otherwise, they could not be linked in one information set.

I adopt the following conventions for more complicated games. Boxes denote choice nodes, and filled-in circles denote terminal nodes. Chance's nodes are preceded by a capital C. When I use abbreviations for the players' actions, I distinguish the labels as follows: Player 1's actions are given in CAPITALS, Player 2's in lower case, Player 3's (if needed) in *CAPITAL ITALICS*, and Player 4's in *lower-case italics*. If there are more than two players, I continue writing their payoffs in sequence, separated by commas, in the parentheses. I refer to Player 1 as "he," Players 2 and 3 as "she," and Player 4 as "he" for convenience. When I talk about players generically, I use "it." I use some abstract games that have no reference to politics to illustrate points about game theory. In these games, I generally call the moves Up and Down, abbreviated

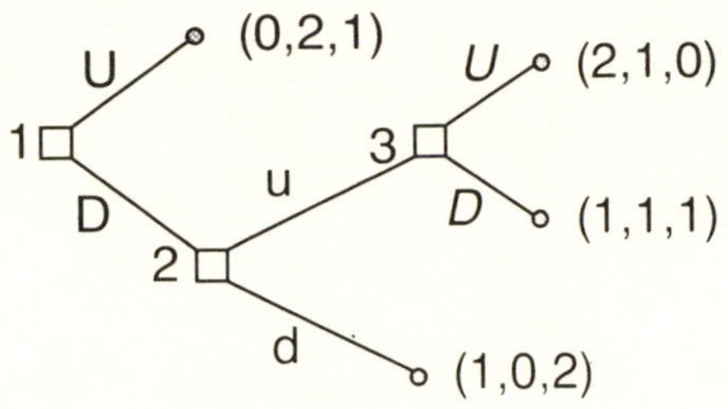

Figure 3.8 Exercise 3.2

U and D or u and d; Left and Right, abbreviated L and R or l and r; or Front and Back, abbreviated F and B or f and b.

> Exercise 3.1: Draw the extensive form of the following bargaining game. The players are trying to divide \$6. Player 1 can first offer either \$4 or \$2 to Player 2. Player 2 then chooses to either accept or reject this first offer. If she rejects Player 1's offer, they flip a coin. If the coin comes up heads, Player 1 receives \$3 and Player 2 receives \$1. If the coin comes up tails, Player 1 receives \$1 dollar and Player 2 receives \$3 (i.e., if they do not agree, it costs them \$2 to flip the coin).

> Exercise 3.2: Describe the game in Figure 3.8 in words.

> Exercise 3.3: Draw the game tree for the first two moves of tic-tac-toe, one move for each player.[1] (Hint: Be sure to exploit the symmetry of the game; for example, there are only three possible initial moves, a corner box, the middle box, or one of the boxes in the middle of the sides.)

Three terms are used to describe the information the players may have when playing a game.

> **Definition**: A game is played under **perfect information** if all information sets are singletons. A game is played under **complete information** if all the players' payoffs are common knowledge. A game is played under **incomplete information** if some player's payoff is its private information.

Perfect information means that all players' information sets contain only one node, and so all players know the history of the game whenever they make

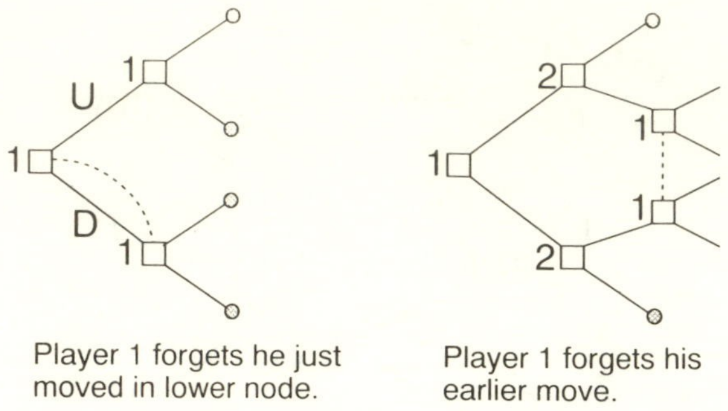

Figure 3.9 Game Trees That Violate Perfect Recall

a move. Among common parlor games, chess and checkers are played under perfect information, while bridge and poker are not. In bridge and poker, there is a chance move, the deal, at the start of the game that is not completely revealed to the players until the end of play. Perfect information covers situations where the players know everything that has happened before each move in a game. Complete information means that all players know one another's payoffs. The deterrence game is played under incomplete information because the challenger does not know the result of the chance move when it moves. We model that incomplete information with imperfect information. The information sets with multiple nodes reflect the uncertainties the players face. As in the deterrence game, uncertainty can be introduced into a game by an initial chance move followed by imperfect information about the result of that chance move.

We also assume that the players remember their prior moves and any information that they knew at an earlier node. This assumption is known as perfect recall.

Definition: A game is played under **perfect recall** when

1. no information set in the game contains both a node and one of its predecessors; and

2. for any two nodes x and x′ in an information set for player i, if x″ is a predecessor of x in an information set for player i, then there exists a predecessor node of x′, y, in the same information set as x″ such that player i takes the same action from y to x′ as it does from x″ to x. (Note: nodes x″ and y could be the same node.)

The first part of the definition requires players to distinguish current moves from future moves. The game fragment on the left of Figure 3.9 violates this condition: Player 1 forgot that he just moved if he chooses D. Player 1's information set in this game connects his first choice node with his choice node that results if he plays D from his first choice node. Because he cannot distinguish his first node from this succeeding node, he has forgotten that he chose D at his first node. The second part of the definition is more complicated and excludes several types of forgetfulness. It excludes situations where a player forgets earlier moves, as in the game on the right of Figure 3.9. It also excludes situations where the players forget moves by other players (including Chance) that they knew earlier in the game. There are no examples of games in political science that I know of where the players do not have perfect recall. Bridge is an example of a game without perfect recall if you think of it as a two-player game between the two teams of players, North-South and East-West. During the bidding, each "player" temporarily forgets what cards it has seen after a hand bids. After North bids, then the player North-South forgets what cards are in North's hand when South must bid.

Extensive forms can be inconvenient to write out for some games. If the players have an infinite array of moves, drawing an infinite number of branches could take some time. For example, the range of possible policies that could be adopted on an issue is often modeled as the points along a line, as opposed to a finite set. Those who make policy choose from an infinite number of possible policies. Games with an infinite but well-specified set of moves are often described in **time line form**. The time line form of a game parallels the extensive form. It specifies the order of the players' decision nodes, what choices are available to a player at each choice node, what information a player has when he or she must move, how the choices produce the outcomes, and the players' utility functions over the outcomes. A time line form lists the nodes in order, specifying who moves, the available choices, and what information is available to that player at that node. Terminal nodes give the outcomes and the players' utility functions.

The idea of time captured in both time line and extensive forms is decision time, rather than strict chronological time. There is no assumption that nodes are equally spaced in time or even that the nodes must occur after their predecessors. Moves can be simultaneous, as in the Matching Pennies game. These forms strive to capture the decision environment of choices. What do the players know? How do their decisions interact to produce outcomes? Although temporal sequence can affect what the players know and how their choices lead to outcomes, what matters is the decision environment, not the temporal sequence.

Games in Strategic Form

Even very simple games quickly become quite complicated when expressed in extensive form. Consequently, games are often analyzed in a reduced form, called the strategic form (also known as the normal form). In the strategic form, we reduce each player's choice to the selection of a complete plan for playing the game. The choice of a strategy is assumed to be made before the game begins.

> **Definition**: A **strategy** S_i for player i assigns one move to each of i's information sets in a given game.

A strategy is a complete plan for playing a game for a particular player. It specifies what moves that player would make in any situation. Imagine that the players are scheduled to play the game at a set time. However, one player has a pressing commitment at the time they are to play. The referee asks that player for a comprehensive plan to play his or her position. That plan must specify a move for all possible moves that the player could make, even those that the player thinks will not occur. Then the referee can simply play for the missing player by following the player's strategy. Players can make probabilistic moves by specifying a probability distribution over the available actions at an information set. Strategies that do not include any probabilistic moves are called **pure strategies**.

We use players' strategies to reduce a game to an interaction of their pure strategies. Once we know the players' pure strategies, we can mechanically trace out their interactions in the extensive form and derive the outcome of the game. It is as if all players mailed in their strategies at the start of the game. We just open the envelopes and follow their instructions to determine the outcome of the game.

> **Definition**: An **n-person game in strategic form** is an n-dimensional array of all the players' pure strategies with each entry of the array filled with the players' utilities for the outcome (which could be a probability distribution of outcomes) that results from that combination of strategies.

> Example: To find the strategic form of Matching Pennies, we specify each player's pure strategies. Each player has one information set with two possible moves. Thus each player can have only two possible strategies, heads or tails. These two strategies create a two-by-two table, shown in Figure 3.10. To find the outcomes that result from each pair of the players' strategies, we trace out the result of the game if the players play those strategies. In the upper left-hand cell, Player 1 plays heads and Player 2 also plays heads. According to the rules of the game, Player 1 wins both pennies, and Players 1 and 2 have payoffs 1 and -1, respectively, for this outcome. The figure gives the complete strategic form.

		Player 2	
		h	t
Player 1	H	(1,-1)	(-1,1)
	T	(-1,1)	(1,-1)

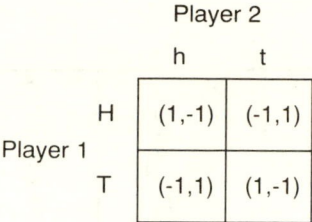

Figure 3.10 Strategic Form of Matching Pennies

Exercise 3.4:

a) Draw the extensive form of Matching Pennies if Player 1 must reveal his move before Player 2 chooses hers.

b) Find the strategic form of this game. (Hint: Does Player 2 still have only two possible strategies?)

More complicated extensive forms create larger strategic forms. Consider the deterrence game discussed at the beginning of the chapter and presented as a tree in Figure 3.5. Begin with the challenger's strategies. The challenger has two moves at each of its two information sets. It thus has four possible strategies. I list these strategies by its move at its first node, followed by its move at its second node: Not Challenge, Press; Not Challenge, Back Down; Challenge, Press; and Challenge, Back Down. The defender also has two moves at each of its two information sets, giving it four possible strategies. Call these strategies: Always Resist; Resist If Resolute, Do Not Resist If Irresolute; Do Not Resist If Resolute, Resist If Not Resolute; and Never Resist. Recall that the defender is resolute (or resolved—I use the two terms interchangeably) in the upper branch of the tree. Its second strategy is to play Resist in the upper branch and Not Resist in the lower branch. I have summarized this strategy as Resist If Resolute, Do Not Resist If Not Resolute, to give a better intuitive flavor for what the strategy directs the player to do.

I did not specify two elements of the extensive form of the deterrence game in my description: the probabilities in the chance move at the beginning of the game that determined whether the defender was resolute or not, and the players' utilities for the outcomes. Assume the probabilities are a $\frac{1}{2}$ chance that the defender is resolute and a $\frac{1}{2}$ chance it is not resolute. For the players' utilities, I write $u_{CH}(O)$ and $u_D(O)$ for the challenger's and defender's utilities, respectively, for outcome O.

The strategic form of the deterrence game requires a four-by-four array because each player has four possible strategies. Figure 3.11 shows this array. We trace the consequences of each pair of strategies to determine the players'

Challenger

Defender	Challenge, Press	Challenge, Back Down	Do Not Challenge, Press	Do Not Challenge; Back Down
Always Resist	$\frac{1}{2}u_{CH}(W)+\frac{1}{2}u_{CH}(W^*)$, $\frac{1}{2}u_D(W)+\frac{1}{2}u_D(W^*)$	$\frac{1}{2}u_{CH}(BD)+\frac{1}{2}u_{CH}(BD^*)$, $\frac{1}{2}u_D(BD)+\frac{1}{2}u_D(BD^*)$	$\frac{1}{2}u_{CH}(SQ)+\frac{1}{2}u_{CH}(SQ^*)$, $\frac{1}{2}u_D(SQ)+\frac{1}{2}u_D(SQ^*)$	$\frac{1}{2}u_{CH}(SQ)+\frac{1}{2}u_{CH}(SQ^*)$, $\frac{1}{2}u_D(SQ)+\frac{1}{2}u_D(SQ^*)$
Resist if Resolute, Do Not Resist if Irresolute	$\frac{1}{2}u_{CH}(W)+\frac{1}{2}u_{CH}(C^*)$, $\frac{1}{2}u_D(W)+\frac{1}{2}u_D(C^*)$	$\frac{1}{2}u_{CH}(BD)+\frac{1}{2}u_{CH}(C^*)$, $\frac{1}{2}u_D(BD)+\frac{1}{2}u_D(C^*)$	$\frac{1}{2}u_{CH}(SQ)+\frac{1}{2}u_{CH}(SQ^*)$, $\frac{1}{2}u_D(SQ)+\frac{1}{2}u_D(SQ^*)$	$\frac{1}{2}u_{CH}(SQ)+\frac{1}{2}u_{CH}(SQ^*)$, $\frac{1}{2}u_D(SQ)+\frac{1}{2}u_D(SQ^*)$
Do Not Resist if Resolute, Resist if Irresolute	$\frac{1}{2}u_{CH}(C)+\frac{1}{2}u_{CH}(W^*)$, $\frac{1}{2}u_D(C)+\frac{1}{2}u_D(W^*)$	$\frac{1}{2}u_{CH}(C)+\frac{1}{2}u_{CH}(BD^*)$, $\frac{1}{2}u_D(C)+\frac{1}{2}u_D(BD^*)$	$\frac{1}{2}u_{CH}(SQ)+\frac{1}{2}u_{CH}(SQ^*)$, $\frac{1}{2}u_D(SQ)+\frac{1}{2}u_D(SQ^*)$	$\frac{1}{2}u_{CH}(SQ)+\frac{1}{2}u_{CH}(SQ^*)$, $\frac{1}{2}u_D(SQ)+\frac{1}{2}u_D(SQ^*)$
Never Resist	$\frac{1}{2}u_{CH}(C)+\frac{1}{2}u_{CH}(C^*)$, $\frac{1}{2}u_D(C)+\frac{1}{2}u_D(C^*)$	$\frac{1}{2}u_{CH}(C)+\frac{1}{2}u_{CH}(C^*)$, $\frac{1}{2}u_D(C)+\frac{1}{2}u_D(C^*)$	$\frac{1}{2}u_{CH}(SQ)+\frac{1}{2}u_{CH}(SQ^*)$, $\frac{1}{2}u_D(SQ)+\frac{1}{2}u_D(SQ^*)$	$\frac{1}{2}u_{CH}(SQ)+\frac{1}{2}u_{CH}(SQ^*)$, $\frac{1}{2}u_D(SQ)+\frac{1}{2}u_D(SQ^*)$

Figure 3.11 Strategic Form of the Deterrence Game with Uncertainty about Two Types of Defenders

expected utility for those strategies, including the effects of the chance move on the outcome in the expected utilities. For instance, what expected utilities result when the challenger plays Challenge, Press, and the defender plays Resist If Resolute, Do Not Resist If Not Resolute (the second cell down in the first column)? The result of the chance move affects the outcome, both by changing the move the defender makes in response to the challenge and by changing the outcome itself. If the defender is resolved, it resists the challenge, leading the challenger to press the challenge, producing an outcome of W. If the defender is not resolved, it does not resist the challenge, leading to the C* outcome. Each of these possibilities occurs with a probability of $\frac{1}{2}$. The challenger's expected utility for this pair of strategies is $\frac{1}{2}u_{CH}(W) + \frac{1}{2}u_{CH}(C^*)$; the defender's expected utility is $\frac{1}{2}u_D(W) + \frac{1}{2}u_D(C^*)$. The figure gives the strategic form for the deterrence game.

It may strike you as strange that I differentiate between the Not Challenge, Press strategy and the Not Challenge, Back Down one for the challenger. After all, the game is over if the challenger does not challenge in its first move. These two strategies always produce the same outcome. These strategies are equivalent because they have the same consequences regardless of the defender's strategy.

> **Definition**: Two strategies s_i and s_i' for player i are **equivalent** iff they lead to the same probability distribution over outcomes for all pure strategies of i's opponents.

Because equivalent strategies always have the same consequences, a set of equivalent strategies can be collapsed into just one strategy. This strategy represents the entire set of equivalent strategies. One can then reduce a strategic-form game into a reduced strategic form by collapsing all equivalent strategies into one. In the deterrence example, I separate the equivalent strategies of the challenger for the sake of completeness. I prefer seeing all the feasible strategies. As we will see later, it makes little difference whether equivalent strategies are collapsed for the purpose of analyzing a game.

A game in strategic form consists of the following:

1. a set of n players, indexed from 1 to n;
2. n sets of pure strategies S_i, one for each player; and
3. n payoff functions M_i, one for each player.

The payoff to player i from the strategies $s_1,s_2,\ldots,s_n$ is written $M_i(s_1;s_2;\ldots;s_n)$. All the players' payoffs from the strategies $s_1,s_2,\ldots,s_n$ is written $M(s_1;s_2;\ldots;s_n) = [M_1(s_1;s_2;\ldots;s_n), M_2(s_1;s_2;\ldots;s_n), \ldots, M_n(s_1;s_2;\ldots;s_n)]$. The payoff functions incorporate both strategy choices leading to outcomes and the utility evaluation of those outcomes.

Exercise 3.5: Find the strategic forms of the games in

a) Exercises 3.1.
b) Exercises 3.2.

The above notation can be used to define strategic-form games for games with infinite pure strategies. Such games cannot be written as an array. Instead, we define strategic-form games with infinite strategy sets by using payoff functions. These functions give each player's payoff as a function of the strategies that the players select.

Classical game theory analyzes strategic-form games, but extensive-form games are more fundamental than strategic forms. Strategic forms are reductions of extensive forms. Many commonly used strategic-form games assume a particular extensive form that does not capture the sequence of strategic interaction. The extensive form underlying all strategic-form games is such that the players select their strategies simultaneously. If the players do not select their moves simultaneously in the extensive form, they can react to earlier moves of other players. Extensive forms show us the sequence of moves clearly. Strategic forms submerge this sequence in the set of strategies. When players have sequential moves, their strategies must specify multiple responses to the other players' earlier moves. As in Exercise 3.4, changing the sequence and information of the players changes the strategies they can play and thus changes the strategic form.

Occasionally, different extensive forms reduce to the same strategic form. Consider the two extensive-form games in Figure 3.12. Both of these games have the strategic form in Figure 3.13. The strategic form here has eliminated a critical difference between the two games. In the extensive-form game on the right-hand side of Figure 3.12, Player 2 knows what Player 1 has done when she must decide on her move. In the other game, she does not know. The strategic-form array in Figure 3.13 does not show this difference. It is true that since both games produce the same consequences, you can argue that Player 2's move at the upper node in the extensive-form game on the left-hand side of Figure 3.12 is a nonmove because the payoffs are 1 for both players regardless of what Player 2 chooses if her upper node is reached. However, as we will see later, Player 2's ignorance of Player 1's move when she must choose in the game on the left can change what moves are strategically defensible.

The choice of extensive form is probably the most critical step in any game theory model; it determines the players' choices and how the players interact strategically. All too often, scholars have assumed that strategic-form games are fundamental, but one should always remember that they are derived from a more detailed account of the game.

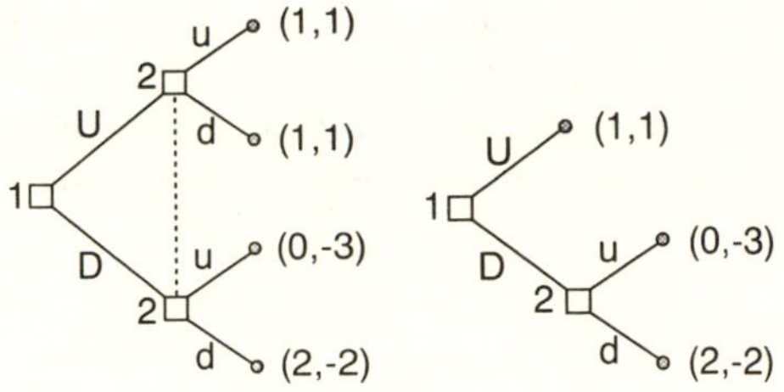

Figure 3.12 Two Different Extensive Forms
That Produce the Same Strategic Form

		Player 2	
		u	d
Player 1	U	(1,1)	(1,1)
	D	(0,-3)	(2,-2)

Figure 3.13 Strategic Form of
the Games in Figure 3.12

Review

This chapter has explained how games are specified. The extensive form is the basic specification of a game. It consists of nodes, divided into choice and terminal nodes. The choice nodes are divided among the players, with one player for each, and Chance is considered a player. An outcome is assigned to each terminal node. There are moves from each choice node that lead to other nodes. All of Chance's moves have assigned probabilities for each move. Each player has a utility function over the outcomes. Information sets may collect several of a player's nodes to signify that the player cannot verify which node it is at when it must move. Finally, the game is assumed to be common knowledge among the players.

Games in the strategic form have the players choose strategies at the beginning of the game, and their chosen strategies produce payoffs for the players. Strategies are complete plans to play the game; they must specify a move for every information set that the player has in the extensive form. The payoffs combine both the outcome that a set of chosen strategies produces and the utilities the players have for that outcome. Strategic forms are commonly given in an array of strategies and payoffs.

I stress two main substantive points about using game models in this chapter. First, the design of a game is the most important stage in modeling a situation.

The game captures a host of assumptions about the situation; think carefully when you make those assumptions. Second, strategic-form games are reductions of extensive-form games. Strategic-form games may assume a particular extensive form that does not represent the situation being modeled.

Further Reading

Most of the textbooks reviewed in the Further Reading section of Chapter One have useful chapters on the definition of games. Kreps's (1990) Chapter Eleven is probably the best because he takes time to discuss how a simple game attempts to capture the logic of a duopoly. However, the reader should expect to find parts of this chapter to be highly abstract. Luce and Raiffa (1957) present an accessible, but at times dated, discussion of the parts of the definition of an extensive form.

The discussion of the deterrence game draws on the literature on modeling deterrence as an extensive-form game. I recommend Wagner 1989 as a first source for modeling deterrence as an extensive-form game. Wagner (1983) discusses the misuse of games as representations of arguments in international politics.

Chapter Four
Classical Game Theory

This chapter presents the classical approach to game theory and its basic results. In classical game theory, we analyze how players choose their strategies given the strategic form. It may seem strange that I begin by analyzing games in the strategic form when I have argued that the extensive form is fundamental. I do this for two reasons. First, the concept of equilibrium arose from games of pure competition, zero-sum games, in the strategic form. Second, the intuition behind the idea of an equilibrium is easily explained in the strategic form. Chapter Five begins the analysis of equilibria in extensive forms. That analysis assumes the reader is already familiar with equilibrium in classical game theory.

The central idea of this chapter is Nash equilibrium. In a Nash equilibrium, neither player has an incentive to change its strategy unilaterally. This idea comes from two-person, zero-sum games. The pure competition of such games drives the players to adopt strategies such that neither can exploit the other. The equilibria of two-person, zero-sum games have several nice properties. The notion of Nash equilibrium generalizes this concept to the non–zero-sum setting, where the players have some complementary interests. However, moving this idea to non–zero-sum games comes at a cost. It eliminates some of the nice properties of equilibrium in two-person, zero-sum games.

This chapter moves between two-person, zero-sum games and non–zero-sum games with two or more players to explain the idea of equilibrium in classical game theory. The chapter begins with the definition of a zero-sum game and a discussion of the distinction between cooperative and noncooperative game theory. It then discusses Nash equilibrium in two-person, zero-sum and two-person, non–zero-sum games. I use two-person games to illustrate Nash equilibrium in non–zero-sum games for convenience; the concept of a Nash equilibrium for n-person, non–zero-sum games is identical. The discussion of Nash equilibrium introduces three important ideas: dominated strategies, best replies, and mixed strategies. One strategy dominates another strategy for a player when the first is always at least as good as and sometimes better than the second. A player's best reply to a particular strategy of the other player is the strategy that gives the first player its highest payoff against the particular strategy of the other player. The notion of mixed strategies adds the idea that the players may have incentives to make their actions unpredictable to the other player.

The chapter returns to two-person, zero-sum games to state the Minmax Theorem. This theorem proves the general existence of equilibria in those games and the desirable properties those equilibria have. I next discuss the weaknesses of the Nash equilibrium concept. Nash equilibria of non–zero-sum (no matter how many players) games do not have all of the desirable properties of the equilibria of two-person, zero-sum games. Nash equilibria assume that players share a common conjecture about how the game will be played; the consequences of this idea and some principles for selecting among Nash equilibria are discussed. Rationalizable strategies provide an idea of what could happen in a game when the players lack a common conjecture. I compare these strategies, which are produced by the repeated elimination of dominated strategies, to Nash equilibria.

I end the chapter with a pair of examples about elections and a brief discussion of cooperative game theory. The first example is a simple model of political reform in democracies. The second example presents the spatial model of candidate competition as a two-person, zero-sum game. It presents the Median Voter Theorem, the germinal result in formal models of elections and legislatures. The Nash bargaining solution and a brief introduction to n-person game theory represent cooperative game theory. The Nash bargaining solution is my first discussion of bargaining. It is closely tied to the first noncooperative model of bargaining I present in Chapter Five, the Rubinstein bargaining model. These two models together demonstrate some of the differences between cooperative and noncooperative game theory. I provide a brief introduction to the ideas of n-person game theory. They have been important in political science. I do not cover them in detail because to do so would lead me far from my focus on noncooperative game theory. The chapter closes with a review of the central ideas of classical game theory.

I am quite brief in my coverage of the topics in this chapter. Entire textbooks have been written about each of the three branches of classical game theory: two-person, zero-sum games; two-person, non–zero-sum games; and n-person games. This chapter strives to acquaint the reader with the basic logic of the classical theory as a basis for understanding noncooperative game theory. I also expect that you will be able to solve simple strategic-form games after completing this chapter. I do not expect that you will emerge from this chapter as an expert on classical game theory. My discussion here focuses on explaining the basic concepts and on showing how they are used to solve simple games.

Defining the Terms of Classical Game Theory

Two-person, zero-sum games are games of pure competition between the players.

Definition: A game is **zero-sum** iff

$$\sum_{i=1}^{n} M_i = 0,$$

that is, if and only if the sum of the payoffs to all players equals zero.

In a zero-sum game, everything won by one player must be lost by another player. With only two players, this is a game of pure competition. The players have no interest in communicating or coordinating their strategies to their mutual benefit because there is no mutual benefit in these games. In a two-person, zero-sum game, the payoff to Player 2 is just the opposite of Player 1's payoff. We simplify the strategic form by writing down only Player 1's payoff, with the assumption that Player 2's payoff is the opposite of Player 1's payoff. Zero-sum games can have more than two players. In such games two or more players can have an interest in coordinated action to take advantage of another player (or several other players).

Two-person, zero-sum games are poor models of most social phenomena. Almost all interesting social phenomena create mixed motives for the parties involved. There are very few situations in which two actors have directly opposed interests—perhaps only candidate competition and the military maneuvers of warfare. Even in those situations, it may be inaccurate to describe the situation as zero-sum. It may appear at first that two-candidate races are zero-sum because one must win and the other lose. But the candidates may have to answer to constituencies other than just the voters. It may be in their interest to take divergent positions on the issues to satisfy their parties, independent of any benefits they derive from their parties in this election. They may have aspirations to higher office in future elections. Such aspirations could create motivations beyond vote maximization in this election. Non–zero-sum games capture these mixed motivations. They represent situations in which the sides have both competitive and cooperative interests. No longer is one player's gain automatically the other player's loss.

Because non–zero-sum games create the possibility of cooperative behavior between the players, we must consider the players' ability to coordinate their strategies through communication. Non–zero-sum games fall into two classes, based on the enforceability of agreements.

Definition: In a **cooperative** game, players can make binding agreements before and during the play of the game, and communication between the players is allowed. In a **noncooperative** game, binding agreements cannot be made by the players, although communication may or may not be allowed.

The difference between cooperative and noncooperative games is not the players' behavior in these games. Rather, the terms under which the players can make arrangements in their common interest separates cooperative and noncooperative games. Cooperative games allow the players to coordinate their strategies through binding agreements. In noncooperative games, the players must enforce any coordination of strategy through the game itself. An agreement can be enforced only through the interests of the agreeing parties.

One of the great disputes in game theory concerns the primacy of noncooperative games. Harsanyi and Selten (1988) contend that noncooperative games are more fundamental than cooperative games because they explicitly model the means of enforcement of agreements. Cooperative games, they argue, make it too easy for the players to make agreements; the players can bind themselves to agreements that may not be enforceable. Noncooperative games force us to consider how collaboration among players is implemented in the game and what incentives the players have to violate such agreements. I agree with this argument. Three of the key questions game theory should address is when, how, and why the players cooperate to their mutual benefit. The enforcement of agreements (or alternatively why people honor agreements at a short-run cost) is a critical question, and cooperative game theory assumes away that critical question. Consequently, this book focuses on noncooperative game theory. Nevertheless, cooperative game theory has been important in the development of game theory and its application to political science. I introduce some important ideas from cooperative game theory at the end of this chapter. I also provide further sources on cooperative game theory at the end of this chapter.

A traditional distinction between cooperative and noncooperative games is that the latter do not allow any communication between the players. Each player must determine its own strategy on its own. Over time, game theorists have found the question of whether communication is allowed less important than whether agreements are binding. If agreements cannot be enforced by an outside agency, then communication is irrelevant in some situations. Noncooperative game theorists argue that communication should be explicitly modeled in the game. Early discussions of communication in games allowed the players to discuss anything openly before playing. But interest has grown in analyzing the strategic effects of communication. To do so, the messages have to be incorporated as moves within the game itself. Allowing the players to say anything was simply too ill defined to evaluate the strategic role of communication. It is common now to model communication explicitly in noncooperative games. Still, such highly formalized communication is not as rich as language. In Chapter Eight, I provide several examples of the formal analysis of communication within a game.

		Player 2	
		s_1	s_2
Player 1	S_1	-1	2
	S_2	4	3

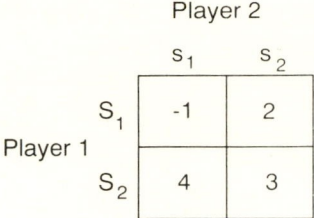

Figure 4.1 A Two-Person, Zero-Sum Game

Domination, Best Replies, and Equilibrium

How should the players play a game? Sometimes, one strategy is always better for a player than any of its other strategies. Consider the two-person, zero-sum game in Figure 4.1. Regardless of which strategy Player 2 plays, Player 1 is always better off playing S_2. If Player 2 plays s_1, Player 1's payoff is -1 if he plays S_1 and 4 if he plays S_2. If Player 2 plays s_2, Player 1's payoff is 2 if he plays S_1 and 3 if he plays S_2.

Because S_2 is always better for Player 1 than S_1, we say that S_2 dominates S_1.

Definition: A strategy S_1 **strongly (or strictly) dominates** another strategy S_2 for Player 1 iff

$$M_1(S_1;s_j) > M_1(S_2;s_j) \text{ for all } s_j.$$

A strategy S_1 **weakly dominates** another strategy S_2 for Player 1 iff

$$M_1(S_1;s_j) \geq M_1(S_2;s_j) \text{ for all } s_j$$

and

$$M_1(S_1;s_j) > M_1(S_2;s_j) \text{ for some } s_j.$$

We call S_2 in this situation a **weakly dominated strategy**. If S_1 strongly dominates all other strategies S_i, we call S_1 a **dominant strategy**. If both players have dominant strategies, the resulting equilibrium is called a **dominant strategy equilibrium**.

There are similar definitions of domination for Player 2. Strongly dominated strategies are always inferior. A player always does better by playing the strategy that dominates it. A player should never play a strongly dominated strategy. A weakly dominated strategy is never better and sometimes worse than the strategy that dominates it.

		Player 2	
		s_1	s_2
Player 1	S_1	(5,5)	(-10,10)
	S_2	(10,-10)	(-5,-5)

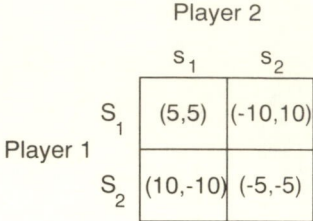

Figure 4.2 Prisoner's Dilemma

If a player has a dominant strategy, it should always play that strategy because it does worse by playing any other strategy. If both players have dominant strategies, then we have a dominant strategy equilibrium, a very strong prediction for the outcome of a game. Both players have a strong incentive to play their dominant strategies, regardless of what the other player does.

> Example: A classic two-person, non-zero-sum game is Prisoner's Dilemma. Prisoner's Dilemma is typically presented with the following cute story. Two criminals are arrested, but the district attorney does not have enough evidence to convict either of them for serious charges unless one or both confess to the crime. The district attorney separates the two and makes the following offer to each: "If you confess and your partner does not, I will grant you immunity, and you will walk out free. However, if your partner squeals, and you don't, I'm going to throw the book at you. If neither of you confesses, then I'll have to settle for misdemeanor charges, which will get you each a brief prison term. If you both confess, I'll get you both on felony charges, but I'll argue for shorter sentences than if you do not confess and your partner does. Think about it and tell me what you want to do."

Figure 4.2 gives the payoff matrix for Prisoner's Dilemma (let S_1 be no confession and S_2 be a confession). A complete equilibrium must specify both players' strategies. I adopt the notation of listing the players' strategies sequentially, with semicolons separating their strategies. When the players must specify multiple moves in their strategies, I use commas to separate the different moves in a player's strategy.

Prisoner's Dilemma has a dominant strategy equilibrium, $(S_2;s_2)$: both crooks should squeal. But both players are better off at $(S_1;s_1)$ than at $(S_2;s_2)$. A deal to play $(S_1;s_1)$ would be in both players' interest. But their self-interest leads both players to cheat on such a deal. This is the dilemma in the Prisoner's Dilemma. Communication alone cannot solve the dilemma. Even if both criminals are dragged off to the interrogation rooms screaming, "I'll

a)

		Player 2	
		s_1	s_2
Player 1	S_1	2	3
	S_2	0	1

b)

		Player 2	
		s_1	s_2
Player 1	S_1	(3,4)	(5,-1)
	S_2	(3,-2)	(-5,-4)

c)

		Player 2		
		s_1	s_2	s_3
	S_1	(1,1)	(-2,0)	(4,-1)
Player 1	S_2	(0,3)	(3,1)	(5,4)
	S_3	(1,5)	(4,2)	(5,2)

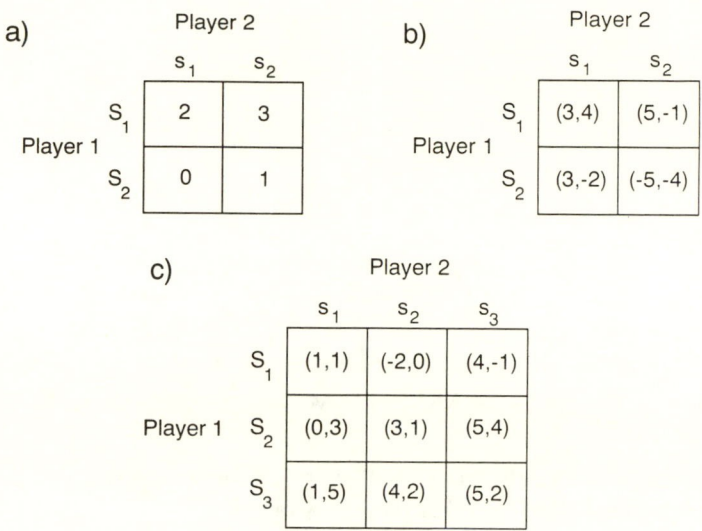

Figure 4.3 Exercise 4.1

never squeal," each is always better off confessing, regardless of what the other does. The players need a binding agreement or some way to enforce a deal to solve the Prisoner's Dilemma. In Chapter Nine, I discuss the play of Prisoner's Dilemma when the game is played repeatedly. Iterated Prisoner's Dilemma is a very different game from Prisoner's Dilemma.

> Exercise 4.1: Find any dominated strategies in the games in Figure 4.3. Are there any dominant strategy equilibria in these games?

Unfortunately, most games do not have a dominant strategy equilibrium. The game in Figure 4.1 does not; although S_2 is a dominant strategy for Player 1, Player 2 does not have a dominant strategy. If Player 1 plays S_1, Player 2 prefers playing s_1, giving her a payoff of 1. (Recall that Player 2's payoff is the opposite of Player 1's payoff in a two-person, zero-sum game.) If Player 1 plays S_2, Player 2 prefers playing s_2, giving her a payoff of -3. The strategy that is best for Player 2 depends upon what strategy Player 1 plays. The strategy that is best for a player against a particular strategy of the other player is the first player's best reply to that particular strategy.

> **Definition**: A strategy S_i is a **best reply** to strategy s_j for Player 1 iff for all other strategies S available to Player 1,
>
> $$M(S_i;s_j) \geq M(S;s_j).$$
>
> A strategy S_i is a **strict best reply** to strategy s_j for Player 1 iff for all other strategies S available to Player 1,

		Player 2	
		s_1	s_2
Player 1	S_1	(1,4)	(0,2)
	S_2	(-1,0)	(5,1)

Figure 4.4 A Two-Person, Non–Zero-Sum Game without Dominant Strategies

$$M(S_i;s_j) > M(S;s_j).$$

There are parallel definitions for Player 2. A dominant strategy is a strict best reply against all of the other player's strategies.

Return to Figure 4.1. Player 1 has a dominant strategy, S_2. Player 2's best reply to Player 1's dominant strategy is s_2. The pair of strategies (S_2; s_2) is stable. Neither player wants to change his or her strategy given that they know what strategy the other player is playing. Assuming that both players know the game and reason about how the other will play the game, Player 2 should anticipate that Player 1 will play S_2. She should then play s_2.

In some games, neither player has a dominant strategy. Neither player has a dominant strategy in the two-person, non–zero-sum game in Figure 4.4. S_1 and S_2 are Player 1's best replies to s_1 and s_2, respectively. Similarly, s_1 and s_2 are Player 2's best replies to S_1 and S_2, respectively. Each player's best strategy depends upon the other player's chosen strategy.

We define a Nash equilibrium as a situation where each player's strategy is a best reply to the other player's strategy. When both players are playing best replies against each other's strategies, they have no incentive to change their strategies. The game in Figure 4.4 has two Nash equilibria in pure strategies, (S_1;s_1) and (S_2;s_2). S_1 is Player 1's best reply to s_1, and s_1 is Player 2's best reply to S_1. Similarly, S_2 is Player 1's best reply to s_2, and s_2 is Player 2's best reply to S_2.

> **Definition**: A pair of strategies S_i and s_j forms a **Nash equilibrium** iff the strategies are best replies to each other. Alternatively, a pair of strategies forms a Nash equilibrium iff
>
> $$M_1(S_i;s_j) \geq M_1(S; s_j) \text{ for all } S \neq S_i$$
>
> and
>
> $$M_2(S_i;s_j) \geq M_2(S_i;s) \text{ for all } s \neq s_j.$$

A Nash equilibrium is stable because neither player has an incentive to deviate unilaterally from its equilibrium strategy. Either player reduces its payoff if it defects from its equilibrium strategy. However, this observation does not imply that an equilibrium is the best outcome for either player. Nor are equilibria "fair" in any common meaning of "fairness." Instead, Nash equilibrium is a minimal condition for a solution to a game if the players can correctly anticipate each other's strategies. Nash equilibria entail stable, mutual anticipations of other players' strategies. If such anticipations exist, neither player has an incentive to change its strategy unilaterally. To do so would reduce its payoff.

Nash equilibria in pure strategies can be found easily from the strategic form. Player 1 can choose the row of the strategic form, and Player 2, the column. Sometimes Players 1 and 2 are called Row and Column for this reason. Within a given column, that is, for a fixed strategy for Player 2, Player 1's best reply is the strategy that produces the largest payoff for him in that column. Within a given row, Player 2's best reply is the strategy that produces the largest payoff for her in that row. Nash equilibria can be found, then, by searching for outcomes where the first payoff is the greatest in its column and the second payoff is the greatest in its row. The strategies that produce such outcomes form a Nash equilibrium in pure strategies.

> Exercise 4.2: Find the Nash equilibria in pure strategies for the games in Figure 4.5.

In a two-person, zero-sum game, the players' payoff at an equilibrium must be the greatest in its column and the least in its row. Player 1 has control over the row chosen and can benefit by defection if some outcome in the same column has a greater payoff. Conversely, Player 2 wishes to minimize Player 1's payoff (recall that $M_2 = -M_1$ in a zero-sum game) and has control over the column chosen within a given row. Equilibria of zero-sum games are sometimes called minmax points because they are simultaneously row minima and column maxima.

> Exercise 4.3: Find the equilibria of the two-person, zero-sum games in Figure 4.6.

Mixed Strategies

Some games do not have Nash equilibria in pure strategies. Figure 4.7 gives the strategic form of the Matching Pennies game from Chapter Three (using the convention for payoffs in zero-sum games). Matching Pennies does not have a Nash equilibrium in pure strategies. Player 1's best replies to h and t are H and T, respectively; Player 2's best replies to H and T are t and h, respectively.

a)

Player 1 \ Player 2	s_1	s_2
S_1	(0,0)	(-5,10)
S_2	(10,-5)	(5,5)

b)

Player 1 \ Player 2	s_1	s_2
S_1	(3,4)	(-3,5)
S_2	(10,-2)	(5,-5)

c)

Player 1 \ Player 2	s_1	s_2
S_1	(3,4)	(5,-1)
S_2	(3,-2)	(-5,-4)

d)

Player 1 \ Player 2	s_1	s_2	s_3
S_1	(1,1)	(-2,0)	(4,-1)
S_2	(0,3)	(3,1)	(5,4)
S_3	(1,5)	(4,2)	(5,2)

e)

Player 1 \ Player 2	s_1	s_2
S_1	(1,1)	(1,1)
S_2	(2,-1)	(-10,-2)
S_3	(-1,-2)	(0,-1)

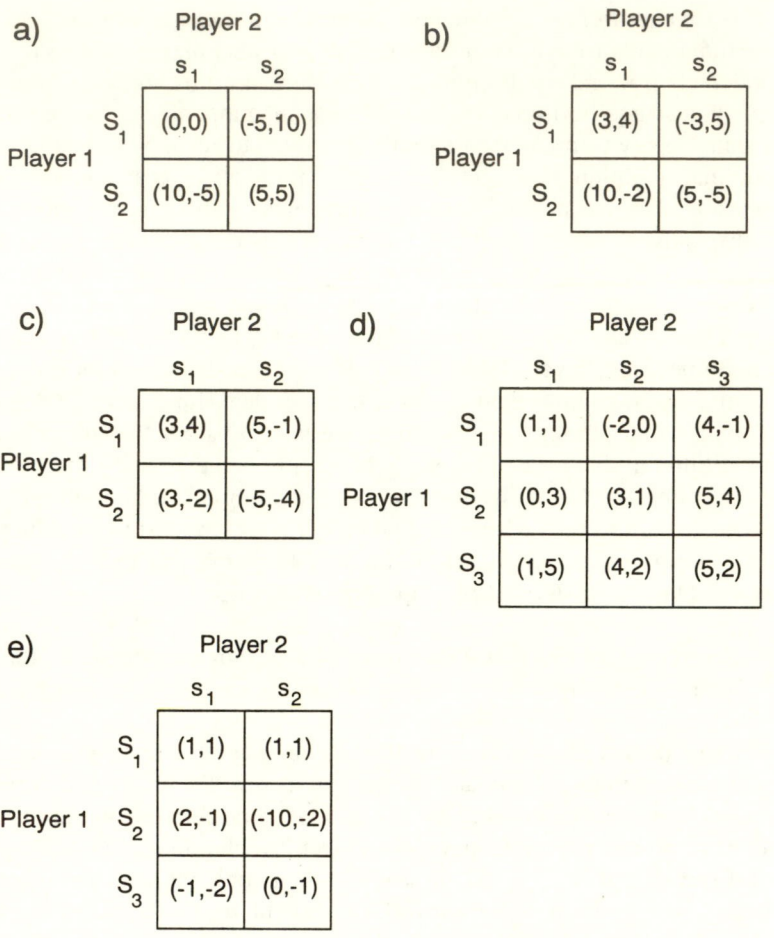

Figure 4.5 Exercise 4.2

Put simply, Player 1 wants to match Player 2's strategy, and Player 2 wants to avoid matching Player 1's strategy. How should they play this game?

Each player wants to make the other player uncertain about which strategy he or she will play. If a player can predict whether the other player will play heads or tails, the first player can take advantage of that prediction to win the game. We use probabilities to represent degrees of uncertainty about what strategy the other player will play.

Definition: A **mixed strategy** for a player is a probability distribution on the set of its pure strategies. Mixed strategies are denoted by $(p_1S_1, \ldots, p_nS_n)$, where p_i is the probability of playing strategy S_i where the player has n pure strategies and

a)

		Player 2	
		s_1	s_2
Player 1	S_1	2	0
	S_2	4	-1

b)

		Player 2	
		s_1	s_2
Player 1	S_1	3	4
	S_2	-3	-18

c)

		Player 2	
		s_1	s_2
Player 1	S_1	-3	-4
	S_2	12	-5

d)

		Player 2		
		s_1	s_2	s_3
	S_1	1	4	-1
Player 1	S_2	2	3	3
	S_3	-2	-1	5

d)

		Player 2		
		s_1	s_2	s_3
	S_1	-1	4	-1
Player 1	S_2	-1	3	-1
	S_3	-2	-6	-5

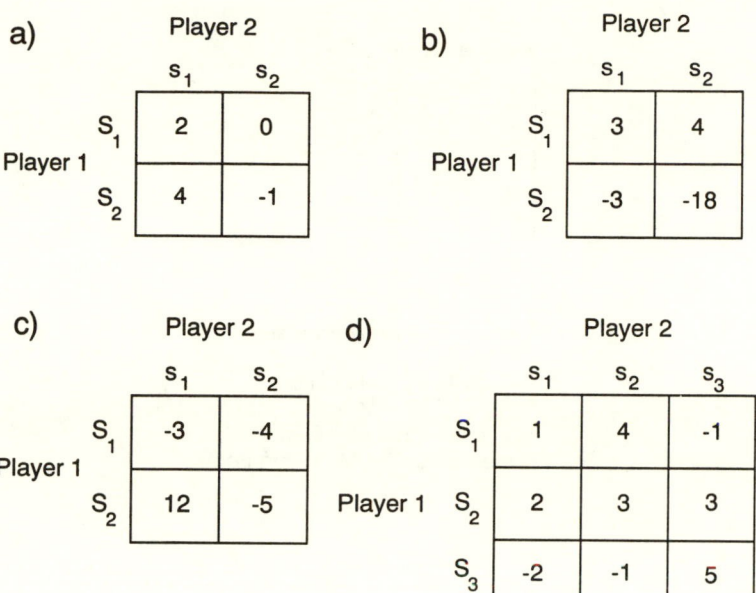

Figure 4.6 Exercise 4.3

		Player 2	
		h	t
Player 1	H	1	-1
	T	-1	1

Figure 4.7 Matching Pennies

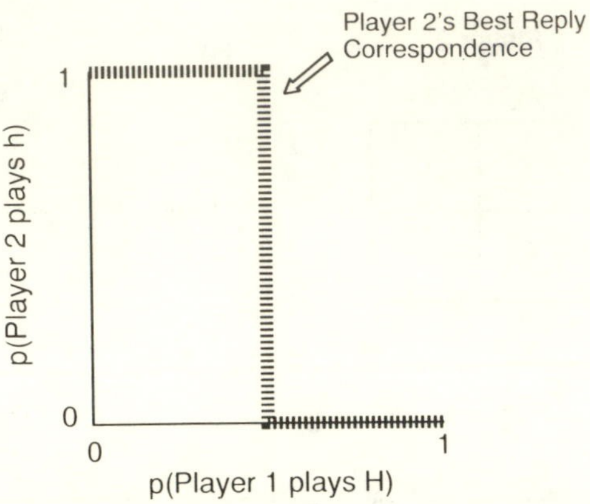

Figure 4.8 Player 2's Best Reply Correspondence for Matching Pennies

$$\sum_{i=1}^{n} p_i = 1.$$

A player's set of mixed strategies includes all of its pure strategies; $(1S_1, 0S_2, \ldots, 0S_n)$ is the same strategy as S_1.

A player's best reply to a mixed strategy of the other player can be calculated with expected utilities. In Matching Pennies, calculate Player 2's best reply if Player 1 plays a mixed strategy of $(\frac{1}{4}H, \frac{3}{4}T)$. If she plays h, her expected utility against Player's 1 mixed strategy will be the following:

$$\begin{aligned} u_2(h) &= p(H)[-M(H;h)] + p(T)[-M(T;h)] \\ &= \frac{1}{4}(-1) + \frac{3}{4}(1) = \frac{1}{2}. \end{aligned}$$

If she plays t, her expected utility against Player's 1 mixed strategy will be the following:

$$\begin{aligned} u_2(t) &= p(H)[-M(H;t)] + p(T)[-M(T;t)] \\ &= \frac{1}{4}(1) + \frac{3}{4}(-1) = -\frac{1}{2}. \end{aligned}$$

Because $u_2(h) > u_2(t)$, heads is Player 2's best reply against this mixed strategy for Player 1.

A best reply correspondence maps out a player's best reply to every mixed strategy of the other player. Figure 4.8 gives Player 2's best reply

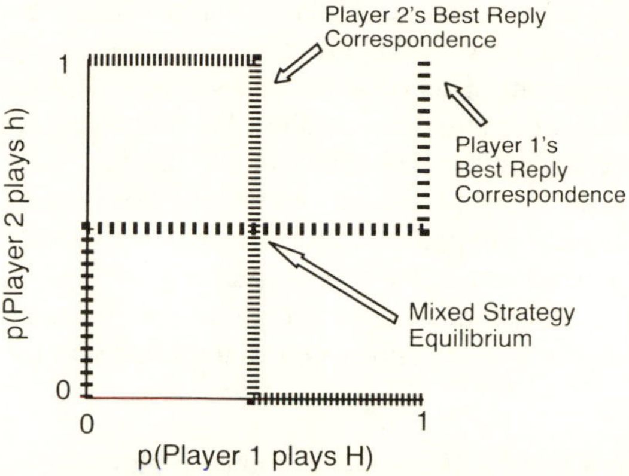

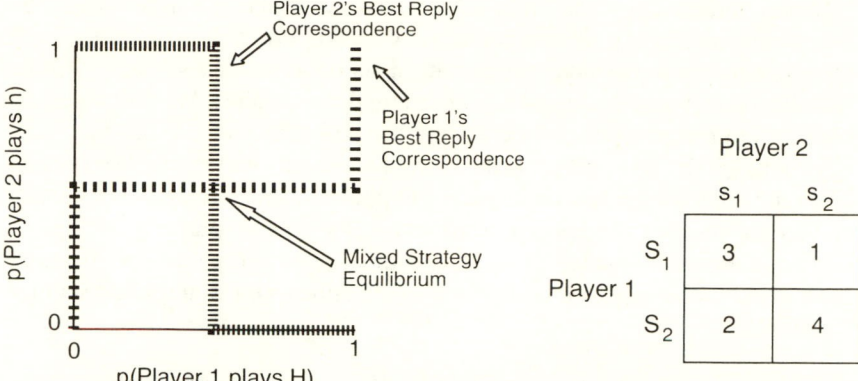

Figure 4.9 Both Players' Best Reply Correspondences for Matching Pennies

		Player 2 s_1	Player 2 s_2
Player 1	S_1	3	1
	S_2	2	4

Figure 4.10 A Two-Person, Zero-Sum Game without a Pure Strategy Nash Equilibrium

correspondence for Matching Pennies. The horizontal axis of Figure 4.8 gives the probability that Player 1 will play H in a mixed strategy. Player 1's pure strategies correspond to the end of this axis. When p(H) = 0, he plays T; when p(H) = 1, he plays H. The vertical axis gives the probability that Player 2 will play h in her mixed strategy. Each point in Figure 4.8 specifies a pair of mixed strategies, one for each player. The thick, dashed line gives Player 2's best reply correspondence. She should play h if she believes the chance that Player 1 will play H is less than one-half and t if that chance is greater than one-half. If she thinks there is exactly a one-half chance that Player 1 will play h, then *any* strategy she plays, mixed or pure, is a best reply.

We can also calculate Player 1's best reply correspondence. Figure 4.9 maps it on the same diagram as Player 2's best reply correspondence. The two correspondences intersect when both players play heads half the time and tails the other half. These strategies form the **mixed strategy equilibrium** $[(\frac{1}{2}H, \frac{1}{2}T); (\frac{1}{2}h, \frac{1}{2}t)]$. They are mutual best replies.

In some sense, this mixed strategy equilibrium is natural and obvious. In Matching Pennies, you want the other player to think you are equally likely to play either heads or tails. If the other player can predict your move, he or she can take advantage of you. But what happens in a more complicated zero-sum game?

> Example: The game in Figure 4.10 has no pure strategy equilibria. No matter what pair of pure strategies we select, one of the two players has an incentive to change strategy. What is the mixed strategy equilibrium of this game?

When pure strategy equilibria do not exist, each player may wish to introduce some uncertainty about what strategy it will play. This uncertainty forces the other player to consider playing all of its undominated strategies. Otherwise we cannot find strategies that are mutual best replies. We find a player's equilibrium mixed strategy by choosing the probability of picking each strategy such that the other player is indifferent among its undominated strategies. Then the other player has no incentive to play any one strategy over another, and any of those strategies is a best reply to the mixing player's strategy. To find such a mixed strategy in a game with two pure strategies, we calculate the other player's expected utility for playing either pure strategy and set them equal.

Example: In the game in Figure 4.10, Player 2 wants to play s_2 if Player 1 plays S_1 and play s_1 if Player 1 plays S_2. To calculate Player 1's mixed strategy that makes Player 2 indifferent between her two strategies, let p be the probability that he will play S_1. Player 1 plays the mixed strategy $[pS_1, (1-p)S_2]$. Find p such that Player 2 is indifferent between playing s_1 and s_2:

$$-3p + (-2)(1-p) = -1p + (-4)(1-p)$$
$$-p - 2 = 3p - 4$$
$$p = \frac{1}{2}$$

Then $(\frac{1}{2}S_1, \frac{1}{2}S_2)$ is Player 1's mixed strategy that makes Player 2 indifferent between her two pure strategies.

We can find a player's expected value for playing the game from the other player's mixed strategy. We calculate what payoff the player expects from playing the game against the other player's mixed strategy. This expected value is often called the player's **value** for the game. The players' values for a game can vary with the equilibrium in a non–zero-sum game. In a pure strategy equilibrium, the players' values are just their payoffs from that equilibrium.

Example: Either side of the first equality above gives Player 2's value for the game against Player 1's mixed strategy. Substitute $\frac{1}{2}$ for p in either side, and we get Player 2's utility if Player 1 plays its mixed strategy. From the left side of the equality above, we have the following:

$$v_2 = (-3)(\tfrac{1}{2}) + (-2)(1 - \tfrac{1}{2}) = -2\tfrac{1}{2}$$

Exercise 4.4: Find Player 2's mixed strategy to make Player 1 indifferent between his two strategies and his value for the game in the above example.

There is a critical observation about mixed strategies that must not be missed here. *Mixed strategies are calculated to neutralize the other player's choice of strategy,* not to maximize the mixing player's payoff. Mixed strategies expand the set of strategies that are a best reply for the other player. When a player is indifferent among its undominated strategies, any of them is a best reply. When both players play their mixed strategies, the pair of strategies forms a Nash equilibrium. Game theory is about strategic interaction; the strategic effect of a player's strategy on the other player's choice of strategy is as important as the immediate consequences of that strategy for the player's payoffs.

Whenever a mixed strategy is a best reply to a given strategy, every pure strategy in the mixed strategy is also a best reply to the given strategy. Whenever we have a mixed strategy equilibrium, each player plays its mixed strategy in order that the other player can play its mixed strategy. If a player deviates from its equilibrium mixed strategy, then the other player's best reply is no longer its equilibrium mixed strategy.

Mixed strategy equilibria can be understood in two ways. First, they could be exact instructions to randomize over pure strategies. In Matching Pennies, Player 2 could tell Player 1 that she is going to flip her coin to make her move after Player 1 has selected his move. Mixed strategies with more complicated probabilities could be carried out by drawing lots. Second, mixed strategies can be interpreted as representing the other player's uncertainty about what strategy the mixing player will play. A mixed strategy under this interpretation does not give random chances of the pure strategies. Rather, it delineates the uncertainty in the mind of the other player about the mixing player's strategy. The other player's indifference between its strategies captures the degree of uncertainty where the other player cannot exploit the mixing player.

What happens when a player plays a mixed strategy? Mixed strategies make one's actions unpredictable. When a player can profit by knowing the other player's strategy, the latter must obscure its intentions to prevent the former from taking advantage of its knowledge. Sports contains many examples of mixed strategies; for example, calling plays in football is a zero-sum game. If a pure strategy equilibrium existed in football, each team would always run the same play and set the same defense conditional on the down, distance, and score. But they don't. Football coaches say that if you know the play, there is a perfect defense to stop it, and if you know the defense, a perfect play to attack it. There is no pure strategy equilibrium in football.[1] Both sides should choose randomly among their plays and defenses to prevent the other side from predicting what they are planning on any given play. The exact set of plays and defenses used in a team's mixed strategy involves careful judgments about the

a)

Player 1 \ Player 2	s_1	s_2
S_1	3	-4
S_2	-2	1

b)

Player 1 \ Player 2	s_1	s_2
S_1	-3	1
S_2	0	-5

c)

Player 1 \ Player 2	s_1	s_2
S_1	5	-4
S_2	1	2

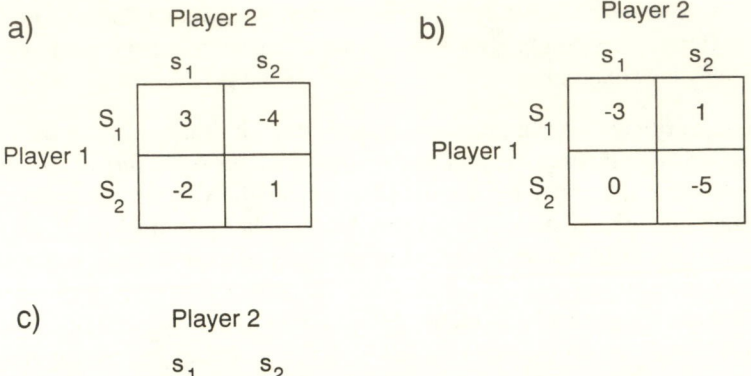

Figure 4.11 Exercise 4.5

a)

Player 1 \ Player 2	s_1	s_2
S_1	(4,2)	(-5,6)
S_2	(-1,5)	(0,-2)

b)

Player 1 \ Player 2	s_1	s_2
S_1	(1,1)	(0,4)
S_2	(-1,3)	(3,-5)

Figure 4.12 Exercise 4.6

strengths and weaknesses of a team and its opponent. The set of plays also should vary with the down, distance, and score. Both of these judgments make football a fascinating strategic game.

Exercise 4.5: Find the mixed strategy equilibria and values of both players in the two-person, zero-sum games in Figure 4.11.

Exercise 4.6: Verify that the two-person, non–zero-sum games in Figure 4.12 do not have Nash equilibria in pure strategies. Find a Nash equilibrium in mixed strategies and the value of the game for both players in the mixed strategy equilibrium for each game in Figure 4.12.

The Minmax Theorem and Equilibria of Two-Person, Zero-Sum Games

Mixed strategies expand the set of strategies available to the players. We have found Nash equilibria in mixed strategies. Do equilibria always exist in the set of mixed strategies? To answer this question, I begin with two-person, zero-sum games.

Two-person, zero-sum games are very special. It is common knowledge that the players' interests are perfectly opposed. Both players' self-interest dictates that they try to reduce the opponent's payoff. A player's **security level** for a strategy S_i is the minimum payoff it can obtain if it declares in advance that it will play S_i. The security level of a strategy is important for two-person, zero-sum games because a player must assume that its opponent will strive to limit it to its minimum payoff. Players in a two-person, zero-sum game should choose their strategies to maximize their security levels.

> Example: In the game in Figure 4.10, Player 1's security level for S_1 is 1. If Player 2 knows that Player 1 is playing S_1, she will play s_2. Similarly, Player 1's security level for S_2 is 2. Player 2's security levels for her pure strategies are -3 for s_1 and -4 for s_2. But the players' mixed strategies that were calculated to make the other player indifferent between its pure strategies have higher security levels than those of their pure strategies. The mixed strategy $(\frac{1}{2}S_1, \frac{1}{2}S_2)$ provides Player 1 with a security level of $2\frac{1}{2}$, and $(\frac{3}{4}s_1, \frac{1}{4}s_2)$ provides Player 2 with a security level of $-2\frac{1}{2}$.

This example illustrates the Minmax Theorem, the basic result about two-person, zero-sum games. All two-person, zero-sum games have at least one equilibrium in mixed strategies. The equilibrium strategies maximize both players' security levels.

> **Theorem** (the Minmax Theorem): For every two-person, zero-sum game with a finite number of pure strategies, there exists a number, v, a mixed strategy for Player 1 that guarantees him a total payoff of at least v, and a mixed strategy for Player 2 that guarantees that Player 1 gets at most v. These mixed strategies are in equilibrium, and any pair of mixed strategies that are in equilibrium yield v for Players 1 and 2 and are also in equilibrium with the equilibrium strategies that produce v.

The Minmax Theorem is immensely powerful for the special case of two-person, zero-sum games. Every two-person, zero-sum game can be solved in mixed strategies. If there are multiple equilibria, all equilibria produce the same value, and any equilibrium strategy for one player is in equilibrium with any equilibrium strategy for the other player. In other words, all equilibrium strategies are interchangeable and produce the same value. The interchangeability of strategies makes the practical solution of two-person, zero-sum games easier. Any equilibrium strategy is in equilibrium with any equilibrium strategy of the other player. If an equilibrium strategy is found, we need look no further for strategic purposes; it is equally effective against any equilibrium strategy the opponent plays.

The proof of the Minmax Theorem can be sketched as follows. For any pair of strategies, find each player's best reply in the set of mixed strategies to the other player's strategy in that pair. This process defines a best reply transformation in the space of mixed strategies from the original pair of strategies to the pair of best replies to them. There are theorems in mathematics that state that all such transformations have a fixed point, a pair of strategies that is mapped onto itself by the transformation. The fixed point of the best reply transformation is the equilibrium; it is a pair of strategies that are best replies to each other. Given that an equilibrium exists, then the statements about the value of the game and interchangeability of equilibrium strategies follow from some inequalities.

However, the Minmax Theorem states only that an equilibrium exists and does not explain how to find that equilibrium. To give you an idea of the limits of the Minmax Theorem, chess is a two-person, zero-sum game. Thus there is an equilibrium for chess. There exists a strategy for chess that guarantees either a victory for one side or a draw for both. Strategically, then, chess is not an interesting game. Of course, determining this strategy is not a trivial problem, which is why chess is an interesting game to play. No one has ever solved for the optimal chess strategy for either player. The strategy space is immense, and the interaction of the players' strategies extraordinarily complex.

The Minmax Theorem does not hold for all possible two-person, zero-sum games. For example, games with infinite strategy sets can fail to have equilibria:

> Example: The game in which each player picks a number and the higher number wins. This game has no equilibrium because for any number chosen, any larger number is a best reply. There is no pair of numbers that are best replies to each other in this game, so no pure strategy equilibrium exists. Similarly, there is no mixed strategy equilibrium. If there were such a mixed strategy equilibrium, either player would be better off reducing the probability of playing the least number it might play and raising the probability of any number greater than the lowest number that the opponent plays in its mixed strategy.

The Minmax Theorem fails to hold for this case because the players have an infinite set of pure strategies and the payoff function is not, as mathematicians say, "well-behaved." There are theorems that apply to games with infinite strategy sets that explain how "well-behaved" the payoff function must be for Nash equilibria to exist in pure and mixed strategies. See Fudenberg and Tirole 1991 (34–36, 484–89) for some such theorems.

Characteristics of Nash Equilibria

The previous section discussed two-person, zero-sum games. Equilibria of two-person, zero-sum games have many nice properties. Nash equilibrium is the extension of equilibrium in two-person, zero-sum games to non–zero-sum games. Both types of equilibria require players' strategies to be mutual best replies. Unfortunately, most of the nice properties of equilibria of two-person, zero-sum games do not extend to Nash equilibria in non–zero-sum games. This section identifies and illustrates which properties of the equilibria of two-person, zero-sum games no longer hold in Nash equilibria of non–zero-sum games.

In a Nash equilibrium, neither player can better itself acting on its own. Nash equilibria are stable from unilateral defections. However, they may not be stable against coordinated defections. Both players could benefit if they both changed their strategies together. Such coordinated defections are never desirable in a zero-sum game because the players have opposed interests. If one player benefits from the joint shift in strategies, the other must lose from that shift.

> Example: The game in Figure 4.13 has two Nash equilibria in pure strategies, (S_1;s_1) and (S_2;s_2). But (S_2;s_2) is not stable against both players' defecting at the same time. Both players prefer shifting from (S_2;s_2) to (S_1;s_1).

Non-zero-sum games with multiple Nash equilibria pose problems that two-person, zero-sum games with multiple equilibria do not. If a two-person, zero-sum game has multiple equilibria, all the equilibria produce identical values for the players and all equilibrium strategies are interchangeable. Neither proposition is true for non–zero-sum games with multiple equilibria.

> Example: Battle of the Sexes. The Battle of the Sexes game has a cute slice of life in the 1950s built into its story. As Luce and Raiffa (1957, 91) put it, " A man, player 1, and a woman, player 2, each have two choices for an evening's entertainment. Each can either go to a prize fight [S_1 and s_1] or to a ballet [S_2 and s_2]. Following

		Player 2	
		s_1	s_2
Player 1	S_1	(2,2)	(0,0)
	S_2	(0,0)	(1,1)

Figure 4.13 A Two-Person, Non–Zero-Sum Game with Two Nash Equilibria

		Player 2	
		s_1	s_2
Player 1	S_1	(2,1)	(0,0)
	S_2	(0,0)	(1,2)

Figure 4.14 Battle of the Sexes

the usual cultural stereotype, the man much prefers the fight and the woman the ballet; however, to both it is more important that they go out together than that each see the preferred entertainment." In the 1990s version of this game, now called "Contest of the Individuals with Neither Gender nor Sexual Orientation Specified," Chris and Pat decide whether they wish to vacation at the beach or in the mountains.[2] No matter what we call this game, both players want to coordinate their strategies, but they disagree about which outcome is better. Figure 4.14 gives the strategic form of Battle of the Sexes. This game has two Nash equilibria in pure strategies: $(S_1;s_1)$ and $(S_2;s_2)$.

Battle of the Sexes illustrates how Nash equilibria lack many of the nice properties of the equilibria of two-person, zero-sum games. First, different Nash equilibria of the same game can have different values. In Battle of the Sexes, each player's value for the game at equilibrium is different across the two equilibria. Unlike the equilibria of two-person, zero-sum games, different Nash equilibria of a game can have different values for a player.

Second, equilibrium strategies are not interchangeable. $(S_1;s_2)$ is not a Nash equilibrium of Battle of the Sexes, even though both S_1 and s_2 are equilibrium strategies for some pure strategy Nash equilibrium of the game.

Exercise 4.7: Find a mixed strategy equilibrium and its value to both players for Battle of the Sexes.

Nash equilibria do not possess all the nice properties of the equilibria of two-person, zero-sum games. But Nash equilibria always exist in mixed strategies.

Theorem (Nash): Every finite non–zero-sum game has at least one Nash equilibrium in mixed strategies.

The proof of the existence of Nash equilibria parallels the proof of the Minmax Theorem. The best reply transformation must have a fixed point, and that

		Player 2 S_1	Player 2 S_2
Player 1	S_1	(5,5)	(0,10)
	S_2	(10,0)	(-5,-5)

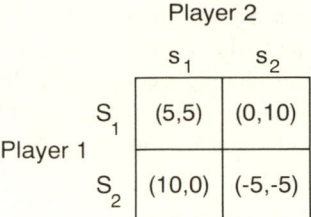

Figure 4.15 Chicken

fixed point is a Nash equilibrium. But the proof does not tell us how to find Nash equilibria—only that they exist. There are no general techniques for finding Nash equilibria other than simple searches and basic intuition. One way to find Nash equilibria is to think about how each player should play the game and look for strategy pairs where neither player can benefit by changing its strategy.

Example: Another classic game, Chicken. Chicken, like Prisoner's Dilemma and Battle of the Sexes, has a cute story attached to it. Back in the 1950s, teenaged males suffering from excessive hormones would engage in a contest of manhood known as Chicken. The two contestants would meet on a deserted stretch of road, each driving their favorite machine. They would face each other at some distance and drive their cars directly at each other until one driver "chickened" out by swerving off the road. The other would be the winner and proclaimed the man with the most hormones on the block. Sometimes neither driver would chicken out, and many hormones would be spilt on the pavement. Let S_1 be a driver's choice to swerve and S_2 the choice to hold firm to the course. Figure 4.15 gives the strategic form of Chicken. The best outcome is to win the game by having your opponent "chicken" out, but better to be a live chicken than a dead duck.

Exercise 4.8:

a) Find the pure strategy Nash equilibria of Chicken.

b) Are there any mixed strategy equilibria? If so, what are they, and what value do they produce for the players?

Classic two-by-two games, such as Prisoner's Dilemma and Chicken, are often used as models of strategic interaction in international relations. Although such simple models can illustrate some important strategic problems, they have two significant limitations as models. First, two-by-two games assume simultaneous moves for the players. Some games, such as Prisoner's Dilemma, are unchanged by adding an order to the players' moves. Others, such as Chicken, are completely changed by introducing a sequence to the moves. The assumption of simultaneous moves also prevents the analysis from addressing the question of how the players respond to earlier moves.

Exercise 4.9:

a) State the strategic form of Chicken when the second player can observe the first player's move before choosing her move.

b) What are the pure strategy Nash equilibria of this game?

c) Do all these Nash equilibria make sense to you?

Second, strategic situations with only two choices are quite limited. Although all game models are simplifications of reality, reducing the players' choices to two may abstract questions of strategic interest into nonexistence. All too often, two-by-two games have been seen as the only possible models. Analysts have used those games to make inappropriate arguments about situations with more than two relevant strategic choices.

Nash Equilibria and Common Conjectures

Many games have multiple Nash equilibria. How do the players know which equilibrium to play, and how do they coordinate their expectations to play that equilibrium? In a two-person, zero-sum game, the players do not have to worry about multiple equilibria. All equilibria produce the same value, and all equilibrium strategies are interchangeable. The players do not have to try to predict which equilibrium the other player will use when choosing their own strategy. Any of a player's equilibrium strategies is in equilibrium with all of its opponent's equilibrium strategies, and all those equilibria produce identical values for the players. But Nash equilibrium strategies are not interchangeable in non–zero-sum games. Nash equilibrium strategies are best replies to each other; they are not necessarily best replies to any other Nash equilibrium strategy of the other player. The players need to know the other players' strategies to know that their own strategy is a best reply in a non–zero-sum game.

The concept of a Nash equilibrium assumes that the players hold a **common conjecture** about how the game is going to be played. In a Nash equilibrium, a player cannot make itself better off by deviating from its equilibrium strategy if it knows that the other player will play its corresponding equilibrium strategy. When players hold a common conjecture, they correctly anticipate one another's strategies.

		Player 2	
		s_1	s_2
Player 1	S_1	(2,2)	(0,0)
	S_2	(0,0)	(1,1)

Figure 4.16 A Two-Person, Non–Zero-Sum Game with Two Nash Equilibria

Common conjectures could arise for many reasons. This section discusses two possible sources of common conjectures, communication and focal points. The common conjecture assumed may also distinguish some Nash equilibria from others in games with multiple Nash equilibria. The exact common conjecture used can help us choose among multiple Nash equilibria of a game.

When the players have identical interests in a game, communication may be sufficient to create the common conjecture needed for a Nash equilibrium. The game in Figure 4.16 has two Nash equilibria in pure strategies: $(S_1;s_1)$ and $(S_2;s_2)$. If the players can communicate, one would expect them to agree to play $(S_1;s_1)$.

If pregame communication is the source of the common conjecture, then one would expect players to coordinate on a Pareto-optimal equilibrium. The players should not choose an equilibrium if both can do better in another equilibrium. Some game theorists suggest Pareto optimality as a condition for selecting among multiple Nash equilibria.

> **Definition**: An outcome x **Pareto dominates** an outcome y iff for all players i, $u_i(x) \geq u_i(y)$ and for some player j, $u_j(x) > u_j(y)$. Outcome x **strictly Pareto dominates** outcome y iff for all players i, $u_i(x) > u_i(y)$.

In the game in Figure 4.16, there are two Nash equilibria in pure strategies. $(S_1;s_1)$ strictly Pareto dominates $(S_2;s_2)$. It seems implausible that the players would play $(S_2;s_2)$ over $(S_1;s_1)$ if they communicate to agree on their strategies.

Pareto optimality is not as useful to select among Nash equilibria when the players do not have identical interests. Battle of the Sexes has two pure strategy equilibria, but neither Pareto dominates the other. Further, communication alone may not create a common conjecture for Battle of the Sexes. Suppose the players quarreled about which pure strategy equilibrium to play, with Player 1 holding out for $(S_1;s_1)$ and Player 2 arguing for $(S_2;s_2)$? What strategies do you think they would play after such an argument?

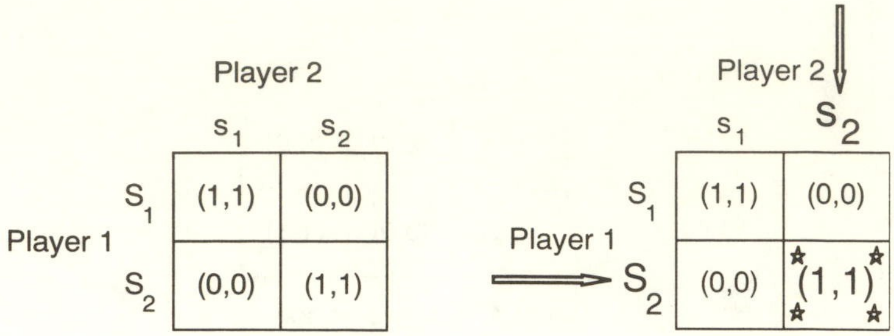

Figure 4.17 The Effect of a Focal Point in a Game with Two Identical Equilibria

Second, factors beyond the game may create a common conjecture. The players may share ideas that lead them to focus on some strategy pairs over others. For example, the two games in Figure 4.17 are the same. They have two Nash equilibria in pure strategies: $(S_1;s_1)$ and $(S_2;s_2)$. If the players cannot communicate and they play the game using the strategic form on the left, we might expect them to play $(S_1;\ s_1)$ simply because S_1 comes before S_2. If they use the strategic form on the right, $(S_2;\ s_2)$ seems more likely. The stars, arrows, and large print make that equilibrium more salient to the players. In real life, Schelling's (1960, 55–57) famous example of where to meet in New York City illustrates the idea of focal points. His audience in New Haven, Connecticut, selected Grand Central Station, their focal point in Manhattan.

This observation captures the idea of focal points. If there are multiple Nash equilibria, some may be distinguished in ways that lead the players to those equilibria over the others. Focal points could be distinctive outcomes that attract attention out of a large set of Nash equilibria. If the players have played the game before, their prior experiences could create a common conjecture about how the game should be played. A common culture could lead the players toward some strategies over others.

Symmetry can be thought of as a focal point. Consider the game where two players can divide one hundred dollars if they can agree on how to divide it. Each player must simultaneously write down how they will divide the sum. If the two entries match, the players get the money, divided in the way they have agreed. Any division of the money is a Nash equilibrium of this game. But we might expect that the players would choose to divide the money equally. Equal division is a natural focal point in the set of equilibria.

If we accept symmetry as a focal point, symmetric games should have symmetric equilibria. If a game treats the two players the same—gives them the same choices and produces the same outcomes from the corresponding choices—the equilibrium should reward them with the same outcome.

Definition: A game is **symmetric** iff both players have the same strategy set, S, and for all $s_i, s_j \in S, u_1(s_i;s_j) = u_2(s_j;s_i)$.

A game is symmetric if the game does not change when we relabel the players. The players must have identical strategy sets. When we exchange the strategies the players play, the players also reverse payoffs. Both Chicken and Battle of the Sexes are symmetric games. The players differ only in their labels.[3] Symmetric games should have equilibria where the players receive equal payoffs. Such games provide no way to differentiate the players except through the labels we give them. One argument for equilibrium selection holds that Nash equilibria of symmetric games where the players receive different payoffs should be discarded.

Neither Chicken nor Battle of the Sexes has a pure strategy Nash equilibrium that satisfies the symmetry criterion. Instead, the mixed strategy equilibria of the two games are selected. They do produce equal payoffs for the players. However, the symmetry condition conflicts with Pareto optimality in Battle of the Sexes. Both players are better off in either of the pure strategy equilibria than they are in the mixed strategy equilibrium.

Game theory does not have a theory of focal points at this time. One would have to explain how focal points arise from cultural influences, shared experiences, or moral systems. But focal points draw our attention to an important point about Nash equilibria. Nash equilibria assume that the players share a common conjecture about what strategies they each will play. Otherwise, the players cannot know that their strategies are best replies to each other. Focal points could be one source of a common conjecture.

How strong does the common conjecture have to be for a Nash equilibrium? Two theorems set forth by Aumann and Brandenburger (1991) clarify what shared knowledge is needed for Nash equilibrium. Before looking at these theorems, we have to define the term *mutual knowledge*. Recall the definition of common knowledge from Chapter Three. Something is common knowledge if all players know it, all players know that all other players know it, and so on. A weaker level of knowledge is mutual knowledge.

Definition: An aspect of a game is **mutual knowledge** if all players know it.

Mutual knowledge, unlike common knowledge, does not require that the players know that the other players know it. In this sense, events that are mutual knowledge are not as well known as those that are common knowledge.

For pure strategy Nash equilibria, mutual knowledge of strategies is sufficient to guarantee that the players know their strategies are mutual best replies.

> **Theorem**: If the players are rational and the pure strategies they are playing are mutual knowledge, then those strategies must form a Nash equilibrium.

If strategies are mutual knowledge, then rational players must select best replies. Strategies that do not form a Nash equilibrium cannot be mutual knowledge among rational players.

Mixed strategy Nash equilibria require greater knowledge. The players are uncertain about what pure strategy the other players will play in a mixed strategy Nash equilibrium. Consequently, they cannot be certain that their mixed strategies are best replies.

> **Theorem**: For two-person zero-sum games, if the game, the rationality of the players, and their mixed strategies are mutual knowledge, then those mixed strategies form a Nash equilibrium.

As in the previous theorem, if the mixed strategies are mutual knowledge, they must form a Nash equilibrium. Otherwise, one of the players would not be playing a best reply, and it would wish to change its strategy. However, this theorem does not generalize for games with three or more players. Stronger knowledge is needed. I suggest you see Brandenburger 1992 for a further discussion of Nash equilibrium and common conjectures.

Rationalizability

What happens when the players do not share a common conjecture about how the game will be played? Are there are any limits on what strategies rational players would play? Recall the idea of a strictly dominated strategy. When a player has a strictly dominated strategy, it always does better by playing the strategy that dominates its dominated strategy. A rational player would never play a strictly dominated strategy, no matter what it conjectures about the other players' strategies.

Rational players can use common knowledge of the game being played and their rationality to restrict the set of strategies from which they choose. Rational players will not play strictly dominated strategies, and they know other rational players will not play such strategies. They need only focus their attention on undominated strategies. If a player eliminates another player's strictly dominated strategies, it could find that some of its strategies are now strictly dominated within the smaller game left after the elimination. It should not play a strategy that has become strictly dominated; there are no strategies that the other players will consider where such a strategy is at least as good as another strategy.

This observation suggests a way of reducing games to those strategies that rational players could select, an iterated dominance-elimination procedure. In a

		Player 2		
		s_1	s_2	s_3
	S_1	(0,1)	(-2,3)	(4,-1)
Player 1	S_2	(0,3)	(3,1)	(6,4)
	S_3	(1,5)	(4,2)	(5,2)

Figure 4.18 A Game to Illustrate the Elimination of Dominated Strategies

		Player 2		
		s_1	[redacted]	s_3
	[redacted]	[redacted]	[redacted]	[redacted]
Player 1	S_2	(0,3)	[redacted]	(6,4)
	S_3	(1,5)	[redacted]	(5,2)

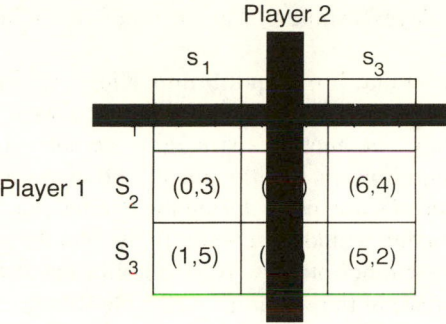

Figure 4.19 The Game in Figure 4.18 after Dominated Strategies Are Eliminated

dominance-elimination procedure, we eliminate all strictly dominated strategies from the game, and then continue searching for strategies that are now dominated in the set of remaining strategies. This procedure is carried out until no more strategies can be eliminated. The process is an **iterated dominance-elimination procedure**. If an iterated dominance-elimination procedure ends in only one strategy per player, the game is **dominance solvable**. Prisoner's Dilemma is dominance solvable.

Example: Conduct an iterated dominance-elimination procedure on the game in Figure 4.18. S_1 is strictly dominated by S_3: Player 1 always does better playing S_3 rather than S_1. If we delete S_1 from consideration, then s_1 strictly dominates s_2 for Player 2. In Figure 4.19 blacks these two eliminated strategies and the payoffs they produce are blacked out.

Figure 4.19 cannot be reduced further by an iterated dominance-elimination procedure. Neither S_2 nor S_3 strictly dominates the other for Player 1. Neither s_1 nor s_3 strictly dominates the other for Player 2. The game in Figure 4.18 is not dominance solvable, then.

The strategies that result from an iterated dominance-elimination procedure are called **rationalizable**.[4] A rational player could hypothesize strategies for the other players where a rationalizable strategy is a best reply. In the reduced game in Figure 4.19, either player can rationalize both of its remaining strategies given the proper hypothesis about the other player's strategy. If Player 1 thinks that Player 2 will play s_3, he prefers playing S_2. If he thinks that she will play s_1, he prefers playing S_3. Similarly, if Player 2 thinks that Player 1 will play S_2, she prefers playing s_3. Simultaneous choices of S_2 and s_1 can be rationalized if both players' hypotheses about the other's strategy are incorrect; in this case, Player 1 thinks that Player 2 will play s_3, and Player 2 thinks Player 1 will play S_3. If either player knew its hypothesis about the other player's strategy was incorrect, it would want to change its strategy.

Rationalizability, unlike Nash equilibrium, allows for incorrect hypotheses about the other player's strategy. In Nash equilibrium, we assume that the players' hypotheses about one another's strategies are correct. Any strategy that is part of a Nash equilibrium is rationalizable. If it were not, then it would be strictly dominated at some point during the iterated dominance-elimination procedure. That strategy would be a better reply than the player's Nash equilibrium strategy to the other players' Nash equilibrium strategies. Nash equilibria, then, are a subset of the set of rationalizable strategy pairs. Many games have multiple Nash equilibria. The set of rationalizable strategy pairs always includes all Nash equilibria and typically is larger than the set of all Nash equilibria.

Exercise 4.10: Conduct an iterated dominance-elimination procedure on the game in Figure 4.20. Is this game dominance solvable? If so, what are the resulting strategies? If not, what does the game look like after the procedure, and what are the Nash equilibria of the remaining game?

In general, there is no completely satisfactory solution concept for two-person, non–zero-sum games. Nash equilibria often provide multiple solutions with no commonly accepted way to judge among them. The logic of mutual best replies alone does not explain why the players share a common conjecture about how the game should be played. Because non–zero-sum games involve mixed motives for all players, threats and bargaining strategies are common in them. But the exploration of threats and bargaining tactics requires the specification of the nature of communication among the players and a greater knowledge of the structure of the game. Different sequences of moves can affect

		Player 2				
		s_1	s_2	s_3	s_4	s_5
	S_1	(4,-1)	(3,0)	(-3,1)	(-1,4)	(-2,0)
	S_2	(-1,1)	(2,2)	(2,3)	(-1,0)	(2,5)
Player 1	S_3	(2,1)	(-1,-1)	(0,4)	(4,-1)	(0,2)
	S_4	(1,6)	(-3,0)	(-1,4)	(1,1)	(-1,4)
	S_5	(0,0)	(1,4)	(-3,1)	(-2,3)	(-1,-1)

Figure 4.20 Exercise 4.10

greatly the efficacy of threats and bargaining tactics. I leave these topics for my discussion of games in the extensive form. Now I present two examples of games applied to electoral politics.

Political Reform in Democracies

Reform of the civil service has been a recurrent problem in democracies. Patronage is the traditional source for government employees. Victorious parties reward their workers and followers with government jobs. Patronage often leads to inefficiency and corruption, and the demand for reform soon follows. But civil service reform is difficult to achieve after the demand for it arises. The fight to establish merit-based hiring over patronage is often blocked by established political parties. Why is the move to meritocracy difficult to achieve? This section presents two simple models from Geddes 1991 that help us understand the political motivations behind the success and failure of civil service reform in democracies.

Reform occurs only if politicians approve of it. The models here focus on the incentives that politicians face when the issue of political reform arises in competitive democracies. Both patronage and reform have electoral value to politicians seeking office. Patronage is a reward for loyal campaign workers and so produces a cadre of veterans for the political organizations of parties in office. Reform is an effective campaign issue with voters when the inefficiencies of patronage become obvious to all. The two models here address the questions of when politicians use the promise of patronage jobs to their campaign workers and when they support reform as an issue in their campaigns.

The model shown in Figure 4.21 displays the incentives of politicians to use patronage, that is, promise their workers jobs, during a campaign. Exam-

		Politician 2: Do Not Use Patronage	Politician 2: Use Patronage
Politician 1	Do Not Use Patronage	$(p, 1-p)$	$(p-v_2, 1-p+v_2)$
	Use Patronage	$(p+v_1, 1-p-v_1)$	$(p+v_1-v_2, 1-p-v_1+v_2)$

Figure 4.21 Game of Electoral Competition between Two Politicians with Patronage

ination of this array answers the question, will candidates voluntarily commit themselves to merit-based hiring in the absence of civil service laws enforcing it? Consider electoral competition between two politicians, colorfully named Politician 1 and Politician 2. The game in Figure 4.21 is a simple representation of such competition. Each candidate can choose to use patronage in the campaign or not. If neither candidate uses patronage, then Politician 1's chance of winning is p and Politician 2's chance is $1 - p$. Patronage provides an advantage to the candidate using it. Politician 1's chance of winning rises by v_1 if he uses patronage, and Politician 2's chance rises by v_2 if she uses it in her campaign. Each candidate's advantage from patronage reduces its opponent's chance of winning. Figure 4.21 gives the complete game.

This game is a constant-sum game because both players' payoffs sum to a constant, here, 1, in all cells of the strategic form. Constant-sum games are strategically identical to zero-sum games. We can transform the payoffs of a constant-sum game to make it a zero-sum game. Because the total payoff is a constant, what one player gains, the other player must lose. The equilibrium of the game in Figure 4.21 is (Use Patronage;Use Patronage). Further, (Use Patronage;Use Patronage) is a dominant strategy equilibrium. When left to their own devices, politicians employ patronage. Competitive pressures require them to do so. Because there is an electoral benefit to using patronage in a campaign, reform requires that politicians not be able to use patronage. Meritocratic civil service laws do that.

But if patronage helps a candidate's chances of winning, why would parties support reforms that would deny them the exercise of patronage? The answer is that supporting reform can provide an electoral benefit. Cleaning up corruption is a familiar theme in any reform campaign. But reform requires convincing those that hold power that reform advances their electoral chances better than does "business as usual." The model shown in Figure 4.22 has two actors, a majority party and a minority party. Without the support of the former, civil service reform cannot pass. With that support, it passes. Each party can now support or oppose reform. If the majority party supports reform, reform laws

		Minority Party: Support Reform	Minority Party: Oppose Reform
Majority Party	Support Reform	$(p,1-p)$	$(p+e,1-p-e)$
	Oppose Reform	$(p+v_1-v_2-e,$ $1-p-v_1+v_2+e)$	$(p+v_1-v_2,$ $1-p-v_1+v_2)$

Figure 4.22 Game of Electoral Competition between Two Parties with Civil Service Reform

pass, and neither party can use patronage in its campaigns. Each side's chance of winning depends on its underlying chance of winning, p for the majority party and $1 - p$ for the minority party. If the majority party opposes reform, both parties can and will use patronage in their campaigns, even if they support reform. They use patronage because of the logic of the first model. However, there is a benefit to supporting reform when the other party does not, given by e in the game in Figure 4.22. This benefit arises from advancing reform even if the party goes on to use patronage in its campaign. If both parties support reform, neither gains an electoral advantage from doing so.

Whether reform passes depends on the electoral value of patronage relative to supporting reform. If $v_1 - v_2 < e$, then (Support Reform;Support Reform) is the equilibrium of the game in Figure 4.22. If $v_1 - v_2 > e$, (Oppose Reform; Support Reform) is the equilibrium. Supporting reform is a dominant strategy for the minority party; it is always better off supporting reform. This conclusion seems to fit the observation that reform is a common theme with challengers.

But successful reform requires the assent of the majority party. The inequality $v_1 - v_2 < e$ specifies when the majority party supports reform. The smaller the left-hand side, $v_1 - v_2$, the more likely that it supports reform. This difference is the electoral value of patronage to the majority party. The greater its control over patronage benefits and the greater those benefits, the larger this difference will be, and the less interested the majority party will be in reform. This difference should be smaller when the parties are more equal in electoral strength and when they have had more equal access to civil service jobs in the past. If the majority party is much stronger than the minority party, it should expect greater benefits from patronage and consequently be less willing to agree to reforms that end patronage. If the majority party has had disproportionate access to patronage in the past, it should have many entrenched workers, increasing its benefit from patronage. Both of these reasons reduce the majority party's interest in reform. Reform requires relative equality of the parties.

The right-hand side, e, increases with the demand for reform. After scandals about the inefficiency and corruption of patronage, the public's demand for reform is highest. Successful reform, then, is more likely after scandals. Scandals produce a competitive reason for the parties to support reform. That competitive logic operates most strongly when the parties are equally matched in electoral competition. When one party consistently dominates the other in elections, even large scandals are unlikely to produce reform. Electoral success produces clear control of the bureaucracy, and so patronage has greater benefits for the party in power. That party can ignore the calls for reform caused by a major scandal and still win reelection.

These models have provided some quick insights into the question of political reform in democracies. The question of political reform is, of course, more elaborate than these simple models can capture. Nevertheless, they do structure our understanding of the problem and lead to testable hypotheses, which appear to be supported by the history of reform in Latin America and the United States.[5] Often, simple models can provide great gains in the understanding of politics.

Candidate Competition in the Spatial Model of Elections

The Median Voter Theorem is one of the central results of political science. It is the foundation of most rational choice models of candidate competition and legislative process. The Median Voter Theorem asserts that the position of the median voter can defeat any alternative over a single issue in a pairwise vote. It does not hold if alternatives can address multiple issues, except under special conditions. This section presents the Median Voter Theorem as a two-person, zero-sum game of candidate competition.

One Issue

Spatial models of elections examine how the decisions of candidates and those of voters influence each other. I assume that voters vote to achieve their preferred issue positions and that candidates attempt to maximize their chances of winning the election. (Alternatively, candidates may be interested in maximizing the number of votes they win.) I treat the competition between two candidates as a two-person, zero-sum game. I focus on the competition between the candidates and their issue positions at the expense of examining voters' decisions in detail.

In the spatial model, candidates compete for votes by adopting positions on issues. Assume for now that there is one issue; it could be a general liberal-conservative split. We represent this issue and all possible positions on it by a line. All possible positions are points on the line, and we use numbers to label each position on the issue. Each voter's preferred position on the issue is called its **ideal point**. A voter's utility for other positions decreases as the distance from its ideal point grows. Voters vote for the candidate who adopts

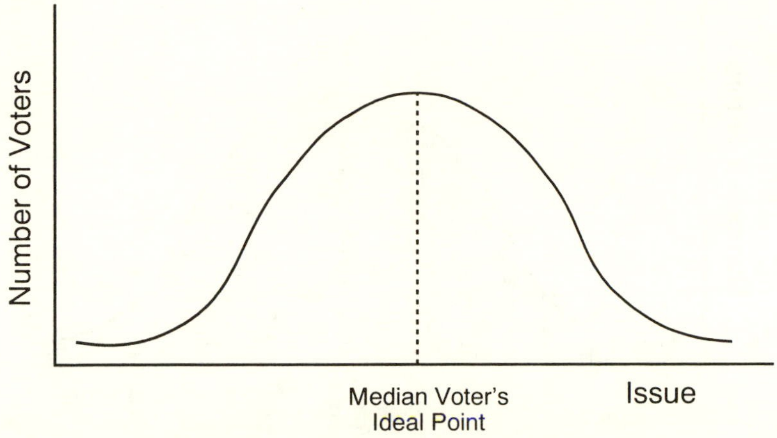

Figure 4.23 The Median Voter's Ideal Point in a Distribution of Voters' Ideal Points

the position closest to their ideal point. If the candidates are equally distant or adopt the same position, assume that the voter flips a coin between the two. We assume that voters always vote; there are no abstentions. The electorate can be represented by the distribution of voters' ideal points. This distribution is a set of finite points if the number of voters is small (as in the application of the spatial model to legislatures). If the number of voters is large, a continuous distribution gives the spread of the voters' ideal points. The one-humped curve in Figure 4.23 gives a continuous distribution of voters' ideal points on the issue. The height of the curve for a given position on the issue denotes the number of voters holding that position as their ideal point. The area under the curve between any two positions gives the number of voters who hold ideal points between those two positions.

The candidates wish to increase their chances of winning the election. This competition makes the game between them zero-sum. Let the candidates' utility for winning the election be 1, and their utility for losing be -1. I assume that candidates are free to choose any position they wish. When selecting their positions, candidates consider only how their position affects their chances of winning.

One may object to this model, arguing that real voters do not vote solely, or even primarily, on the issues, that candidates are not free to choose any position they wish, and that candidates have policy motivations as well as electoral motivations. This model is a simple introduction to the spatial model. Many variations of the spatial model exist, some of which account for the objections above. Other variations place the candidates in a more realistic institutional framework by modeling primaries, pressure groups, and parties explicitly. But this simple model illustrates the basic feature of spatial competition.

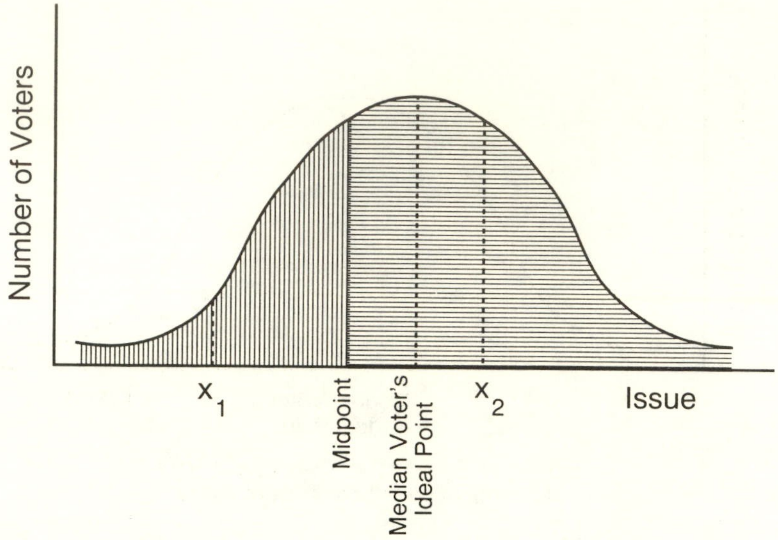

Figure 4.24 Candidates' Vote Shares in a Spatial Model

What position should each of the two candidates adopt to maximize the chance of winning the election? Figure 4.24 adds positions for both candidates to the distribution of voters shown in Figure 4.23. Candidate 1 adopts x_1 as his position, and Candidate 2 takes x_2 as her position. The heavy vertical line between the two shaded regions denotes the midpoint between their two positions, $(x_1 + x_2)/2$. All voters to the left of the midpoint vote for Candidate 1; all those to the right vote for Candidate 2. The area under the curve to the left of the midpoint line (shaded with vertical lines) gives the size of the vote for Candidate 1. The area under the curve to the right of the midpoint line (shaded with horizontal lines) gives the size of the vote for Candidate 2. Because the latter area is bigger than the former in Figure 4.24, Candidate 2 wins this election.

Generalizing from the example in Figure 4.24, we calculate the players' payoffs given their positions. The median voter divides the electorate into two equal halves. A candidate wins if he or she receives the votes of the median voter and all voters on one side of the median. If the candidates adopt positions on opposite sides of the median voter, as in Figure 4.24, the candidate whose position is closer to the median voter's ideal point wins, Candidate 2 in Figure 4.24. If the candidates adopt positions on the same side of the median voter, again the candidate closer to the median wins. The closer candidate gets the median voter and all voters on the other side of the median from the candidates. Candidate 1's payoff is 1 if Candidate 1's position is closer to the median than Candidate 2's position, -1 if it is farther, and 0 if both positions are equally distant from the median voter. Formally, if Candidate 1 adopts x_1, Candidate

2 adopts x_2, and the median voter's position is y_m, then the payoff function is as follows:

$$m = \begin{cases} 1 \text{ if } |x_1 - y_m| < |x_2 - y_m| \\ 0 \text{ if } |x_1 - y_m| = |x_2 - y_m| \\ -1 \text{ if } |x_1 - y_m| > |x_2 - y_m| \end{cases}.$$

Given that Candidate 2 adopts x_2 as her position, what is Player 1's best reply? If x_2 is not the ideal point of the median voter, any position closer to the median than x_2 will produce a victory for Candidate 1. The distance between Candidate 2's position and the median voter's ideal point is $x_2 - y_m$ if $x_2 > y_m$ and $y_m - x_2$ if $y_m > x_2$. If Candidate 2 adopts the median voter's ideal point as her position, Candidate 1 should also adopt that position. If he does so, all voters will be indifferent and flip coins to determine their votes. He will have a one-half chance of winning if he adopts the median as his position. Any other position loses. Candidate 1's best reply correspondence is as follows:

If $x_2 < y_m$, choose x such that $x_2 < x < 2y_m - x_2$.

If $x_2 > y_m$, choose x such that $2y_m - x_2 < x < x_2$.

If $x_2 = y_m$, choose $x = y_m$.

Candidate 2's best reply correspondence is similar. Adopt the median if he does; otherwise, choose a position closer to the median than he does.

Are there positions for both candidates that are mutual best replies? Yes, they should both adopt the median voter's ideal point. Each candidate plays a best reply to the other's strategy, then. Any other position leads to defeat given that the other candidate adopts the median position. No other positions can be mutual best replies. If a candidate adopts a position other than the median, the other candidate should adopt a position closer to the median. But then the former's position is not a best reply to the latter's position.

Exercise 4.11: Consider the case with a finite number of voters and two candidates who wish to maximize their vote totals. Assume that there are $2n - 1$ voters with ideal points, y_i labeled $y_1 < y_2 \ldots < y_{2n-1}$. The voter furthest left is labeled 1, the next most left voter is labeled 2, and so on, with voter $2n - 1$ being furthest right on the issue. Also assume that the candidates' utility for an election is the margin of victory over the other candidate. Negative payoffs denote margins of defeat.

a) Specify the payoff function given the positions of the candidates. You may assume $x_1 < x_2$ for convenience.

b) Find Candidate 1's best reply to Candidate 2's position x_2 with $y_i \leq x_2 < y_{i+1}$.

c) What is the equilibrium of this model? Discuss; what should candidates do according to this model?

Exercise 4.12: Now assume that there is a continuous distribution of voters, as in Figure 4.23, and that candidates maximize their vote totals.

a) Find Candidate 1's best reply to Candidate 2's position if it exists.

b) What is the equilibrium of this model?

In all three cases, candidates adopt the ideal point of the median voter in equilibrium. There is a best position for the candidates to adopt, and we should expect the candidates to move to it. Convergence to the median is the winning strategy in models of spatial competition (unless we introduce some other twists, such as voter alienation or the possible entry of third candidates).

Convergence of candidates to the median voter's ideal point is a special case of one of the central results in political science, the Median Voter Theorem. This theorem addresses all cases where the voters face one issue, have single-peaked preferences on that issue, and make pairwise comparisons of positions.

Theorem (the Median Voter Theorem): If all voters vote and their preferences are single-peaked on a single dimension, then the median ideal preference can defeat all other positions in a pairwise vote.

The Median Voter Theorem provides us with a powerful way to characterize voting in many settings. It is the engine that pulls many models in political science. In discussing congressional committees, we can summarize the positions of committees and the floor as single ideal points. Even though there are many individuals on a committee and on the floor, the Median Voter Theorem allows us to summarize each group's votes by the ideal point of its median voter. The median voter is always on the winning side. By focusing on how the median voter will vote on proposals, we can summarize how a group will vote.

Four assumptions about how actors vote are sufficient for the Median Voter Theorem. First, voter preferences are single-peaked. The preferences of a voter are given by its ideal point, its most preferred outcome. Its preference for alternatives falls off in both directions around its ideal point. The falloff need not be symmetric around the ideal point, so a voter may prefer a position on one side of its ideal point to another position on the other side that is closer to its ideal point. The important point here is that voter's preferences fall off around

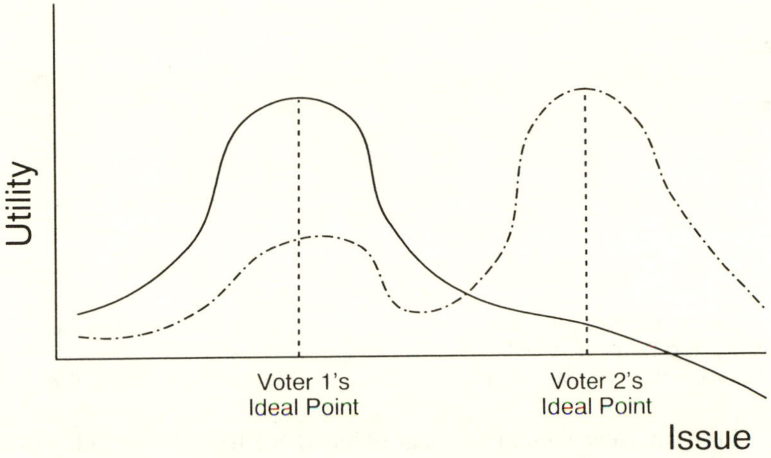

Figure 4.25 Single-Peaked and Non–Single-Peaked Utility Functions

an ideal point. In Figure 4.25, the utility function drawn with the solid line is single-peaked, and the utility function drawn with a broken line is not.

Second, we assume that all voters vote. There are no costs to voting in the Median Voter Theorem. In some models of candidate competition, voters may become alienated and not vote if both candidates' positions are "too far" from their ideal points. There can be an incentive, then, to diverge from the median if there are large numbers of voters far from the median.

Third, voters are assumed to make pairwise comparisons between alternatives. In the candidate competition model, there are only two candidates. If we look at races between more than two candidates, the incentive to congregate at the median ideal point can disappear. If two of the candidates converge to the median ideal point, then a third candidate can win a plurality of the votes by moving just off the median to either side.

Fourth, we assume only one issue is on the agenda. What happens with more than one issue?

Multiple Issues

We consider two issues now. More than two issues is essentially the same as two issues, and three dimensions do not fit well on two-dimensional paper. Assume that voters have ideal points and vote for the candidate whose position is closest to their ideal points. This assumption implies the issues are separable (the outcome of one does not affect what outcome is preferred on the other) and equal in importance. These assumptions are strong (i.e., it is unlikely that they are met in the real world), but more general spatial preferences do not produce greatly different results. These assumptions also create circular indifference

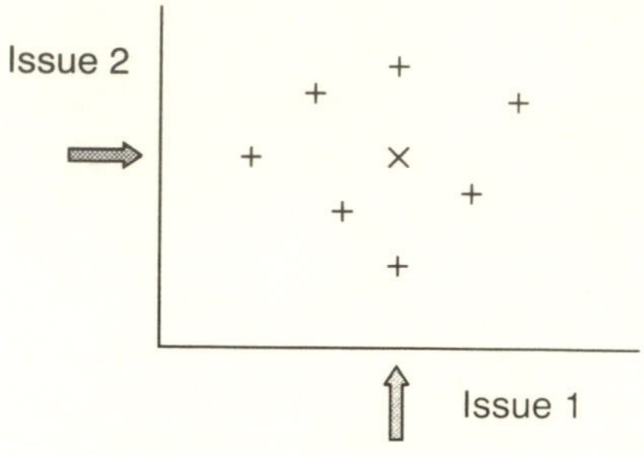

Figure 4.26 Separate Issue Medians in a Distribution of Seven Ideal Points over Two Issues

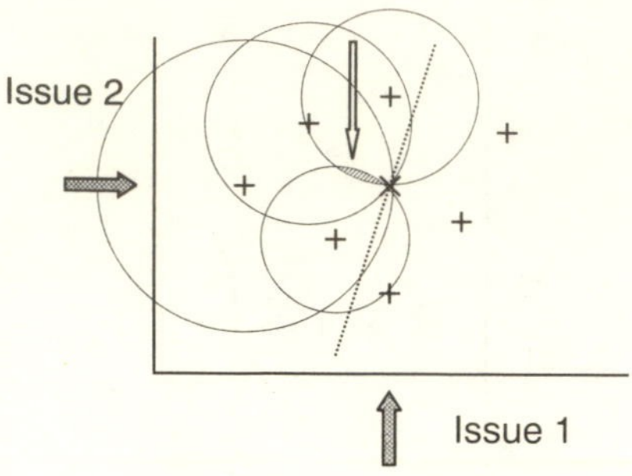

Figure 4.27 Positions That Can Defeat the Median on Both Issues in Figure 4.26

curves for each voter around its ideal point. If we trace the set of positions among which a voter is indifferent, we get a circle around its ideal point. I present the case of separable issues to simplify the discussion. Otherwise, we would need greater mathematical precision to argue carefully.

Two issues are quite different from one issue. We cannot just extrapolate from the case of one issue to two issues. If we could, the ideal point of the median voter would be an equilibrium. But what is a median in two dimensions? For example, examine the distribution of seven voters' ideal points denoted by crosses in Figure 4.26. The arrows give the median position for each issue separately, and x gives their intersection.

But x in Figure 4.26 is not an equilibrium point. Draw any line through x that does not intersect an ideal point, and you will find four voters on one side of the line and three voters on the other. The broken line in Figure 4.27 is one possible line through x. I have drawn the indifference curves of the four voters with ideal points to the left of the line through x. Each voter prefers all the points inside these circles to x; they are closer to its ideal point. The shaded set just to the left of x and indicated by the hollow arrow is the set of all points that all four of these voters prefer to x. It is inside all four indifference curves. Any point in this set defeats x in a pairwise vote because all four of those voters prefer it to x. There exists a large number of positions on the side of the line with four voters that can defeat a candidate at x. In contrast to the single issue case, x does not mark the spot.

There are distributions of ideal points that lead to an equilibrium with multiple issues, but they must satisfy stringent restrictions. Figure 4.28 gives one such case. One voter's ideal point is the median position, and the other voters pair up on lines drawn through the median. Now the median position defeats all others in pairwise votes. The voter whose ideal point is the median will, of course, always vote for it over any other alternative. The other voters will pair with the voter on the line through their ideal points and the median. One votes for the median and the other for the alternative.

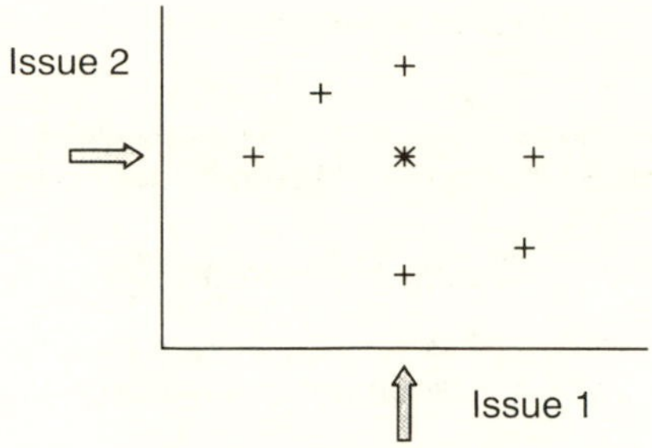

Figure 4.28 A Distribution of Ideal Points on Two Issues That Has an Equilibrium

There is no pure strategy equilibrium to candidate competition with multiple issues in general. The intuition here is that coalitions can be split if there are multiple issues. A candidate creates a coalition when it announces its position. Any candidate who does so in advance can be beaten if the other candidate selects the appropriate counterposition. The appropriate counter splits off part of the first candidate's coalition and joins it to other voters.

There is an equilibrium to this game, but it is a mixed strategy equilibrium. Candidates should attempt to obscure their issue positions. The candidate who can be everything to everyone stands the best chance of winning.[6] If incumbents are fixed to their position by their record, they should always lose. Of course, incumbents do not always lose, suggesting that incumbents possess other advantages not captured in this simple model. Correcting this limitation of the model leads to a more complicated and realistic model, which is how formal models progress.

A Very Brief Introduction to Cooperative Game Theory

In cooperative games, the players can sign binding agreements. Once the players sign an agreement, they must follow its terms. Enforcement of agreements is assumed in cooperative games. When Prisoner's Dilemma is played as a cooperative game, the dilemma disappears. The players can sign an agreement to play (S_1;s_1). Some cooperative games also have **transferable utility**; the players can transfer utility (e.g., money) after the outcome of the game among themselves. Such transfers are called **side payments**. The players should sign an agreement to choose the strategies that produce the maximum total payoff. From any other agreement, both players can always be made better off by signing an agreement to get the maximum utility and then divide the additional utility equally. In cooperative games without transferable utility, the players can redistribute payoffs by choosing among different strategy pairs that produce different payoffs for the players.

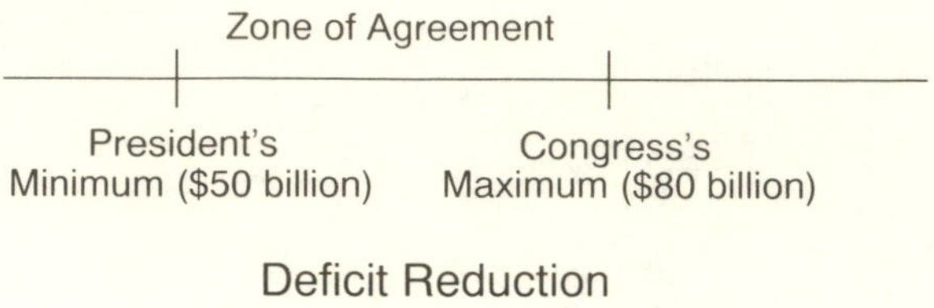

Figure 4.29 Reservation Levels and the Zone of Agreement in a Negotiation

The critical question in cooperative games is how the players divide the surplus above the minimum they can each achieve on their own. Cooperative game theory focuses on what bargains the players will strike to divide surplus among themselves. I discuss the basics of cooperative game theory in two-person and n-person games. The Nash bargaining solution illustrates the former, and a brief discussion of n-person games in characteristic function form illustrates the latter.

The Nash Bargaining Solution

Actors bargain when there are many outcomes that both are willing to accept over the alternative to an agreement and they disagree about which of those outcomes is best. Bargaining in politics occurs between nations in international crises and economic affairs, among political parties when they try to form coalition governments in multiparty democracies, and between legislatures and executive agencies. In Chapters Five and Eight, I introduce noncooperative game models of bargaining and contrast them to the Nash bargaining solution.

For the discussion here, I model negotiation between the president and the Congress over deficit reduction in the budget.[7] For convenience, assume that the range of possible budget deals can be modeled by the set of points on a line. You can think of each point as specifying an amount of deficit reduction. The Nash bargaining solution allows the set of outcomes to have multiple dimensions, but the explanation is easier with outcomes restricted to one dimension. If the sides fail to reach an agreement, the automatic budget cuts in the Gramm-Rudman bill take effect. The outcome that results if the parties do not reach an agreement is called the **conflict point**. (In international crisis bargaining, war is the conflict point.)

Each side has a **reservation level**, or **reservation point**, that expresses its value for a no-agreement outcome. A side's reservation level is the bargain it sees as equivalent to the conflict point. It is the minimal deal that it would accept. Figure 4.29 shows the reservation points of the president and Congress on the range of possible deficit reduction deals. Assume that the president wants reductions of at least $50 billion a year and the Congress wants at most $80 billion a year. If Congress does not offer at least $50 billion a year in cuts, the

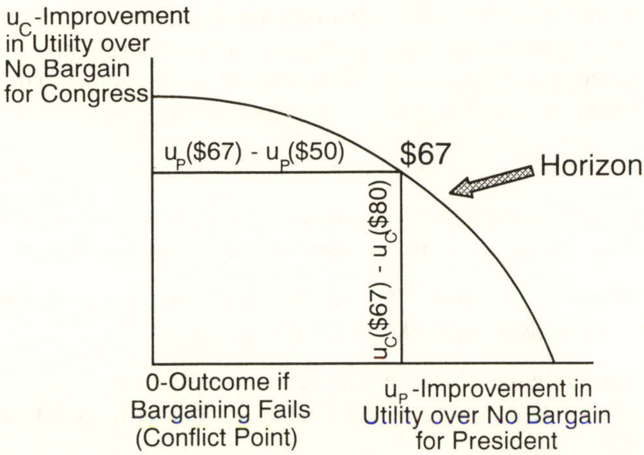

Figure 4.30 Nash Bargaining in Utilities

president prefers that the automatic cuts go into effect. In between the reservation levels of the two sides is a **zone of agreement**. This zone gives all the bargains that both parties prefer to the conflict point. Both the president and Congress prefer any budget deal that reduces the deficit between \$50 billion and \$80 billion a year over invoking the automatic cuts. If there is no zone of agreement, then the parties can never reach an agreement: there are no deals that both prefer to the conflict point.

We transfer the problem from the bargained dimension—here, amount of deficit reduction—to utility space. Figure 4.30 plots each side's added utility from each possible deal over no agreement (all the dollar figures represent billions of dollars). Consider a possible bargain, a reduction of \$67 billion a year. For each possible deal, we calculate how much utility over no agreement each player gains from that deal. We plot each player's utility gain on one of the axes of Figure 4.30. The president's utility gain for the \$67 billion deal is u_P(\$67 billion) − u_P(\$50 billion) and is plotted on the horizontal axis; Congress's utility gain for the \$67 billion deal is u_C(\$67 billion) − u_C(\$80 billion) and is plotted on the vertical axis. The general proposition for this is as follows: for bargain x between Players 1 and 2, with reservation levels c_1 and c_2 respectively, the gains in utility from agreeing to x are $u_1(x) - u_1(c_1)$ for Player 1 and $u_2(x) - u_2(c_2)$ for Player 2. The **horizon**, or **frontier**, shown in the figure gives the limit of all possible bargains available to the players. Any point on or under the frontier is a possible bargain. The frontier is the set of all Pareto-optimal deals. For any deal below the frontier, there is a deal on the frontier that both players prefer.

The Nash bargaining solution uses a different logic than the strategic logic of noncooperative game theory. We define a set of properties that a solution should have, and then determine what bargains meet these conditions. Rather than modeling optimal bargaining strategies, the Nash bargaining solution asks what should typify bargaining between equal strategic actors. The Nash bargaining solution requires bargains to meet the following four conditions

1) **Joint efficiency**: The solution must be located on the utility frontier.

2) **Symmetry**: If the two bargainers have the same utility function, they divide the difference between their reservation points equally.

3) **Linear invariance**: The solution should be invariant under linear transformations of each player's utility function.

4) **Independence of irrelevant alternatives**: If we eliminate possible bargains while retaining the solution and the conflict point, the solution should be unchanged.

The first condition states that the players reach Pareto-optimal bargains. Otherwise, both could be made better off by a different bargain. The second condition asserts that the bargaining process is neutral between the two players. Utility functions are determined up to a linear transformation; the third condition asserts that the Nash bargaining solution should be invariant to such transformations. The fourth condition requires that the solution not be altered by adding or deleting alternatives that the parties agree are inferior to the solution.

There is only one solution that satisfies the four conditions above, the Nash bargaining solution:

> **Theorem** (Nash bargaining solution): There is a unique solution satisfying the four conditions above, calculated as follows. Choose x on the frontier to maximize the product of the two sides' utilities. In symbols, using the sides' utility functions, u_1 and u_2, and reservation points, c_1 and c_2, choose x to maximize $[u_1(x) - u_1(c_1)][u_2(x) - u_2(c_2)]$.

The Nash bargaining solution equates each side's marginal utility loss from a shift in the solution relative to the utility gain at the solution. Shifting the solution in either player's favor hurts the other player equally whether we shift the solution toward Player 1 or toward Player 2. Shifts along the frontier from the Nash bargaining solution cost one player in utility what the other player gains in utility from the shift. The Nash bargaining solution operates like an arbitration procedure within the limits of each side's utility for the outcomes.

The proof of the theorem proceeds by showing that if the four conditions hold, we must arrive at the above formula. Let x be the Nash solution for a given bargaining problem. Carry out a linear transformation of u_1 and u_2 to

u_1^* and u_2^* such that $u_1^*(x) = u_2^*(x) = 1$. Then we expand the game to include all points y such that $u_1^*(y) + u_2^*(y) \leq 2$. The solution to this game must be (1,1) by symmetry. Then by linear invariance and independence of irrelevant alternatives, the solution to the original game is the transformation of (1,1) back into the original game—x. Thus x is the only possible solution because the above transformation of any other solution cannot be a solution of the game where $u_1^*(y) + u_2^*(y) \leq 2$.

Example: Find the Nash bargaining solution when two players bargain over the difference between 0 and 1, with $u_1(x) = x^2, u_2(x) = -x, c_1 = .5$, and $c_2 = .8$. This problem is the deficit reduction bargain, with x measured in units of $100 billion.

To find x to maximize the product of the utilities,

$$[u_1(x) - u_1(c_1)][u_2(x) - u_2(c_2)] = [x^2 - (.5)^2][-x - (-.8)]$$

$$= -x^3 + .8x^2 + .25x - .2,$$

first differentiate the expression above and set it equal to zero:

$$-3x^2 + 1.6x + .25 = 0.$$

Then solve this equation by using the quadratic formula:

$$x = \frac{-1.6 \pm \sqrt{(1.6)^2 - 4(-3)(.25)}}{2(-3)} \approx \frac{1.6 \pm 2.36}{6},$$

and discard the negative root, because the answer must fall between c_1, .5, and c_2, .8. This will yield

$$x \approx .66.$$

Player 1 has done better in the division of the surplus .3 units (.16 to Player 1 and .14 to Player 2). Player 1 is risk acceptant and can use that advantage to gain a better division of the surplus from Player 2.

Exercise 4.13: Find the Nash bargaining solution for the following situations:

a) $u_1(x) = 2x - 5, u_2(x) = 2 - 3x, c_1 = 0, c_2 = 1$. Why should you expect this answer? (Hint: Check the assumptions of the Nash bargaining solution.)

b) $u_1(x) = \sqrt{x}, u_2(x) = -x^2, c_1 = 0, c_2 = 1$.

The Nash bargaining solution has a number of important limitations. First, it ignores the structure of bargaining. The parties are treated equally in the Nash bargaining solution. But in many cases, bargaining environments are structured to the advantage of one side. Different styles of auctions produce different outcomes even when the bidders and sellers have the same values for the goods at auction. A Dutch auction, which starts with a high price and lowers it until a bidder agrees to buy, can lead to different prices than those in a competitive auction. Noncooperative bargaining deals explicitly with this issue and allows us to see how different bargaining structures affect the outcome of bargaining. Harsanyi has shown that the Nash bargaining solution assumes a fixed bargaining structure. The player facing a greater risk should the negotiations break down makes a small concession to the other player, and negotiations continue until the two sides meet in a final agreement. Harsanyi 1977 has an excellent technical discussion of this process.

Second, are the axioms of the Nash bargaining solution reasonable? The Nash bargaining solution can be viewed as either a description of what outcomes bargaining will reach or as an optimal arbitration scheme. In either case, certain axioms can be seen as unreasonable. As a description, we have already mentioned that bargaining structures can introduce asymmetries between the players. The "independence of irrelevant alternatives" condition may be too strong. Unreachable outcomes may be useful as either threats or distractions to undermine a possible bargain. The Nash bargaining solution can be modified to include the possibility of threats, but the basic version excludes many threats, particularly those that hurt both sides, and the credibility of those threats.

A final objection is that the Nash bargaining solution always reaches an agreement whenever one is possible. But often actual bargaining breaks down even when agreement is possible because one party decides that continuing negotiations would be fruitless. In Chapter Five, I return to the Nash bargaining solution and compare it to a simple bargaining model in noncooperative game theory.

N-Person Games

This section provides a very brief introduction to the basic ideas and concepts of n-person cooperative games. These games have been applied to political science although interest in applying them has waned with the development of noncooperative game theory. I recommend Chapters Seven through Nine of Ordeshook 1986 as the place to begin further reading on n-person games and how they have been applied to political science.

When we move to games with more than two players, cooperative game theory focuses on coalition formation. A **coalition**, denoted by C, is a nonempty subset of the set of all players. Coalitions form when a set of players agrees to coordinate their strategies for their mutual benefit. We assume the players in a coalition coordinate their strategies to maximize their total payoff and that utility is transferable between members of a coalition. The former assumption eliminates the question of how members of a coalition actually coordinate their behavior. The second assumption eliminates the problems of dividing the gains of the coalition. The coalition divides its "pot" of transferable utility at the end of the game, and the players can make binding commitments about the division of their payoff when they form a coalition.

An n-person cooperative game can be described by the utility each coalition can secure for itself. The **characteristic function** of an n-person game is a real-valued function, v, on all the subsets of the players (including the empty set) such that

$$v(\emptyset) = 0,$$

and

$$v(R \cup S) \geq v(R) + v(S) \text{ if } R \cap S = \emptyset.$$

The v function gives the "pot" of utility that each coalition can guarantee itself if it forms. Characteristic functions satisfy two constraints. First, the empty set can neither obtain utility nor lose it. Second, if we merge two coalitions with no members in common, then the new coalition must be able to secure at least as much as the sum of what each would secure by acting separately.

A characteristic function describes each coalition's ability to ensure a total payoff to its members. The outcome of a game is how the players divide up the payoffs. An **imputation** for the n-person game with characteristic function v is a vector $(x_1, x_2, \ldots, x_n)$ such that

$$\sum_{i \in N} x_i = v(N),$$

and

$$x_i \geq v(i) \text{ for all players i.}$$

Imputations are possible divisions of the payoff among the players. Although the set of imputations does not constitute a solution, we expect that any solution would be drawn from the set of imputations. Imputations satisfy two rationality conditions. The first is group rationality, or efficiency—the players divide all the payoff available to them and leave nothing on the table. The second restriction is individual rationality—no player accepts less than it can guarantee itself acting alone.

Some games are uninteresting because they provide their players with no motivation to form coalitions. A game is **essential** if the value of the game to the coalition of all exceeds the sum of the value of the game to the players operating by themselves; if not, it is **inessential**. Some coalition in an essential game must guarantee its members a greater total payoff than they could obtain acting on their own. Inessential games provide no motivation to their players to form coalitions and so are uninteresting.

Imputations are a set of possible solutions to a game. To solve a game, we need to know what imputations would actually occur. Solution concepts specify sets of imputations that have additional desirable properties beyond the basic rationality conditions of imputations. These additional properties reflect possible reasons for forming coalitions.

Coalitions form because their members have an interest in banding together. One imputation, **x**, **dominates** another, **y**, **through a given coalition**, C, if and only if (1), every member of C receives a higher payoff in x than in y and (2), the sum of the payoffs to the members of C is not greater than the value coalition C can guarantee itself if it forms. When both these conditions occur, we expect that the coalition C would form and overturn the second imputation in favor of the first. In other words, one imputation dominates another through a coalition if and only if the change is preferred by every member of the coalition (the first condition) and the change can be enforced by the coalition (the second condition, explained below).

The concept of domination allows us to specify some imputations that are more likely to form than others. Any undominated imputation cannot be replaced by another. If a n-person game is played through the suggestion of different imputations, which are then replaced by other imputations that dominate them, we arrive at the first solution concept for n-person games, the **core**. The core of a game is the set of all undominated imputations of the game. If a core imputation is proposed, no coalition that objects to it can enforce its will. The core is also the Pareto-optimal set of a n-person game. No player (or coalition) can be made better off without depriving some other player or coalition, which will block such a move. If a core imputation exists, then for every possible coalition, the sum of its members' payoffs must be at least as great as the total payoff that coalition can achieve acting on its own. The core has one major limitation as a solution concept. It does not always exist. There are many n-person games without a core.

It is disturbing that cores do not exist for every game, particularly for a large set of interesting games, such as constant-sum games. Many other solution concepts—the kernel, the nucleolus, the bargaining set, and the competitive solution—incorporate different reasons why some coalitions will form and not others. I discuss the Von Neumann–Morgenstern solution (also known as stable sets) and a somewhat different idea of solution, the value.

Von Neumann–Morgenstern solutions are sets of imputations that satisfy two conditions. The first is internal stability; no imputation inside a Von Neumann–Morgenstern solution is dominated by any other imputation in that solution. Once inside a Von Neumann-Morgenstern solution, the players will not shift around inside the solution. The second condition, external stability, states that every imputation not in the solution is dominated by some imputation in the solution. There can be imputations outside the solution that dominate some imputations inside the solution, but if the players leave the solution by proposing an imputation that dominates an imputation in the solution, then some other imputation in the solution must dominate the imputation outside the solution, returning the players to the solution. Von Neumann–Morgenstern solutions are stable in the sense that players pass through them regularly during the course of bargaining and coalition formation. We cannot say which imputation in the solution will occur, but we can say that the outcome should fall within the solution. If a game has a core, then the core must be included in any Von Neumann–Morgenstern solution to satisfy external stability.

Von Neumann–Morgenstern solutions have four main weaknesses. First, multiple Von Neumann–Morgenstern solutions often exist to any one game. Which one should we use? Second, the idea of solution here is quite weak. A Von Neumann-Morgenstern solution gives a set that the players should pass through frequently in the process of negotiation. It does not say they should end their negotiations in the set. Third, most Von Neumann–Morgenstern solutions include multiple imputations. Even if we end up in a Von Neumann–Morgenstern solution, we cannot predict which of those imputations in the solution will occur. Finally, there exist games without any Von Neumann-Morgenstern solutions.

Power indices capture an alternative way to solve an n-person game. Power indices specify each player's expectation for playing an n-person game. Assume that coalitions are formed by adding players randomly until the coalition of all players is formed. Each player's power or value is its expected marginal contribution to the coalition's payoff when it joins across all possible orders of coalition formation.

Power indices also have their limitations. First, there are several different ways to calculate power indices, which produce different answers in different situations. Second, players do not form coalitions randomly, but power indices assume they do.

Review

Chapter Four discusses a host of topics from classical game theory. But three concepts must not be missed—best replies, Nash equilibrium, and mixed strategies. A player's best reply against a strategy of the other player is the strategy that produces the highest payoff for the player against that strategy of the other player. If one player knows what strategy the other player will play, it should play its best reply against that strategy of the other player.

A Nash equilibrium is a pair of strategies that are best replies to each other. If the players share a common conjecture that each will play its Nash equilibrium strategy, then that Nash equilibrium is self-enforcing. Neither player has an incentive to change its strategy unilaterally.

Some games do not have Nash equilibria in pure strategies. But they do have Nash equilibria in mixed strategies. Mixed strategies represent the players' uncertainty about what pure strategy the other player will play. In a mixed strategy Nash equilibrium, each player is indifferent among the pure strategies that can be played in its mixed strategy.

Further Reading

My presentation in this chapter broadly matches the standard texts on non-cooperative game theory. Brandenburger 1992 is an excellent first source on common conjectures and Nash equilibrium.

The literature on the spatial theory of elections is massive, and much of it begins with Downs 1957. Formal spatial theory of elections begins in the mid-1960s. Ordeshook 1986 and Enelow and Hinich 1984 provide good surveys of the topic. Enelow and Hinich 1990 is a collection of recent contributions to spatial theory.

The model of political reform is taken directly from Geddes 1991. I refer the reader to this article for the full development of the model and a discussion of the evidence from Latin American democracies.

Once again, the standard references are good on n-person games. Ordeshook 1986 should be your first source for n-person game theory and its applications to political science. Owen 1982 is the best technical textbook on n-person game theory. Harsanyi 1977 provides a very good treatment of the Nash bargaining solution, including extensions of the Nash bargaining solution and explication of the links between it and the Zeuthen bargaining model (a behavioral model where the player with the greatest risk makes the next small concession).

Chapter Five
Solving Extensive-Form Games: Backwards Induction and Subgame Perfection

Chapters Five through Nine analyze games in their extensive form rather than their strategic form. The extensive form of a game is more fundamental than its strategic form because it specifies all of the moves and their order. Nash equilibria analyze the interaction of strategies in the strategic form. Henceforth in this book, we analyze individual moves in the extensive form. Working with extensive-form games reinforces the connection between utility theory and game theory. Each individual move in a game is treated as a separate decision under uncertainty. A player projects what responses are likely to be made to each of its possible moves and chooses the move that produces the best final outcome. A player assumes the other players are rational and uses its knowledge of the game to project other players' future moves. Often, a player cannot be certain what the other players have done or will do. Players in such cases calculate expected utilities by using subjective probability distributions that express their beliefs about what has occurred or what will occur in the game.

This chapter and the next two present the central equilibrium concepts for extensive-form games—subgame perfect, perfect Bayesian, sequential, and perfect equilibrium. All four eliminate Nash equilibria that allow the players to make unreasonable moves. These equilibrium concepts reduce the number of Nash equilibria by imposing additional rationality conditions. Perfect Bayesian equilibrium is the most widely used definition of equilibrium. It is more general than subgame perfect equilibrium and easier to solve for than sequential or perfect equilibria. Figure 5.1 gives a Venn diagram that relates these four types of equilibria and Nash equilibrium. Any equilibrium that is perfect must also be sequential, perfect Bayesian, subgame perfect, and Nash. Any subgame perfect equilibrium is also a Nash equilibrium. All types of equilibria are strategy pairs (or sets for games with more than two players).

Extensive forms allow a more detailed analysis of the strategic interaction between the players than strategic forms do. Nash equilibria compare complete strategies of the players to see if they are optimal against each other. But the sequence of a game should affect how the players play the game. How do prior moves affect a player's decisions? What expectations about the other players' future moves does a player form during the game? How do its anticipations change as the game progresses?

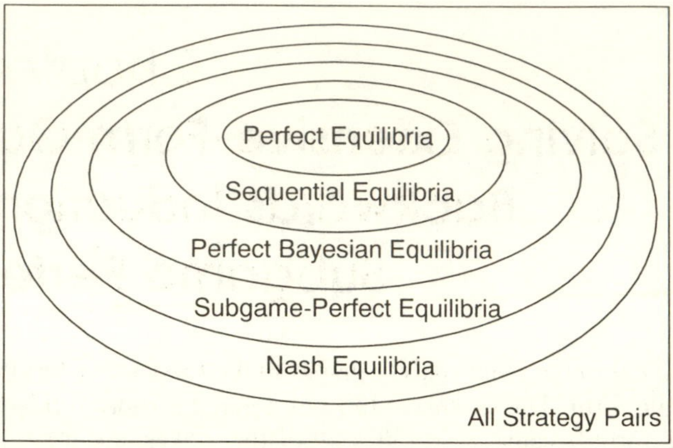

Figure 5.1 The Relationship of Five Different Types of Equilibria

The moves the players make at nodes reached in an equilibrium are called their behavior **on (or along) the equilibrium path**. Decisions about moves at nodes that are not reached in an equilibrium are behavior **off the equilibrium path**. Nash equilibria examine the rationality of moves on the equilibrium path. Sometimes, a player's choice on the equilibrium path depends on another player's choice off the equilibrium path. The latter player could make an irrational move off the equilibrium path and thus alter the first player's choice on the equilibrium path in a Nash equilibrium.

In Nash equilibria, players can precommit themselves to carrying out incredible threats and promises. The strategic form assumes that players choose complete strategies before the game begins. The players can precommit themselves at the start of the game to make moves in the future. A player can commit itself to threats and promises that are against its own interest to carry out. A precommitment to an incredible threat could induce the other player to move so that the threat does not need to be carried out. But games are sequential strings of decisions: players cannot make moves until they reach them. Precommitment—making a binding commitment to a move before that move has been reached—violates the idea of a game as a sequence of decisions. Subgame perfection, unlike Nash equilibrium, tests the credibility of moves on and off the equilibrium path.

I begin with subgame perfection in this chapter, introduce perfect Bayesian equilibrium in Chapter Six, and discuss sequential and perfect equilibrium in Chapter Seven. To introduce subgame perfection, I present backwards induction first. Backwards induction is a simple way to solve for the subgame perfect equilibrium of a game of perfect and complete information. In such games, a player always knows all prior moves and the other players' payoffs when it must move. It can anticipate future moves of the other players if it assumes they will play rationally. Backwards induction analyzes the game "backwards"—

begin with the players' choices that lead directly to terminal nodes, choose their best moves at those nodes, and then work "backward" to determine which preceding moves are optimal by using the projections of moves later in the tree.

Backwards induction requires that the players always make optimal moves from each node in the tree. In a game of complete and perfect information, optimal moves can be judged because players can anticipate future moves. Subgame perfection generalizes this idea to some moves in games of imperfect information. A subgame is a portion of a game, starting at a single node and including all subsequent nodes, that forms a game by itself. Subgame perfection requires players to play Nash equilibria in all subgames of a game: players must make optimal moves at all nodes that begin a subgame. Unfortunately, not all nodes begin subgames. To test the rationality of moves at such information sets, we need the concept of beliefs, which are central to perfect Bayesian equilibrium. That is the focus of Chapter Six.

The solution concepts developed for extensive-form games provide a way to solve games with limited information, where the players do not know some aspect of the game. A player forms conjectures about the uncertainties of the game. It revises these conjectures as it learns about the game from the moves of the other players. These games are particularly interesting models of political and social behavior because actors rarely know the exact situation they face. Bluffing and other strategic misrepresentations are common in these games. Limited-information games allow us to analyze communication formally, as well as misrepresentation and deception. Chapter Eight introduces these games.

A quick review of the elements of extensive-form games from Chapter Three should help you recall the detailed structure of those games. Game trees specify the players' moves in sequence. Choices are given as branches out of nodes, the decision points in the tree. Each node is assigned to one and only one player, including Chance as a player. Each player's nodes may be grouped into information sets that express the player's knowledge of prior moves. Terminal nodes give endpoints of the game, and a payoff for each player is associated with each terminal node. We assume the game is common knowledge. Perfect information means that a player knows all prior moves whenever it must move (i.e., all information sets are singletons); complete information that all players' payoffs are common knowledge.

This chapter illustrates backwards induction with several models from legislative studies. Models in legislative studies were using backwards induction before noncooperative game theory entered political science. Legislative agendas often require multiple votes to resolve an issue. I begin with sophisticated voting, where voters consider how the outcome of earlier votes affects later votes. Because the order of the agenda can influence the outcome, control of the agenda can be powerful. Both sophisticated voting and agenda control are essential for understanding structure-induced equilibria, a model of legislative rules. I discuss a very simple model of noncooperative bargaining, the Rubinstein

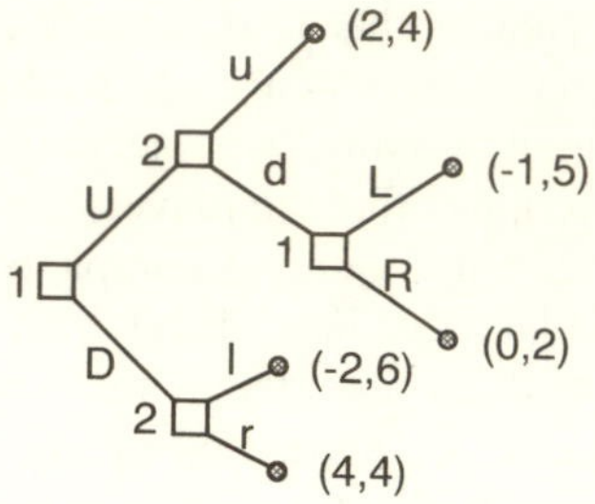

Figure 5.2 An Example for Backwards Induction

bargaining model, and connect it to the Nash bargaining model discussed in Chapter Four. The last example extends the logic of the Rubinstein bargaining model to bargaining in Congress. This model provides a second argument about why congressional rules exist and how they shape outcomes. This chapter concludes with a discussion of the limitations of backwards induction.

Backwards Induction

Solving a sequential game with perfect information is easy. We begin with decisions that lead only to terminal nodes of the game, choose the action that maximizes the utility of the player choosing at that node, and then work backwards through the earlier nodes of the game. Each player can predict what the other players will do at subsequent nodes, so it can predict the exact consequences of its possible moves from each node. For earlier nodes, we substitute the eventual outcome that will be reached for each move, using the anticipated future moves of the other players. We can determine all players' optimal choices by working backwards in this fashion. Because every information set is a singleton under perfect information, the players know all prior moves and can anticipate all future moves when they must choose their moves.

> Example: Solve the game in Figure 5.2 by backwards induction. Begin with Player 1's final move. He will choose Right, labeled R in Figure 5.2, over Left, labeled L; his payoff for choosing Right is 0 and for Left it is -1. Player 2 will choose left, labeled l, in her lower move; she gains a payoff of 6 instead of 4 for choosing right, labeled r. At Player 2's upper move, she gains a payoff of 4 if she chooses up (u). If she chooses down (d), then Player 1 will choose Right, and Player 2's payoff will be 2. She chooses up over down, then. Player 1's initial move depends on Player 2's future moves. If he plays up (U), she will play up (u), giving him a payoff of 2. If he plays Down (D), she will play left (l), giving Player 1 a payoff

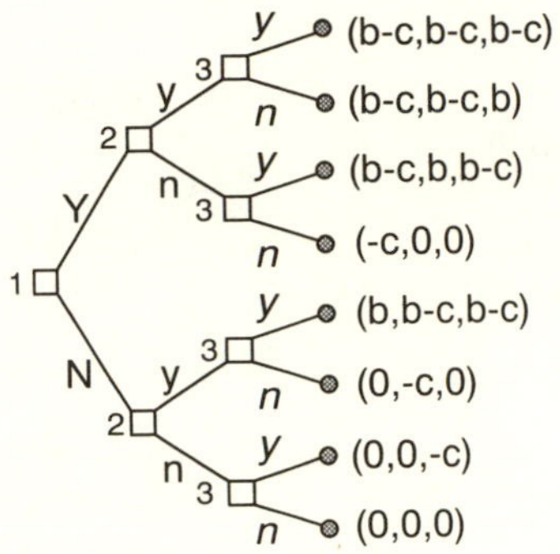

Figure 5.3 The Pay Raise Voting Game

of −2. Player 1 prefers Up. The result is (U,R;u,l) producing an outcome of (2,4).

Backwards induction is so simple that one may think that it cannot provide any interesting insights. But consider the following problem.

> Example: Three legislators are voting on whether to give themselves a pay raise. All three want the pay raise; however, each faces the same small cost in voter resentment, c, if he or she votes for the pay raise. The benefit for the raise, b with b > c, exceeds the cost of voting for it. If they vote sequentially on the raise, is it better to vote first or last?

At first blush, you might think that voting last is preferable because then you can decide whether the raise passes if the first two members split their votes. The extensive form in Figure 5.3 represents this game. Label the players 1, 2, and 3, according to the order in which they vote on the pay raise. Each player can vote yes (Y, y, or *y*) or no (N, n, or *n*) on the pay raise. They vote sequentially; Player 3 knows the votes of Players 1 and 2 when she must vote. The pay raise passes if two of the three vote yes. Any player voting yes pays cost c regardless of whether the raise passes. Each of the eight terminal nodes gives a different combination of votes, with the players' payoffs.

The backwards induction begins with Player 3's vote. If both or neither of Players 1 and 2 vote for the raise, she votes against it. In the former case (her top node), her payoff for voting yes is b − c; for voting no, it is b. In the latter case (her bottom node), her payoff is −c for voting yes and 0 for voting no. If Players 1 and 2 split their votes on the pay raise (her two middle nodes), Player 3 votes yes. Her payoff for voting yes is b − c, versus a payoff of 0 for voting no.

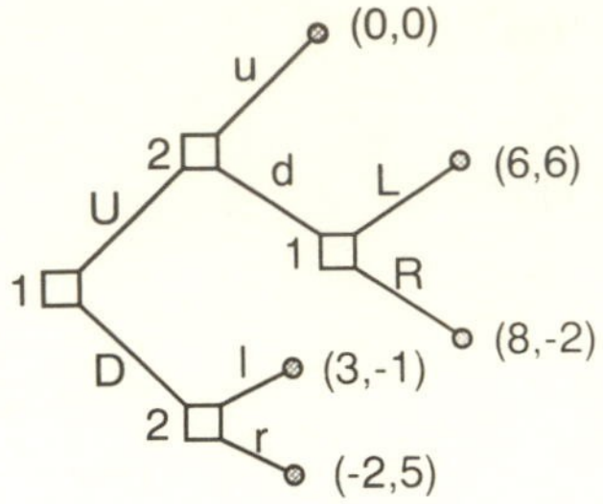

Figure 5.4 Exercise 5.1a

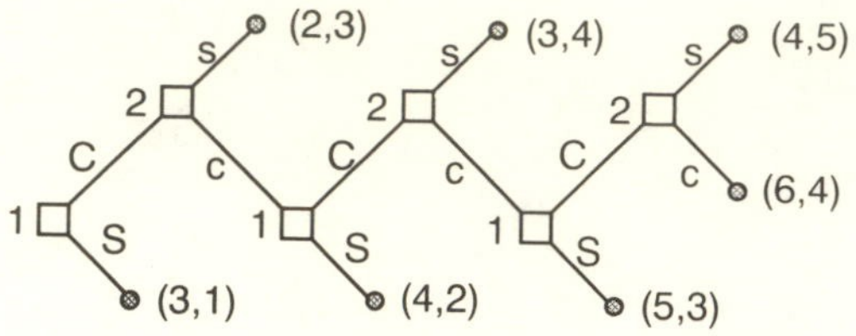

Figure 5.5 Exercise 5.1b: The Three-Level Centipede

Player 2 considers how Player 3 will vote when she casts her vote. At her upper node (when Player 1 has voted yes), Player 3 will vote yes if Player 2 votes no, producing a payoff of b for Player 2. If Player 2 votes yes from her upper node, Player 3 will vote no, giving Player 2 a payoff of b − c. Voting no is better than voting yes for Player 2 if Player 1 has already voted yes. If Player 1 votes no (Player 2's lower node), Player 3 will vote yes if Player 2 votes yes, leading to a payoff of b − c for Player 2. If Player 2 votes no, Player 3 will also vote no, producing a payoff of 0 for Player 2. Player 2 prefers voting yes when Player 1 votes no.

Finally, Player 1 can anticipate the votes of Players 2 and 3 when he votes. If he votes yes, Player 2 will vote no and Player 3 will vote yes, leading to a payoff of b − c for him. If he votes no, Players 2 and 3 will vote yes, giving him a payoff of b. Voting no is better for Player 1.

Write down a set of strategies for the game in Figure 5.3 as follows: (Player 1's vote; Player 2's vote if Player 1 votes yes, Player 2's vote if Player 1 votes no; Player 3's vote if Players 1 and 2 vote yes, Player 3's vote if Player 1 votes yes and Player 2 votes no, Player 3's vote if Player 1 votes no and Player 2 votes yes, Player 3's vote if Players 1 and 2 vote no). The equilibrium of the game in Figure 5.3 is (N;n,y;*n,y,y,n*). In equilibrium, Player 1 votes against the raise, forcing Players 2 and 3 to vote in favor of it. Voting first is better than voting last; you can force the others to take the heat and still get the raise.

Exercise 5.1: Solve the games in Figures 5.4 through 5.6 using backwards induction.

a) Solve the game in Figure 5.4.

b) Solve the game in Figure 5.5. This game is called the three-level centipede. Each move of s stops the game, and each move of c continues it. The three levels are the three repetitions of the basic choice of stopping or continuing the game.

c) Solve the game in Figure 5.6.

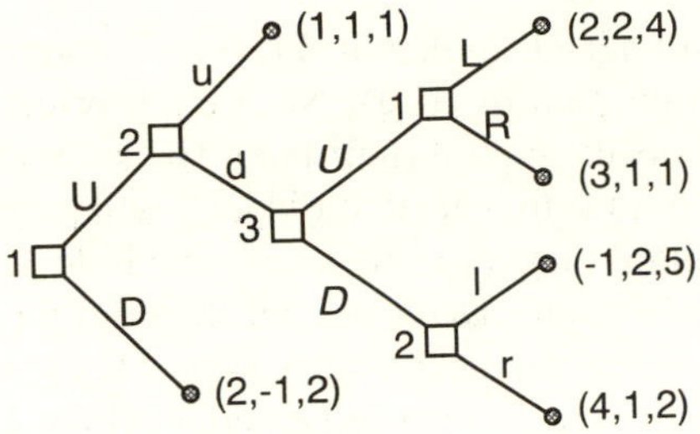

Figure 5.6 Exercise 5.1c

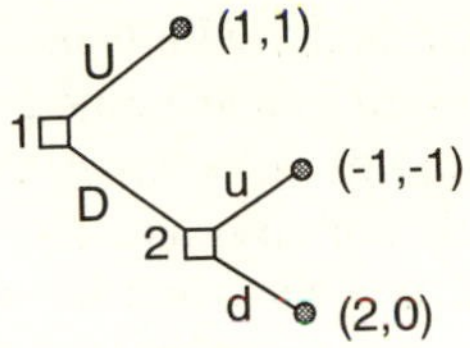

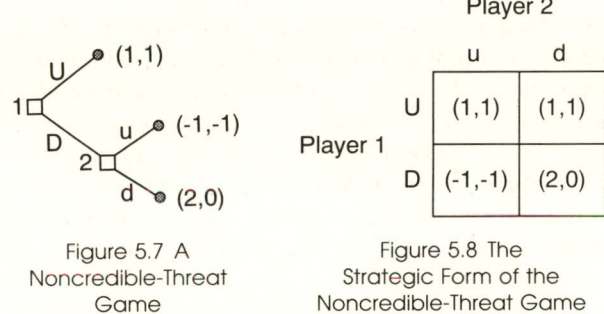

Figure 5.7 A Noncredible-Threat Game

Player 2

Player 1	u	d
U	(1,1)	(1,1)
D	(-1,-1)	(2,0)

Figure 5.8 The Strategic Form of the Noncredible-Threat Game

How does the result of a backwards induction compare to the Nash equilibria of a game? Backwards induction always produces a Nash equilibrium, but some Nash equilibria are not found by a backwards induction. Nash equilibrium assesses the rationality only of moves on the equilibrium path. Backwards induction assesses the rationality of all moves in a strategy, both on and off the equilibrium path. Thus Nash equilibria where a player plays irrationally off the equilibrium path will not be found by a backwards induction.

> Example: Perform a backwards induction on the game in Figure 5.7. Player 2 chooses down, d, if she has to move because a payoff of 0 is better than -1. Anticipating her move, Player 1 prefers Down, D, to Up, U. Backwards induction leads to a strategy pair of (D;d).

But the game in Figure 5.7 has two Nash equilibria: (U;u) and (D;d). Figure 5.8 gives the strategic form of this game. Consider how each of these Nash equilibria translates into behavior in the extensive form in Figure 5.7. (D;d) corresponds to the backwards induction above. In (U;u), Player 2 uses the threat of u to coerce Player 1 into playing U. But this threat is not credible because Player 2 will prefer to play d if Player 1 chooses D. However, if Player 1 plays U, Player 2 never has to choose. The Nash equilibrium (U;u) allows

Player 2 to precommit herself to play u. Player 2's noncredible threat to play u is off the equilibrium path of (U;u). Nash equilibrium does not judge the rationality of moves off the equilibrium path. Backwards induction does and finds that Player 1 should anticipate that Player 2 will play d if she must move.

Nash equilibria allow players to make noncredible threats provided they never have to carry them out. Decisions on the equilibrium path are driven in part by what the players expect will happen off the equilibrium path. If those expectations are based on bizarre behavior off the equilibrium path, we can produce bizarre behavior on the equilibrium path. The players should play optimally even in portions of the game that they do not expect to reach in equilibrium. Backwards induction requires rational play at all nodes when we can specify what the other players will do in future moves.

Backwards induction can be a useful tool in solving more complex games. Often the analysis of a problem begins with a model with complete and perfect information. Later, the model can be revised to add limited information. We can ascertain the effects of those uncertainties on behavior in the model. Models under complete and perfect information often produce conclusions at variance with reality. But such models should be seen as first steps in the modeling process rather than as definitive representations. Such first steps are also helpful in providing some intuition about what the later models under limited information may look like.

Subgame Perfection

Backwards induction requires that the players make optimal choices from each node in the game. However, it can only judge an optimal move when the precise outcome of each available move can be determined. Information sets with multiple nodes confound a backwards induction. A player moving at an information set with multiple nodes cannot determine which node it is at in the information set. If it prefers different moves for different nodes of the same information set, it cannot determine which move is best from that information set.

Subgame perfection generalizes the idea of checking the optimality of all moves to some moves in games with information sets that contain multiple nodes. Subgame perfection includes backwards induction but is more general. Players should choose optimally from every point in the game whether those nodes are reached in equilibrium or not. To formalize this idea, we need to know what "from every point in the game" means.

> **Definition**: A **proper subgame** is a subset of the nodes of a game starting with an initial node and including all its successors that preserves all information sets of the game and over which a (new) game is defined by the restriction of the original game elements (acts, payoffs, chance moves, information sets, etc.) to these nodes.

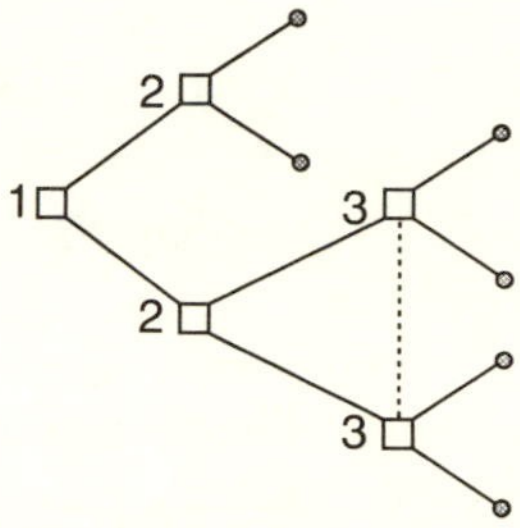

Figure 5.9 A Game Tree That Illustrates Subgames

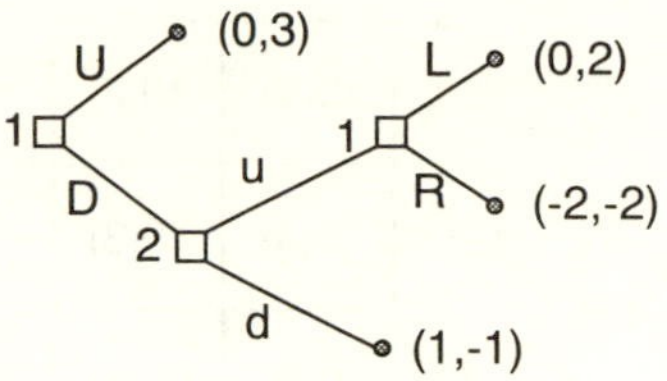

Figure 5.10 A Game of Complete and Perfect Information

Proper subgames are parts of a game that can be treated as games in their own right—hence the name *subgame*. In the game in Figure 5.7, Player 2's move alone constitutes a proper subgame. The entire game is also a subgame of itself.

> Example: The game tree in Figure 5.9 has three proper subgames, the two sections of the game starting at either of Player 2's nodes and the entire game itself. I have deliberately left out the strategies and payoffs to focus on the game tree. No proper subgame can be started at either of Player 3's nodes. Player 3's information set would be split. Subgames, like all games, must begin with a single node.

To ensure that each player is rational at all stages of the game, we require strategies to be optimal in all proper subgames. To see if a Nash equilibrium is subgame perfect, decompose the game into all its subgames, and then check whether the restriction of the equilibrium strategies to each subgame constitutes a Nash equilibrium for that subgame.

> **Definition**: A set of strategies is **subgame perfect** if for every proper subgame, the restriction of those strategies to the subgame forms a Nash equilibrium.

> Example: The game in Figure 5.10 has four Nash equilibria in pure strategies: (U,L;u), (U,R;u), (D,L;u), and (D,R;d). You can find them in Figure 5.11, which gives the strategic form of this game. How many of these Nash equilibria are subgame perfect?

The game in Figure 5.10 has three subgames: the entire game, the second and third moves, and the third move alone. The subgame consisting of just the third move has only one Nash equilibrium, L. The subgame of the second and third moves has two Nash equilibria, (L;u) and (R;d). Figure 5.12 gives the

		Player 2: u	d
Player 1	U,L	(0,3)	(0,3)
	U,R	(0,3)	(0,3)
	D,L	(0,2)	(1,-1)
	D,R	(-2,-2)	(1,-1)

Figure 5.11 The Strategic Form of Figure 5.10

		Player 2: u	d
Player 1	L	(0,2)	(1,-1)
	R	(-2,-2)	(1,-1)

Figure 5.12 The Strategic Form of a Subgame of Figure 5.10

strategic form of this subgame. Thus any subgame-perfect equilibrium must have (L;u) for its last two moves. For example, (U,R;u) is not subgame perfect because the restriction of it to either of the proper subgames is not a Nash equilibrium of that subgame. R is not a Nash equilibrium of the subgame of just the third move, and (R;u) is not a Nash equilibrium of the subgame of the last two moves. Thus there are two subgame-perfect equilibria in pure strategies, (D,L;u) and (U,L;u).

Exercise 5.2: Find the Nash equilibria of the games in Figures 5.13 through 5.17. You do not need to search for mixed equilibria, except in Figure 5.17. Determine which of these Nash equilibria are subgame perfect and which are not.

a) Find the Nash equilibria for the game in Figure 5.13. Which ones are subgame perfect?

b) Find the Nash equilibria for the game in Figure 5.14. Which ones are subgame perfect?

c) Find the Nash equilibria for the game in Figure 5.15. Which ones are subgame perfect? Does your analysis change if Player 2 cannot tell what Player 1's move has been when she must decide? (Hint: What game is this?)

d) Find the Nash equilibria for the game in Figure 5.16. Which ones are subgame perfect?

e) Find the Nash equilibria for the game in Figure 5.17. Which ones are subgame perfect? (Hint: Start by finding the Nash equilibria for the subgame that Players 3 and 4 play in the last two moves. Extra Hint: What well-known game are Players 3 and 4 playing? For each of those equilibria, calculate the values of Players 1 and 2

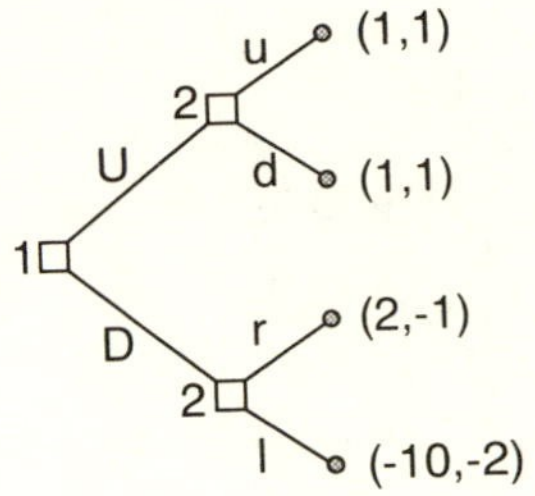

Figure 5.13 Exercise 5.2a

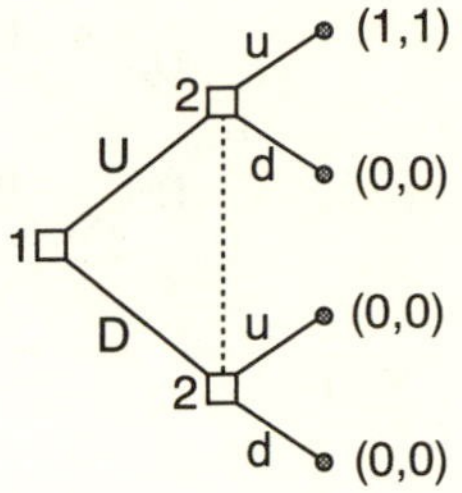

Figure 5.14 Exercise 5.2b

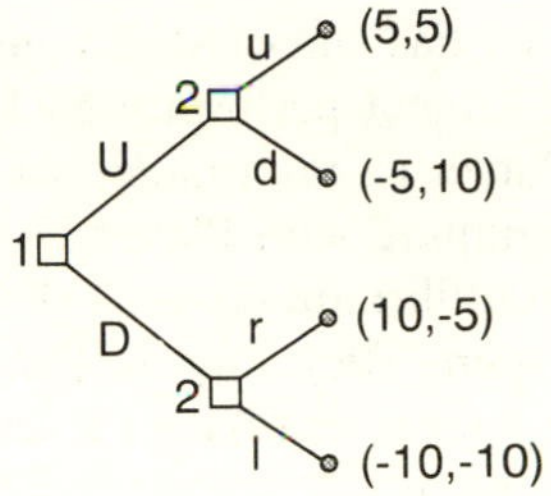

Figure 5.15 Exercise 5.2c

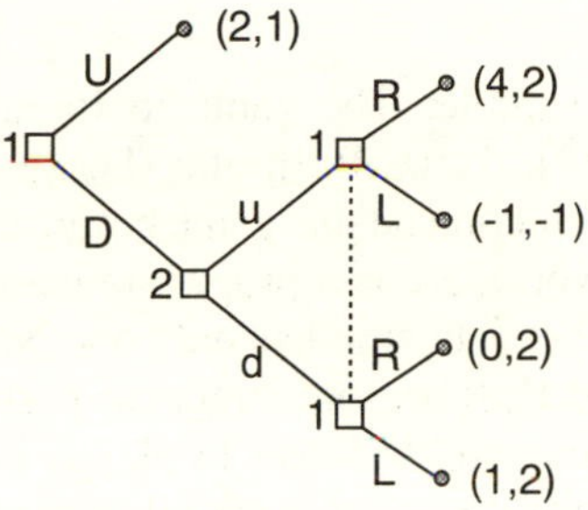

Figure 5.16 Exercise 5.2d

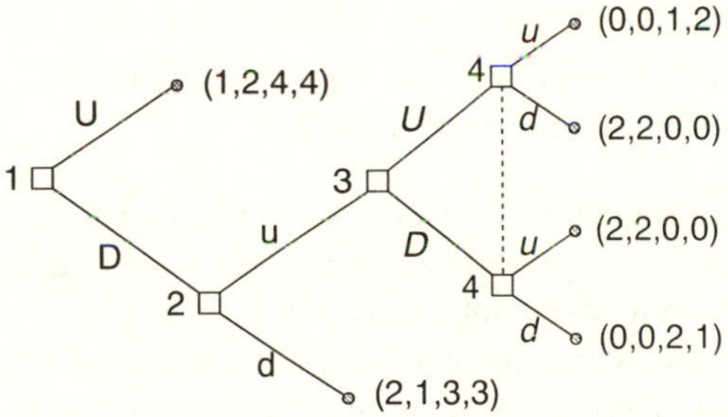

Figure 5.17 Exercise 5.2e

for that subgame before determining their Nash equilibria over the first two moves.)

Backwards induction is a special case of subgame perfection. Games with perfect information decompose into proper subgames from every node. Backwards induction, like subgame perfection, requires equilibrium play in each of those subgames. But subgame perfection is stronger than backwards induction. It can eliminate Nash equilibria where backwards induction is powerless by ruling out equilibria where a player makes an noncredible threat in a subgame containing an information set with multiple nodes.

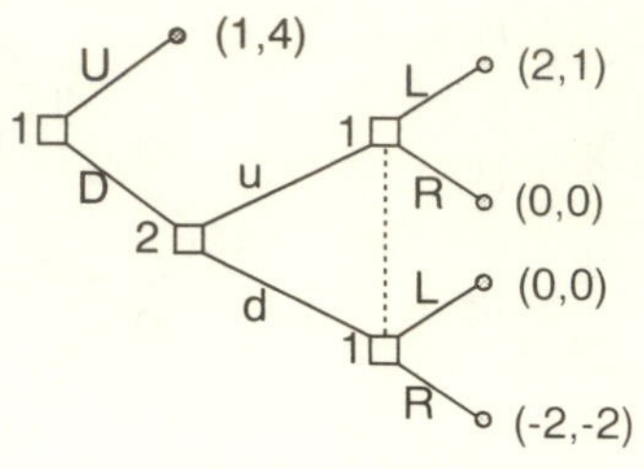

Figure 5.18 An Example of Subgame Perfection

Example: The game in Figure 5.18 has three Nash equilibria: (U,L;d), (U,R;d), and (D,L;u). We cannot perform a backwards induction on this game because of Player 1's information set. However, there is a proper subgame beginning with Player 2's move. This subgame has only one Nash equilibrium, (L;u). (U,L;d) and (U,R;d) are not subgame perfect, then. They rely on Player 2's noncredible threat to play d in the subgame. (D,L;u) is the only subgame-perfect equilibrium of this game.

As the following theorem states, subgame-perfect equilibria always exist in mixed strategies.

Theorem: Every finite n-person game has at least one subgame-perfect equilibrium in mixed strategies.

The equilibrium concepts that I discuss in Chapter Six and Seven, perfect Bayesian, sequential, and perfect equilibria, always produce subgame-perfect equilibria. The theorem above follows because finite games always have those types of equilibria and consequently must have subgame-perfect equilibria.

Backwards induction leads to a stronger result. Games of perfect and complete information not only have equilibria; they typically have an unique equilibrium in pure strategies.

Theorem (Kuhn-Zermelo): Every finite n-person game of perfect and complete information typically has a unique subgame-perfect equilibrium in pure strategies. There may be multiple pure strategy equilibria if a player is indifferent between two or more of its pure strategies.

The first version of this theorem, formulated by Zermelo (1913), is the first result in game theory. Zermelo showed that chess has a winning strategy: White can force a victory, Black can force a victory, or either can force a draw.

He used backwards induction. Players could foresee the ultimate consequences of their moves by using backwards induction from the first move. Of course, the actual calculation of the backwards induction that solves chess is beyond the abilities of any human or computer known to date.

Multiple equilibria are possible if a player is indifferent between two or more of its strategies from any node of the game. For example, the game in Figure 5.10 has two subgame-perfect equilibria. Player 1 is indifferent between (U,L) and (D,L) given that Player 2 will play u. Both (U,L;u) and (D,L;u) are subgame-perfect equilibria of this game, as are all mixed strategies where Player 1 mixes between these two strategies.

The Kuhn-Zermelo theorem does not hold if there are an infinite number of strategies or an infinite number of possible moves. It does not hold, then, for games with a continuum of strategies. For example, consider the game where I name a number between 0 and 1 exclusive, then you name a number between 0 and 1 exclusive, and the person naming the smaller number wins. This game does not have an equilibrium because no matter what number I choose between zero and one, you can always find a smaller number between 0 and 1.

Backwards induction has been important in the development of formal theory in political science. The following sections of this chapter present several models that use backwards induction and subgame perfection.

Sophisticated Voting

We typically assume that individuals vote for their most preferred outcomes. We call this sincere voting because their votes are sincere expressions of their interests. But procedures with multiple votes raise the question of the actors' expectations across votes. Individual actors may benefit by voting against their preferences in the earlier votes if they can anticipate the outcome of later votes. Sophisticated (or strategic) voting can lead to a preferred outcome for those actors.

> Example: Assume there are three alternatives—x, y, and z—and three voters—Players 1, 2, and 3—with the following preferences:
>
> Player 1: xPyPz;
>
> Player 2: yPzPx; and
>
> Player 3: zPxPy.
>
> Sincere voting requires each actor to vote according to its preferences in any pairwise comparison of alternatives. An actor casts a sophisticated vote when it votes against its preferences in a pair-

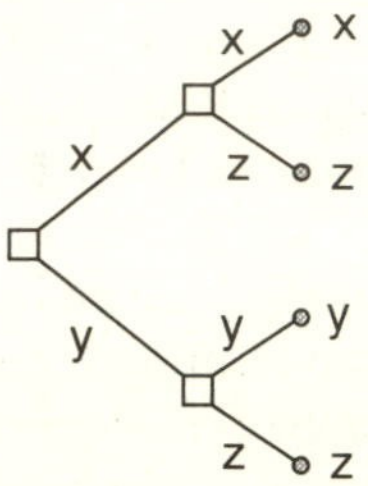

Figure 5.19 A Voting Tree with Three Alternatives

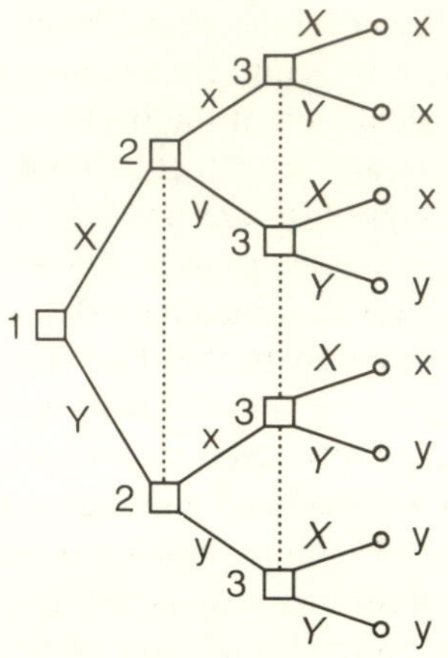

Figure 5.20 The Extensive Form of a Round of Voting

wise comparison. For example, Player 1 casts a sophisticated vote if it votes for y over x.

The three alternatives are voted in pairwise comparisons: first x versus y, and then the winner of that vote versus z. The tree in Figure 5.19 expresses this sequence of votes. This tree is not a game tree because the boxes here represent votes, the branches represent the alternatives that win the preceding vote, and the termini represent the final outcomes of the process. Nevertheless, this voting tree formalizes the voting game. I refer to each separate possible vote as a round of the game. Each round has the game form in Figure 5.20 because everyone votes simultaneously. I have chosen a pairwise comparison of x and y for illustration. For convenience, I list the players' votes in numerical order, but all votes in a round are simultaneous because of the information sets. Each player has one vote, and the alternative that receives two or more of the three votes cast wins. We assume that players always vote.

Exercise 5.3: Demonstrate that in the final round of voting, sincere voting between the pair of alternatives offered is a dominant strategy for all three voters in the game in Figure 5.19.

In the final round of voting, each voter votes sincerely. This observation allows the voters to anticipate the outcome of the last vote when they vote in the earlier rounds. The first vote in the vote tree determines what alternative faces z in the final vote. They should then vote for the alternative they wish to see face z in the second vote.

Exercise 5.4: Show that (Y,X,Y;y,z,y;*X*,*Z*,*Z*) is a subgame-perfect equilibrium of the voting game described above. The strategies are read as the vote to be cast between x and y, between x and z, and between y and z.

Player 1 votes strategically in the first round of this equilibrium. He votes for y instead of his most preferred outcome, x. The end result of his strategic vote, y, is better for Player 1 than the outcome if he votes sincerely in the first vote. If Player 1 voted for x over y in the first round, x would face z in the second round. Players 2 and 3 then would vote for z over x, and Player 1 would get its least preferred outcome, z. By voting for y over x in the first round, Player 1 shifts the final outcome from z to y, a shift he prefers. No other player has an incentive to vote strategically in this example.

Exercise 5.5: Find the sophisticated voting equilibrium of the following situation: There are four alternatives: x, y, z, and w. There are three voters: 1, 2, and 3. The sequence of votes is x versus y, z versus w, and then a vote between the two winners to determine the final outcome. The voters' preferences are as follows:

Voter 1: xPyPzPw;

Voter 2: yPwPzPx; and

Voter 3: wPzPxPy.

You need only list each player's vote for the first two votes (x versus y and z versus w) to specify an equilibrium because all voters vote sincerely in the final round.

Agenda Control

Voting procedures with multiple rounds of voting force the voters to consider the subsequent votes when they cast their votes. The order of comparison of outcomes is critical to the players' choices and the final outcome. Agendas can determine the outcome of multistage voting procedures.

Example: Return to the example of the previous section, but change the agenda to an initial vote between y and z, followed by a vote between the winner and x. Under the latter agenda, (X,X,Y;y,z,z;*X*,*Z*,*Z*) is an equilibrium. Again, the strategies are read as the vote to be cast between x and y, between x and z, and between y and z. Player 2 casts a sophisticated vote for z in the first round because y, its most preferred outcome, will lose to x in the second round.

Different agendas favor different players. The original agenda produced y, Player 2's most preferred outcome, and the agenda above produces z, Player 3's most preferred outcome. Voting on x versus z first and then on the winner versus y produces x as the outcome, and thus favors Player 1. Control of an agenda can be an immensely powerful tool. By figuring out the consequences of each possible agenda, a player with control of the agenda can secure its most preferred outcome.

Example: In Exercise 5.5, both Voters 1 and 2 prefer the agenda given in the problem because it produces y for the final outcome. Given that Players 2 and 3 vote for w or z over x in the final round, achieving y is the best possible outcome for Player 1. Player 3 can produce its most preferred outcome, w, by proposing a vote between y and z first, followed by a vote between x and w, and ending with a vote between the two winning alternatives.

Exercise 5.6: Demonstrate that the above agenda produces w as the outcome. (Hint: Multiple strategic votes may be cast; it matters whether y or z is chosen before x or w.)

You may wonder about the range of power that control of the agenda provides. With all parties voting sincerely and more than one issue, any outcome is possible generally. The following theorem was set forth by both McKelvey (1976) and Schofield (1976):

Theorem (the Chaos Theorem): If there are two or more issues, and three or more voters with spatial preferences, all voters vote sincerely at all times, and no equilibrium position exists, then for any two points x and y, there exists a finite agenda of alternatives, $(x_i)_{i=1}^n$, such that x_1 defeats x, x_{i+1} defeats x_i, and y defeats x_n in majority votes.

In general, you can find an agenda that will get you from any outcome to any other outcome if there is no equilibrium. In Chapter Four, we saw that equilibrium in majority voting for two or more dimensions is unlikely. The Chaos Theorem states that whoever controls the agenda can produce any outcome it wants.

This result is driven by sincere voting. If there is no equilibrium, any alternative can be beaten by some other alternative under sincere voting. The path from the starting point, x, to the desired endpoint, y, is constructed by finding a sequence of intermediate alternatives, which slowly take the voters away from

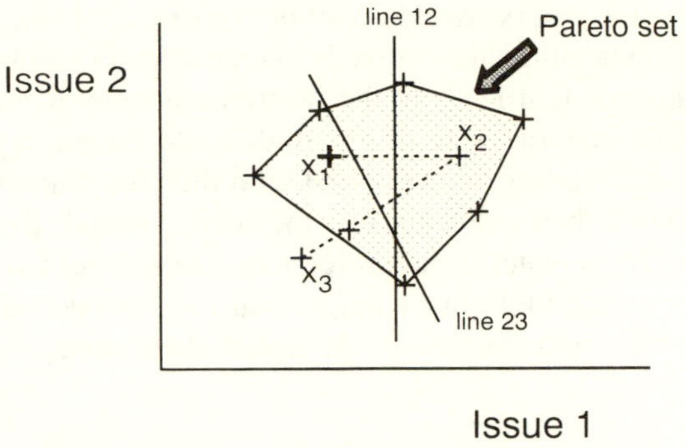

Figure 5.21 An Illustration of the Chaos Theorem

the Pareto set of their ideal points. The Pareto set (the shaded area in Figure 5.21) is the polygon produced by connecting all the voters' ideal points. No voter can be made better off without making some other voter worse off inside the Pareto set. This wandering path is found by proposing an alternative that can beat the current alternative on the "other side" of the distribution. That new alternative is then defeated by a third alternative even further from the Pareto set. For example, x_1 in Figure 5.21 is beaten by x_2. Line 12 is the perpendicular bisector of the line between x_1 and x_2. The three voters on the left side of line 12 vote for x_1, and the four voters on its right side vote for x_2. Similarly, x_3 defeats x_2 in a pairwise vote among sincere voters. There are four voters on the lower-left side of line 23, the perpendicular bisector of the line between x_2 and x_3, and only three voters on the upper-right side of line 23. The agenda from x_1 to x_3 takes us from a point in the Pareto set to one outside the Pareto set.

With sophisticated voting, the voters anticipate when the agenda serves only to lead them down the garden path. They compare the effects of each choice in terms of the final outcome it produces rather than the immediate outcome of the current vote. They vote for a choice that they may not prefer to the immediate alternative because they prefer the ultimate consequence of that vote. When voters are sophisticated, they anticipate future votes, greatly reducing the ability of the agenda to determine outcomes. The following theorem was stated by Shepsle and Weingast (1984):

> **Theorem**: If there are two or more issues, voters have spatial preferences, all voters cast sophisticated votes at all times, and no equilibrium position exists, then for any two points x and y, an agenda from x to y exists only if y defeats x in a majority vote with sincere voting or there exists an alternative z such that z beats x and y beats z in a majority vote with sincere voting.

With sophisticated voters, agendas can be constructed from one point to another only when some other alternative beats the starting point and loses to the endpoint. The agenda that leads to the desired outcome depends on whether y can defeat x in a majority vote. If it can, then the agenda is just y versus x. If it cannot, the agenda is y versus x first, and then the winner against z. If x wins the first round, then z defeats x in the second round. But y defeats z in a pairwise vote. Those voters who prefer x to y to z should vote strategically for y in the first round. Only those points that can be reached in a two-stage agenda are possible replacements for the initial alternative.

Legislative Rules and Structure-Induced Equilibria

As we saw in Chapter Four, there is generally no equilibrium in pure strategies under majority voting when there are two or more issues. For every position, there exists at least one other position that a majority of voters prefer to it. This conclusion has important implications for legislatures as well as elections. In elections, candidates choose positions, and the voters vote for the candidates whose positions they prefer. In a legislature, proposals are made by the members according to the rules of the body. If an equilibrium position did exist, we could predict legislative outcomes from the actors' preferences. The equilibrium position would defeat any other proposal. Once proposed, it could not be displaced. However, we cannot predict legislative outcomes from actors' preferences alone when there is no equilibrium position. Any proposal can be defeated by some other proposal. Furthermore, an individual with control of the agenda can obtain any outcome from sincere voters and a large set of outcomes from sophisticated voters in the absence of an equilibrium.

Although agenda control occasionally allows an actor to run rampant and force its will on a majority, we must ask why this does not happen more often. One possible answer is that legislatures have rules that structure the agenda and give some set or sets of actors an additional role in the process. In the U.S. Congress, for instance, the committee system regulates what bills are sent to the floor for a vote and in what fashion they are advanced. The following model, drawn from the work of Shepsle (1979), addresses this situation.

Assume we have two issues, each of which can be represented by a continuum, creating a two-dimensional space. There are five members of the legislative body—call them 1 through 5. Figure 5.22 shows their ideal points, x_1 through x_5, and their coordinates on each issue. Members 1, 2, and 3 form one committee with control of all possible bills on the first dimension, and Members 3, 4, and 5 form a committee with control over the other dimension. Bills—that is, possible changes in the status quo—must pass through the relevant committee before all members can vote on them.

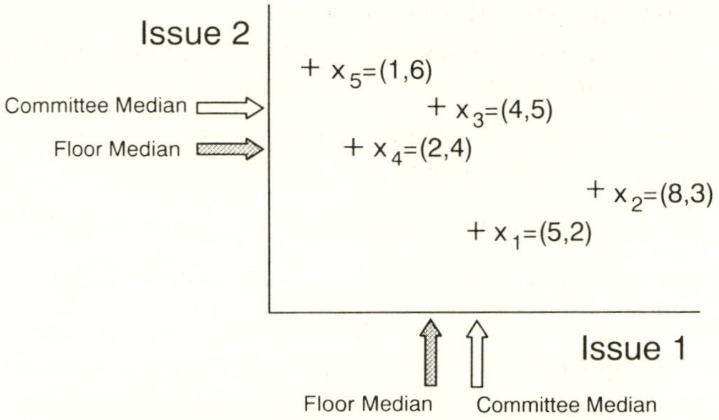

Figure 5.22 An Example of Structure-Induced Equilibrium with Five Voters and Two Issues

The open arrows in Figure 5.22 give the medians of the relevant committee for each issue, and the shaded arrows give the medians of the floor for each issue. For Issue 1, Member 3's position, 4, is the floor median, and Member 1's position, 5, is the committee median. Member 4's position, 4, is the floor median for Issue 2, and Member 3's position, 5, is the committee median. A median position on an issue is the position with an equal number of relevant voters on both sides.

We assume that a status quo outcome occurs unless the legislature takes action. The committee chair can propose bills—that is, propose changes in the status quo—on the dimension his or her committee controls. The committee votes on whether to send that bill to the floor. The floor leader can then propose amendments to the bill, depending upon the rules of the body. (The roles of committee chair and floor leader are not those found in the U.S. Congress. They are a fiction I have created to stipulate who may propose bills and offer amendments.) The rules control amendments to those bills once they reach the floor. We assume that there are three disjunctive rules, as follows. Under the open rule, any amendment on either dimension can be made to bills on the floor. Under the germaneness rule, amendments can be offered only on the dimension of the bill. Under the closed rule, no amendments can be offered. The sequence of votes is as follows. First, the committee decides whether to send a bill to the floor, and if so, what bill. Next, the floor can amend the proposed bill under the appropriate rule. Finally, the bill or its amended version faces the status quo position. The time line games below capture this sequence, including all the procedure for each of the possible rules. For ease of exposition, these time line games concern bills by the first committee on Issue 1; similar time lines exist for the second committee. In these games, x is an outcome of Issue 1 and y an outcome of Issue 2. The subscripts denote whether that outcome is the status quo, SQ, a proposed bill, P, or an amended bill, A.

The Legislating Game under the Open Rule

1. Committee chair chooses whether or not to propose a bill (x_P,y_{SQ}) and chooses x_P if it does so.

2. Committee votes on whether to send proposed bill to the floor. If it votes not to do so, the game ends.

3. Floor leader can propose amendment (x_A,y_A) to the bill.

4. Floor votes on the amendment, (x_A,y_A) versus (x_P,y_{SQ}).

5. The winner of stage 4 faces the status quo, (x_A,y_A) versus (x_{SQ},y_{SQ}) if the amendment won and (x_P,y_{SQ}) versus (x_{SQ},y_{SQ}) if the amendment lost.

The Legislating Game under the Germaneness Rule

1. Committee chair chooses whether or not to propose a bill (x_P,y_{SQ}) and chooses x_P if it does so.

2. Committee votes on whether to send proposed bill to the floor. If it votes not to do so, the game ends.

3. Floor leader can propose amendment (x_A,y_{SQ}) to the bill.

4. Floor votes on the amendment, (x_A,y_{SQ}) versus (x_P,y_{SQ}).

5. The winner of stage 4 faces the status quo, (x_A,y_{SQ}) versus (x_{SQ},y_{SQ}) if the amendment won and (x_P,y_{SQ}) versus (x_{SQ},y_{SQ}) if the amendment lost.

The Legislating Game under the Closed Rule

1. Committee chair chooses whether or not to propose a bill (x_P,y_{SQ}) and chooses x_P if it does so.

2. Committee votes on whether to send proposed bill to the floor. If it votes not to do so, the game ends.

3. The bill faces the status quo, (x_P,y_{SQ}) versus (x_{SQ},y_{SQ}).

Consider the ideal points given in Figure 5.22 under the germaneness rule. Let Member 1 be the chair of the first committee and Member 5 the chair of the second committee. Make Member 3 the floor leader. Solve the game by backwards induction. The alternative closest to the relevant median voter wins a pairwise comparison in spatial voting models. Floor medians win on the floor, and committee medians win in committee. The floor approves any bill—whether it has been amended or not—that is closer to the floor median on Issue 1 than the status quo. Member 3's position ($x_3 = 4$) is the floor median on

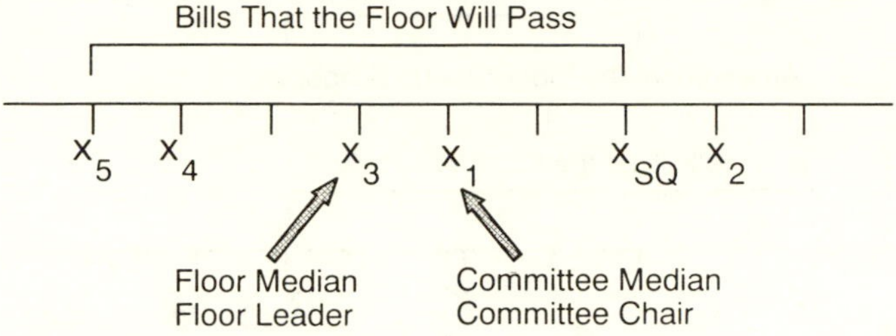

Figure 5.23 Bills That Pass the Floor on Issue 1 under the Germaneness Rule

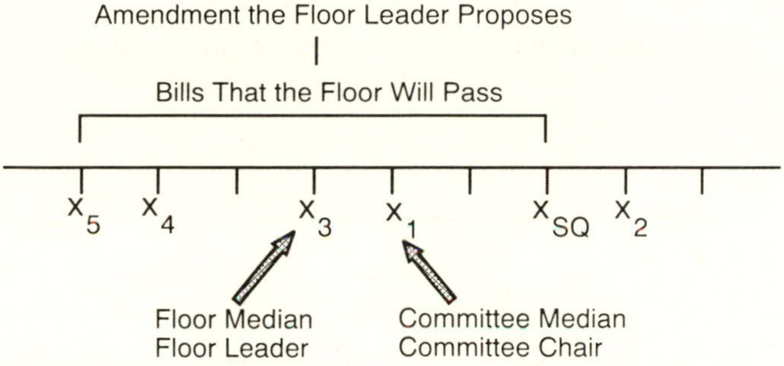

Figure 5.24 The Amendment That the Floor Leader Proposes

Issue 1. If the current bill is closer to Member 3's position than the status quo, it passes. The range of bills that the floor prefers to the status quo ($x_{SQ} = 7$ in this example) is given in Figure 5.23.

An amendment passes if it is closer to the floor median than the proposed bill is to the floor median. No matter which version of the bill advances to face the status quo, the median voter on the floor prefers the alternative closest to its ideal point. The floor leader should offer an amendment to the bill that is closest to its ideal point and will defeat the status quo and the current bill on the floor. Because Member 3, the floor leader, is also the floor median, she will propose her ideal point, which will pass unless the status quo is already at her position on Issue 1. Figure 5.24 shows the floor leader's proposed amendment. If her ideal point were different from the floor median, she would propose the amendment closest to her ideal point that would beat first the original bill and then the status quo.

The committee sends a bill to the floor if it prefers the amended version of the bill to the status quo. In this case, the committee anticipates that any bill it sends to the floor will be amended to the floor median and that the amended version will pass. Thus the committee sends a bill to the floor only when the median voter of the committee prefers the floor median to the status quo. In

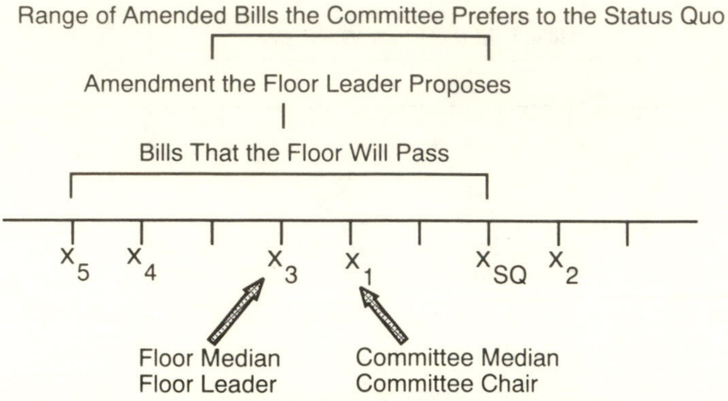

Figure 5.25 Bills the Committee Prefers to the Status Quo

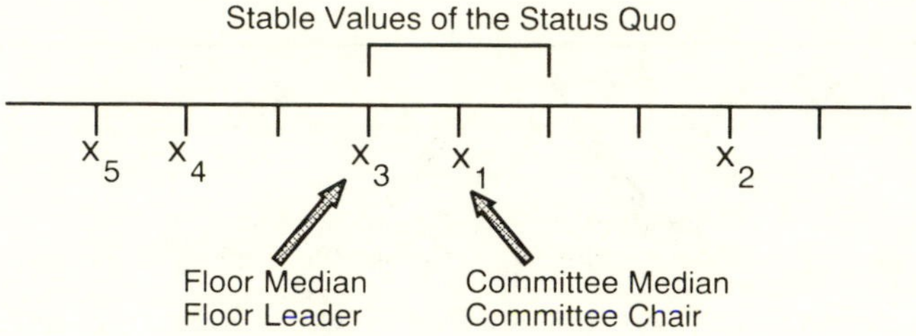

Figure 5.26 Structure-Induced Equilibria of Issue 1 under the Germaneness Rule

this example, the committee median is Member 1's ideal point, $x_1 = 5$. The median voter of the committee prefers the status quo when the status quo is closer to its ideal point than the floor median is to its ideal point, that is, when $|x_{SQ} - x_1| \leq |x_{SQ} - x_3|$. Substituting the values of this example shows that the committee will not send a bill to the floor when $x_3 = 3 \leq x_{SQ} \leq 7 = x_1 + (x_1 - x_3)$. For all other values of the status quo, the committee prefers the amended bill to the status quo. Figure 5.25 shows the range of amended bills that the committee prefers to the status quo. The amendment the floor leader will propose falls in this range, so the committee will send a bill to the floor.

Finally, the committee chair proposes a bill only when it prefers the final amended version of the bill to the status quo, provided that the committee will send it to the floor. The committee chair is the median voter of the committee in this example, so it proposes a bill whenever the committee will send the bill to the floor.

To summarize this example, no bill is proposed if the committee chair prefers the status quo to the floor median on Issue 1. Here, the committee chair blocks legislation when the status quo falls between x_3 and $2x_1 - x_3$ (between 4 and 6 in this case). Figure 5.26 shows the range of status quo values where the com-

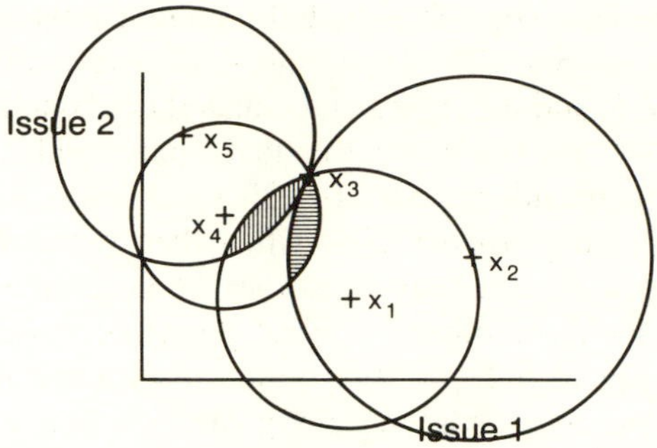

Figure 5.27 Bills that Pass on the Floor under the Open Rule

mittee chair will block legislation. When no bill is proposed, we say that the status quo is **stable**. Otherwise, the committee proposes a bill that is amended to the floor median, which then defeats the status quo. Some of these stable points diverge greatly from the floor median, and some of them are substantially greater than the committee chair's position. The committee system stabilizes these points. The committee chair anticipates that sending a bill to the floor will lead to an amended version of the bill that it will like even less than the status quo. Therefore it never proposes a bill to change that dimension. If the status quo is stable on both dimensions, it is a **structure-induced equilibrium**.

Exercise 5.7:

a) Find the set of stable values for the status quo on Issue 2 in this example under the germaneness rule.

b) Find the final outcome for unstable values of the status quo.

The open rule is analyzed in the same fashion as the germaneness rule, except now amendments can be made on both dimensions. Amended bills that a majority of voters prefer to the status quo will pass on the floor. The floor leader will offer an amendment to move the bill as close to its ideal point as is possible. Now amendments can alter the bill on both dimensions. This gives the floor leader additional flexibility. The floor leader proposes his or her ideal point as the amendment to a bill unless a majority of voters prefer the status quo to the floor leader's ideal point. Graphically, we can find the set of positions that a majority prefers to the floor leader's ideal point, as shown in Figure 5.27. For each member, we draw the circle (assume separable preferences between two equally salient issues, producing circular indifference curves) centered at the member's ideal point and through Member 3's ideal point, x_3. Each member prefers all points inside its circle and votes for those points over Member 3's ideal point in a pairwise vote. The shaded regions are the points that at least three members prefer to x_3. The left petal, shaded vertically, is preferred by Members 1, 4, and 5, and the right petal, shaded horizontally, is preferred by Members 1, 2, and 4. Any bill sent to the floor from outside the shaded regions will be successfully amended to Member 3's ideal point.

The committee chairs propose bills when they prefer Member 3's ideal point to the status quo. The only outcomes both committee chairs, Members 1 and 5, prefer to Member 3's ideal point are those in the vertically shaded region in Figure 5.27. In that region, each chair desires to propose a bill that will move the status quo along the jurisdiction of its committee (i.e., the dimension it controls) to the border of the vertically shaded region closest to its ideal point. Any bill that proposes further change will be amended to Member 3's ideal point, and the committee chair prefers an outcome along the boundary of the vertically shaded region to Member 3's ideal point.

In summary, the only stable point under the open rule is Member 3's ideal point. If the status quo lies outside the vertically shaded region, a bill will be offered, amended to Member 3's ideal point, and passed on the floor. If the status quo lies in the vertically shaded region, one of the two committee chairs offers a bill that moves the status quo along the jurisdiction of its committee to the boundary of that region. The open rule reduces the range of stable status quo outcomes, the set of structurally induced equilibria, relative to the germaneness rule. The reduced range of amendments under the germaneness rule stabilizes outcomes that are not stable under the open rule.

Exercise 5.8: Find the set of structure-induced equilibria under the closed rule for this example. Under the closed rule, no amendments can be offered to the committee's bill on the floor. The game form is given earlier in this section. The instructions below lead you through the backwards induction step by step.

a) For each dimension, find the set of bills that defeat the status quo in a vote on the floor.

b) Find the set of bills from those that can defeat the status quo on the floor (those from part a) that each committee is willing to send to the floor.

c) From the set of bills the committee is willing to send to the floor, find the bill each committee chair will propose.

Those ranges (apparent from part c) where the committee chair is unwilling to send a bill to the floor are the structure-induced equilibria.

Exercise 5.9: Assume the following situation: The legislative body has seven members, with ideal points such that $x_1 = (6,2)$, $x_2 = (5,1)$, $x_3 = (2,5)$, $x_4 = (4,4)$, $x_5 = (2,2)$, $x_6 = (1,7)$, and $x_7 = (7,6)$, and two committees, (1,2,3) and (5,6,7), with jurisdictions over the first and second dimensions, respectively. The committee chairs are Members 1 and 5, respectively. The floor leader is Member 4.

a) Find the structure-induced equilibria under the closed rule.

b) Find the structure-induced equilibria under the germaneness rule.

The Rubinstein Bargaining Model*

In Chapter Four, I discussed bargaining using the Nash bargaining solution. The idea behind the Nash bargaining solution was to give a set of postulates that characterized bargains. The Nash approach does not attempt to explain why the sides reach the bargain they do; rather, it tries to predict what bargains are reached. This section begins to present the noncooperative approach to bargaining. We consider the actors' incentives in the bargaining and ask what offers they should make and when they should accept those offers. Rather than ask what rational bargains look like, we ask how rational actors bargain. The noncooperative approach allows us to explore bargaining behavior as well as the final bargain reached. This section presents a simple noncooperative model of bargaining, the Rubinstein (1982) bargaining model.

Real bargaining is very complicated. There is no well-defined game form that describes all possible ways actors bargain. There are no rules for bargaining. Sometimes actors can make take-it-or-leave-it offers; sometimes they make offers simultaneously; and other times they just shout at one another. How they bargain can have a profound effect on the final outcome. A side with control of how offers are made can manipulate the situation to its advantage. Formalizing bargaining requires us to define a game that will capture certain aspects of bargaining. Here, we analyze one very general form of bargaining—the players alternate offers sequentially. One side makes an offer that the other can accept or reject. If the offer is rejected, the second side can then make a counteroffer of its own, and the first side accepts or rejects that counter. If the counteroffer is rejected, the bargaining continues with another offer by the first side, and so on. Each offer and response is one **round** of bargaining.

*This section uses limits and differential calculus.

The players bargain over the division of 100 units.[1] For convenience, we assume that the units are transferable utility. We also assume that the players prefer reaching a bargain sooner than later. They discount the final bargain for each additional round of bargaining using discount factors δ_1 and δ_2, with $0 < \delta_i < 1$. The time line of a sequential bargaining game with three rounds of alternating offers is given below. Each round of bargaining consists of two moves, an offer and a response. For ease of exposition, each offer is the amount Player 1 receives in that offer. Player 2 gets the remainder.

Sequential Bargaining Game

1. Player 1 offers Ω_1, with $0 \leq \Omega_1 \leq 100$.

2. Player 2 accepts or rejects Ω_1. If she accepts, the game ends, Player 1 receives Ω_1, and Player 2 receives $100 - \Omega_1$.

3. Player 2 offers Ω_2, with $0 \leq \Omega_2 \leq 100$.

4. Player 1 accepts or rejects Ω_2. If he accepts, the game ends, Player 1 receives $\delta_1\Omega_2$, and Player 2 receives $\delta_2(100 - \Omega_2)$.

5. Player 1 offers Ω_3, with $0 \leq \Omega_3 \leq 100$.

6. Player 2 accepts or rejects Ω_3. Game ends. If Player 2 accepts Ω_3, Player 1 receives $\delta_1^2\Omega_3$, and Player 2 receives $\delta_2^2(100 - \Omega_3)$. If Player 2 rejects Ω_3, Players 1 and 2 receive 0.

What is the subgame perfect equilibrium of the three-round sequential bargaining game? This game can be solved with a backwards induction. Player 2 accepts any offer in the final move. Rejecting a offer leads to a payoff of 0, so even accepting $\Omega_3 = 100$, leaving 0 for Player 2, is equally good. Anticipating this, Player 1 offers $\Omega_3 = 100$ in the fifth move, and 0 for Player 2. In the fourth move, Player 1 accepts any offer of at least $100\delta_1$. By rejecting Ω_2, he can obtain $100\delta_1$ in the final round—Ω_3 discounted for the additional round of bargaining. Any offer at least that good should be accepted. Player 2 offers $\Omega_2 = 100\delta_1$ in the third move, leaving $100(1 - \delta_1)$ for herself. In the second move, Player 2 accepts Ω_1 if it gives her at least $100\delta_2(1 - \delta_1)$. If she rejects Ω_1, she can get $100(1 - \delta_1)$ in the second round; the discounted value is $100\delta_2(1 - \delta_1)$. Finally, Player 1 offers $\Omega_1 = 100[1 - \delta_2(1 - \delta_1)]$ because Player 2 accepts that offer and he cannot do better. If Player 1 offers himself more than $100[1 - \delta_2(1 - \delta_1)]$, Player 2 rejects that offer leaving Player 1 with $100\delta_1$ in the second round. He prefers $100[1 - \delta_2(1 - \delta_1)]$ to $100\delta_1$ because $\delta_1 < 1$. In equilibrium then, Player 1 offers $\Omega_1 = 100[1 - \delta_2(1 - \delta_1)]$, and Player 2 accepts this offer. The equilibrium must also specify the strategies off the equilibrium path to show why this behavior is optimal. The offer that Player 1 makes depends on what Player 2 will accept, and her acceptance of an offer depends on what offer Player 1 would accept from her in the second round, and so on. The later offers that are never made in equilibrium are every bit as much a part of the equilibrium as the offer made and accepted.

> Exercise 5.10: Show that Player 1 prefers Ω_1 to Ω_2 in the equilibrium above.

What happens when we allow the players to bargain forever? We remove Player 1's ability to force Player 2 to accept nothing in the final round because there is no final round in open-ended bargaining. If Player 1 offers Player 2 nothing, she will reject such a miserly offer and continue the game. First, consider the Nash equilibria of this game. Any division of the 100 units can be supported on any round of the game as a Nash equilibrium. For example, the following strategies support a division where Player 1 gets 1 unit and Player 2 gets 99 units on the forty-second round. Both players offer themselves all 100 units on rounds one through forty-one. They reject any offer before the forty-second round unless it gives them all 100 units. On the forty-second round and every round thereafter, Player 2 offers 1 unit to Player 1, leaving 99 for herself, and he accepts. These strategies form a Nash equilibrium because neither player can better its payoff by changing its strategy unilaterally. Using similar strategies, any division of the payoff on any round is supported by some Nash equilibrium.

We can solve for the subgame-perfect equilibrium of the infinite sequential bargaining game by using a simple trick.[2] The game that follows from any offer Player 1 makes is the same. Player 2 can reject the offer and make a counteroffer, and there are still an infinite number of rounds of bargaining left. Thus Player 1 always makes the same offer in every round. Let M be Player 1's optimal offer. From the logic of the three-round bargaining model, Player 1 should offer $100 - \delta_2(100 - \delta_1 M)$ two rounds earlier.

> Exercise 5.11: Show that Player 1 offers $100 - \delta_2(100 - \delta_1 M)$ two offers before offering M. (Hint: Just follow the same calculations of indifference given in the model with three rounds of bargaining.)

Because Player 1 always makes the same offer in every round, M is the value such that M equals $100 - \delta_2(100 - \delta_1 M)$. We can solve for the optimal offer by equating the two expressions, and then solving for M:

$$M = 100 - \delta_2(100 - \delta_1 M)$$

$$M = 100\left(\frac{1 - \delta_2}{1 - \delta_1\delta_2}\right).$$

In equilibrium, Player 1 offers $\Omega_1 = 100[(1-\delta_2)/(1-\delta_1\delta_2)]$, and Player 2 accepts it, receiving $100\{[\delta_2(1-\delta_1)]/(1-\delta_1\delta_2)\}$. I have not solved for Player 2's offers, but they follow from the logic above.

This equilibrium has a number of intuitive and counterintuitive features. Begin with the intuitive features. First, each player's impatience, as captured in its discount factor, affects its share of the bargain. More impatient players have lower discount factors; future payoffs are worth less to them. Decreasing δ_1 decreases the equilibrium offer; decreasing δ_2 increases the equilibrium offer, which lowers Player 2's share. The only thing that drives the players to agree to a deal is their impatience. If there were no discount factors, there would be no loss from delaying agreement indefinitely.

Second, Player 1 has the advantage of making the first offer. If we allow Player 2 to make the first offer, Player 1's share goes down and Player 2's share goes up. Player 1 generally receives a greater share of what is divided than Player 2 does. If they have the same discount factor ($\delta_1 = \delta_2 = \delta$), Player 1 receives $100[1/(1+\delta)]$ and Player 2 receives only $100[\delta/(1+\delta)]$. Because $\delta < 1$, Player 1 receives more than Player 2. The first offer provides an advantage because Player 2 must wait and suffer the effect of a discounted counteroffer. Taking advantage of this power, Player 1 offers Player 2 less than she would ask for in the second round. Player 2 accepts less because she cannot do better by waiting and making a counteroffer.

Third, the greater the pressure for an immediate deal (i.e., the smaller δ_1 and δ_2), the larger the share Player 1 receives. As closing the deal quickly becomes more important, Player 1 can exploit that pressure to extract a larger share from Player 2.

The main counterintuitive feature of the equilibrium is its uniqueness. There are no other subgame-perfect equilibria. There is only one rational way to bargain in this situation. None of the tactics that we associate with bargaining—take-it-or-leave-it offers or lying about one's real position, for instance—occur in the equilibrium. The Rubinstein bargaining model cannot explain the bargaining we observe in the world. Further, there is no real bargaining in the equilibrium. The first offer is always accepted; there is no exchange of offers before a settlement.

The outcome of the Rubinstein bargaining model also corresponds to the Nash bargaining solution. Imagine that we let the time of the rounds go to 0; you can think of the players shouting offers back and forth instantaneously. Let the time between offers be t. The discount factors for each round become δ_i^t. Player 1 receives $100\,[(1-\delta_2^t)/(1-\delta_1^t\delta_2^t)]$ and Player 2 receives $100\,\{[\delta_2^t(1-\delta_1^t)]/(1-\delta_1^t\delta_2^t)\}$ in equilibrium. Player 1's share of the 100 units goes to the following as t approaches 0 in the limit (using L'Hôpital's Rule to find the limit):

$$\lim_{t\to 0} 100\left(\frac{1 - \delta_2^t}{1 - \delta_1^t\delta_2^t}\right) = \lim_{t\to 0} 100\left(\frac{-\ln\delta_2(\delta_2^t)}{-\ln\delta_1(\delta_1^t\delta_2^t) - \ln\delta_2(\delta_1^t\delta_2^t)}\right)$$

$$= 100\left(\frac{\ln\delta_2}{\ln\delta_1 + \ln\delta_2}\right)$$

In like manner, Player 2 receives $100[\ln\delta_1/(\ln\delta_1 + \ln\delta_2)]$ in the limit as t goes to 0. This division corresponds to the Nash bargaining solution. If the players have equal values for reaching an agreement, $\delta_1 = \delta_2$, they divide the 100 units equally, as in the Nash bargaining solution. Binmore (1992, 180–212) has a complete discussion of the correspondence between the Nash bargaining solution and the Rubinstein bargaining model.

Even with its weaknesses, the Rubinstein bargaining model is a starting point for understanding bargaining. It directs our attention to other aspects of bargaining, such as incomplete information, that it does not capture. It alerts us to the consequences of how players bargain for the bargain struck. It provides a noncooperative motivation for the Nash bargaining solution.

Bargaining in Legislatures

Bargaining in the legislative setting differs from the bilateral bargaining discussed in the previous section. First, legislatures have more than two members, so bargaining is multilateral, rather than bilateral. Second, voting rules generally require only a simple majority of the legislators to enact an outcome, unlike the unanimity required in bilateral bargaining. A simple majority can pass bills that deny benefits to the minority, and the minority is powerless to stop that bill. In bilateral bargaining, each party holds veto power over any possible deal. Third, legislative rules shape the order of offers and acceptances. In the previous section, I assumed alternating offers.

Legislative bargaining is regulated by rules of recognition and amendment. Here, I examine the effects of a simple random rule of recognition and open and closed rules of amendment, using a model from Baron and Ferejohn 1989. Unlike the earlier section of this chapter about committee systems, this section focuses on bargaining on the floor of a legislature, not bargaining between a committee and the floor. Open and closed rules of amendment here change the ability of a recognized member to change the current proposal on the floor.

I begin with a three-member legislature, with two rounds of proposals. The results of this very simple model are then generalized to n members and unlimited proposals. Refer to the three members as 1, 2, and 3. Each member represents a separate district. They will bargain over the distribution of one unit, which we can think of as legislative "goodies" or "pork barrel projects" to be brought back to each district. Those who believe that ideological concerns are more central in legislation can think of the distribution of the unit as a way to represent whose ideological interests are served more closely by the legislation: the greater a member's share, the closer the bill reflects his or her ideological goals. To return to our original, crasser formulation, the members wish to increase the "pork" they bring home to their own districts to raise their chance of reelection. A **proposal** (or bill), $x = (x_1,x_2,x_3)$, is a distribution of the unit across the three members; $x_1 + x_2 + x_3 = 1$ because the members will divide all the available "pork."[3] The members receive no benefits if no proposal passes. They prefer reaching agreement sooner rather than later. The three members have a common discount factor, $\delta \leq 1$, across rounds of proposals. Their values for proposal x if it passes on the second round are δx_1, δx_2, and δx_3 for Members 1, 2, and 3, respectively.

The recognition rule determines who can make a proposal in each round of the game. For simplicity's sake, I assume that each member has an equal probability of being recognized. The probability that a member will be recognized, then, is $\frac{1}{3}$. The recognized member can then make a proposal, on which the three members will vote. I assume that proposals are voted under a closed rule. Each proposal goes to a immediate vote, with no chance for amendment.

Proposals require two of the three votes in order to pass. To simplify the problem of how members vote when they are indifferent between the current proposal and continuing the game, I assume that members always vote for proposals if they are indifferent between accepting and rejecting the current proposal.[4] The time line form of the game is as follows:

1. Chance selects which member will make the first proposal. Call the recognized member M_1.

2. M_1 makes proposal x^1.

3. The members vote on x^1. If two or three members vote yes, x^1 passes, the game ends, and the members receive payoffs x_i^1. Otherwise, x^1 is defeated.

4. If x^1 is defeated, Chance selects which member will make the second proposal. Call the recognized member M_2.

5. M_2 makes proposal x^2.

6. The members vote on x^2. If two or three members vote yes, x^2 passes, and the members receive payoffs δx_i^2. Otherwise, x^2 fails and all three members receive payoff 0.

The game above can be solved by backwards induction. In the final move of the game, all three voters will vote for any proposal even if they receive 0 in that proposal. Because voters vote for proposals when they are indifferent and their payoff if x^2 is rejected is 0, they always vote for x^2. In move 5, M_2, knowing that any proposal will pass, makes a proposal that gives the entire unit to himself.

In move 3, voters must compare their payoff from the current proposal to their expected payoff if the game continues. In the latter case, each player has a $\frac{1}{3}$ probability of being recognized in the second round of the game. If recognized, the voter will propose that it receive the entire unit. If not recognized, the voter will receive 0 in the second proposal. Each voter then expects a payoff of $\frac{1}{3}\delta$ ($\frac{1}{3}$ for the probability of being recognized, 1 for its value for the second proposal, and δ for the discounted value of the second proposal) from continuing the game. Voters will vote for any proposal in the first round that gives them at least $\frac{1}{3}\delta$.

Anticipating these votes, M_1 will offer one other voter $\frac{1}{3}\delta$ and keep $1 - \frac{1}{3}\delta$ for itself in the second move. It does not matter to which voter M_1 offers this deal. This proposal will always pass; the game always ends on the first proposal in equilibrium. The following proposition presents the entire equilibrium:

Proposition: The subgame-perfect equilibrium of the two-round, three-member legislative bargaining game under the closed rule is as follows:

1) In the first round, M_1 proposes that it receive $1 - \frac{1}{3}\delta$ and another member receive $\frac{1}{3}\delta$. M_1 and the other member vote for the proposal, and it passes.

2) In the second round, M_2 proposes that it receive 1 and the other members receive 0. All three members vote for the proposal, and it passes.

<u>Exercise 5.12</u>: Find the subgame-perfect equilibrium of the two-round legislative bargaining model when there are $2n + 1$ members of the legislature. Proposals pass with $n+1$ votes. The probability of recognition in each round is now $1/(2n + 1)$ because each member has an equal chance of recognition.

<u>Exercise 5.13</u>: Find a subgame-perfect equilibrium of the open-ended legislative bargaining game with three members under the closed rule.

a) Begin by using backwards induction to find the equilibrium of the game with three rounds of proposals possible.

b) Find the equilibrium of the game with n rounds of proposals possible.

c) Find an equilibrium of the open-ended legislative bargaining game. (Hint: Do the results of parts a and b suggest what this equilibrium looks like?)[5]

The open rule in this model allows for possible amendments to a proposal. After a bill is proposed, another member is recognized; consecutive recognition is not allowed. That member can either move the previous question or amend the current proposal. The former action brings the current proposal to a vote, and the latter substitutes a new proposal for the old one. Each time a new or amended bill is proposed counts as a round of the model, which discounts the payoffs. All the members then share an interest in approving a proposal sooner rather than approving the same proposal later. The legislative game with the open rule has the following time line form for each round:

1. Chance selects which member will make the proposal. Call the recognized member M_1.

2. M_1 makes proposal x^1.

3. Chance recognizes a member other than M_1, who can move or amend x^1. Call this recognized member M_2.

4. M_2 makes proposal x^2. If $x^2 = x^1$, M_2 is said to move the question. Otherwise, M_2 amends the current proposal, and the next round begins at move 3, with the amended proposal as x^1 of the next round.

5. If M_2 moves the question, the members vote on x^1. If two or three members vote yes, x^1 passes, the game ends, and the members receive payoffs x_i^1. Otherwise, x^1 is defeated, and the next round begins with move 1.

Payoffs are discounted by the number of rounds played. For example, player i receives payoff $\delta^3 x_i^1$ if proposal x^1 passes on the third round.

The open rule adds a strategic complication to the model. Under the closed rule, recognized members propose bills that assign sufficient benefits to a majority to secure their passage, and then give themselves the remainder of the benefits. All members not in that majority receive nothing. Under the open rule, members of the majority will move the question if they are recognized after a proposal is made. But any minority member who is recognized will offer an amendment instead. The amendment will delay the approval of a proposal at least one round, which costs all members. Proposers face a trade-off under the open rule in how many members they include in their proposal. If all members receive benefits equal to what they expect if the game continues, then any member will move the question and the proposal will pass. But the benefits extended to all the members come out of the proposer's payoff. Including benefits for more members raises the chance that a proposal will pass quickly at the cost of reducing the proposer's share of the total payoff. Including benefits for fewer members raises the proposer's payoff at the cost of raising the chance that one of the excluded members will be recognized next, propose an amendment, and so delay the passage of a bill.

The answer to how many members will receive positive benefits in a proposal depends on the relative impatience of the members. When discount factors are low, approving a bill quickly is more important because more is lost through delay. We expect to see proposals provide positive benefits for more members when discount factors are low. When discount factors are high, the members are patient, and a proposer is willing to take the risk of delay inherent in excluding members from their proposal. The equilibrium under the open rule should capture this intuition.

I solve this problem for a three-member legislature. The general case with n members is similar; I refer you to Baron and Ferejohn 1989 for the details. We wish to ascertain the values of δ for which M_1 offers benefits to both of the other members as opposed to just one. I calculate the values of offering benefits to one versus two other members. Begin by calculating the players' values if the proposer offers benefits to both other members. The proposer offers V to each of the other two members, retaining $1 - 2V$ for himself. As before, the proposer should choose V to make the other members indifferent between moving the question and proposing an amendment. Recall that I have assumed that members always vote for proposals and move the question whenever they are indifferent.

$$V = \delta(1 - 2V).$$

If the recognized member accepts the current proposal, she receives V. If she offers an amendment, she becomes the new proposer and receives $1 - 2V$ a round later. Solving for V, I get the following:

$$V = \frac{\delta}{1 + 2\delta}.$$

The following proposition gives the complete equilibrium when the proposer offers benefits to both other members.

> **Proposition**: The subgame-perfect equilibrium of the open-ended, three-member legislative bargaining game under the open rule when all three members receive benefits is as follows:
>
> **1)** In any round, M_1 proposes that it receive $1/(1 + 2\delta)$ and the other members receive $\delta/(1 + 2\delta)$. M_1 and the other members vote for the proposal, and it passes.

2) In any round, M_2 moves the question. All three members vote for the proposal, and it passes.

Proposals where only two members receive benefits are more complicated. The member who does not receive benefits in the proposal on the floor will propose an amendment if he or she is recognized. Call the three members the proposers, the included member, and the excluded member, based on what they receive from the current proposal. Let y be the amount that the proposer offers the included member, reserving $1 - y$ for itself. Amendments create the possibility that the current proposal will be delayed or changed. The players' values for a proposal are not exactly the amounts they receive in that proposal. Although the proposer receives $1 - y$ if its proposal passes, there is a $\frac{1}{2}$ chance that the excluded member will be recognized next and offer an amendment. Let the amount the proposer expects from the game be V_p, the value to the included member be V_i, and the value to the excluded member be V_e.

The proposer should offer enough to make the included member indifferent between moving the question and offering a proposal of its own.

$$y = \delta V_p.$$

The value of the game to the proposer is determined by who is recognized next. The included member moves the question, in which case the proposer receives $1 - y$. The excluded member offers an amendment offering benefits to the included member and excluding the proposer. The proposer has value V_e a round later for this amendment.

$$V_p = \tfrac{1}{2}(1 - y) + \tfrac{1}{2}\delta V_e.$$

The value of a proposal to the included member before M_2 is recognized varies with who is recognized next. As before, the included member moves the question, and the excluded member offers an amendment. But the included member is offered benefits in the amended proposal.

$$V_i = \tfrac{1}{2}y + \tfrac{1}{2}\delta V_i.$$

The value of a proposal to the excluded member also depends on who is recognized next. The included member moves the bill, leaving the excluded member with nothing. The excluded member itself becomes the proposer in the next round if he or she is recognized.

$$V_e = \tfrac{1}{2}(0) + \tfrac{1}{2}\delta V_p = \tfrac{1}{2}\delta V_p.$$

The four equations in four unknowns, y, V_p, V_i, and V_e, are solved simultaneously, which in this case is easier than it sounds. Substitute the first and the fourth equations for y and V_e in the second equation to solve for V_p:

$$V_p = \tfrac{1}{2}(1 - \delta V_p) + \tfrac{1}{2}\delta(\tfrac{1}{2}\delta V_p) = \tfrac{1}{2} - \tfrac{1}{2}\delta V_p + \tfrac{1}{4}\delta^2 V_p$$

$$V_p = \frac{2}{4 + 2\delta - \delta^2}.$$

Substituting the value of V_p into the first, third, and fourth equations leads to the values of y, V_i, and V_e:

$$y = \delta V_p = \frac{2\delta}{4 + 2\delta - \delta^2},$$

$$V_i = \tfrac{1}{2}y + \tfrac{1}{2}\delta V_p = \frac{2\delta}{(2 - \delta)(4 + 2\delta - \delta^2)},$$

and

$$V_e = \tfrac{1}{2}\delta V_p = \frac{\delta}{4 + 2\delta - \delta^2}.$$

The following proposition pulls all these pieces together into a complete statement of this equilibrium:

> **Proposition**: The subgame-perfect equilibrium of the open-ended, three-member legislative bargaining game under the open rule when two members receive benefits is as follows:
>
> **1)** In move 2 of any round, M_1 proposes that it receive $(4-\delta^2)/(4+2\delta-\delta^2)$ and the included member receive $2\delta/(4+2\delta-\delta^2)$.
>
> **2)** In move 4 of any round, if M_2 is the included member, it moves the question, M_1 and M_2 vote for the proposal, and it passes. If M_2 is the excluded member, it proposes as an amendment that it receive $(4-\delta^2)/(4+2\delta-\delta^2)$ and the included member receive $2\delta/(4+2\delta-\delta^2)$.

Now that we know what each player receives if the proposer includes one or two other members in its proposal, we can determine whether the proposer includes one or two other members. The proposer receives $1/(1+2\delta)$ if it includes both other members and expects $2/(4+2\delta-\delta^2)$ if it includes only one. The point where the proposer is indifferent between the two forms of proposal is found by setting these two terms equal and solving for δ. This calculation yields $\sqrt{3}-1 \approx .71$. The proposer includes both other members in its proposal

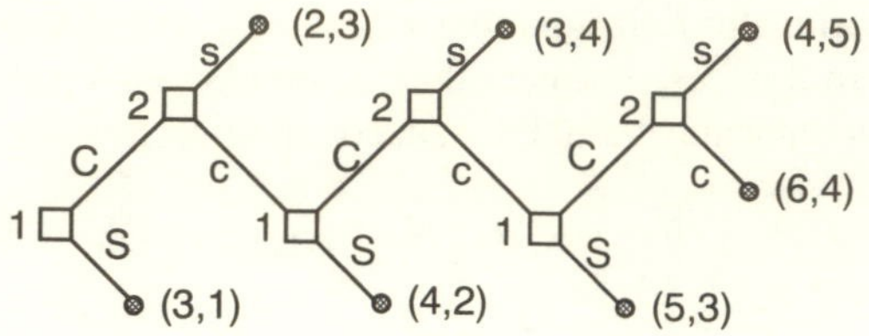

Figure 5.28 The Three-Level Centipede Game

for lower discount factors and includes only one other member in its proposal for higher discount factors. This conclusion mirrors the intuition discussed earlier in this section. When the pressure to reach a quick agreement is high (i.e., when discount factors are low), proposers include more members in a bill to forestall the threat of delay through amendments. When the pressure to reach a quick agreement is low, bills exhibit the same majoritarian logic found under the closed rule.

This last observation brings us to the final point I wish to make with this model, another reason for the closed and open rules. The open rule allows the members greater input into legislation because amendments can be made to objectionable proposals. A cost of this flexibility is the possibility of delay by amendments. Delay under the open rule can be eliminated by including more members in a proposal. But universalistic proposals reduce the benefits the proposers receive from legislation. The closed rule has neither of these problems: agreement in the model is instantaneous, and proposers always receive a maximal share of the benefits. But the loss of amendment power restricts the ability of other members to modify proposals. Consequently, we would expect that the floor would be reluctant to adopt closed rules, favoring them only when time is of the essence and the issue is likely to lead to an amendment battle.

Why Might Backwards Induction Yield Counterintuitive Results?

Backwards induction has strong intuitive appeal, and we have seen how backwards induction can be used to solve problems relevant to politics. But there are situations where the results of backwards induction can violate our intuition about how to play a game.

> Example: The game in Figure 5.28 is called the three-level centipede game. (You might recall it as part b of Exercise 5.1.) The basic structure of all centipede games is that the players sequentially choose whether to end the game or continue it. This game is a three-level centipede because each player gets three chances to

> end the game. Both players' payoffs rise for every time that they both agree to continue the game. But both players receive a bonus if they end the game. These bonuses are large enough that either player wants to end the game if it knows that the other player will end the game in the next move. If I know you will continue the game, I want to continue the game. The problem here appears to be trust. If I continue the game, will you continue it in return?

If you solve the three-level centipede game by backwards induction, the only equilibrium is (S,S,S;s,s,s)—both players always stop the game whenever they have the chance. In the last move of the game, the moving player always ends the game to gain the bonus for ending the game. In the next-to-last move, the moving player ends the game. The other player will end the game in the last move, and the moving player is better off ending the game itself rather than letting the other player end the game in the last move. This calculation zippers back through the game. At every move, the moving player should anticipate that the other player will end the game in the next move. Then the moving player is better off ending the game now instead of continuing.

Backwards induction creates this chain of logic no matter how long the centipede game lasts. Imagine a hundred-level centipede game, where each player has one hundred moves instead of the three moves in the game in Figure 5.28.[6] The same logic above holds in the hundred-level game. The first player ends the game in his first move. Both players anticipate that the other player will end the game in its next move if the moving player does not end the game now.

But this equilibrium conflicts with the play we expect from "reasonable" players. The gain from continuing the game for many rounds, say, fifty or more in the hundred-level centipede game, is very large compared to the loss if you continue the game and the other player ends it in its next move. Why not take a chance and continue the game? Experiments where subjects play the centipede game are almost never finished on the first move. Instead, both players continue the game during the early moves.

The difference between the equilibrium of the centipede and "reasonable" play of the game may be the failure of backwards induction. Backwards induction requires the players to anticipate all future moves. Such anticipations may be unrealistic in very complicated or long games. Do the players actually look two hundred moves down the tree in the hundred-level centipede game? The simple anticipation that the other player will continue the game in response to your continuing the game seems more plausible. Is the concept of backwards induction inherently flawed because it requires players to form anticipations that are unreasonable?

I think not. There are two responses to this argument. The first is formal and is developed more fully in Chapter Nine. Backwards induction can be performed only in games of complete information. But it may be unreasonable to believe that both players know each other's payoffs with certainty. Every real situation is clouded with uncertainty about other actors' exact motivations and goals. If we introduce some uncertainty into the players' knowledge of each other's payoffs, we can find equilibria of the centipede game where both players continue the game for many moves. We create a small probability that one player always has to continue the game in every move. This uncertainty breaks the backwards induction and creates incentives for normal players to continue the game. A full treatment of this argument requires the concepts that are developed in the next three chapters and must wait for Chapter Nine. It also adds noticeably to the mathematical complexity of these models. But one solution to the paradox of the centipede game introduces uncertainty.

This uncertainty could represent a failure of common knowledge of the rationality of the players (Reny 1992). Backwards induction requires that the rationality of the players be common knowledge. Otherwise, they may have rational incentives to act "irrationally." If a player is not certain the other player is rational, the latter may benefit by acting "irrationally" even if it is rational. In the centipede game, I may rationally want to continue the game if you are not certain that I am rational. You might continue the game in your next move in the hope that I am "irrational."

There is another response to this dilemma. Models are tools that we use to simplify political situations so that we can understand them. Concepts of equilibrium are how we represent choices within such settings. Neither is meant to be a literal description of situations or choices. Actors do anticipate one another's actions in politics. Backwards induction is a way to formalize such anticipations within a game. We can gain insight into some problems in politics with models of complete and perfect information solved by backwards induction. The proof of such models lies in the conclusions they produce. Even such simple models have provided important insights about political problems. Further, models of perfect and complete information often form the starting point for models with incomplete information. Chains of models that improve on their predecessors can increase our understanding. Such chains have to start with a first model.

The problem of anticipations within a game is complex. Chapter Six advances the idea of anticipations in a game by introducing the concept of beliefs in a game. Beliefs summarize what the players know about the prior history of the game. Because the prior history of a game includes clues about the other players' strategies, beliefs are useful when forming anticipations about the other players' future moves. But that is the subject of the next chapter.

Review

This chapter has presented subgame perfection and applied it to several topics in political science. A subgame starts at a node of a larger game, includes all subsequent nodes, and forms a game on its own. A subgame-perfect equilibrium requires players to play a Nash equilibrium of every subgame of a game. Backwards induction is an easy way to find subgame-perfect equilibria in a game of complete and perfect information. Subgame perfection begins to test the rationality of moves off the equilibrium path. It allows us to examine the credibility of some threats and promises that the players will not have to carry out in equilibrium.

Further Reading

Backwards induction can be traced back to Zermelo (1913). Subgame perfection, the common formalization of backwards induction, is due to Reinhart Selten, and Selten 1975 has a good presentation of both subgame perfection and the idea of perfect equilibrium. Fudenberg and Tirole's (1991) Chapter Three provides a good treatment of backwards induction and subgame perfection.

Ordeshook 1986 is a solid reference for sophisticated voting, agenda control, and structure-induced equilibria. For those interested in further reading, the original source for sophisticated voting is Farquharson 1969. On agenda control, the original sources for the Chaos Theorem are McKelvey 1976 and Schofield 1976. The result on agenda control under sophisticated voting comes from Shepsle and Weingast 1984. You should also see Banks 1989a, Ordeshook and Palfrey 1988, and Ordeshook and Schwartz 1987 on agenda control under sophisticated voting. The section on bargaining in legislatures is taken from Baron and Ferejohn 1989.

The Rubinstein bargaining model comes from Rubinstein 1982. Kreps (1990a, 556–65) presents a very good and accessible treatment of this model. He shows that the division of the cake depends on the assumptions of how the bargaining is structured. Binmore (1992, 180–212) gives a thorough treatment of the Nash bargaining solution, the Rubinstein bargaining model, and how the latter provides a noncooperative foundation for the former.

If you are interested in the centipede game and other examples of the limitations of backwards induction, Reny 1992 is the best accessible treatment. I also recommend Kreps's (1990b, 77–82, 147–48) discussion. Kreps is a proponent of uncertainty as a solution to the paradoxes of backwards induction and has developed that position in his work.

Legislative Studies

The study of the U.S. Congress has been fruitful ground for game theory models. I present three different models of congressional rules, and models have been published of many other aspects of Congress. Shepsle and Weingast 1994 is a good place to start learning this literature. It surveys the available models of Congress. Krehbiel 1988 is an earlier survey that is still useful. Black 1958 is the source that began the formal study of committee decisions.

The structure-induced equilibrium model has generated a large literature. Historically, the notable papers are Shepsle 1979, Shepsle and Weingast 1987, and Weingast 1989. Hammond and Miller (1987) use this approach to analyze the organization of Congress given in the U.S constitution.

The model of bargaining in legislatures by Baron and Ferejohn (1989) has led to a set of papers analyzing the distributive effects of congressional policies (Baron 1989a, 1991b).

The third model of congressional structure is informational; it is presented in Chapter Eight. Krehbiel 1991 is the place to begin; Gilligan and Krehbiel (1987, 1989, 1990) present their models of an informative committee structure. Huber (1992) uses models of congressional rules to explain differences between the legislatures of France and the United States.

The other institutions of Congress have also been modeled. Calvert (1987) uses the Chain Store Paradox (see Chapter Nine) to analyze legislative leadership. McKelvey and Riezman (1992) explain why legislators use the seniority system to distribute committee positions. Austen-Smith (1990) and Austen-Smith and Riker (1987, 1990) present models of legislative debate based on signaling theory. Sullivan (1990) presents a simple model of bargaining between the president and the Congress. The section on models of bureaucracy and administration in Chapter Nine of this book includes models of legislative-agency relations. These models analyze congressional oversight and control of agencies.

Ainsworth and Sened (1993) and Austen-Smith (1993) present models of lobbying as an information source for legislators. Austen-Smith (1992) considers how legislative constituencies could restrict sophisticated votes in both chambers of congress.

Chapter Six
Beliefs and Perfect Bayesian Equilibria

Perfect Bayesian equilibrium unites a new concept, beliefs, with strategies to create a more powerful idea of equilibrium. So far, equilibria have been combinations of strategies that are best replies to one another. Chapter Five added the idea that best replies should be judged off the equilibrium path as well as on it. Backwards induction and subgame perfection provided one way to judge best replies off the equilibrium path. But information sets with multiple nodes often frustrate those techniques. Because we cannot do a backwards induction through information sets with multiple nodes, backwards induction is powerless to deal with many games. Subgame perfection can help in some of these cases but not all.

Information sets with multiple nodes reflect a player's inability to verify the node it is located at when it must choose. It cannot determine the consequences of its moves because of this uncertainty. When a player chooses at an information set with multiple nodes, it uses what information it has about which node it is likely to be at when it chooses. We represent these judgments about what has happened with conditional probabilities. A player thinks to itself, *What is the probability that I am at the top node in this information set given that I must make a move from this information set?*

These conditional probabilities on the nodes of an information set with multiple nodes are called **beliefs**. They summarize a player's judgment about what has probably happened up to that point in the game. Beliefs express the likelihood that the moving player is at each node in such an information set. We use beliefs to calculate a player's expected utility for each action from an information set with multiple nodes. For each action, we weigh the utility of the outcome that results from that action from each node in the information set by the probability the player is at that node.

Not just any probabilities can be considered rational beliefs in the context of a particular equilibrium. Beliefs should reflect what the players know about the game and the common conjecture they hold about the strategies they are playing. They capture the moving player's hypotheses about the history of play that led to this information set. A player's beliefs reproduce what it believes the other players are likely to have done before it must move.

Further, we assume that players make optimal use of the information available to them. We model how players use information to revise their beliefs with

Bayes's Theorem from probability theory. When actors are uncertain, they use new information to update their beliefs about underlying states of the world. Rarely is new information decisive for judging the state of the world. Instead, it shifts the player's judgment about the likelihood of different states. Bayes's Theorem explains how new information should be used to update beliefs about underlying states of the world. It weighs the ability of the new evidence to discriminate among different states and the strength of prior beliefs to arrive at updated beliefs.

The states in a game are all the moves that have been made earlier in the game. If a player knew what moves had been made, it could determine which node it is at when it must move. When it cannot verify what moves have been made, it uses the other players' equilibrium strategies to judge at which node it is likely to be. A player updates its beliefs by combining what it can observe with the likelihood in the equilibrium that the other players' would make each possible move. Bayes's Theorem is the formal tool for this updating. Rational beliefs, then, depend on the players' strategies. Along the equilibrium path, the beliefs should be calculated from the known probabilities of chance moves and the players' strategies by means of Bayes's Theorem.

A perfect Bayesian equilibrium consists of beliefs and strategies that support one another in equilibrium. Given the beliefs and the other players' strategies, each player's strategy is optimal at every node in the game and all beliefs are consistent with the equilibrium strategies along the equilibrium path.

The addition of beliefs reinforces the tie between game theory and decision theory. Expected utility calculations model decisions in the sequence of the game. Beliefs add a concept that seems very natural for analyzing games. We can analyze how beliefs and actions are related in equilibrium. We can trace how actions change beliefs and how beliefs lead to actions in a perfect Bayesian equilibrium. Beliefs provide an intuitive way to discuss how players deal with incomplete information and incorporate a form of learning into a game.

The difficulty of the material steps up here. Like most of game theory, the mathematics are not difficult, generally requiring just algebra. But careful attention to the mathematics is required here even though the ideas are quite simple and intuitive. Translating those ideas into a careful formal argument requires close attention to the mathematical details. Calculations of both expected utility and Bayesian updating are necessary to find equilibria. These calculations are not difficult, but there is no substitute for them. Further, strategic logic can be complex. Figuring out the equation that expresses the correct strategic calculation is often more difficult than solving that equation. Formal solutions are necessary here precisely because intuition alone is often wrong. The discipline of formalization is needed to structure and shape our intuition.

Working through these models compels us to think carefully about the incentives the players face and what strategies can best achieve their goals.

This chapter begins by reviewing Bayes's Theorem. Bayes's Theorem is essential for updating beliefs in a perfect Bayesian equilibrium. I follow Bayes's Theorem with an example of Bayesian decision theory, the preference for biased information. Bayesian decision theory links expected utility calculations and Bayesian updating of beliefs to see how new information can change decisions. I then introduce beliefs with a classic example from Selten 1975. I define perfect Bayesian equilibrium next. The chapter ends with an example drawn from nuclear deterrence.

Bayes's Theorem*

Deciders are often uncertain about the consequences of their actions. We represent their uncertainty by subjective probabilities over the possible states of the world. These probabilities represent a decider's degree of belief about the likelihood of each different state. The higher the subjective probability of a state, the more likely is the decider to believe that state is the true state of the world.

These beliefs should change as a decider gains new information about the state of the world. Sometimes, that information may convince the decider about the true state of the world. If event E can happen only when A is the state of the world, then observing E is sufficient to conclude that A is the state of the world. But new information rarely allows such strong conclusions. Typically, an event could occur under several different states of the world with differing probabilities. Actors use the probabilities of an observed event's occurring given each possible state to update their probabilities about the state of the world. The subjective probabilities of each state before consideration of new information are called **prior (or initial) beliefs (or probabilities)**. Updating considers both the prior beliefs and the probabilities that the event will occur given each state. The updated beliefs are called **posterior beliefs (or probabilities)**. Some events are more likely under some states of the world than under others. Observing an event provides information that increases beliefs about states of the world where it is more likely to occur.

Beliefs are conditional probabilities. Let A be a state of the world and B an event. The probability of B given A, written $p(B|A)$, specifies the likelihood that B will occur given that A is the state of the world. Bayes's Theorem uses the conditional probabilities of events given states to deduce the conditional probabilities of states given events. For instance, the latter would be the conditional probability of A given B, written $p(A|B)$.

*This section uses conditional probabilities.

Theorem (Bayes's Theorem): Let $(A_i)_{i=1}^n$ be the set of states of the world, and B an event. Then

$$p(A_i|B) = \frac{p(A_i)p(B|A_i)}{\sum_{i=1}^{n} p(A_i)p(B|A_i)}$$

If there are only two states of the world, A and not A (abbreviated $\sim$ A), the above formula simplifies to

$$p(A|B) = \frac{p(A)p(B|A)}{p(A)p(B|A) + p(\sim A)p(B|\sim A)}$$

Bayes's Theorem determines the posterior probability of a state by calculating the probability that both the event and the state will occur and dividing it by the probability that the event will occur regardless of state (determined by summing across all states). An event, B in the formula, changes beliefs about the underlying state of the world, A in the formula, because different states produce different probabilities of the event's occurring. We learn about the state of the world by observing events that are more likely to occur under one state than under others. If an event is equally likely under all states, prior beliefs will not change after observing the event. Events with greater differences in probability given each state discriminate more effectively across the states than events with small differences.

Bayes's Theorem follows directly from the definition of a conditional probability. The probability of A given B, written $p(A|B)$, is the probability of (A and B) divided by the probability of B, p(A and B)/p(B). The probability of (A and B) is $p(A)p(B|A)$, from the definition of the conditional probability of B given A, $p(B|A)$ = p(A and B)/p(A). The probability of B is the sum of the probabilities that (A and B) occur and that [(not A) and B] occur. These probabilities are $p(A)p(B|A)$ and $p(\sim A)p(B|\sim A)$, respectively. Substituting these probabilities into the conditional probability of A given B gives us Bayes's Theorem.

Example: Commissioner Crackdown wants to rid baseball of all players using drugs through drug testing. A particular test detects drug use successfully 90 percent of the time, but gives a false positive (i.e., a player tests positive even though that player has not used drugs) 10 percent of the time. If 10 percent of all players use drugs, what is the probability that a randomly selected player who tests positive is using drugs?

Let D signify that a player uses drugs, ~D signify that a player does not use drugs, and + signify that a player had a positive test result. We want to know p(D|+), the probability that a player uses drugs given that that player has tested positive.

$$p(D|+) = \frac{p(D)p(+|D)}{p(D)p(+|D) + p(\sim D)p(+|\sim D)} = \frac{(.1)(.9)}{(.1)(.9) + (.9)(.1)} = .5.$$

There is a 50 percent chance that a player testing positive has used drugs.

Example: In a certain city, 30 percent of the people are conservatives, 50 percent are liberals, and 20 percent are independents. Records show that in the latest election, 65 percent of the conservatives, 82 percent of the liberals, and 50 percent of the independents voted. If a person in the city is selected at random and it is learned that he or she did not vote in the last election, what is the probability that he or she is a liberal?

We want to know p(L|~v), where L signifies that the voter is a liberal and ~v signifies that he or she did not vote.

$$p(L|\sim v) = \frac{p(L)p(\sim v|L)}{p(C)p(\sim v|C) + p(L)p(\sim v|L) + p(I)p(\sim v|I)}$$
$$= \frac{(.5)(.18)}{(.3)(.35) + (.5)(.18) + (.2)(.5)} = \frac{18}{59}.$$

Exercise 6.1: A bag contains a thousand coins. One of the coins is badly loaded, so that it comes up heads $\frac{3}{4}$ of the time. A coin is drawn at random. What is the probability that it is the loaded coin if it is flipped and turns up heads without fail

a) three times in a row?

b) ten times in a row?

c) twenty times in a row?

In game theory, the states are the other players' strategies, and the events are the moves observed. If one player knows another player's strategy, it can predict all of the other player's future moves (up to any randomization through mixed strategies). A player's moves can reveal its strategy to the other players. Mixed strategies lead to partial, rather than total, revelation of strategy. Other players can use the information in the observed moves to infer the strategy of the first players. Those other players can then adjust their own strategies in response. Bayes's Theorem is the formal tool used to model this updating in a game. Each player has an initial probability distribution over the other players' pure strategies that reflects its beliefs about what they will do. Each strategy specifies a probability for each action at each node (pure strategies give probabilities of 0 and 1 for each action). After observing a move by another player, a player uses its prior beliefs, the set of possible strategies, and Bayes's Theorem to calculate new probabilities for each strategy of the moving player.

The Preference for Biased Information

Bayesian decision theory gives us a way to explore how information affects choices. Does new information change a decider's choice from the one it would make without that information? Bayes's Theorem allows us to update the decider's subjective probability distribution and thus determine if its decision changes. I explore a related question in this section, the choice among different sources of information. Given a choice among possible sources of information, which source is most likely to affect a decision? If consulting sources of information is costly, which sources should be consulted? The best source is the one that is most likely to shift one's decision from what would be chosen in the absence of new information. The following model is a simplification of Calvert 1985.

Consider the position of a decider choosing between two courses of action, A_1 and A_2, in the face of uncertainty about the desirability of each course of action. The actual desirability of each course of action, denoted by x_1 and x_2, respectively, is either 0 or 1. The decider's payoff is the desirability of the chosen action: x_1 if A_1 is chosen or x_2 if A_2 is chosen. The actual values of x_1 and x_2 are not observed by the decider. Instead, it can consult an advisor who produces a recommendation about the desirability of each course of action based on the actual desirability of each.

The decider believes x_1 is better before receiving any advice. We represent this in the decider's prior beliefs. It believes that A_1 is more likely to produce a desirable outcome than A_2. This bias is best thought of as the decider's existing belief that A_1 is more effective than A_2. This bias may be an understanding that A_1 is generally a better option than A_2. Extensive experience with both options in prior settings could create such an understanding. It should not be thought of as a blind prejudice of the decider. The decider's initial beliefs are as follows:

$$p(x_1 = 1) = \tfrac{2}{3} \qquad p(x_1 = 0) = \tfrac{1}{3}$$

$$p(x_2 = 1) = \tfrac{1}{3} \qquad p(x_2 = 0) = \tfrac{2}{3}$$

An advisor can provide a "good" or "bad" recommendation for each alternative after observing its true desirability. Advisors are not strategic actors. An advisor produces recommendations based on the desirability of an action and a built-in bias, α, it has in favor of A_1 and against A_2. Any advisor makes some errors in its recommendations. Advisors sometimes say that an option is "bad" when $x_i = 1$ and that it is "good" when $x_i = 0$ for $i = 1, 2$. Formally, we have the following probabilities for recommendations:

$$p(A_1 \text{ good}|x_1 = 1) = \left(\tfrac{2}{3}\right)^{\frac{1}{\alpha}} \qquad p(A_1 \text{ good}|x_1 = 0) = \left(\tfrac{1}{3}\right)^{\frac{1}{\alpha}}$$

$$p(A_2 \text{ good}|x_2 = 1) = \left(\tfrac{2}{3}\right)^{\alpha} \qquad p(A_2 \text{ good}|x_2 = 0) = \left(\tfrac{1}{3}\right)^{\alpha}$$

The probabilities of bad recommendations are 1− (probability of a good recommendation).

The parameter α gives an advisor's bias in favor of A_1 and against A_2. If $\alpha = 1$, the advisor gives neutral recommendations. The probability of a "good" recommendation by an unbiased advisor is $\frac{2}{3}$ and the probability of a "bad" recommendation is $\frac{1}{3}$. As $\alpha > 1$ increases, the advisor is more likely to say that A_1 is "good" regardless of the true value of x_1 and less likely to say that A_2 is "good." However, biased advisors are honest in the sense that they are more likely to say an option A_i is "good" when $x_i = 1$ than when $x_i = 0$ for both options.

We want to know what action the decider selects after receiving advice from the different advisors. If collecting advice is costly, then the decider benefits from advice only when that advice convinces it to change its decision. We compare the advice from two possible advisors, one unbiased and one biased in favor of A_1. For each possible piece of advice, we calculate the decider's updated distribution of the efficacy of each action. It chooses the action with the higher expected outcome.

Consider the unbiased advisor first. If the unbiased advisor recommends that A_1 is "good," we calculate the decider's posterior probabilities for x_1. Bayes's Theorem is used as follows to calculate these posterior probabilities:

$$\begin{aligned} p(x_1 &= 1|A_1 \text{ good}) \\ &= \frac{p(x_1 = 1)\,p(A_1 \text{ good}|x_1 = 1)}{p(x_1 = 1)\,p(A_1 \text{ good}|x_1 = 1) + p(x_1 = 0)\,p(A_1 \text{ good}|x_1 = 0)} \\ &= \frac{(\frac{2}{3})(\frac{2}{3})}{(\frac{2}{3})(\frac{2}{3}) + (\frac{1}{3})(\frac{1}{3})} = \frac{4}{5}. \end{aligned}$$

The probability that $x_1 = 0$ given that the unbiased advisor recommends that A_1 is "good" is $1 -$ (the probability above) $= \frac{1}{5}$.

With the posterior probability distribution, we calculate the decider's expectation for choosing A_1 after receiving a "good" recommendation. We sum the value of each possible outcome by the probability of its occurring after the decider receives the unbiased advisor's recommendation that A_1 is "good":

$$E(A_1|A_1 \text{ good}) = p(x_1 = 1|A_1 \text{ good})x_1 + p(x_1 = 0|A_1 \text{ good})x_1$$

$$= \left(\frac{4}{5}\right)(1) + \left(\frac{1}{5}\right)(0) = \frac{4}{5}.$$

We calculate the decider's expectation for choosing each action after receiving each possible recommendation about that action in parallel fashion. Calculate the posterior distribution after receiving each recommendation, and use those probabilities to calculate an expected value. These three expectations are as follows:

$$E(A_1|A_1 \text{ bad}) = \tfrac{1}{2} \quad E(A_2|A_2 \text{ good}) = \tfrac{1}{2} \quad E(A_2|A_2 \text{ bad}) = \tfrac{1}{5}$$

Exercise 6.2: Verify that each of the three expectations above is correct.

Because the decider can choose only one course of action, it always chooses A_1. Its expected utility for choosing A_1 is always at least as great as that for choosing A_2, even if the neutral advisor advises that A_1 is "bad" and A_2 "good." If advice is costly, the decider should never consult the neutral advisor. Advice from the neutral advisor never leads the decider to change its chosen action from its prior belief. Why pay for advice that makes no difference?

But what about the biased advisor? Let $\alpha = 2$. Once again, we calculate the decider's expectation for each course of action after receiving each type of recommendation from the biased advisor. For a "good" recommendation for A_1, we have the following calculation for the decider's belief about the efficacy of A_1:

$$p(x_1 = 1|A_1 \text{ good})$$

$$= \frac{p(x_1 = 1)p(A_1 \text{ good}|x_1 = 1)}{p(x_1 = 1)p(A_1 \text{ good}|x_1 = 1) + p(x_1 = 0)p(A_1 \text{ good}|x_1 = 0)}$$

$$= \frac{(\frac{2}{3})(\frac{2}{3})^{\frac{1}{2}}}{(\frac{2}{3})(\frac{2}{3})^{\frac{1}{2}} + (\frac{1}{3})(\frac{1}{3})^{\frac{1}{2}}} = \frac{2\sqrt{2}}{2\sqrt{2} + 1} \approx .74.$$

With this probability, we can calculate the decider's expected utility for choosing A_1 after it receives a "good" recommendation:

$$E(A_1|A_1 \text{ good}) = p(x_1 = 1|A_1 \text{ good})x_1 + p(x_1 = 0|A_1 \text{ good})x_1$$
$$= \left(\frac{2\sqrt{2}}{2\sqrt{2}+1}\right)(1) + \left(\frac{1}{2\sqrt{2}+1}\right)(0) = \frac{2\sqrt{2}}{2\sqrt{2}+1} \approx .74.$$

For a good recommendation for A_2, the calculation is similar, as follows:

$$p(x_2 = 1|A_2 \text{ good})$$
$$= \frac{p(x_2 = 1)p(A_2 \text{ good}|x_2 = 1)}{p(x_2 = 1)p(A_2 \text{ good}|x_2 = 1) + p(x_2 = 0)p(A_2 \text{ good}|x_2 = 0)}$$
$$= \frac{(\frac{1}{3})(\frac{2}{3})^2}{(\frac{1}{3})(\frac{2}{3})^2 + (\frac{2}{3})(\frac{1}{3})^2} = \frac{2}{3},$$

so

$$E(A_2|A_2 \text{ good}) = p(x_2 = 1|A_2 \text{ good})x_2 + p(x_2 = 0|A_2 \text{ bad})x_2$$
$$= (\tfrac{2}{3})(1) + (\tfrac{1}{3})(0) = \tfrac{2}{3}.$$

The following results are found by carrying out the calculations for the remaining two cases:

$$E(A_1|A_1 \text{ bad}) = \frac{2(\sqrt{3} - \sqrt{2})}{3\sqrt{3} - 2\sqrt{2} - 1} \approx .46,$$

and

$$E(A_2|A_2 \text{ bad}) = \tfrac{5}{21}.$$

Exercise 6.3: Verify that each of the two expectations above is correct.

The biased advisor can produce decisive advice. The decider will choose A_2 if the biased advisor says A_1 is "bad" and A_2 is "good". The biased advice may be worth paying for (depending on its price). This result may seem strange—the best advisors may be those who share the same biases as the decider. The practical advice is to surround yourself with advisors who share your biases but still retain some integrity. The intuition behind this result is that people discount different sources of information when they know the biases of those sources. The biased source is more useful than the neutral source because it is unlikely to say that A_1 is "bad" and A_2 is "good." When it does, the decider's beliefs about the value of both options shift dramatically. That recommendation is sufficient to overwhelm the initial bias of the decider in favor of A_1 and cause it to choose A_2. Because the biased advisor rarely produces such a recommendation, that recommendation carries much weight in the eyes of the decider. The neutral source, in a sense, sends too many signals. The decider discounts its recommendations for A_2 and against A_1 because such signals are common. Those recommendations from the neutral source are sufficiently frequent that they fail to convince the decider that A_1 is a bad option compared to A_2. The amount of information such signals convey is insufficient to overcome the decider's existing bias in favor of A_1.

This result is particularly interesting because it goes against common sense. Psychological studies show that individuals often rely on sources of information that share the individual's biases–behavior referred to as "bolstering." Some have argued that bolstering is evidence that individuals are irrational because "rational" actors should look for neutral sources of information. This model suggests that the rational selection of information sources is not so simple. Biased sources may often be the best sources because advice against their biases is a clear signal to change actions. During the Vietnam War, it was no surprise to President Johnson that Senator Fulbright was opposed to the war. Consequently, Fulbright's opposition to the war carried little weight with Johnson. But when Robert McNamara came out against the war in 1967, the change in position by an original "hawk" in favor of the war had a strong effect on Johnson's evaluation of the war. Of course, this observation requires that the biased source must retain some honesty. A flunky who always provides an optimistic review of the options is useless.

It is not clear how general is the preference for biased information. This result depends upon the specific assumptions of this model. Changing some of the details of the model makes the unbiased source preferable. However, the intuition does seem general. Consider sources with a bias opposite from the decider's preexisting judgment. When you know a source of information is opposed to your own inclination, you expect the source will produce recommendations against your bias. One should rationally discount recommendations from such a source; it is biased. Any unusual recommendation from that source merely reinforces your confidence in your existing bias. Individuals may be quite rational when they select sources of information that share their own biases. Only those sources can produce evidence that will convince them to change their position on the options.

Perfect Bayesian Equilibria

Subgame perfection forces players to be rational in every subgame. But not every move begins a proper subgame, and subgame perfection cannot judge the rationality of behavior at such moves. For example, no proper subgame can begin at an information set that includes more than one node. A player could make a noncredible threat at that information set and use that threat to deter the other player at a preceding node. How can we judge whether moves at such information sets are rational?

Perfect Bayesian equilibrium resolves this problem by introducing the concept of beliefs. When a player reaches a singleton information set, it knows the entire history of the game to that point. It decides which move is optimal by using the other players' strategies to predict their future moves, and thus predict the outcome of each possible move. It calculates its expected utility for each available move to choose its move. When a player reaches an information set with multiple nodes, its optimal move often varies with the node reached. A move may be optimal from one node but not from another. We cannot be certain which move is optimal from that information set because we do not know at which node the player is.

Beliefs solve this problem by allowing us to weigh the different nodes in an information set, and then calculate the player's expected utility from that information set. A player's beliefs are represented by a probability distribution over the nodes in an information set. For a given information set, they specify the probability that the player is at each node if the information set is reached. The player's expected utility for each available move is calculated by using these probabilities. We weigh the expected utility of each available action from each node in the information set by the player's belief that it is at that node, and then sum across all nodes in the information set. A player chooses the action that maximizes its expected utility.

Beliefs for an information set capture the players' hypotheses about the current state of the game. Beliefs are required to be consistent with equilibrium strategies wherever possible. On the equilibrium path, beliefs are the probabilities each node will be reached in the equilibrium. Off the equilibrium path, beliefs reflect hypotheses about what defections from the equilibrium led to those nodes. Beliefs reflect judgments about both the outcomes of prior, but still secret, chance moves and prior, yet unknown, strategy choices of the other players. The players use one another's strategies to predict the consequences of their own moves in any form of equilibrium. A player's judgments about the other players' strategies are captured in its beliefs and moves. Perfect Bayesian equilibria, then, create a symbiotic relationship between strategies and beliefs; in equilibrium, strategies are optimal given the beliefs, and the beliefs are consistent with the strategies.

Before formalizing this notion of equilibrium, I present an example of how beliefs can address the rationality of moves in games with information sets with multiple nodes.

Example: Consider the game in Figure 6.1 from Selten 1975. One Nash equilibrium of this game is (D;a;*L*). Each player's move is a

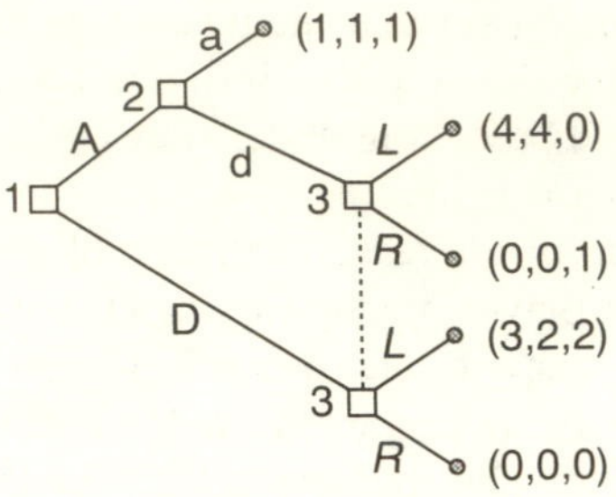

Figure 6.1 Selten's Game

best reply on the equilibrium path. If Player 2 will play a and Player 3 will play *L*, then Player 1 prefers D to A. D produces a payoff of 3 for him, whereas A gives him a payoff of 1. If Player 1 plays D, Player 2's move is off the equilibrium path. In a Nash equilibrium, any move off the equilibrium path is a best reply. Player 3's move is optimal for her if Player 1 plays D. Then Player 3 will have to move, and she will be at her lower node. *L* produces a payoff of 2 for Player 3, while *R* produces 0 for her.

Consider Player 2's position in this Nash equilibrium. If Player 2 has to make a move, then Player 1 must have played A. Player 2's move should be based solely on her expectation about Player 3's move. If Player 3 plays *L* with probability greater than $\frac{1}{4}$, Player 2 should play d instead of a. But (D;d;*L*) is not a Nash equilibrium, Player 1 wants to change his strategy from D to A, leading Player 3 to change from *L* to *R*, and so on. However, Player 2 never plays a in (D;a;*L*), so playing a is rational as a Nash equilibrium. Subgame perfection does not eliminate this equilibrium because the game fragment starting at Player 2's move is not a subgame—it breaks Player 3's information set.

The other Nash equilibrium to this game is {A;a;[p*L*, (1 − p)*R*]}, with $p < \frac{1}{4}$. Player 3 credibly threatens Players 1 and 2 by playing *R* to force them to play A and a in this equilibrium. These strategies form a Nash equilibrium. If Player 2 plays a and Player 3 plays *L* with probability $p < \frac{1}{4}$, Player 1 prefers A to D. A secures him a payoff of 1, while D leads to a payoff of 3p for him. If Player 1 plays A and Player 3 plays *R* with probability $p < \frac{1}{4}$, a is Player 2's best reply. Her move is now on the equilibrium path. Choosing a gives her a payoff of 1, while d gives her a payoff of 4p, which is less than 1. Player 3's move is off the equilibrium path; when Players 1 and 2 play A and a, Player 3 never makes a move. Any move by Player 3 can be part of a Nash equilibrium.

Players 1 and 2 can collaborate to take advantage of Player 3's lack of knowledge of their moves in this game. If they can convince Player 3 to play *L* in the hope of obtaining the (3,2,2) outcome, they can exploit Player 3's inability to verify their moves and play A and d, leading to the (4,4,0) outcome. Consequently, Player 3 must play it safe by playing *R*, which keeps Players 1 and 2 honest. All three players are hurt by Player 3's lack of information. If we break Player 3's information set so that Player 3 can verify the prior moves of Players 1 and 2, this game has a Pareto-superior solution to the second Nash equilibrium.

> Exercise 6.4: Verify that (D;a;*R*,*L*) is a subgame-perfect equilibrium for the game in Figure 6.1 if Player 3's information set is broken into separate nodes. (Note: The strategy above gives Player 3's moves for both nodes—*R* at the upper node and *L* at the lower node.)

The (D;a;*L*) equilibrium solves the information problem by allowing Player 2 to make a noncredible commitment to play a to Player 3. But Players 1 and 2 have an incentive to undermine that commitment, and Player 3 cannot verify that they have honored or broken that commitment. Why should Player 3 believe Player 2's commitment? To capture the intuition here, we introduce the concept of beliefs. We can then calculate how Player 3's beliefs about the moves of Players 1 and 2 drive her own move.

> **Definition**: A set of **beliefs**, μ, for a game is a set of probability distributions with one distribution for each information set in the game.

Beliefs allow us to calculate expected utilities for each possible choice in a game. A belief for a given node is the conditional probability that the node is reached if the information set containing the node is reached during play of the game. Subgame perfection allows us to examine the rationality of moves within proper subgames but is powerless in the face of an information set that cannot be divided into a proper subgame. A set of beliefs specifies for each information set the probability that the player is at a given node in the information set for every node in the information set. Beliefs at a singleton information set must equal 1 by the laws of probability. For an information set with multiple nodes, the sum of the probabilities of all nodes in that information set must be 1. A player's expected utility is calculated by weighing its expected utility for each action at every node in the information set by the actor's belief that it is at that node. Actors then maximize expected utility at every information set, using their beliefs.

> Example: Return to the game in Figure 6.1 and examine the rationality of the Nash equilibrium (D;a;*L*). Assume that Player 3's

belief that she is at her upper node is $\frac{2}{3}$ and her belief that she is at her lower node is $\frac{1}{3}$. The beliefs of Players 1 and 2 are both 1 because they have only singleton information sets. For Player 3, calculate expected utilities for each move given the above beliefs:

$$u(\text{Play } L) = (\tfrac{2}{3})(0) + (\tfrac{1}{3})(2) = \tfrac{2}{3};$$

$$u(\text{Play } R) = (\tfrac{2}{3})(1) + (\tfrac{1}{3})(0) = \tfrac{2}{3}.$$

Player 3 is indifferent between *L* and *R* and any mixed strategy of the two given these beliefs. Here, we choose the pure strategy *L*. Player 3 prefers *L* to *R* whenever her belief that she is at the lower node if her information set is reached is greater than $\frac{1}{3}$. There is a wide range of beliefs for which Player 3 prefers *L* to *R*.

One of the advantages of beliefs is that we can now check the rationality of any move in a candidate equilibrium, including those that are not contained in a proper subgame. Player 2's move of a was problematic before; now we can check whether that move is rational. The technique is similar to backwards induction. We trace the likely consequences of each of Player 2's available moves, and then calculate the expected utility of each. If Player 2 chooses a, she receives a payoff of 1. If she chooses d, Player 3 will choose *L*, and Player 2 receives a payoff of 4. Clearly, Player 2 prefers d to a. Thus a is not a rational move once beliefs allow us to carry out backwards induction through information sets.

For Player 1, the utilities of playing A and D are 1 and 3, respectively. (Recall that Player 2 plays a in the candidate equilibrium.) Player 1's move is rational given the other players' moves in the candidate equilibrium. Player 1's beliefs, like Player 2's, are irrelevant in calculating his expected utility because his information set is a singleton. However, Player 2 prefers d to a once beliefs allow us to perform a backwards induction from all information sets. Adding beliefs for Player 3 did not change the rationality of her move. Instead, this addition allowed us to see that Player 2's move was not rational. Beliefs permit us to evaluate all moves using expected utility calculations. I now define "rationality" with beliefs.

Definition: A pair of beliefs and strategies is **sequentially rational** iff from each information set, the moving player's strategy maximizes its expected utility for the remainder of the game given its beliefs and all players' strategies.

Exercise 6.5: Verify that (A;a;*R*) is sequentially rational for the game in Figure 6.1 for any set of beliefs where Player 3 places at least probability $\frac{2}{3}$ that she is at her upper node if her information set is reached.

We can describe the idea behind beliefs intuitively. A player who is uncertain about prior moves (i.e., at an information set with multiple nodes) creates hypotheses about those prior moves. I say hypotheses here because the beliefs for one information set may involve speculation about prior, unobserved moves by several players, including moves by Chance. Player 3's beliefs at such a point depend upon conjectures about what both of the other players have done. These hypotheses could assert that one particular node has been reached in the information set. The beliefs then must place probability 1 on a node in the information set. They might assume that one of several nodes has been reached. Beliefs summarize what the player thinks has happened in the game before the current information set.

What beliefs are reasonable in the context of a given equilibrium? The beliefs should be based on the chance moves in the game and the other players' moves in the equilibrium whenever possible. Bayes's Theorem provides the mechanism for updating probabilities, and beliefs are just sets of conditional probabilities across the nodes of different information sets. The hypotheses a player uses to determine its beliefs should be based on the expectation of equilibrium behavior by the other players. As in Nash equilibrium, we assume that the players share a common conjecture that they are playing their equilibrium strategies. The players (and we) can calculate the probability that each node is reached from those equilibrium strategies. At a minimum, the beliefs must equal these conditional probabilities along the equilibrium path. Otherwise, the players' beliefs would diverge from their expectations about one another's behavior.

Example: Return yet again to the game in Figure 6.1. What beliefs does the (D;a;*L*) equilibrium produce for Player 3? We calculate the chance that her upper node is reached given that her information set is reached in this equilibrium. Player 3's upper node is reached if Player 1 plays A and then Player 2 plays d; her lower node is reached if Player 1 plays D. Denote "Player 3's upper node reached" by 3's un and "Player 3's information set reached" by 3's inf. We use Bayes's Theorem to calculate the probability that Player 3's upper node is reached if her information set is reached as follows:

$$p(\text{3's un}|\text{3's inf}) = \frac{p(A,d)p(\text{3's inf}|A,d)}{p(A,d)p(\text{3's inf}|A,d) + p(D)p(\text{3's inf}|D)}$$

$$= \frac{(0)(1)}{(0)(1) + (1)(1)} = 0$$

Player 3 should not believe that she is at her upper node if her information set is reached; she must believe that she is at the lower node. When Player 1 plays D and Player 2 is committed to playing a, the only way Player 3's information set can be reached is her lower node.

Along the equilibrium path, we can calculate beliefs. But we cannot make such a calculation when a player must make a decision at an information set that has probability zero in an equilibrium. Instead, we allow the players to create a plausible hypothesis to explain what has happened. Something that should not happen in equilibrium has happened, and the players need some hypothesis to explain the defection. Using this hypothesis, each player can maximize its expected utility and continue playing. For now, we place minimal restrictions on such hypotheses.

> **Definition**: A **perfect Bayesian equilibrium** is a belief-strategy pairing such that the strategies are sequentially rational given the beliefs and the beliefs are calculated from the equilibrium strategies by means of Bayes's Theorem whenever possible.

I am being vague deliberately about beliefs off the equilibrium path when I say "whenever possible." Rather than stating technical definitions of what restrictions are placed on beliefs off the equilibrium path in perfect Bayesian equilibria, I discuss some of the issues here. First, the players continue to use the equilibrium strategies to update their beliefs after moves off the equilibrium path. Defection does not lead the players to abandon the common conjecture of equilibrium behavior. Instead, they assume that one defection does not increase the chance that other players will play "irrationally" off the equilibrium path. Second, in games with three or more players, we assume that if one player defects from its equilibrium strategy, the other players use the same conjecture about its defection. If they have the same beliefs prior to the defection, they must have identical beliefs after the defection. Third, players "cannot signal what they do not know." A defection by Player 1 does not lead Player 2 to change her beliefs about what Player 3 has done before 1's defection.

Perfect Bayesian equilibria, like Nash and subgame-perfect equilibria, always exist in mixed strategies.

> **Theorem**: Every finite n-person game has at least one perfect Bayesian equilibrium in mixed strategies.

This theorem is true because finite games always have perfect equilibria, and any perfect equilibrium is also perfect Bayesian.

There is no easy method for finding perfect Bayesian equilibria. I find the best technique is to think about how the game should be played, formulate a possible equilibrium, and check to see if the strategies are optimal given the beliefs and the beliefs follow from the strategies along the equilibrium path. Backwards induction can be very helpful in seeing what strategies might be in equilibrium and what beliefs are needed to sustain them. Alternatively, look for Nash equilibria, determine what beliefs follow along the equilibrium path, and see if the strategies are sequentially rational given the beliefs.

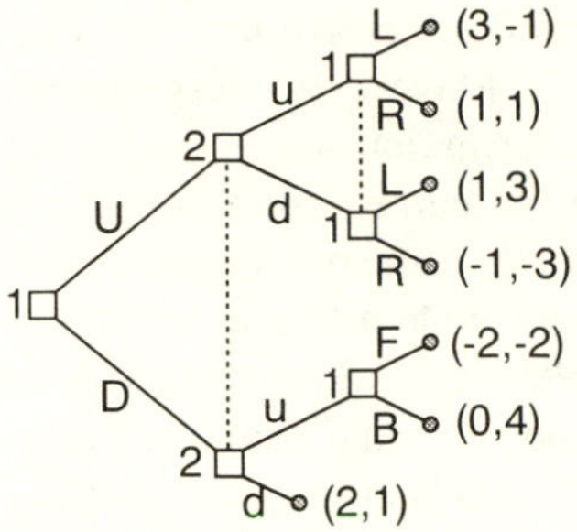

Figure 6.2 An Example of Perfect Bayesian Equilibrium

Example: Find the perfect Bayesian equilibria of the game in Figure 6.2. Specify a belief-strategy pair for this game as follows: (Player 1's move in the first node, Player 1's move in the upper information set, Player 1's move in the lower branch; Player 2's move: Player 1's belief that he is at the upper node of his information set in the upper branch if that information set is reached; Player 2's belief that she is at the upper node of her information set). We do not need to specify the beliefs for the singleton information sets. In general, I state strategies in a perfect Bayesian equilibrium before the beliefs. Strategies are specified using the same notation as for a Nash equilibrium; Player 1's complete strategy followed by the other players' strategies in order. The players' beliefs are listed after a colon; the beliefs of each player are separated from those of the other player(s) by semicolons. Individual moves within a player's strategy and beliefs for each information set within a player's set of beliefs are separated by commas.

Begin the analysis in the lower branch. Here, we have a classic example of subgame perfection. Player 1 would like to use the threat of F to force Player 2 to play d, but the threat is not credible. In equilibrium, Player 1 must play B at his lower node, and so Player 2 wants to play u if she is at her lower node.

In the upper branch, L is a dominant strategy for Player 1. Regardless of his beliefs at that information set, he prefers to play L. To see this, let p be Player 1's belief that he is at the upper node of the information set. Calculate expected utilities for both possible moves:

$$u(\text{Play L}) = p(3) + (1 - p)(1) = 1 + 2p;$$

$$u(\text{Play R}) = p(1) + (1 - p)(-1) = -1 + 2p$$

Playing L is better for any possible value of p. Anticipating that Player 1 will play L, Player 2 prefers playing d if she is at the upper node of her information set.

Now the trick in the game comes in—Player 2 does not know which node she is at when she must make her decision. She prefers playing d at the upper node and u at the lower node. We look for beliefs that make Player 2 indifferent between playing u and d, allowing her to employ a mixed strategy. Let q be Player 2's belief she is at the upper node. Then we have the following when she is indifferent between playing u and d:

$$\begin{aligned} u(\text{Play u}) &= u(\text{Play d}); \\ q(-1) + (1-q)(4) &= q(3) + (1-q)(1) \\ q &= \tfrac{3}{7}. \end{aligned}$$

Note that Player 2 anticipates Player 1's future moves when she calculates her utility for each move. The consequences of playing u is the (3,−1) outcome from the upper node because Player 1 will play L and the (0,4) outcome from the lower node because he will play B. If she chooses d, the outcomes will be (1,3) from her upper node and (2,1) from her lower node. If Player 2 believes she is at the upper node with probability $\frac{3}{7}$, then she is indifferent between playing u and d and can play any mixed strategy.

To produce these beliefs, Player 1 must play U with probability $\frac{3}{7}$ and D with probability $\frac{4}{7}$. Otherwise, Player 2's beliefs are not consistent with his equilibrium strategy. Because this information set must lie on the equilibrium path (both of Player 1's initial moves lead to Player 2's information set), Player 2's beliefs must be the same as the conditional probabilities each node is reached in equilibrium.

For Player 1 to mix his strategy in his first move, he must be indifferent between playing U and D. Player 2 can create this indifference by choosing a mixed strategy in her move. Let r be the probability that Player 2 chooses u in her move. Calculate Player 1's expected utilities for U and D and equate them:

$$\begin{aligned} u(\text{Play U}) &= u(\text{Play D}); \\ r(3) + (1-r)(1) &= r(0) + (1-r)(2) \\ r &= \tfrac{1}{4}. \end{aligned}$$

Once again, Player 1 anticipates Player 2's and his own future moves when calculating his utility for each strategy.

Putting all this together, $[(\frac{3}{7}U,\frac{4}{7}D),L,B;(\frac{1}{4}u,\frac{3}{4}d):\frac{1}{4};\frac{3}{7}]$ constitutes a perfect Bayesian equilibrium for this game. The beliefs follow directly from the strategies. Player 1 plays U with probability $\frac{3}{7}$ and D with probability $\frac{4}{7}$. Then Player 2's beliefs must be $\frac{3}{7}$ on the upper node and $\frac{4}{7}$ on the lower node. Similarly, Player 1's beliefs for his information set also follow directly from Player 2's strategy. In this game, Player 1 mixes his strategy to produce the beliefs that allow Player 2 to mix her strategy in a fashion that makes Player 1 indifferent at his first move, allowing him to mix his strategy. This interdependence of mixed strategies is common in these games. If either player deviates from the equilibrium strategy, the other player will take advantage of that defection.

Finally, we must check that no pure strategy equilibrium exists where Player 2 knows that she is at one of the two nodes in her information set. Player 1's moves later in the tree are fixed at L and B by the same logic as before. If Player 1 plays U for certain, Player 2 will believe she is at her upper node (consistency of beliefs again) and will play d. But then Player 1 would prefer to shift from U to D, so (U,L,B;d:1;0) is not a perfect Bayesian equilibrium. Similarly, (D,L,B;u:0;1) is not a perfect Bayesian equilibrium because Player 1 would like to change from D to U. If he does, Player 2 wants to change to d.

Beliefs allow us to judge the sequential rationality of moves from information sets with multiple nodes. In this example, Player 2's optimal move from her information set depends on her beliefs. In the example in Figure 6.1, beliefs allowed us to judge the rationality of Player 2's move at a singleton information set before Player 3's information set with multiple nodes. Sequential rationality judges the rationality of all moves in a game.

<u>Exercise 6.6</u>: For each of the Nash equilibria in Exercise 5.2 (page 130), determine which are perfect Bayesian equilibria. Find the beliefs that support each perfect Bayesian equilibrium.

<u>Exercise 6.7</u>: Find the perfect Bayesian equilibria for each of the games in Figures 6.3 through 6.5. Be certain to specify the beliefs and the strategies off the equilibrium path as well as the equilibrium behavior.

a) Find the Nash equilibria of the game in Figure 6.3 and compare them to the perfect Bayesian equilibria.

b) C denotes a chance move in the game in Figure 6.4. Find the perfect Bayesian equilibria.

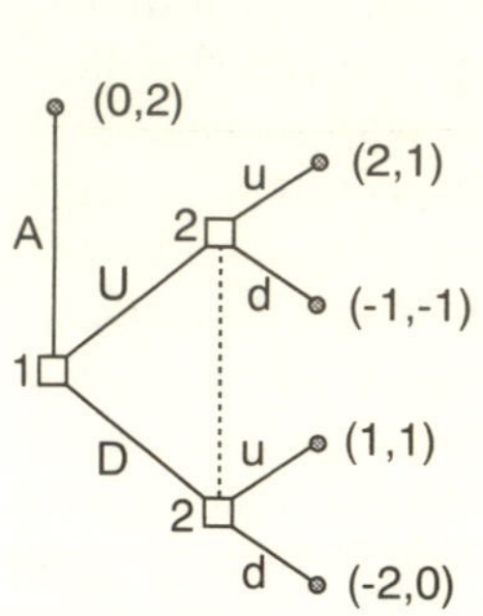

Figure 6.3 Exercise 6.7a

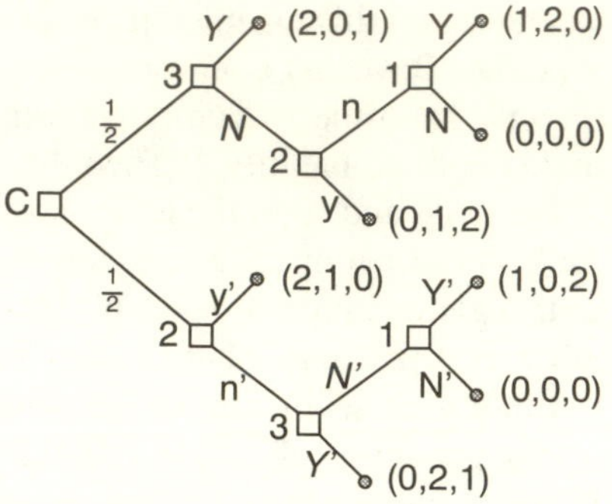

Figure 6.4 Exercise 6.7b

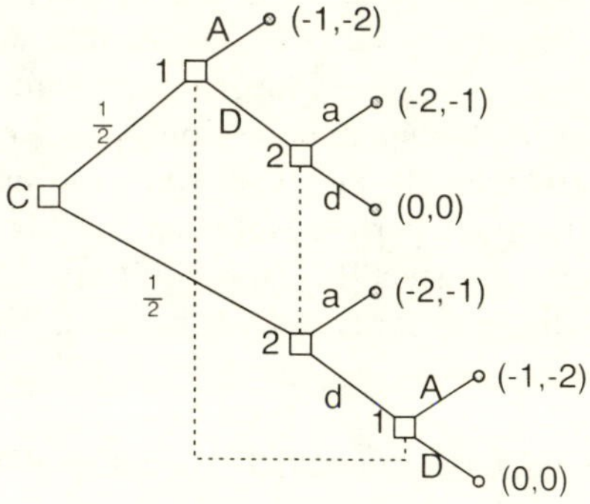

Figure 6.5 Exercise 6.7c

c) Each player has only one information set in the game in Figure 6.5. Each must choose its move without knowing the chance move that determines which player moves first. Find the perfect Bayesian equilibria.

Nuclear Deterrence

I now turn to some simple analysis of the strategic questions in nuclear war. All responsible parties agree that nuclear war would be an unparalleled disaster, but under what conditions might a government think about the unthinkable? To set the scene, I present the following greatly simplified discussion of some issues in nuclear strategy drawn from Powell 1990.

Some rational leaders might consider launching a nuclear first strike if that strike would disarm the other side, preventing any response (assuming that long-run ecological damage would not impose serious costs on the striking side). But during the Cold War, both the United States and the former Soviet Union had nuclear arsenals that made a first strike that disarmed the other side highly improbable. From the mid-1960s on, each side had a secure second-strike capability; that is, both the United States and the Soviet Union could have responded to any initial nuclear strike with a devastating retaliatory strike, primarily from submarine-based missiles, but also from surviving land-based missiles. First strikes were deterred by this credible threat of retaliation. This case illustrates the general one: neither side will be willing to launch a first strike when such an attack will only lead to its own destruction through nuclear retaliation.

This conclusion has a disturbing side effect. It eliminates the use of nuclear weapons for extended deterrence—the protection of allies from external threats through nuclear threats. For example, during the Cold War, the United States threatened to use strategic nuclear weapons if the Soviet Union invaded Western Europe—but if such a nuclear first strike would necessarily have led to the devastation of the United States by Soviet nuclear retaliation, the threat of initiating nuclear war to defend Western Europe would not have been credible. For nuclear weapons to have political utility beyond the deterrence of nuclear war, both sides must believe there is some chance that nuclear war could start. Otherwise, the threat is hollow.

Schelling (1960) proposed one solution to this problem, the reciprocal fear of surprise attack.[1] Assume there is some advantage in striking first if nuclear war occurs: the side that strikes first is somewhat less devastated than the other. Both sides can still launch devastating second strikes. But it is better to strike first than second because the first strike takes out some of the other side's missiles. Each side might contemplate a first strike, not because it expected to win by attacking, but rather because it feared that the other side was preparing to attack and it wished to gain the first strike advantage for itself. These fears could build upon one another in a vicious circle, creating the reciprocal fear of surprise attack. Nuclear war might then be launched, not because either side thought it could win, but because each feared the other was about to launch an attack.

This argument places several restrictions on possible models. Neither side must know that the other side has committed itself to not attacking when it must decide whether to launch an attack itself. If neither side decides to attack, the status quo, the best outcome for both sides, should prevail. If a first strike is launched, the other side retaliates, but the side that strikes first suffers less. The game in Figure 6.6 is one model of the argument. The A and a actions are nuclear first-strike attacks, and the D and d actions delay the launching of a first strike. The a payoffs are for launching a first strike, and the r payoffs are for receiving such a strike and then retaliating. The difference between the two measures the first-strike advantage. The larger (r − a) is, the greater the advantage to striking first. If neither player attacks, the status quo holds—the 0 payoff. We assume that striking first is preferable to receiving a first strike, but that no nuclear war is preferable to any nuclear war (i.e., $0 > -a_1 > -r_1$

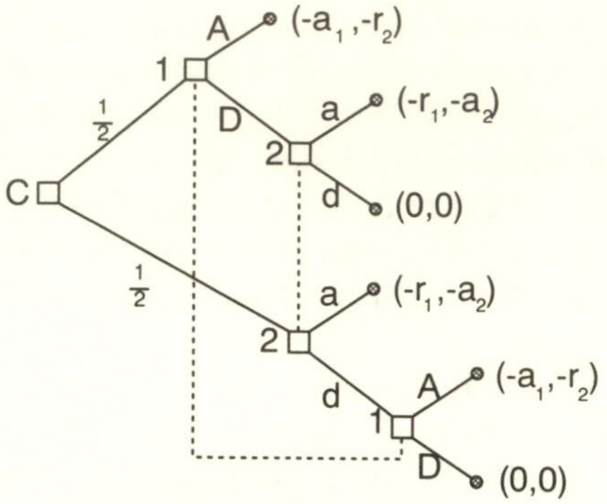

Figure 6.6 A Game with the Reciprocal Fear of Surprise Attack

and $0 > -a_2 > -r_2$). The chance move and information sets capture the idea that neither player knows whether the other is preparing a first strike when it must choose whether to launch a first strike of its own. Neither player knows whether delaying a strike ends the game at the status quo or gives the other player the opportunity to launch its own strike.

Specify an equilibrium of the game in Figure 6.6 by (Player 1's move; Player 2's move: Player 1's belief that he has the first move if his information set is reached; Player 2's belief that she has the first move if her information set is reached). The above game has three perfect Bayesian equilibria:

$$(\mathrm{A;a{:}1;1}), (\mathrm{D;d{:}}\tfrac{1}{2};\tfrac{1}{2}),$$

and

$$\left[\left(\frac{2a_2}{a_2 + r_2}\mathrm{A}, \frac{r_2 - a_2}{a_2 + r_2}\mathrm{D}\right); \left(\frac{2a_1}{a_1 + r_1}\mathrm{a}, \frac{r_1 - a_1}{a_1 + r_1}\mathrm{d}\right): \frac{a_1 + r_1}{2r_1}; \frac{a_2 + r_2}{2r_2}\right].$$

In the first equilibrium, each side attacks if it wins the draw because each knows that if it does not attack, the other side will attack in its turn. This equilibrium gives the reciprocal fear of surprise attack run amok. Each player attacks out of the fear that the other will attack if it does not. In the second equilibrium, neither side attacks because each knows that the other side will not attack in its turn. Here, we have "mutual confidence in restraint"; neither player launches an attack because they both believe the other player will not launch one.

To see that the first strategy-belief pair forms a perfect Bayesian equilibrium, consider a player's best reply given its beliefs and the other player's strategy. Call the player i for convenience. It believes that it has the initiative to strike first if it gets to move. Its utility for attacking is $-a_i$. If it delays its attack, the other player will attack, giving Player i a payoff of $-r_i$. Because $-a_i > -r_i$, it prefers attacking. Its beliefs follow from the players' strategies and Bayes's Theorem. Let "i mf" (or "j mf") stand for "Player i moves first" (or "Player j moves first"), which has probability $\frac{1}{2}$ based on the initial chance move. Let "i isr" stand for Player i's information set reached. If Player i has the first move, its information set is always reached, $p(\text{i isr}|\text{i mf}) = 1$. If Player j has the first move, i's information set is never reached in this equilibrium because j always attacks, $p(\text{i isr}|\text{j mf}) = 0$. Calculate the probability that Player i has the first move if its information set is reached:

$$p(\text{i mf}|\text{i isr}) = \frac{p(\text{i mf})p(\text{i isr}|\text{i mf})}{p(\text{i mf})p(\text{i isr}|\text{i mf}) + p(\text{j mf})p(\text{i isr}|\text{j mf})}$$

$$= \frac{(\frac{1}{2})(1)}{(\frac{1}{2})(1) + (\frac{1}{2})(0)} = 1.$$

In the third equilibrium, both sides play mixed strategies, with each side's probability of attacking increasing as the other side's first-strike advantage $(r - a)$ decreases. If the third equilibrium seems bizarre, remember that each side's probability of attacking is chosen to make the other side indifferent between attacking and not attacking. One might think that the greater the first-strike advantage, the more attractive a first strike. However, there are two motivations for attacking in this model: to gain the first-strike advantage and fear of the other player's attacking in turn. The mixed strategy equilibrium offsets these two motivations. When the advantage from striking first is large, the motivation to strike first from fear must be reduced. Otherwise, the other player will always launch a first strike. The best reply is to attack against mixed strategies that use a higher probability of attacking than the equilibrium strategy does. When the opponent has a strong motivation to seize the first-strike advantage, you must try not to provoke it. Lowering the probability of launching one's own first strike lowers the level of provocation.

Exercise 6.8: Demonstrate that

$$\left(D;d:\frac{1}{2};\frac{1}{2}\right)$$

and

$$\left[\left(\frac{2a_2}{a_2+r_2}A, \frac{r_2-a_2}{a_2+r_2}D\right);\left(\frac{2a_1}{a_1+r_1}a, \frac{r_1-a_1}{a_1+r_1}d\right): \frac{a_1+r_1}{2r_1};\frac{a_2+r_2}{2r_2}\right]$$

are perfect Bayesian equilibria of the game in Figure 6.6.

The model in Figure 6.6 formalizes the logic of the reciprocal fear of surprise attack. Both sides are willing to attack if each fears that the other side is about to attack. If you break both sides' information sets and play the game under perfect information, the reciprocal fear of surprise attack disappears. Each side knows then whether it is moving first or second when it must decide whether to attack. When it is moving second, it knows that the other side has not attacked. When it is moving first, it knows that the other player will know that it has not launched an attack when the other player moves. Only uncertainty about the other side's actions can create the reciprocal fear of surprise attack. If nuclear war were like tennis, where everyone knows who serves and in what order they serve, it would be less of a problem. Unfortunately, nuclear war is not tennis.

> Exercise 6.9: Show that (D,D;d,d) is the only subgame-perfect equilibrium of the game in Figure 6.6 played under perfect information (read the strategy as Player 1's move if he moves first, Player 1's move if he moves second; Player 2's move if she moves first, Player 2's move if she moves second).

The model above provides no reason why either side would contemplate using nuclear weapons in the first place. Typically, nuclear strategists assume that some crisis would precede any thought of using nuclear weapons. A nuclear threat could be considered as a way to extort a favorable resolution of the crisis. In the model in Figure 6.6, there is nothing at stake between the two sides except nuclear war. If we add some stakes beyond the prevention of nuclear war to the model, each side has another option—to end the crisis by surrendering the stakes to the other side. I call this option Quit (abbreviated Q and q). The outcome of quitting the crisis is that the side that quits surrenders the stakes to the other. Winning the stakes is preferable to the status quo; surrendering the stakes is worse than the status quo but better than any nuclear war. Let the value of the stakes be s_i for Player i. Then $0 > -s_1 > -r_1 > -a_1$, and $0 > -s_2 > -r_2 > -a_2$. Figure 6.7 presents the game with this added option.

This game has only one perfect Bayesian equilibrium, (D;d:$\frac{1}{2}$;$\frac{1}{2}$) (using the same notation as for the previous game). Once we add the option of ending the crisis by surrendering the stakes, neither player has an incentive to attack because quitting the crisis is always preferable to starting a nuclear war. Consequently, the reciprocal fear of surprise attack disappears for both sides. If one side begins to fear that the other is planning to attack, it should quit the crisis instead of launching its own first strike. The logic of mutual assured destruction says that nuclear war, even when you strike first, is worse than any non–nuclear war outcome, including surrendering the stakes at hand. Thus the reciprocal fear of surprise attack should not occur. Not only should I surrender if I fear you are planning to attack, but I should also expect you to surrender if you fear I am planning to attack. Further, nuclear threats cannot be used in

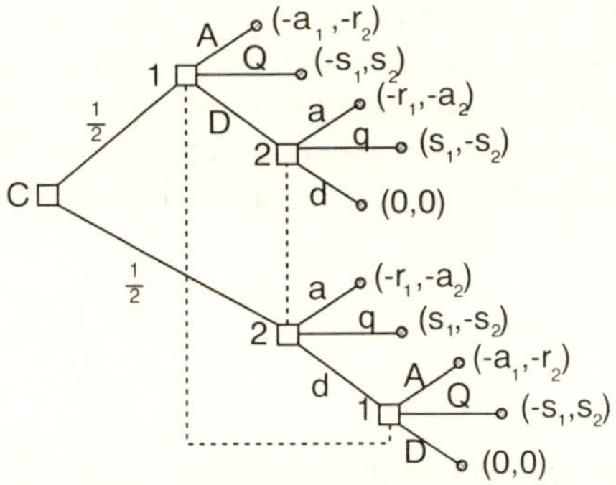

Figure 6.7 The Opportunity to Quit Added to a Game with the Reciprocal Fear of Surprise Attack

this model to coerce the other side to surrender the stakes. Both sides expect that the other side will not attack. There is no reason to surrender the stakes to eliminate the threat of war—that threat does not exist. Again we return to the argument that nuclear weapons cannot be used to defend other interests or extort concessions from the other side. Some real threat of nuclear war is necessary for either extended deterrence or nuclear extortion to be possible.

Exercise 6.10: Show that (D;d:$\frac{1}{2}$;$\frac{1}{2}$) is the only perfect Bayesian equilibrium of the above game.

a) First show that (D;d:$\frac{1}{2}$;$\frac{1}{2}$) is a perfect Bayesian equilibrium of the game.

b) Show that Q strictly dominates A (and q strictly dominates a). Consequently, A and a can never appear in a perfect Bayesian equilibrium strategy.

c) Show that once neither player ever attacks (play A or a), D strictly dominates Q (and d strictly dominates q). Thus only the given belief-strategy pairing can be a perfect Bayesian equilibrium.

The critical point of this example cannot be emphasized too strongly: *the results of a model depend upon the choices you give the players and how you structure them.* Breaking the information sets eliminated the problem, but that modification of the model seems implausible. The reciprocal fear of surprise attack depends upon each player's not knowing whether the other was preparing to attack. Eliminating that uncertainty denied a central premise of the argument. Adding the choice of quitting the crisis and sacrificing the stakes undermines the reciprocal fear of surprise attack, and that modification of the model does not violate the assumptions of the reciprocal fear argument. It may be that the sides do not have the option to surrender in a specific situation. This variation does not demonstrate that the reciprocal fear of surprise attack can never occur. It does demonstrate that in this model the reciprocal fear of surprise does not occur when the option of surrendering is available. The only way to judge what are reasonable models is to understand the situation, build the models, and solve for their consequences.

Review

This chapter has introduced the ideas of beliefs and perfect Bayesian equilibrium. Beliefs allows us to perform backwards induction through information sets with multiple nodes. This is sequential rationality. Each player's moves must maximize its expected utility given its beliefs and the other players' strategies. Beliefs allow us to judge sequential rationality from information sets with multiple nodes. We weigh the utility of a move from each node in an information set by the probability that the moving player believes it is at that node when it moves. Unlike Nash or subgame-perfect equilibrium, sequential rationality allows us to check best replies at all information sets in a game.

Beliefs must be consistent with the players' equilibrium strategies whenever possible. Players use the equilibrium strategies and Bayes's Theorem to calculate the probability that each node in an information set with multiple nodes is reached. Bayes's Theorem combines prior beliefs and new information optimally to update probabilities. For information sets off the equilibrium path, players are free to make any conjecture about why defection from equilibrium occurred. However, they must share that conjecture and continue to use Bayes's Theorem and the equilibrium strategies after a defection.

Further Reading

Most statistics textbooks contain sections on Bayes's Theorem. DeGroot 1970 is a textbook on Bayesian decision theory. The model of preference for biased information is loosely adapted from Calvert 1985.

The discussion in this chapter draws on Selten 1975 and Kreps and Wilson 1982. Both of these papers are highly mathematical, very difficult reading, and immensely rewarding. I have drawn freely from their carefully crafted examples and terse discussions of their solution concepts. The three-player game is a well-known example from Selten 1975. The textbooks in noncooperative game theory provide more accessible treatments of perfect Bayesian equilibrium.

The section on nuclear war draws heavily on the work of Robert Powell, in particular Chapter Five of Powell 1990. The other chapters of Powell 1990 deal with other issues in nuclear deterrence.

Comparative Politics

Formal work in comparative politics typically draws on models of U.S. politics. The strongest area of application is the politics of advanced industrial democracies. Most democracies are multiparty ones. Laver and Schofield 1990 is an excellent place to begin reading the formal literature on multiparty democracy. Although it does not present formal models, it draws heavily on models. Multiparty systems change both electoral competition and government formation. Austen-Smith and Banks (1988) address the question of how voters' decisions are affected by their considering the effects of their votes on the government that forms. Austen-Smith and Banks (1990) and Laver and Shepsle (1990) model government formation and portfolio allocation. Baron (1991a) modifies the model of bargaining in legislatures discussed in Chapter Five to investigate whether moderate parties are more likely than others to be included in coalition governments. Baron (1993) shows that a multiparty system leads the parties to adopt distinct policy positions in campaigns and in office. Greenberg and Shepsle (1987) analyze how the possible entry of new parties leads existing parties to adopt different positions.

Variations in electoral and legislative rules across countries has also been modeled. Palfrey (1989) explains Duverger's law—that single-member districts with winner-take-all elections give rise to only two competing parties in each district. Cox (1990) considers how different electoral laws change party positions in elections. Huber (1992) compares the legislative rules of France and the United States, using formal models of legislative structure.

There are models of other issues in comparative politics. Wallerstein (1989, 1990) studies questions of union organization and corporatism. Pool (1991) examines the strategic incentives that official languages create. Kuran (1991) looks informally at the problems involved in judging when a population is ready for a revolution. Bates and Lien (1985) show that political leaders can gain by granting policy concessions and rights to their subjects. Geddes's (1991) model of political reform was covered in Chapter Four. Putnam's (1988) two-level game model connects domestic politics and foreign policy. Tsebelis (1990) uses linked models to analyze the dual internal and external incentives leaders face.

Chapter Seven
More on Noncooperative Equilibrium: Perfect and Sequential Equilibria

This chapter deals with further refinements of equilibrium in noncooperative game theory. Sequential equilibrium is similar to perfect Bayesian equilibrium but adds some restrictions on beliefs off the equilibrium path. All hypotheses that could explain defection from equilibrium behavior are seen as equally plausible in perfect Bayesian equilibria. Sequential equilibrium places a minimal restriction on beliefs off the equilibrium path.

Perfect equilibrium refines the set of Nash equilibria in a different way from that of sequential equilibrium. The idea is simple and quite intuitive. Optimal strategies should be optimal given small chances that the other players will defect from the equilibrium at any given move. We call these small chances "trembles." Trembles can be thought of as small probabilities of error in making moves, of "irrationality" by other players, or of a lack of knowledge of the common conjecture needed in equilibrium. Regardless of why trembles occur, perfect equilibrium requires that players' strategies be best replies against some possible trembles. Such perfect strategies are optimal responses not only on the equilibrium path but also against small deviations from the equilibrium. Although perfect equilibrium is very attractive in the abstract, it can be difficult to solve for perfect equilibria of a game. Many different types of trembles are possible from any given Nash equilibrium, and we are free to choose whatever set of trembles we like.

Perfect equilibrium also includes another refinement of Nash equilibria, elimination of equilibria with weakly dominated strategies. Recall that a weakly dominated strategy is never better and sometimes worse than the strategy that dominates it for that player. There are perfect Bayesian equilibria where a player plays a weakly dominated strategy. Only outcomes where the player is indifferent between this strategy and the strategy that dominates it occur in equilibrium. Perfect equilibrium eliminates these equilibria because there is a small chance that a tremble will lead that player to a node where the dominating strategy produces a better outcome for the player. The dominated strategy cannot be a best reply to the tremble, then. This consequence of perfect equilibrium can be realized by eliminating equilibria where one of

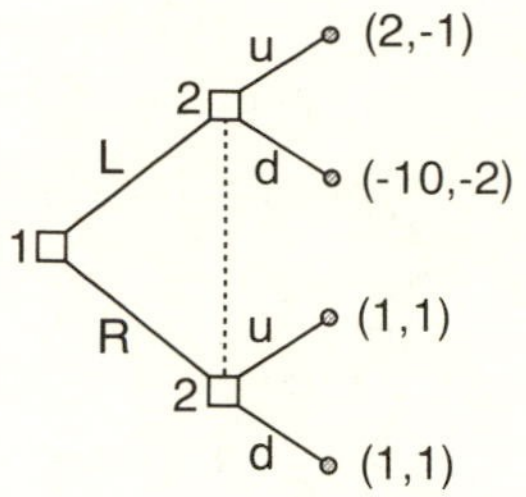

Figure 7.1 A Game Tree Illustrating
Elimination of Weakly Dominated Strategies

the players plays a weakly dominated strategy. However, eliminating weakly dominated strategies can lead to unusual results.

This chapter proceeds in reverse order from the discussion above. I begin with the elimination of equilibria with weakly dominated strategies, move on to perfect and sequential equilibria, and end with two examples, one from deterrence and the other from voting behavior. These concepts have historical importance in the development of noncooperative game theory. Perfect equilibrium was the first refinement of Nash equilibrium. The formalization of beliefs began with sequential equilibrium. Perfect Bayesian equilibrium has supplanted sequential equilibrium in the literature. Both are descendants of perfect equilibrium, developed to provide many of the benefits of the latter with less pain. I have given perfect Bayesian equilibrium precedence as a practical tool for solving games, but you should still be familiar with the ideas behind these other types of equilibria.

Elimination of Weakly Dominated Strategies

A weakly dominated strategy is never better and sometimes worse than the strategy that dominates it. But there are situations where it is just as good; otherwise, it would be strongly dominated. A weakly dominated strategy can be part of an equilibrium if only situations where it is just as good as the strategy that dominates it occur on the equilibrium path. One simple refinement of Nash equilibria eliminates equilibria with weakly dominated strategies.

> Example: The game in Figure 7.1 has two Nash equilibria, (L;u) and (R;d). You may wish to write down the strategic form of the game to check this. Player 2 plays a weakly dominated strategy in (R;d) because u is at least as good for her if Player 1 plays R and better if he plays L. But u is in Nash equilibrium with R. If we eliminate this dominated strategy, the only equilibrium is (L;u). Eliminating Player 2's dominated strategy cannot hurt Player 2 and would help her if Player 1 played L. Playing u protects Player

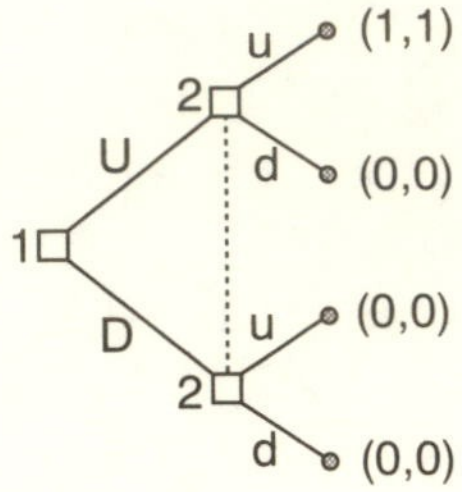

Figure 7.2 An Intuitive Example of the Elimination of Weakly Dominated Strategies

2 against a defection by Player 1 if they are playing (R;d). If Player 1 realizes this and eliminates Player 2's dominated strategy, then he will always want to play L.

(R;d) is a perfect Bayesian equilibrium of this game. The only belief consistent with Player 1's playing R is that Player 2 is at her lower node. Given that Player 2 believes she is at her lower node, playing d is a best reply for her. Both of the Nash equilibria here are perfect Bayesian.

Player 2 is hurt by eliminating the (R;d) equilibrium in the example above, so we might imagine her telling Player 1, "I am going to play d because you will then play R to avoid your −10 payoff, and I will not be hurt by playing d then." But Player 1 could respond, "That could be true, but there is a chance that I may make an error and play L. You will regret playing d then. Despite your speech, I believe you intend to play u to protect yourself against such a mistake and that your speech is just a ploy to convince me to play R. Your ploy did not work; I am going to play L." We cannot resolve such imaginary speeches here. Playing (R;d) makes sense for Player 2 only when she is absolutely certain that Player 1 will play R. She has an incentive to tell Player 1 that she is convinced, and he has an incentive to respond that he is not convinced by her statements.

Eliminating Nash equilibria with weakly dominated strategies provides protection against possible defections from equilibrium. The elimination of equilibria with dominated strategies provides a strategic logic to eliminate some Nash equilibria in some games. Further, the consequences of eliminating equilibria with weakly dominated strategies is positively intuitive in some cases.

Example: The game in Figure 7.2 has two equilibria, (U;u) and (D;d). Why would anyone ever play (D;d) in this game? Down is weakly dominated for both players. There is no penalty and a very likely reward to playing Up here. As in the previous example, the strange Nash equilibrium—(D;d) here—is also a perfect Bayesian equilibrium.

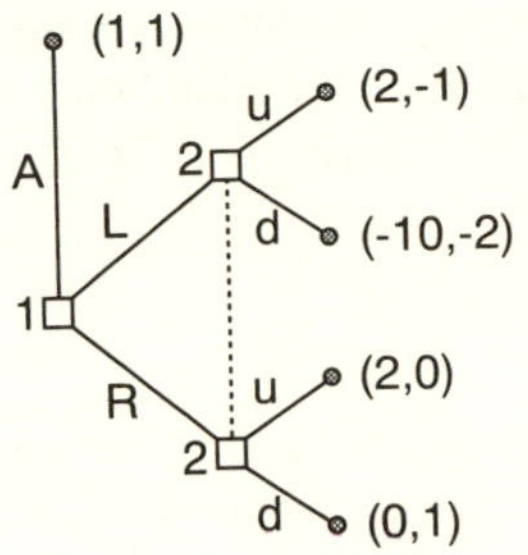

Figure 7.3 Exercise 7.1

		Player 2	
		l	r
Player 1	U	(1,0)	(0,1)
	D	(0,0)	(0,2)

Figure 7.4 A Game Where the Order of Elimination of Weakly Dominated Strategies Matters

Exercise 7.1: Find the Nash equilibria of the game in Figure 7.3. Would any of these equilibria be eliminated because they include weakly dominated strategies?

You have to be careful with the elimination of weakly dominated strategies, though. Rationalizability, described in Chapter Four, iterates the elimination of strongly dominated strategies. If you iterate the elimination of weakly dominated strategies, you can produce paradoxical situations. The order of elimination of strategies can be critical.

Example: Consider the strategic-form game in Figure 7.4 (from Fudenberg and Tirole 1991, 461). D is weakly dominated by U for Player 1, and l is strongly dominated by r for Player 2. If we eliminate D first and then l, the result is (U;r). If we delete l first, D then weakly dominates U for Player 1, and the result is (D;r). The Nash equilibrium of this game is (U;r).

Exercise 7.2: The game of Burning Money is another example of the limitations of iterated elimination of weakly dominated strategies. In Burning Money, two players are playing the two-by-two game Battle of the Sexes given in Chapter Four. Before they choose their moves, Player 1 is given an opportunity to burn publicly one unit of utility as a sign of his commitment. All of his payoffs are reduced by one if he does so Player 2 knows whether he has done so when she chooses her moves.

a) Write out an extensive form for Burning Money.

b) Find the strategic form of Burning Money.

c) Find the pure strategy Nash equilibria of Burning Money.

d) Perform an iterated elimination of weakly dominated strategies on Burning Money. What payoffs are possible, and what behaviors can result?

Perfect Equilibrium*

Perfect Bayesian equilibrium requires that beliefs must reflect the equilibrium strategies along the equilibrium path, but beliefs may be chosen freely off the equilibrium path. Subgame perfection requires rational play at information sets that are part of a subgame and off the equilibrium path. But actions from information sets that are not part of a proper subgame are not restricted. I now turn to the question of beliefs off the equilibrium path: what minimal restrictions on such beliefs should we accept? Two concepts, trembling-hand perfection and consistency of beliefs, lead to perfect and sequential equilibrium. These concepts address how beliefs off the equilibrium path are formed in the most general sense. They impose a minimal definition of consistency on those beliefs.

The question is the stability of strategies off the equilibrium path: what sort of conjectures are the players allowed to use when they form their beliefs off the equilibrium path? The solution is novel: we investigate the stability of strategies by examining each player's best reply to strategies very similar to the equilibrium strategy. The players assume there is a small chance that the other players play randomly rather than rationally at any particular move. These small chances of errors are called **trembles.** These trembles explain why a player might make a suboptimal move. Once off the equilibrium path, each player assumes that the other players will continue to play rationally except for the trembles in its next move. Players assume, then, that one deviation from rationality does not lead to another.

Return to the three-player game discussed in detail in Chapter Six and shown in Figure 6.1. Player 2's strategy in the (D;a;*L*) Nash equilibrium was not robust against small variations in the other players' strategies. When a player moves, it should consider only its position at that point, including expectations about future play. Off the equilibrium path, players should form hypotheses about what defections from equilibrium behavior brought them to that point. We want equilibria to be stable against small departures from equilibrium behavior. If a player should significantly change its equilibrium strategy when another player's equilibrium strategy "trembles," perfect equilibrium considers that equilibrium unstable and discards it.

To formalize the idea of trembles, I introduce the idea of a completely mixed strategy. In a completely mixed strategy, all players have a nonzero probability

*This section uses limits.

of playing all actions at every information set. Thus all information sets must be reached in a completely mixed strategy.

> **Definition**: A set of strategies, S, is **completely mixed** iff for all acts A in the game, $p(A|S) > 0$, that is, if and only if the probability of playing any A in strategy S is greater than 0.

Completely mixed strategies provide a way to represent trembles around equilibrium strategies. We require that these trembles give positive probability to all possible defections from equilibrium behavior. Trembling-hand perfection requires that an equilibrium be a best reply to trembles from itself.

> **Definition**: A set of strategies, S, is **trembling-hand perfect** iff there exists a sequence of a set of completely mixed strategies $(S_i)_{i=1}^{\infty}$ such that $\lim_{i \to +\infty} S_i = S$ and S is a best reply to each S_i.

Trembling-hand perfection tests the robustness of an equilibrium. It verifies that each player's strategy is a best reply against small deviations. To show that an equilibrium is trembling-hand perfect, we find a sequence of trembles that converges to the equilibrium. If the equilibrium strategies are best replies to all of those trembles, then they are trembling-hand perfect. Trembling-hand perfection dispenses with beliefs. Because all nodes are reached in a completely mixed strategy, we can calculate the probability that each node is reached in each tremble in the sequence that converges to the equilibrium. We calculate that each move maximizes the moving player's expected utility for every move in every tremble.

Ascertaining that an equilibrium is trembling-hand perfect is not quite as much work as it sounds. "Trembling" the other moves in the game and calculating whether a move is still a best reply is the best way to check trembling-hand perfection. But the exact choice of the sequence of trembles is important, and the right choice makes the task easier.

> Example: Return to the (D;a;*L*) equilibrium of the three-player game from Chapter Six. Figure 7.5 reproduces the extensive form. "Tremble" Player 1's strategy to create a small chance of playing A; Player 2's best reply then is to always play d. Give Player 1 a probability of δ of playing A, then $p(D) = 1 - \delta$, and give Player 3 a probability of ϵ of playing *R*, then $p(L) = 1 - \epsilon$. Both δ and ϵ are assumed to be small and to approach 0 in the limit. If Player 2 plays a, it receives the following payoff:
>
> $$(0)(1-\delta)(\epsilon) + (2)(1-\delta)(1-\epsilon) + (1)(\delta) = 2 - \delta - 2\epsilon + 2\delta\epsilon.$$

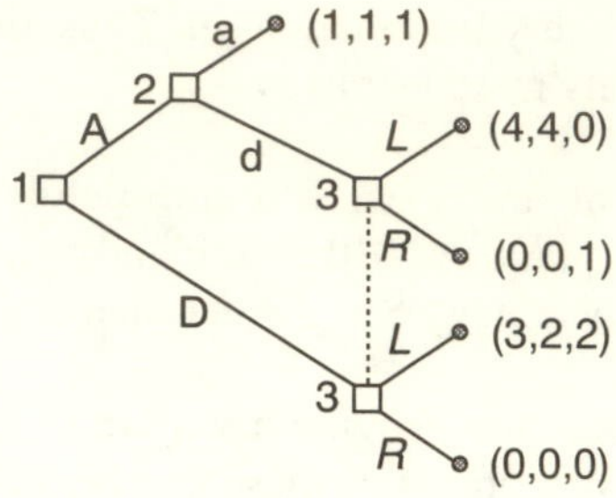

Figure 7.5 Selten's Game

If Player 2 plays d, it receives the following payoff:

$$(0)(1-\delta)(\epsilon) + (2)(1-\delta)(1-\epsilon) + (0)(\delta)(\epsilon) + 4(\delta)(1-\epsilon)$$
$$= 2 + 2\delta - 2\epsilon - 2\delta\epsilon.$$

The payoff for playing d exceeds that of playing a by $(3\delta - 4\delta\epsilon)$. Playing a is not a best reply to trembles of this equilibrium when $\epsilon < \frac{3}{4}$.

To show that the "sensible" (but unfortunate) equilibrium, (A;a;*R*), is trembling-hand perfect, let Player 2's probability of playing d be $2\delta/(1-\delta)$ and the probability of Player 1's playing D be δ. Then Player 3's payoff for playing R is

$$(0)(\delta) + (1)(1-\delta)\left(\frac{1-3\delta}{1-\delta}\right) + (1)(1-\delta)\left(\frac{2\delta}{1-\delta}\right) = 1-\delta,$$

and Player 3's payoff for playing L is

$$(2)(\delta) + (1)(1-\delta)\left(\frac{1-3\delta}{1-\delta}\right) + (0)(1-\delta)\left(\frac{2\delta}{1-\delta}\right) = 1-\delta.$$

Player 3 is indifferent between R and L here, so R is a best reply.

We do not have to show that a possible equilibrium is a best reply to all sequences that converge to it, only that one such sequence exists. I use this freedom to choose the particular sequence above. For example, I chose the trembles of the strategies of Players 1 and 2 to make Player 3 indifferent. It is difficult to know in advance what set of trembles will support an equilibrium. I recommend you try some general trembles, like those in the first part of the example above, to see if any sequence can support the equilibrium.

Any strategy played against completely mixed strategies is automatically trembling-hand perfect because we can use those completely mixed strategies as the sequence of trembles. Thus all equilibria involving only completely mixed strategies is trembling-hand perfect.

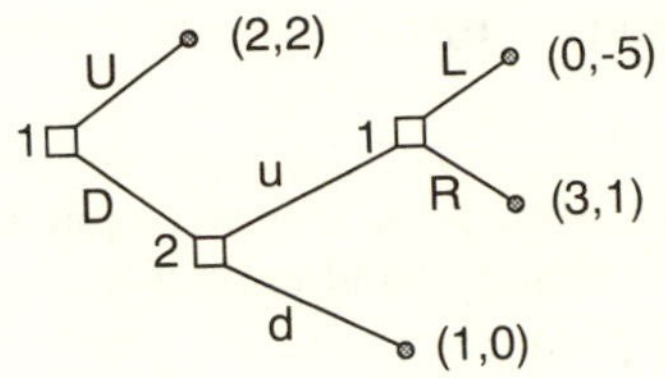

Figure 7.6 A Game with Two Trembling-Hand Perfect Equilibria

Trembling-hand perfection is defined in the strategic form. It addresses small errors in strategies, rather than small errors in moves. There are trembling-hand perfect equilibria that are not subgame perfect.

Example: Figure 7.6 shows a game from Fudenberg and Tirole 1991 (353). The subgame-perfect equilibrium of this game is (D,R;u), as you can see by backwards induction. But it has two trembling-hand perfect equilibria, (D,R;u) and (U,L;d). To demonstrate that (U,L;d) is trembling-hand perfect, let Player 1's strategy "tremble" as follows: $(1-\epsilon-\epsilon^2)$ chance of playing (U,L), ϵ chance of playing (D,L), and ϵ^2 chance of playing (D,R). This strategy is completely mixed because Player 1 has positive probability of playing all moves in equilibrium. Show that d is a best reply for Player 2 against this mix. Her expected utility for playing d against this completely mixed strategy is

$$u_2(d) = 2(1 - \epsilon - \epsilon^2) + 0(\epsilon) + 0(\epsilon^2) = 2 - 2\epsilon - 2\epsilon^2.$$

Her expected utility for playing u is

$$u_2(u) = 2(1 - \epsilon - \epsilon^2) + (-5)(\epsilon) + 1(\epsilon^2) = 2 - 7\epsilon - \epsilon^2.$$

For $\epsilon < \frac{1}{5}$, the expected utility of playing d is higher than u. For Player 2, u is trembling-hand perfect; it is a best reply to this sequence of trembles.

Exercise 7.3: Show that Player 1's strategy of (U,L) is trembling-hand perfect against Player 2's strategy of d. (Hint: You merely have to show that (U,L) is a best reply to the "trembled" strategy.)

The trick in this example is that Player 1's trembles are correlated. If he defects from U in his first move, Player 2 hypothesizes that he is very likely to play L in his second move. But such correlation violates the idea that trembles are random errors. To eliminate this problem, I define perfect equilibria to have independent trembles across moves.[1] By "trembling" each move separately, we prevent the players from drawing inferences about a future defection from an earlier one.

> **Definition**: A set of strategies, S, forms a **perfect equilibrium** iff the strategies are trembling-hand perfect when trembles are independent across the players' moves.

Perfect equilibrium includes subgame perfection. Because every subgame is reached with completely mixed strategies, the players' choices must form a Nash equilibrium on each subgame. Consequently, a perfect equilibrium is subgame perfect.

Perfect equilibrium always exists in mixed strategies for finite games.

> **Theorem** (Selten): Every finite extensive-form game has at least one perfect equilibrium in mixed strategies.

A perfect equilibrium always exists because we can find some sequence of trembles that will converge to an equilibrium for sufficiently small trembles. For a game, G, let a perturbed game, G(ϵ), be one where all moves are made with at least probability ϵ and the probabilities of these trembles are independent across moves. Consider a sequence of perturbed games, G(ϵ_n), where ϵ_n goes to zero as n grows without bound. Each of these perturbed games has an equilibrium by a fixed-point theorem, as in the proof of the Minmax Theorem in Chapter Four. The sequence of equilibria of these perturbed games must have a subsequence that converges as n grows without bound because the game is finite. Further, the strategies at this limit point are mutual best replies. Thus this limit point satisfies the definition of a perfect equilibrium. It is a best reply to a set of trembles, the convergent subsequence, when those trembles are independent across the players' moves.

> Exercise 7.4: For each Nash equilibrium in the games in Exercise 5.2 (page 130), determine which are perfect.

> Exercise 7.5: The game in Figure 7.7 has three Nash equilibria, two of which are subgame perfect. Find the equilibria, and determine which ones are perfect and which one is not.

Sequential Equilibrium

Perfect equilibrium is often difficult to apply. Calculating best replies to trembles can be tedious. But we wish to retain the idea that beliefs off the equilibrium path should be based on some consistent hypotheses about defections from equilibrium. Such hypotheses are captured in perfect equilibrium by the

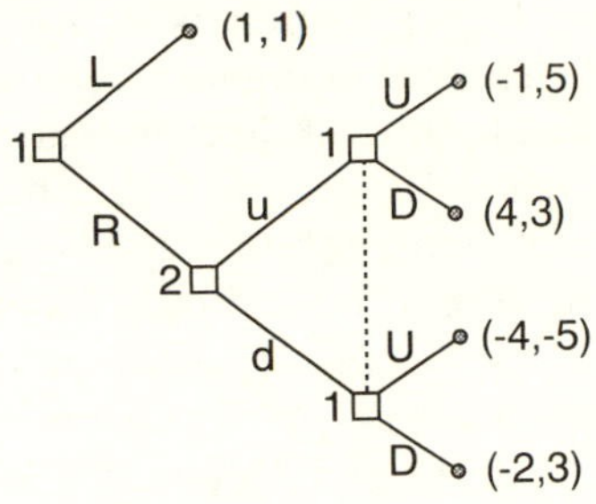

Figure 7.7 Exercise 7.5

sequence of trembles. Sequential equilibrium deals with this problem by requiring consistency between the beliefs in a perfect Bayesian equilibrium and some set of trembles. Sequential equilibrium is preferred to perfect equilibrium because it is easier to solve for and almost all sequential equilibria are perfect.

Here, we make the hypotheses that explain defections explicit in the beliefs. They specify the likelihood of different prior defections. We require that the beliefs be consistent both with some hypothesis that explains defections and with the structure of the game. These restrictions prevent the players from adopting absurd beliefs about the game and then using those absurd beliefs to motivate bizarre behavior.

What restrictions do we place on the beliefs? As in perfect Bayesian equilibrium, beliefs must be determined by Bayes's Theorem and the equilibrium strategies whenever possible. Players update beliefs on the equilibrium path, using the equilibrium strategies and Bayes's Theorem. However, some information sets may never be reached in equilibrium. Updating cannot be done for those information sets.

To solve this problem, we again turn to the set of completely mixed strategies. Trembles, completely mixed strategies that are very close to the equilibrium strategies, generate beliefs off the equilibrium path. The players' beliefs are required to be the limit of some sequence of the beliefs generated by a sequence of these completely mixed strategies that converges to the equilibrium. The definition of consistency of beliefs mirrors the idea of trembling-hand perfection. Small chances of errors provide hypotheses that the players use to account for defections from an equilibrium.

> **Definition**: A pair of beliefs and strategies is **consistent** iff the beliefs are the limit of a sequence of belief-strategy pairings such that the strategies are completely mixed and converge to the equilibrium strategy and the beliefs are calculated from the corresponding strategies by using Bayes's Theorem.

Example: Show that Player 3's beliefs in the (A;a;R:$\frac{2}{3}$) equilibrium of the three-player game in Figure 7.5 are consistent with the equilibrium strategies. In this equilibrium, Player 3's information set should not be reached. We need to find trembles on the moves of Players 1 and 2 that produce the desired beliefs. Let Player 1's probability of playing D be δ, and let Player 2's probability of playing d be $2\delta/(1-\delta)$. Use Bayes's Theorem to find the probability of the upper node given that Player 3's information set is reached. If Player 1 defects from the equilibrium, the lower node will be reached, and if Player 2 defects, the upper node will be reached. We will denote the defections of Players 1 and 2 by the corresponding moves (D and d, respectively), Player 3's information set by "3's inf," the upper node of Player 3's information set as "3's un," and the lower node as "3's ln." We calculate the probability as

$$\text{p(3's un|3's inf)} = \frac{\text{p(d)p(3's un|d)}}{\text{p(d)p(3's un|d)} + \text{p(D)p(3's ln|D)}}$$

$$= \frac{\frac{2\delta}{1-\delta}(1-\delta)}{\frac{2\delta}{1-\delta}(1-\delta)+\delta(1)} = \frac{2\delta}{\delta+2\delta} = \frac{2}{3}$$

As δ goes to 0, Player 3's belief that she is at her upper node if her information set is reached goes to $\frac{2}{3}$.

Exercise 7.6: Find the beliefs that support the perfect equilibrium found in Exercise 7.5.

Sequential equilibrium requires both sequential rationality and consistency of beliefs. We check that each move is optimal given the beliefs and that the beliefs are consistent with the strategy. Formally, we have the following definition of a sequential equilibrium:

Definition: A **sequential equilibrium** is a set of beliefs and strategies for all players that is both sequentially rational and consistent.

Beliefs are consistent with deviations from the equilibrium strategies, and the strategies are optimal given the beliefs. In general, it is easier to determine that beliefs are consistent than it is to determine if the strategies are best replies to their trembles. Sequential equilibria are easier to find and demonstrate than perfect equilibria. The following two theorems were formulated by Kreps and Wilson (1982a):

Theorem: Every extensive-form game has at least one sequential equilibrium.

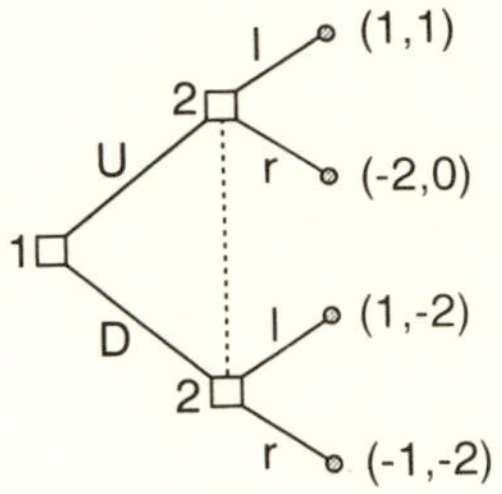

Figure 7.8 A Game with Three Sequential Equilibria, of Which Only One Is a Perfect Equilibrium

Theorem: All perfect equilibria are sequential; almost all sequential equilibria are perfect.[2]

The proof of the first theorem requires the second. Selten proved that every game has at least one perfect equilibrium in mixed strategies. Thus if all perfect equilibria are sequential, every game must have a sequential equilibrium. There are sequential equilibria where a player uses a weakly dominated strategy. Perfect equilibrium eliminates any equilibrium where a weakly dominated strategy is used, so these sequential equilibria are not perfect.

Example: The game in Figure 7.8 has three sequential equilibria, (U;l:1), (D;l:0), and (D;r:0), where the last element specifies Player 2's belief that she is at her upper node when her information set is reached. Of these three equilibria, only (D;l:0) is perfect. Both players have a weakly dominant strategy, D for Player 1 and l for Player 2.

How does sequential equilibrium differ from perfect Bayesian equilibrium? It places somewhat stronger restrictions on beliefs off the equilibrium path. These stronger restrictions can matter in games where players have information sets with more than two nodes or make more than two moves. Fudenberg and Tirole (1991, 345–349) provide a more complete discussion of the differences between the two concepts. For the remainder of this chapter, I turn to applications.

Deterrence and the Signaling of Resolve*

I return to the game of deterrence used in Chapter Three to illustrate the extensive form of a game. In this section, I solve the game and discuss the impli-

*This section uses integral calculus.

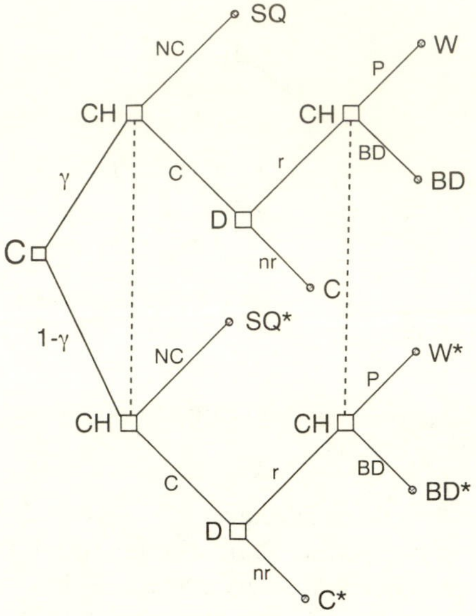

Figure 7.9 The Deterrence Game with Uncertainty about Two Types of Defenders

cations of the equilibrium for the study of deterrence in international politics. This game is also an introduction to the way beliefs are used in the games of limited information that are discussed in Chapter Eight. The lessons about how threats and bluffs work that we can draw from this model also apply to many other situations where actors use threats against one another, such as legislative-executive relations and ultimatums in negotiations.

Figure 7.9 gives the extensive form of the deterrence game. There are two actors, a challenger (CH) and a defender (D). The challenger has the first choice in the game—it can challenge (C) or not challenge (NC). If it does not challenge, the status quo persists (the SQ outcome). If the challenger does challenge, the defender must choose whether it will resist the challenge (r) or grant concessions to end the crisis (nr, for not resisting). Not resisting the challenge produces concessions for the challenger, which I call the C outcome. Resisting the challenge leads to a final decision between war and peace for the challenger. Pressing the challenge, action P in the figure, leads to war, the W outcome. The BD action, backing down from the threat, prevents war at the cost of concessions to the defender and perhaps a loss of "face" for the challenger.

The preferences of each side follow in most cases from the description of the outcomes. The challenger prefers concessions without war to the status quo, which it prefers to backing down. Formally, $1 = u_{CH}(C) > u_{CH}(SQ) > u_{CH}(BD) = 0$. We cannot say where the challenger places W in its preferences other than that concessions are preferred to war. It could prefer war to the status quo, or prefer the status quo to war and war to backing down, or prefer any peaceful outcome, including backing down, to war. I normalize the utilities by setting $u_{CH}(C)$ and $u_{CH}(BD)$ equal to 1 and 0, respectively. Normalization eases the calculations. When interpreting results, we must remember that $u_{CH}(SQ)$ now expresses the challenger's value for the status quo relative to concessions and backing down.

The defender prefers the challenger's backing down to the status quo and prefers the status quo to making concessions itself. Formally, $1 = u_D(BD) > u_D(SQ) > u_D(C) = 0$. Again, there is no obvious assumption about how the defender ranks war relative to the other outcomes. It could prefer war to the status quo, or perhaps war is worse than making concessions in the defender's eyes. The defender's utilities are also normalized.

Rather than making an assumption about the defender's resolve (i.e., its utility for war), the model makes it uncertain. The game begins with a chance move that determines the preferences of the defender. The upper branch of the tree from the chance move is the case of a resolute defender, where $u_D(W) > 0 = u_D(C)$. The lower branch is the case of an irresolute defender, where $u_D(C) = 0 > u_D(W^*)$. The defender is informed about the outcome of the chance move, but the challenger is not. The information sets that connect the challenger's nodes in the top and bottom branches represent the challenger's ignorance of the defender's resolve. The challenger cannot ascertain the defender's resolve. Instead, it has beliefs about the defender's resolve, which it updates as the game progresses. This representation of uncertainty is the fundamental mechanism of games of limited information, the subject of Chapter Eight.

The challenger's initial belief that the defender is resolved is the same as the probability of the upper branch in the initial chance move; this probability is denoted by γ. Beliefs must be consistent with the structure of the game, including chance moves. It may seem strange to think of the game beginning with a chance move that determines the preferences of the defender. After all, the defender is either resolved or not. Instead of this literal interpretation of this model, you should think of the game as representing the uncertainty in the challenger's mind. It does not know whether the defender is resolved. It must consider both possibilities when it makes a move, and the structure of the game represents its uncertainty. This structure forces us as analysts to think about the counterfactual cases that the actors consider when reaching decisions. How might the other side respond? An actor who does not know the other side's motivations precisely must judge the other side's likely responses. This game structure provides a way to think about that problem.

We could also make the defender uncertain about the challenger's utility for war. If there were resolute and irresolute challengers, the chance move would have four possible outcomes for each of the combinations of resolute and irresolute challengers and defenders. Both players would have information sets that reflected their knowledge of their own payoffs and their ignorance of their opponent's payoffs.

Instead of this, I choose to make the challenger's resolve common knowledge. The challenger's preference between war and backing down depends on the defender's resolve. A nation's resolve for war rises with its military capabilities and its willingness to suffer the costs of combat. The more resolved it is, the greater the chance it will win and the less the chance that the other side will win. If the defender is resolute, the chance of the challenger's winning is less because the defender is stronger. I assume that the challenger prefers to back down against a resolute defender. The outcomes without asterisks indicate a resolute defender, so $u_{CH}(BD) = 1 > u_{CH}(W)$. If the defender is irresolute, the challenger is more likely to win, so war is more attractive to the latter. I assume that the challenger prefers war to backing down against an irresolute defender. The outcomes with asterisks indicate an irresolute defender, so $u_{CH}(W^*) > 0 = u_{CH}(BD^*)$. To complete the challenger's preferences, I assume that the status quo, concession, and backing down outcomes are the same regardless of the defender's resolve. Then $u_{CH}(SQ) = u_{CH}(SQ^*)$, $u_{CH}(C) = u_{CH}(C^*) = 0$, and $u_{CH}(BD) = u_{CH}(BD^*) = 1$. The challenger's complete preferences are $u_{CH}(C) = 1 > u_{CH}(SQ) > u_{CH}(W^*) > u_{CH}(BD) = 0 > u_{CH}(W)$.

These preferences capture the argument that each side's resolve affects the other's willingness to go to war. Alternatively, one could argue that the challenger's value for war does not change with the defender's resolve. Then its preferences between war and backing down would not vary across the two branches. I have also assumed here that the challenger prefers the status quo to war, even war against an irresolute defender. These assumptions match a situation where the challenger is probing the defender's resolve. The challenger seeks concessions from the defender and may use the threat of war to gain them. Later, we consider the case where the challenger sometimes prefers war to the status quo in an exercise. Our intuition is that deterrence should be easier in the case I present here than in that exercise; the challenger's resolve is greater in the latter case.

Begin the analysis by first solving each branch under complete information. Often, it helps to solve games of limited information by first solving the corresponding games of complete information. Those solutions also provide a baseline we can compare to the game of limited information. Does the players' uncertainty affect their behavior in the game? The game in Figure 7.10 occurs when the defender is resolved and the challenger knows it. This game can be solved by backwards induction. The challenger prefers BD to W in its last move, so it will back down if that move occurs. Anticipating this, the defender prefers resisting to making concessions in its move. The challenger in its first move expects that the defender will resist and that it will then back down. Preferring SQ to BD, the challenger does not challenge. The equilibrium is (NC,BD;r) and is pictured on Figure 7.10 with arrows.

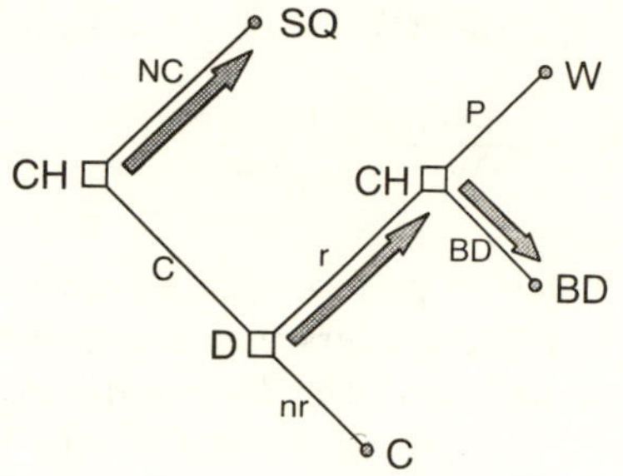

Figure 7.10 Backwards Induction
with a Resolved Defender

Exercise 7.7: Find the equilibrium of the deterrence game under complete information when the defender is irresolute.

Consider the implications of these equilibria under complete information. War does not occur in either case. When the defender is resolute, no crisis occurs. The challenger knows the defender will resist, presenting it with an unpleasant choice between war against a resolute defender or backing down. If you can see that unpleasant choice coming, why start a crisis? When the defender is irresolute, both sides can anticipate that the challenger will go to war if necessary. The defender makes concessions to avoid war. Expecting those concessions, the challenger wants to challenge to gain those concessions. The behavior in both of these equilibria is very different from descriptions of crisis behavior. Each side can clearly anticipate the other's future moves and so knows what action it should take. Much empirical work on deterrence in crisis stresses the difficulty of anticipating how the other side will respond. Other empirical studies emphasize that actors often exhibit overconfidence in their position, underrating the chance that the other side will go to war and ignoring signals of the other side's resolve (e.g., Lebow 1981). Can our model explain these stylized facts if we add uncertainty to it?

Before we can answer that question, we have to solve the model. Proceed by backwards induction, using beliefs. Begin with the challenger's final decision whether to press its threat. Calculate the critical belief that makes it indifferent between backing down and pressing the threat. Let $\bar{\gamma}$ be the challenger's belief at its last move that the defender is resolved. This belief is updated from the challenger's initial belief that the defender is resolved. The bar above the gamma denotes that it is an updated belief. The critical belief, $\bar{\gamma}_{crit}$, occurs when the challenger is indifferent between backing down and pressing its threat. Find this critical belief by equating the challenger's expected utility from backing down to its expected utility for pressing its threat:

$$0 = \bar{\gamma}_{crit}[u_{CH}(W)] + (1 - \bar{\gamma}_{crit})u_{CH}(W^*)$$

$$\bar{\gamma}_{crit} = \frac{u_{CH}(W^*)}{u_{CH}(W^*) - u_{CH}(W)}.$$

If $\bar{\gamma} > \bar{\gamma}_{crit}$, then the challenger prefers backing down to pressing its threat. If $\bar{\gamma} < \bar{\gamma}_{crit}$, then the challenger prefers pressing its threat to backing down. This result matches our intuition. The higher the challenger's belief that the defender is resolved, the less likely that it will press its threat. Similarly, we can deduce conclusions about how the likelihood of the challenger's going to war changes with changes in its utilities for these possible outcomes. Because we may be able to relate these utilities to observable indicators, we may be able to find testable hypotheses for this model.

I omit the derivation of these hypotheses because they are essentially identical to the logic of deterrence presented back in Chapter Two. When I say that extensive-form games parallel expected utility calculations, I mean this similarity between this model and the decision-theoretic deterrence model in Chapter Two. The bases of solutions to extensive-form games of limited information are expected utility calculations. The difference here is that the challenger's belief that the defender is resolved is no longer exogenous. Instead, this belief changes with the defender's actions in the game. The hard part of solving these games comes when we see how actions may be chosen to produce beliefs and must consider how beliefs are updated. Strategic choices to produce beliefs can be more complicated than they seem to be at first glance.

Proceed with the backwards induction by turning to the defender's move. Here, we must consider what move both resolute and irresolute defenders would make. All defenders prefer the challenger's backing down to making concessions themselves to end the crisis. Resolute defenders prefer war to making concessions, so they always resist. Either of the outcomes that result if they resist is better than making concessions in the eyes of a resolute defender. But irresolute defenders must judge the response of the challenger. If the challenger will back down, they wish to resist; if it will press the threat, they wish to make concessions to end the crisis. Find the probability, r, of the challenger's pressing its threat that makes an irresolute defender indifferent between resisting the challenge and making concessions, as follows:

$$0 = r[u_D(W^*)] + (1 - r)(1)$$

$$r = \frac{1}{1 - u_D(W^*)}$$

If the probability that the challenger will press the threat is greater than the indifference probability above, the irresolute defender makes concessions. If that probability is less than the indifference probability, then it resists the challenge.

If the challenger adopts a mixed strategy that presses the threat with the indifference probability and backs down with a probability of 1 minus the indifference probability, irresolute defenders are indifferent between resisting and making concessions. The challenger must have beliefs that equal $\bar{\gamma}_{crit}$—the belief where it is indifferent between pressing the threat and backing down—to play such a mixed strategy. I calculate the defender's mixed strategy that creates these updated beliefs for the challenger. Find the probability, q, of an irresolute defender's resisting the threat that creates the critical belief for the challenger, as follows:

$$\bar{\gamma}_{crit} = \frac{p(\text{D resolute})p(r|\text{D resolute})}{p(\text{D resolute})p(r|\text{D resolute}) + p(\text{D irresolute})p(r|\text{D irresolute})}$$

$$= \frac{\gamma(1)}{\gamma(1) + (1-\gamma)q}$$

$$q = \frac{\gamma(1-\bar{\gamma}_{crit})}{(1-\gamma)\bar{\gamma}_{crit}} = \frac{\gamma[-u_{CH}(W)]}{(1-\gamma)[u_{CH}(W^*)]}$$

γ is the challenger's initial belief that the defender is resolute. The final step in the calculation above is the substitution of the value of $\bar{\gamma}_{crit}$ in terms of the challenger's utilities for the outcomes. This mixed strategy cannot be supported when $\gamma > \bar{\gamma}_{crit}$; the resulting probability of the irresolute defender's resisting is greater than 1. There is a simple intuition behind the math here. When $\gamma > \bar{\gamma}_{crit}$, the challenger will always back down regardless of whether an irresolute defender resists. The challenger is already convinced of the defender's resolve. An irresolute defender should always resist then because it anticipates that the challenger will back down.

So far we have found best reply correspondences for the last two moves in the game. The correspondence in the challenger's last move depends upon its updated beliefs. The correspondence in the defender's move depends on what the challenger's move will be if the last move is reached. To complete the analysis, we must determine what the challenger will do in its first move. When will it challenge, and when will it live with the status quo? If $\gamma > \bar{\gamma}_{crit}$, then the challenger expects that the defender will resist. Recall that we assumed that $u_{CH}(SQ) > u_{CH}(W^*)$—the challenger prefers the status quo to any war, even war with an irresolute defender. Given that all defenders resist challenges, the challenger should live with the status quo when $\gamma > \bar{\gamma}_{crit}$. Deterrence works when the challenger believes that the defender is likely to be resolute. The exact degree of belief that the challenger requires for deterrence depends upon its values for the possible outcomes.

If $\gamma < \bar{\gamma}_{crit}$, the challenger will not be automatically deterred from challenging the status quo. It compares the value of challenging to the value of the status quo. The value of challenging is calculated from the defender's mixed strategy. If the defender resists a challenge, the challenger is indifferent between pressing its threat and backing down. Rather than calculating the challenger's expected utility for its own mixed strategy in the last move, we simply use $u_{CH}(BD)(= 0$ by assumption) for it. Because the challenger is indifferent between pressing its threat and backing down, the utilities of the two options are equal. Either one can be used to represent the challenger's expected utility from the last node, and $u_{CH}(BD)$ is simple to use because it equals 0. The challenger prefers accepting the status quo to challenging it when its utility for the status quo exceeds its expected utility for challenging it as follows:

$$u_{CH}(SQ) > \gamma[u_{CH}(BD)] + (1-\gamma)\{q[u_{CH}(BD)] + (1-q)u_{CH}(C)\}$$

$$> \gamma(0) + (1-\gamma)\left(0\left\{\frac{\gamma[-u_{CH}(W)]}{(1-\gamma)[u_{CH}(W^*)]}\right\}\right.$$

$$\left.+1\left\{\frac{(1-\gamma)u_{CH}(W^*) - \gamma[-u_{CH}(W)]}{(1-\gamma)[u_{CH}(W^*)]}\right\}\right)$$

Solving for γ, we have the following condition for the challenger's initial beliefs:

$$\gamma > \frac{[1-u_{CH}(SQ)]u_{CH}(W^*)}{u_{CH}(W^*) - u_{CH}(W)} = [1-u_{CH}(SQ)]\bar{\gamma}_{crit}.$$

When γ is greater than the right side of the above inequality, the challenger does not challenge the status quo. It does not believe that the chance that the defender will make concessions is great enough to justify the risk of facing the choice between war and backing down. This critical belief has to be smaller than $\bar{\gamma}_{crit}$ because $1 - u_{CH}(SQ) > 0$. General deterrence of crises is more likely in this model as the challenger's value for the status quo rises. The above inequality is more likely to be true as $u_{CH}(SQ)$ rises. The threshold belief needed for deterrence of challenges falls as that value rises.

Pulling all of this analysis together into an equilibrium, we have the following two cases. The equilibria are read as (CH's first move, CH's last move; resolute D's reply, irresolute D's reply: CH's beliefs in its last move). When

$$\gamma > \frac{[1-u_{CH}(SQ)][u_{CH}(W^*)]}{u_{CH}(W^*) - u_{CH}(W)},$$

(NC,BD;r,r:p) with

$$p > \bar{\gamma}_{crit} = \frac{u_{CH}(W^*)}{u_{CH}(W^*) - u_{CH}(W)}$$

is a perfect Bayesian equilibrium. When

$$\gamma < \frac{[1 - u_{CH}(SQ)][u_{CH}(W^*)]}{u_{CH}(W^*) - u_{CH}(W)}$$

$$\left\{C, \left[\frac{1}{1 - u_D(W^*)}P, \frac{-u_D(W^*)}{1 - u_D(W^*)}BD\right]; r, \left[\frac{\bar{\gamma}_{crit} - \gamma}{(1 - \gamma)\bar{\gamma}_{crit}}nr, \frac{\gamma(1 - \bar{\gamma}_{crit})}{(1 - \gamma)\bar{\gamma}_{crit}}r\right] : \bar{\gamma}_{crit}\right\}$$

with

$$\bar{\gamma}_{crit} = \frac{u_{CH}(W^*)}{u_{CH}(W^*) - u_{CH}(W)}$$

is a perfect Bayesian equilibrium.

Exercise 7.8: Find a perfect Bayesian equilibrium to this model when $u_{CH}(C) = 1 > u_{CH}(W^*) > u_{CH}(SQ) > u_{CH}(W) > u_{CH}(BD) = 0$, and all other preferences remain the same:

a) Find the best reply correspondence for CH in its last move.

b) Calculate D's best reply in its move for both resolute and irresolute Ds.

c) Find the critical probability where CH is indifferent between C and NC in its first move.

We can use the equilibrium to compute the probabilities of the outcomes. Assume that all values of γ are equally likely (γ is uniformly distributed on [0,1] is the careful way to say this). Consider a crisis to occur whenever the challenger challenges the status quo. When

$$\gamma > \frac{[1 - u_{CH}(SQ)][u_{CH}(W^*)]}{u_{CH}(W^*) - u_{CH}(W)},$$

no crisis occurs; when

$$\gamma < \frac{[1 - u_{CH}(SQ)][u_{CH}(W^*)]}{u_{CH}(W^*) - u_{CH}(W)},$$

a crisis always occurs. Thus the probability of a crisis is the probability that the latter condition occurs:

$$p(\text{crisis}) = p(\gamma < \gamma^*) = \frac{\int_0^{\gamma^*} 1\,dx}{\int_0^1 1\,dx} = \frac{\gamma^*}{1} = \gamma^*,$$

where

$$\gamma^* = \frac{[1 - u_{CH}(SQ)]u_{CH}(W^*)}{u_{CH}(W^*) - u_{CH}(W)}.$$

The numerator above is the probability that $\gamma < \gamma^*$, and the denominator is the probability of all possible γ. Both probabilities are calculated using definite integrals because γ has a uniform distribution on [0,1]. This probability is just the fraction of the range of γ below γ^*. Because γ is uniformly distributed (all values are equally likely), the fraction of the range gives the probability.

The probabilities of concessions by the defender, the challenger's backing down, and war given a crisis are more complicated to calculate. The probabilities of these events vary with γ. The calculation of the chance each event occurs across all possible γ must account for these changing probabilities. Integrals are necessary to calculate the probabilities. The defender makes concessions with probability

$$(1 - \gamma)\left[\frac{\bar{\gamma}_{crit} - \gamma}{(1 - \gamma)\bar{\gamma}_{crit}}\right] = \frac{\bar{\gamma}_{crit} - \gamma}{\bar{\gamma}_{crit}},$$

where $(1 - \gamma)$ is the probability that it is irresolute and

$$\frac{\bar{\gamma}_{crit} - \gamma}{(1 - \gamma)\bar{\gamma}_{crit}}$$

is the probability that it makes concessions if it is irresolute. The probability that the defender makes concessions if a crisis occurs is

$$p(nr|\text{crisis}) = \frac{\displaystyle\int_0^{\gamma^*} \frac{\overline{\gamma_{crit}} - x}{\overline{\gamma_{crit}}}\,dx}{\displaystyle\int_0^{\gamma^*} 1\,dx} = \frac{\dfrac{\gamma^*\overline{\gamma_{crit}} - (1/2)\gamma^{*2}}{\overline{\gamma_{crit}}}}{\gamma^*} = \frac{2\overline{\gamma_{crit}} - \gamma^*}{2\overline{\gamma_{crit}}}$$

$$= \frac{1 + u_{CH}(SQ)}{2}$$

The probability that war breaks out for a given $\gamma < \bar{\gamma}_{crit}$ is

$$p(\text{D resists})p(\text{CH presses}) = \left(\frac{\gamma}{\bar{\gamma}_{crit}}\right)\left[\frac{1}{1 - u_D(W^*)}\right].$$

This probability grows with γ because the defender is more likely to resist as the challenger's belief that it is resolved grows. An irresolute defender is more likely to bluff as the credibility of its resolve grows. The probability of war given a crisis is

$$p(\text{war}|\text{crisis}) = \frac{\int_0^{\gamma^*} \frac{x}{\bar{\gamma}_{crit}[1 - u_D(W^*)]} dx}{\int_0^{\gamma^*} 1\, dx} = \frac{\frac{\gamma^{*2}}{2\bar{\gamma}_{crit}[1 - u_D(W^*)]}}{\gamma^*}$$

$$= \frac{\gamma^*}{2\bar{\gamma}_{crit}[1 - u_D(W^*)]}$$

$$= \frac{1 - u_{CH}(SQ)}{2[1 - u_D(W^*)]}.$$

War becomes more likely as the resolute defender's value for war increases and the challenger's value for receiving concessions from the status quo increases.

Exercise 7.9:

a) Compute the probabilities that a crisis occurs, that the challenger receives concessions from the defender given that a crisis occurs, and that a crisis escalates to war from the equilibrium you found in Exercise 7.8. Assume that all values of γ are equally likely.

b) The increase in the challenger's utility for war represents an increase in its resolve, whether its increased resolve comes from greater military capabilities or a greater willingness to suffer costs. Discuss the consequences of such increased resolve on what behavior we should expect by comparing the equilibrium of Exercise 7.8 to that in the text. Does greater resolve increase the challenger's chances of securing concessions from the defender without going to war? Does the challenger's greater resolve make war more likely?

What behavior would we observe if the actors were playing this equilibrium? First, the set of crises we would observe is different from the set of all possible crises. No crisis occurs in the first case of the equilibrium in the text; the defender's threat is sufficiently credible to deter the challenger. Crises only occur when the challenger doubts the resolve of the defender. Even then, the defender can convince the challenger of its resolve. The challenger does back down sometimes. The empirical study of crises needs to consider these selection effects in the events we observe. Observed events are not a random sample of the universe of possible events.

Second, when war occurs in the model, it appears that the challenger has ignored the defender's signal of its resolve. If we look only at the war cases in this model, the challenger presses its threat even though there is a substantial chance that the defender is resolute. In many of the war cases, the defender is resolute, and the challenger prefers backing down if it knows that, but war occurs anyway. This behavior resembles the "misperception" often found in empirical studies of crises. The challenger goes to war despite a signal of resolve from the defender. But consider the challenger's position in the face of its uncertainty about the defender's resolve. Even though the defender signals its resolve by resisting the initial threat, the challenger also knows that some irresolute defenders also resist the threat. These bluffs by irresolute defenders reduce the credibility of the signal that resolute defenders send by resisting the threat. The challenger cannot tell which type of defender it faces; it must judge the defender's resolve. Knowing that some irresolute defenders will resist, the defender should partially discount the defender's resistance as a signal of resolve. Nevertheless, this signal does communicate some information to the challenger. Its beliefs about the defender's resolve do change after observing resistance. In some cases, the defender's resistance convinces the challenger to back down. But if we focus only on the war cases, we would find many cases where the challenger goes to war even though a resolute defender has signaled its resolve.

This model suggests that uncertainty creates behavior that looks like "misperception" and "bolstering." The former means that the challenger has misjudged the resolve of the defender; the latter means that the challenger has ignored signals of that resolve. Both occur when the challenger goes to war with a resolute defender.[3] The challenger goes to war when it would not do so if it knew the defender's resolve. Further, it appears to ignore the defender's signal of its resolve. The defender can also appear to misperceive the challenger's intentions. Irresolute defenders resist the challenge sometimes, and the challenger sometimes presses the threat in the face of that resistance. In the model, when a crisis occurs, neither side knows for certain what the other will do in its next move. The clear expectations of the complete information model disappear when we add some uncertainty to the model. Both sides then may make moves that they would not make if they had complete information. But they do not, and we should not be surprised if the actors take actions that appear ill advised in hindsight.

Pushing this point further taxes the ability of this simple model to describe reality. Misperception and other psychological blunders may very well be common occurrences in crises. A complete treatment of these issues is beyond the scope of this model. Case studies that support the idea that misperception is central to crises often look at the politics of decisions within governments. Domestic politics has been abstracted away in this model. My point here is simple: game-theoretic models under uncertainty often produce equilibrium behavior that looks like the actors' misperceiving one another's intentions. It is not clear what evidence would separate the effects of strategic uncertainty from those of psychological misjudgments. At a minimum, game-theoretic models force us to think more carefully about how strategic choices can shape the evidence we can observe. They also serve as a sophisticated baseline for those who wish to argue that "irrational" behavior occurs.

There are two points in this model that may concern you. First, the assumption of only two types of challengers is artificial and creates some of the involved algebra here. In Chapter Eight, I present another model of deterrence, in which the defender's resolve is drawn from a continuous range of possibilities. Modeling uncertainty with a continuous range of types allows a more proper analysis of the effect of increased resolve. That model also eliminates the different cases in the equilibrium in this model.

Second, this model has another equilibrium. The equilibrium (NC,BD;r,r:p) with $p > \bar{\gamma}_{crit}$ is also a perfect Bayesian equilibrium of the model. The challenger's last move is off the equilibrium path. We can choose beliefs off the equilibrium path freely in a perfect Bayesian equilibrium. Here, I have chosen to make the challenger's belief that the defender is resolved sufficiently high to convince the challenger to back down. If the challenger will back down, all defenders, even irresolute ones, resist. The challenger, anticipating that it will back down, prefers to live with the status quo. This equilibrium seems reasonable when $\gamma > \bar{\gamma}_{crit}$, that is, when the challenger begins the game believing that the defender is likely to be resolute. But this equilibrium can be supported for any initial beliefs that challenger can hold. The challenger convinces itself that any defender who resists is resolute before it even tests the defender's resolve with a challenge.

This logic is quite bizarre, but it is an equilibrium. For now, we will rule out this equilibrium when $\gamma < \bar{\gamma}_{crit}$. The challenger's beliefs should change only when it sees evidence that they are incorrect. We can restrict beliefs off the equilibrium path to remain constant. This equilibrium cannot be supported for $\gamma < \bar{\gamma}_{crit}$ when beliefs are restricted in that fashion. With the restriction, $\bar{\gamma} < \bar{\gamma}_{crit}$, and the challenger will wish to press its threat. In turn, irresolute defenders wish to make concessions when they anticipate that the challenger will press its threat. This line of logic leads us to the case of the equilibrium where $\gamma < \bar{\gamma}_{crit}$. This example illustrates the idea of restrictions on beliefs, a refinement of perfect Bayesian equilibria.

"Why Vote?" Redux*

In Chapter Two, I discussed the problem of voter participation, using a simple utility model. The initial observation of such a model is that no one should vote. But people keep on voting in massive numbers; it is hard to argue that measurement error accounts for these discordant observations. I also presented two possible solutions in Chapter Two. One included benefits from the act of voting alone. People vote to gain these general benefits. The other solution invoked prospect theory and argued that people regularly overestimate the probability that their vote will be decisive. This section presents another possible solution to this paradox, based on Ledyard 1984.

This solution grows out of a simple observation. If everyone else votes, then my vote is almost certain to be irrelevant to the outcome. Then I should not vote because the costs of voting exceed any expected benefit from influencing the outcome. But if no one else votes, then I should always want to vote because I can decide the outcome. Neither of these extremes can be an equilibrium.[4] In between them, there is an equilibrium where voters' expectations of whether other voters will vote and the marginal effect of their own vote on the outcome match. Those voters who feel voting is less costly vote; those who face higher costs for voting do not; and the marginal voter is indifferent between voting and not voting. For the marginal voter, the cost of voting matches the benefit from the marginal effect of his or her vote on the outcome of the election.

The model I present here focuses solely on this argument about turnout. I abstract away from the candidates and how their positions drive the voters evaluations of them. A complete model of elections should include the candidates' choices and how those choices create the voters' preferences among the candidates. To simplify the problem, I do not consider the candidates' decisions here.

Each individual voter faces a decision to vote or not to vote, much like the decision presented in the calculus of voting in Chapter Two. There are two candidates, C1 and C2. The benefit for seeing one's preferred candidate elected is B, which I set to 1 for convenience. For every voter, assume he or she has a $\frac{1}{2}$ chance of preferring C1 and a $\frac{1}{2}$ chance of preferring C2. Each voter knows his or her own preferences; these equal probabilities express what they know about other voters' preferences between the candidates. If voter i prefers C1, he or she receives B if C1 wins and 0 if C2. Each voter also faces costs of voting, C_i, with C_i drawn from a uniform distribution on [0,1]. These costs can be thought of as costs relative to the normalized benefit. Costs of voting range from 0 to 1, with all possible values being equally likely. Again, each voter knows his or her own costs of voting, and the distribution of costs

*This section uses the Binomial Theorem.

represents what all voters know about other voters' costs. Finally, there are a total of n members of the electorate. Not all will vote, but n people can vote.

I do not allow costs of voting less than 0 or greater than 1. Any voter with negative costs always votes for his or her preferred candidate. Voters with negative costs have positive net benefits for the act of voting itself. I exclude this possibility to simplify the calculation of a voter's marginal chance of determining the outcome. Including voters with negative costs lowers the chance that voters facing costs determine the outcome. Excluding them reduces the burden of calculation without changing the character of the results greatly. Voters with costs greater than 1 always face costs of voting greater than any possible benefit of voting. Such voters never vote, even when they know they are decisive. Why include them in the model, then?

Similarly, I let the probability of a voter's preferring each candidate equal $\frac{1}{2}$. This assumption covers the case where voters expect a close race. We expect that turnout should be highest when each candidate is supported by an equal share of the electorate. We can vary the expected chances of candidates winning by choosing some other probability that voters prefer C1. I return to this point later in an exercise.

Consider an individual voter's decision as to whether to vote. If the voter does vote, it will obviously be for his or her preferred candidate. (I demonstrated this point with the utility theory model of voting in Chapter Two; the argument is the same here.) Let voter i be indifferent between voting and not voting. All voters j with $C_j < C_i$ vote, and all voters k with $C_k > C_i$ do not vote. The expected number of voters is $C_i n$, where i is the marginal voter. The chance that each voter j votes equals the probability that $C_j < C_i$. Because all values of C_j between 0 and 1 are equally likely, this probability is C_i. If there are n possible voters, the expected number of voters is $C_i n$. For ease of exposition, assume that $C_i n$ is an odd integer.[5] When voter i does not vote, i's preferred candidate (say, C1) wins if $(C_i n + 1)/2$ or more voters vote for C1. If $(C_i n - 1)/2$ voters vote for C1, we have a tie and the winning candidate is selected by chance, with a $\frac{1}{2}$ chance for each candidate. The voter's expected utility for the outcome of the election if he or she does not vote is

$$\sum_{j=\frac{C_i n+1}{2}}^{C_i n-1} \binom{C_i n - 1}{j} \left(\frac{1}{2}\right)^{C_i n-1} + \left(\frac{1}{2}\right) \binom{C_i n - 1}{\frac{C_i n - 1}{2}} \left(\frac{1}{2}\right)^{C_i n-1}.$$

The first term gives that chance that $(C_i n + 1)/2$ or more voters vote for C1; the second term gives the chance that $(C_i n - 1)/2$ voters vote for C1. The benefit to the voter from C1's winning is 1. The second term is multiplied by $\frac{1}{2}$ to account for the chance of C1's winning when there is a tie. In all other cases, C2 is elected, and the voter receives 0 benefit.

If the voter does vote for C1, his or her expected utility is

$$\sum_{k=\frac{C_in-1}{2}}^{C_in-1} \binom{C_in-1}{k}\left(\frac{1}{2}\right)^{C_in-1} - C_i.$$

The first term is the benefit from C1's winning, which occurs when at least $(C_in-1)/2$ other voters vote for C1. The second term is the cost of voting to the voter, which the voter pays regardless of which candidate wins. When less than $(C_in-1)/2$ other voters vote for C1, C2 wins, and our voter pays the cost of voting for no benefit.

As I have assumed that our voter is indifferent, set the two expressions above equal and solve for C_i. Notice that the benefits cancel out whenever more than $(C_in-1)/2$ other voters vote for C1. We should expect this cancellation because our voter is not decisive then. C1 wins regardless of what our voter does. After canceling these cases, we have the following:

$$C_i = \frac{1}{2}\binom{C_in-1}{\frac{C_in-1}{2}}\left(\frac{1}{2}\right)^{C_in-1} = \left[\left(\frac{1}{2}\right)^{C_in}\right]\frac{(C_in-1)!}{\left(\frac{C_in-1}{2}\right)!\left(\frac{C_in+1}{2}\right)!}.$$

The above equality provides an equilibrium condition for C_i. Unfortunately, this expression cannot be solved explicitly for the equilibrium costs, C_i. Nevertheless, we can draw four conclusions about turnout from the above equality, as follows.

First, turnout is positive. C_i cannot be 0 in equilibrium because the right-hand side of the equation above is always positive.

Second, some voters do not vote. The right-hand side is $\frac{1}{2}$ times the probability that all other voters divide their votes equally, which is always less than 1.

Third, turnout declines as the electorate increases. Larger values of n decrease the right-hand side if we hold C_i constant. If we add two voters to the expected turnout, C_in, we multiply the right-hand side by

$$\left[\left(\frac{1}{2}\right)^{2}\right]\frac{(C_in+1)(C_in)}{\left(\frac{C_in+1}{2}\right)\left(\frac{C_in+3}{2}\right)} = \frac{C_in}{C_in+3} < 1.$$

Thus C_i and turnout with it must decline in equilibrium as n increases.

<u>Exercise 7.10</u>: Find the equilibrium condition for voting when C_in is an even integer.

This model does solve the problem of producing a positive turnout with a rational model. But it has other conclusions that some may not believe are an accurate description of turnout in elections. Costs of voting determine who votes in this model. If the time and effort involved in voting are the costs of voting, some have described this model as concluding that only those who live within a block of the polls vote. On a more serious note, this model accounts for why simple barriers to voting can effectively stop groups from voting. Limiting the opportunity to register to vote can stop people from voting even when they believe the benefits of voting are large. It is difficult to know how we can observe the costs of voting. If we include the idea of benefits of voting independent of determining the winner, measuring the costs of voting appears hopeless.

The model also predicts that turnout is always less than $\frac{1}{2}$ and probably quite small. One can argue that this conclusion occurs because I have made the benefits of voting small. There are voters in this model with benefits and costs of voting equal when they know they have the decisive vote. By setting B equal to 1, I have made the benefits of seeing one's preferred candidate elected small. We could increase B and see how the equilibrium turnout changes. We expect that turnout should increase as the benefits of voting increase relative to the costs. In the United States, turnout is higher in presidential elections than in off-year elections. Local elections in this country typically have lower turnout than do national elections. Cross-nationally, turnout is typically higher in countries that reduce the barriers to voting (e.g., registration laws).

> Exercise 7.11: Find the equality expressing the equilibrium relationship for general B. Assume that $C_i n$ is an odd integer. Does turnout increase as B increases?

A complete model would model the candidate's choice of positions as well. If candidates converge on the position of the median voter, the voters' benefits for seeing their preferred candidates elected are reduced. If the candidates adopt the same position, as they do in the spatial model presented in Chapter Four, the voters have no preferences between the two candidates. The assumption of very small benefits for choosing the winning candidate may be quite reasonable in the absence of a solid explanation of why voters believe that the different candidates will have different consequences for postelection policy. The candidates could produce such beliefs by adopting divergent positions. The voters could refuse to believe that the winning candidate will enact the position of the median voter even if he or she adopted it during the campaign. After all, presidents are not free to set policy on their own.

Ideally, all of these motivations should be included in a comprehensive model of elections and government. Such a model would explain how voters form their expectations of the policies that each candidate would adopt once in office, how the candidates choose the strategies that create the voters' expectations about future policy, and how those strategies induce the policies the candidates enact while in office, as well as why voters are willing to vote. Such a model does not exist yet. Several of the parts of that grand model do exist. In Chapter Nine, I present a model of retrospective voting that addresses the question of how retrospective voting disciplines the acts of incumbents. Other models that I do not cover in this book address how voters interpret campaign promises in terms of expected policies should each candidate win.

Review

This chapter presented perfect equilibrium and sequential equilibrium. Both test the robustness of equilibria by assuming that players may "tremble" in their strategies. These small, independent chances of defection create hypotheses that could account for deviations from equilibrium behavior. Perfect equilibrium tests whether strategies are best replies against such trembles. Sequential equilibrium uses trembles to create beliefs off the equilibrium path. Perfect equilibrium eliminates equilibria where a player plays a weakly dominated strategy, while sequential equilibrium does not.

Perfect Bayesian equilibrium is generally used in applications rather than perfect or sequential equilibrium because it is easier to use. Table 7.1 summarizes the different types of equilibrium concepts as a review of the last four chapters. It lists them from the weakest, Nash, at the top of the table, down through increasing strength, ending with perfect equilibrium. The first column lists the equilibrium concepts. The second column states where in a game best replies are judged. The third column describes the robustness of best replies. The fourth column says whether the concept uses beliefs. The final column states how beliefs off the equilibrium path are judged. "Irrelevant" in this column indicates that beliefs are not used in that equilibrium concept.

Nash equilibrium judges best replies only along the equilibrium path. It asks only that moves on the equilibrium path be best replies. Moves off the equilibrium path can be suboptimal for the moving player. Subgame perfection tests best replies within proper subgames. It requires that players play best replies within each subgame. Perfect Bayesian equilibrium adds beliefs to judge the sequential rationality of all moves. Beliefs are always consistent with equilibrium strategies along the equilibrium path. But off the equilibrium path, perfect Bayesian equilibrium allows generally free choice of beliefs. Sequential equilibrium assumes that beliefs off the equilibrium path are consistent with trembles from the equilibrium strategies. Perfect equilibrium tests the robustness of strategies against trembles at all information sets. It does not use beliefs.

This chapter also presented two examples of perfect Bayesian equilibrium in action, one on deterrence and the other on voting. The voting example found

Table 7.1

Equilibrium Concept	Best Replies Are Judged...	Robustness of Best Replies	Uses Beliefs?	Beliefs Off the Equilibrium Path
Nash	Along the Equilibrium Path	Complete Strategies Compared	No	Irrelevant
Subgame Perfect	In Proper Subgames	Strategies within Subgames Compared	No	Irrelevant
Perfect Bayesian	At All Information Sets	Sequential Rationality at All Information Sets	Yes	Can Be Chosen Freely
Sequential	At All Information Sets	Sequential Rationality at All Information Sets	Yes	Consistent with Trembles
Perfect	At All Information Sets	Against Trembles; No Weakly Dominated Strategies	No	Irrelevant

Comparison of Different Equilibrium Concepts

an equilibrium where voters vote despite positive costs of voting. The deterrence example is a game of limited information. The challenger was uncertain about the defender's motivation in the crisis. Games of limited information are the topic of the next chapter. In such games, the concept of perfect Bayesian equilibrium is highly useful.

Further Reading

The standard texts have good discussions of perfect equilibrium and sequential equilibrium. Selten 1975 and Kreps and Wilson 1982a, respectively, are the original sources for these concepts. I recommend Fudenberg and Tirole 1991 for a complete discussion of these concepts.

The model of deterrence draws on the growing literature on limited-information models of crisis bargaining. It is not based on any particular model in the literature. In the Further Reading section of Chapter Eight, I survey some formal models of crisis bargaining.

The voting equilibrium model draws on Ledyard 1984. Palfrey and Rosenthal 1985 is an expansion of Ledyard's model.

Electoral Politics

The theory of elections addresses two related questions: why and for whom do citizens vote, and how do candidates compete in elections? Coughlin (1990) surveys the formal literature on elections. Aldrich (1993) reviews what we know about turnout from rational choice models. Both are good places to begin reading. You should also read the essay on comparative politics in Chapter Six. I survey research on multiparty elections there.

Candidate competition is typically modeled in a spatial framework. Enelow and Hinich 1990 is a collection of recent papers on spatial theory. McKelvey and Ordeshook (1986) examine candidate competition and voting behavior under limited information. Candidates use polls, and voters use endorsements, to assess their relative positions. Kollman, Miller, and Page (1992) examine party competition with a bounded rationality model.

Ledyard's (1984) model includes the candidates' choice of positions in a spatial competition within the model. His model is more general than the simplified version in the text. It is also more pessimistic about voter turnout because the benefits to a voter for determining the winner are smaller as the candidates' positions converge. Palfrey and Rosenthal (1985) expand on Ledyard's model to show its limitations as an explanation of why people in large electorates vote. Lohmann's (1993) model of political activism is closely related to these models of electoral turnout. She models political action as a signaling process.

A different approach to voting in mass elections is retrospective voting, where voters decide whether to retain the incumbent on the basis of his or her performance in office. Ferejohn 1986 is the first game-theoretic model of retrospective voting and is presented in Chapter Nine. Austen-Smith and Banks 1989 is a more advanced model of retrospective voting. Alesina and Rosenthal (1989) turn this argument on its head to claim that elections affect economic performance, rather than economics' driving elections. Retrospective voting is a common element of many models that address the formation of policy by officeholders. Morrow (1991) presents one example of how retrospective voting drives policy on arms control.

Models have been developed of many of the other facets of elections. Austen-Smith (1992) examines lobbying of elected officials by constituents. Lupia (1992) models the initiative process with a signaling model. Myerson and Weber 1993 is the latest in a line of studies examining how voting rules affect electoral competition. Snyder (1990) analyzes campaign contributions and spending patterns as a form of electoral competition.

Chapter Eight
Games of Limited Information and Restrictions on Beliefs

In games of limited or incomplete information, the players lack information about the exact nature of the game. They could be ignorant of the structure of the game, the other players' utility functions, or the exact consequences of their moves. The deterrence game in Chapter Seven is a game of limited information. The challenger did not know the resolve of the defender.

The players generally have different information about these fundamental uncertainties. Up to now, we have assumed that all aspects of the game are common knowledge. Information is common knowledge if all players know that information and all players know that the other players know that information, and so on. A player's **private information** is information known only by that player. The defender's resolve, its preference between war and backing down, was its private information in the deterrence game. Each player's private information determines its **type**. Each player is one of several types; a player knows its own type, and the other players know only the set of types that it could be. In the deterrence game, the defender was one of two types, resolute or irresolute. It knew which type it was, but the challenger only knew that the defender was one of those two types.

In games of limited information, the players make judgments about the other players' types. Their beliefs in a perfect Bayesian equilibrium represent these judgments. A player's beliefs give the probability of the other players' types. In the deterrence game, the challenger had beliefs about the defender's resolve at both of its moves.

A player's private information can affect its moves. A resolute defender always resists a threat in the deterrence game, while an irresolute defender resists only sometimes. A player's moves can reveal its private information to the other players. A player updates its beliefs about another player's type from the latter's moves. A player compares the likelihood that each type of the other player would make the observed move in the equilibrium they are playing. If one type of opponent would make a particular move while another would not, that move reveals the opponent's type. In the deterrence game, the challenger revises upward its belief that the defender is resolute after the defender resists a threat. Resolute defenders are more likely to resist.

The players can communicate their private information through their moves, creating the possibility of strategic deception, bluffing, and signaling. A perfect Bayesian equilibrium of a game of limited information describes both the play of the game in the strategies and the change in the players' beliefs produced by the play of the game. An equilibrium of a game of limited information must specify the strategies and beliefs of all possible types of players. The equilibrium of the deterrence game specified strategies for both resolute and irresolute defenders. If we only specified the strategy of one type of defender, how could the challenger update its beliefs after the defender's move? It would know how likely one type of defender was to resist, but not the other. Because the challenger does not know the defender's type, an equilibrium must solve for both resolute and irresolute defenders. The challenger must consider what both types of defenders will do because it does not know which type it faces. So must we to model the challenger's decision problem.

On the equilibrium path, the equilibrium strategies and Bayes's Theorem define beliefs. But perfect Bayesian equilibrium allows beliefs off the equilibrium path to be chosen freely. This freedom can have profound consequences in a game of limited information. Consider the equilibrium of the deterrence game where the challenger never makes a threat. The defender's response and the challenger's decision as to whether to press the threat are off the equilibrium path. Those moves do not happen in this equilibrium. The challenger's updated beliefs determine its decision as to whether to press the threat. Because this action is off the equilibrium path, we can choose the challenger's belief that the defender is resolute to be sufficiently high that the challenger never presses its threat. If the challenger never presses its threat, then both types of defenders will resist any threat. Anticipating these consequences, the challenger never makes a threat. A player's beliefs about another player's type can determine its moves in a game of limited information. Beliefs off the equilibrium path can thus produce bizarre behavior on the equilibrium path in such games. Restrictions on beliefs are an attempt to deal with this problem.

In Chapter Three, we assumed that the game is common knowledge. We model a game of incomplete information while retaining this assumption with a clever trick developed by Harsanyi (1967–1968). A game of limited information begins with a chance move that determines each player's type. Each player is informed of its own type but not the other players' types. The chance move also produces the players' initial beliefs about the other players' types. All players know the probabilities of each player's type in the chance move. These probabilities are the players' initial beliefs about other players' types. A game of incomplete information consists of a set of identical games. Each of these games is played by a combination of the players' types, and the complete set is defined by all possible combinations of the players' types. The chance move determines which of these games is actually played. The players' uncertainty about the other players' types are modeled by information sets connecting its parallel nodes across games where its type is the same but the other players' types differ. In the deterrence game, there are two types of defenders and one type of challenger. There are two possible games, one between the challenger and a resolute defender and one between the challenger and an irresolute defender. The chance move determines which of the two games is played. The defender knows which game is played, but the challenger does not. Its uncertainty is represented by the two information sets that connect its moves in the two games. This trick allows us to model a game of incomplete information with a game of imperfect information (i.e., information sets with multiple nodes).

This chapter presents five different games of limited information. It introduces signaling games, a particular class of games of limited information, with a game of pretrial bargaining. The informational role of congressional committees is modeled in a signaling game in the second model. Parties bargaining over an agreement typically do not know one another's value for an agreement. The third model is a simple signaling game of bargaining under such uncertainty. The fourth model examines how actions in a crisis could influence the acting nation's reputation. Deterrent actions are signals of future intentions in this model. The fifth model illustrates the problem of beliefs off the equilibrium path. I also include a section on "cheap talk," costless signals of strategic intentions, in this chapter. Although it is not a game of limited information, I can then compare costly and costless signals.

Games of limited information can be used to represent many different uncertainties. Players are often uncertain about one another's payoffs, as in the deterrence game. Congress is uncertain about the results of policies in the model of the workings of congressional committees in this chapter. One can create games where the players "do not know" their own preferences (Morrow 1994a). In these games, the players are uncertain about their preferences over the outcomes. They may know how to achieve each outcome but are uncertain about which outcome is best for them. Each player may have some private information about the value of the outcomes. Such games represent situations where the consequences of policies are very unclear.

Games of incomplete information allow us to analyze strategic communication. We treat communication as messages that the players can send in a game. Sending a message is just a move in the game. Messages may lead the players to change their future moves by altering their beliefs about the game. We can study how communication and actions affect one another in these settings. Some uncertainty is necessary for communication to affect the play of a game. Otherwise, the players do not have beliefs that could be altered by communication. Communication could help the players understand the other players' types in a game of incomplete information. Alternatively, communication could help the players coordinate on one of the multiple equilibria of a game. Imperfect information, that is, uncertainty about the history of the game, is necessary for coordination to play a role. Otherwise, each player can verify what moves the

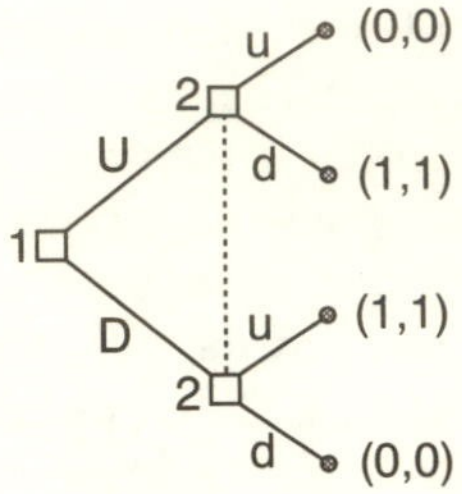

Figure 8.1 A Coordination Game

other has made when it must move, and they do not need communication to signal their moves. The section on "cheap talk" analyzes such coordination.

Communication can have a dramatic effect on the equilibria of a game. It is difficult to say which equilibrium should occur if we do not specify if and how the players can communicate. Nash equilibria require a common conjecture to explain why the players hold mutual expectations about which equilibrium they will play. Communication is one way to provide such a common conjecture. Consider the game in Figure 8.1. If the players cannot communicate, we should expect that they will play the mixed strategy equilibrium, $[(\frac{1}{2}U, \frac{1}{2}D); (\frac{1}{2}u, \frac{1}{2}d)]$. If they can communicate, we expect that they will coordinate on one of the two pure strategy equilibria, (U;d) or (D;u). The outcome of this game depends on whether communication is allowed before the players choose their moves.

Formalizing communication in a game forces us to specify what communication is allowed. We can analyze how different forms of communication affect the equilibria and outcomes of the game. Communication between the players could also be accomplished through moves other than formal opportunities to exchange messages. Actions may indicate the intentions of the acting player, and so speak louder than words. Such communication is often called tacit communication because the players are inferring one another's meanings from their actions. If formal communication is allowed, the extensive form of a game should specify the opportunities to communicate and what messages can be sent. Tacit communication may occur in any dynamic game of limited information.

Signaling Games

Signaling games are a simple way to begin to think about communication. In a signaling game, Player 1, often called the sender, holds private information that affects the decision of Player 2, who is called the receiver. The first player has an opportunity to signal that information to the second player prior to the latter's decision. Consider a legal suit where the defendant knows whether it

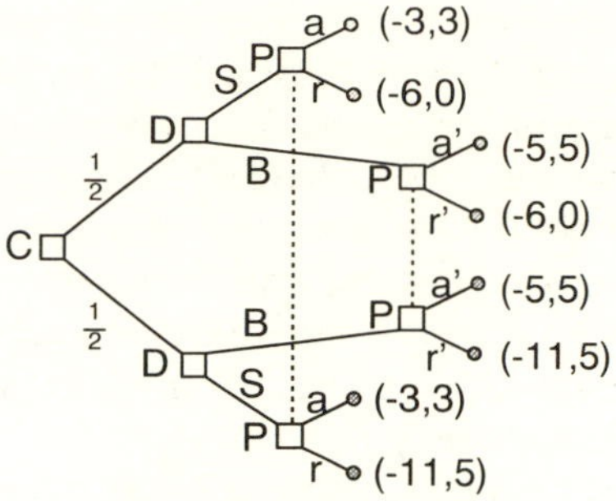

Figure 8.2 A Signaling Game of a Lawsuit

has been negligent, and the plaintiff does not know. The defendant can offer either a small or a large out-of-court settlement to the plaintiff before trial. Going to trial is costly; the defendant prefers reaching a large settlement before the trial to bearing the costs of the trial. But a small settlement is better for the defendant than a large settlement. The settlement offered by the defendant could signal the strength of the defendant's case to the plaintiff, affecting the willingness of the plaintiff to accept the offer. If the settlement offer is rejected by the plaintiff, the case goes to trial, and the defendant's private information is revealed. If the defendant is negligent, the plaintiff is awarded an amount equal to the large settlement.

Figure 8.2 presents a game from Banks and Sobel 1987 that formalizes this situation. Player 1 is the defendant, here called Player D. Player 2 is the plaintiff, here called Player P. The defendant is not negligent in the top branch and negligent in the bottom branch. Moves B and S for the defendant are making a big or a small offer respectively. Moves a and r for the plaintiff represent accepting or rejecting the small offer; moves a′ and r′ represent accepting or rejecting the big offer.

(S,S;a,a′) is a Nash equilibrium of this game. Read the moves as (D's offer if not negligent, D's offer if negligent; P's response to a small offer, P's response to a big offer). The defendant prefers small offers if the plaintiff always accepts them. The plaintiff is always willing to accept small offers because the offer of 3 for certain is better than the gamble of rejecting it and going to court. P's expected utility for rejecting the offer is $\frac{1}{2}(0) + \frac{1}{2}(5) = 2\frac{1}{2}$, which is less than 3. Whether P accepts a big offer is irrelevant to this Nash equilibrium because D never makes a big offer in equilibrium.

> <u>Exercise 8.1</u>: Find the other two Nash equilibria of the above game. (Hint: There are only pure strategy Nash equilibria to this game. Why are there no mixed strategy equilibria on the equilibrium path?)

The next step is to find the beliefs that support each of the Nash equilibria. The combination of those beliefs and the strategies above form perfect Bayesian equilibria of the game. The plaintiff's beliefs specify how strongly the plaintiff believes the defendant is negligent after receiving an offer. Because the plaintiff has two information sets, two sets of beliefs must be specified—one for small offers and one for big offers. The beliefs are calculated from the strategies for any information set reached in the equilibrium. Off the equilibrium path, beliefs can be chosen freely. We will choose beliefs that support the plaintiff's strategy.

In the (S,S;a,a′) equilibrium, the information set after a small offer, S, is on the equilibrium path, and the information set for a big offer is off the equilibrium path. The plaintiff's beliefs after a small offer are calculated from the equilibrium strategies using Bayes's Theorem. Because both types of defendants, negligent and not negligent, always make a small offer, the plaintiff's beliefs must retain the initial probability of each type of defendant in the random move. Thus

$$
\begin{aligned}
&p(\text{D negligent}|\text{S}) \\
&= \frac{p(\text{D negligent})p(\text{S}|\text{D negligent})}{p(\text{D negligent})p(\text{S}|\text{D negligent}) + p(\sim\text{D negligent})p(\text{S}|\sim\text{D negligent})} \\
&= \frac{(\frac{1}{2})(1)}{(\frac{1}{2})(1) + (\frac{1}{2})(1)} \\
&= \frac{1}{2}.
\end{aligned}
$$

The defendant never makes a big offer in this equilibrium. What should the plaintiff believe about the defendant's negligence if she receives a big offer in this equilibrium? Because a big offer should not happen in this equilibrium, perfect Bayesian equilibrium allows the plaintiff to have any beliefs about the defendant's negligence after receiving a big offer. I calculate the range of beliefs that support the plaintiff's strategy of accepting all big offers. Any belief in this range will support this equilibrium. Let p be the plaintiff's belief that the defendant is negligent if he makes a big offer. Calculate the plaintiff's expected utilities for accepting and rejecting a big offer, set them equal, and solve for the belief that makes her indifferent between accepting and rejecting a big offer:

$$
\begin{aligned}
u_P(a'|B) &= p(5) + (1 - p)(5) = 5, \\
u_P(r'|B) &= p(5) + (1 - p)(0) = 5p,
\end{aligned}
$$

and

$$a' I_P r' \text{ implies } p = 1.$$

If $p < 1$, the expected utility of accepting the big offer, 5, is greater than the expected utility of rejecting it, 5p, so she will accept a big offer. In words, the plaintiff must believe that the defendant is negligent for certain for her to reject a big offer. Even then, the plaintiff is indifferent between accepting and rejecting the offer. Any belief less than certainty, $p < 1$, means that the plaintiff accepts all big offers. Because we can choose beliefs off the equilibrium path freely, we can choose any $p \leq 1$, and the defendant will accept big offers.

The plaintiff's beliefs are $(\frac{1}{2}, p)$ with $p \leq 1$ for the (S,S;a,a′) equilibrium, then. The beliefs are read (P's belief that D is negligent after receiving a small offer, P's belief that D is negligent after receiving a big offer).

> Exercise 8.2: Find beliefs that support each of the Nash equilibria you found in Exercise 8.1. Specify the beliefs by giving the conditional probability that D is negligent at each information set.

Both types of defendants make the same offer in all three equilibria. We call an equilibrium where all types play the same strategy a **pooling equilibrium**. A **separating equilibrium** occurs if the types play different strategies and the receiver can tell what type of sender it is facing after observing a move. A **semiseparating equilibrium** occurs when the types neither pool nor separate. The defendant's beliefs change after receiving the offer in a semiseparating equilibrium, but it cannot tell which type it is facing.

The game in Figure 8.2 has only pooling equilibria. The negligent defendants always want to try to convince the plaintiff they are not negligent so that the plaintiff will accept a small offer. The initial beliefs of the plaintiff allow negligent defendants to act as though they were not negligent. The plaintiff's initial belief that the defendant is not negligent is sufficiently high that the plaintiff will accept any offer that either type of defendant makes. The plaintiff learns nothing about the defendant's type in these pooling equilibria. Because all types make the same offer, the plaintiff's beliefs about the defendant's responsibility do not change after she receives the defendant's offer. With different initial beliefs, however, there are separating equilibria of this game.

> Exercise 8.3: Change the chance move in the signaling game in Figure 8.2 to a $\frac{1}{4}$ chance of the defendant's being not negligent and a $\frac{3}{4}$ chance of his being negligent.
>
> **a)** Show that (S,S;a,a′) and (S,S;a,r′) are no longer perfect Bayesian equilibria.
>
> **b)** Find a mixed strategy perfect Bayesian equilibrium of this game where negligent defendants make both types of offers and the plaintiff occasionally rejects small offers. (Hint: Remember

that mixed strategies are calculated to make the other player indifferent between playing its two strategies.)

The semiseparating equilibrium in Exercise 8.3 communicates information about the defendant's type to the plaintiff. Because some negligent defendants make big offers, the plaintiff's belief about the responsibility of the defendant changes after a small offer is made. It is less likely that the defendant is negligent. The plaintiff is less willing to go to trial as a result of the new information. But the plaintiff must still go to trial sometimes after receiving a small offer. If the plaintiff always accepts a small offer, then all defendants will make only small offers. The threat of a trial dissuades negligent defendants from making a small offer all of the time. At the same time, the plaintiff does not want to reject all small offers because nonnegligent defendants make small offers. The plaintiff is better off accepting a small offer from a nonnegligent defendant than rejecting it and losing at trial.

This example illustrates a general principle of equilibrium in signaling games. No type of sender can benefit in equilibrium by acting like a different type. Nonnegligent defendants make small offers, but negligent defendants make large offers sometimes. This principle is called **incentive compatibility**. In equilibrium, the actions of the different types must be compatible with their incentives. Otherwise, some type would prefer sending a different signal than that specified in the candidate equilibrium.

Definition: A strategy pair (σ;a) for signaling game S is **incentive compatible** iff for all player types t and t′,

$$M_t\left\{\sigma(t); a[\sigma(t)]\right\} \geq M_t\left\{\sigma(t'); a[\sigma(t')]\right\},$$

where M_t is the payoff function of type t, $\sigma(x)$ is the signal sent by type x according to strategy σ, and a[σ(x)] is the action taken after observing message $\sigma(x)$ according to strategy a.

Pooling equilibria are always incentive compatible. All types send the same message in a pooling equilibria. The receiver takes the same action regardless of the sender's type; in other words, acting like a different type produces the same action. (Depending on the receiver's beliefs off the equilibrium path, there may be an advantage to sending a message that no type sends in the candidate equilibrium. This question is not one of incentive compatibility, though.) Incentive compatibility is important in testing separating equilibria. The receiver takes different actions after observing the sender's message in a separating equilibrium. Some types of senders benefit from imitation of other types when a strategy pairing is not incentive compatible. We check for incentive compatibility when looking for separating equilibria.

To conclude this section on signaling games, recall the model of political advice that produced a preference for biased information in Chapter Six, and compare it to a signaling game. The advisors in that model are not strategic actors. They produce recommendations without considering the effect of those recommendations on the decider's choice. If they were strategic actors, their recommendations would be chosen to influence the decider to make the choice that the advisor prefers. The next section covers a signaling model of the functioning of the committees of the U.S. Congress. The committee serves as an advisor to the whole body. It knows more about the consequences of policy than does the floor and reports bills that incorporate its superior information. If the committee prefers different policy outcomes from those preferred by the floor, the floor must be wary of accepting the committee's recommendations at face value.

The Informational Role of Congressional Committees

Signaling games provide us with a way to analyze communication between actors. We examine how receivers respond to the sender's signal. Earlier sections in Chapter Five presented models of congressional committees and rules. The argument from structure-induced equilibrium contended that the structure of Congress helped facilitate distributive deals over "pork barrel" programs. Committees provided their members with the ability to block legislation that opposed those members' interests and to send legislation to the floor that would pass unamended. The model of bargaining in legislatures indicated that closed rules were a way to expedite critical legislation when time pressure was high. This section presents a model of a third rationale behind the structure of Congress, drawn from Gilligan and Krehbiel 1987.

The effects of policies are uncertain. The common interest of all members in writing policy that serves their interests (leaving aside the question of how such interests are defined) calls for collecting information to reduce uncertainty. Such information collection requires members who are experienced in particular areas of policy. Committees exist to collect information, develop expertise in areas of policy, and write legislation for the floor based in part on their expertise and information. Legislative rules are used by the floor both to foster expertise and to control the influence of committees. Closed rules favor legislation written by committees, which encourages members to specialize in particular areas of policy. Open rules provide the floor with a way to amend legislation that reflects the particular interests of the committee at the expense of the floor.

The simplified model in this section allows the actors to "change their preferences." Outcomes combine both policy and factors beyond the actors' control. You can think of these exogenous factors as the details of the problem that policy is trying to remedy. Without a detailed knowledge of the specific issues, policies may produce outcomes very different from their intended consequences. This combination of chosen policy and exogenous effects is a way to represent the uncertainty of policy in a formal model. Members have ideal outcomes that they wish to achieve. But without knowledge of the exogenous factors that influence outcomes, actors cannot determine what policy they prefer. Policy preferences can change as members learn about the exogenous factors that influence the outcomes that policies produce. In this sense, the actors' preferences can "change."

Because policy preferences depend upon knowledge of exogenous factors, members have an incentive to gain the expertise needed to judge the consequences of policies. But gaining expertise is costly, and no member can be an expert on all issues.[1] Committees exist to divide the burden of acquiring such expertise. But the preferences of committees may diverge from those of the floor. The floor needs not only to inspire committees to make the effort to collect information but also to control their particular interests. Legislative rules provide one way to do so.

The model has two actors, a committee, C, and the floor, F. Each actor represents the median position of its body. The median voter concept allows us to simplify the choices of each body to that of a single actor. The game analyzes one issue. The issue is represented by a single dimension. The status quo policy is y_{SQ}. Fix the floor's ideal point to be 0 and the committee's ideal point to be $x_C > 0$. A bill gives a policy, y. The outcome combines the final policy with exogenous effects. These exogenous effects are represented by ϵ, a random variable distributed uniformly on $[-1,1]$, that is, distributed so that all values between -1 and 1, inclusive, are equally likely. The outcome is $y + \epsilon$. The players' utility for the outcome is the opposite of the squared difference between the outcome and their ideal point. The further the outcome is from an actor's ideal point, the less preferred it is.

The game begins with a chance move to determine the value of ϵ, which is not revealed to either player. The committee then decides whether to make the effort to collect information on an issue. Collecting information costs the committee c_c and reveals the true value of ϵ to it. The committee then proposes bill y to the floor. Unlike the model using structure-induced equilibrium, this model specifies that the committee must report a bill to the floor. Under the open rule, the floor can then amend the bill freely; call the amended bill y'. The floor chooses between the bill and the status quo. Finally, the outcome is revealed, and the players receive their payoffs. The time line of this game is as follows:

1. Chance determines ϵ, with uniform distribution on $[-1,1]$.

2. C decides whether to observe ϵ. If so, it pays cost c_C from its final payoff. F is informed of whether C decided to observe ϵ.

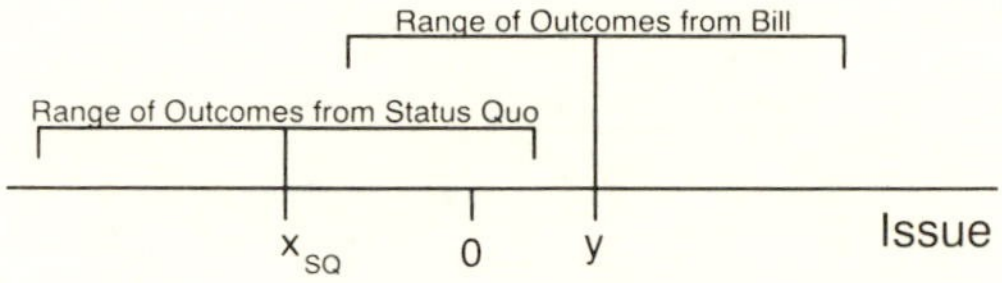

Figure 8.3 Comparing the Status Quo and Policy y with an Uninformed Committee

3. C proposes bill y. F updates its beliefs about ϵ after receiving y.

4. If the game is being played under the open rule, F can amend y to y′. If it is being played under the closed rule, this move is not available to F.

5. F chooses between y (or y′) and y_{SQ}. Call its selection Y.

6. ϵ is revealed to both players. C receives $-(Y + \epsilon - x_C)^2 - c_C$ if it observed ϵ and $-(Y + \epsilon - x_C)^2$ if it did not. F receives $-(Y + \epsilon)^2$.

This model allows us to analyze how the incentives to use committees to collect information vary with the rules, the status quo, and the divergence between the floor and the committee. The greater x_C is, the greater the divergence between the floor's and the committee's ideal points relative to the uncertainty of the issue. ϵ is bounded between -1 and 1. If x_C is large, say, above 10, the uncertainty on the issue is small relative to the divergent preferences. If x_C is small, say $\frac{1}{4}$, the uncertainty is relatively large. Incentives to use committees for information should be greater in the second case than in the first.

I solve the model under the closed rule and leave the open rule to accompanying exercises. Find an equilibrium by breaking the problem into the cases where C chooses to observe ϵ and those where C chooses not to observe ϵ. We can compare the two cases to determine when C prefers to gain expertise on the issue.

Begin with the case where C does not collect information. The analysis of this case parallels the model of structure-induced equilibrium in Chapter Five. F must choose between bill y and x_{SQ}. Because neither F nor C is informed about ϵ, both still believe that ϵ is uniformly distributed on $[-1,1]$. The mean of ϵ is 0, and F prefers y over x_{SQ} if y is closer to 0, F's ideal point, than x_{SQ} is. Figure 8.3 illustrates this logic. All points in each range of outcomes are equally likely. F chooses the range whose center is closer to its ideal point. In Figure 8.3, F prefers the bill to the status quo.[2]

The committee reports the bill to the floor that is closest to its ideal point and can pass the floor. Any bill y closer to F's ideal point than x_{SQ} passes on the floor. Because the committee is uninformed about the true value of ϵ, it prefers any bill to the status quo that is closer to its ideal point. If $x_{SQ} \leq -x_C$, C proposes x_C as the bill. If $-x_C < x_{SQ} < 0$, C proposes $-x_{SQ}$. If $0 \leq x_{SQ} \leq x_C$, C proposes a bill that will not pass the floor, x_C, for example. If $x_C < x_{SQ}$, C

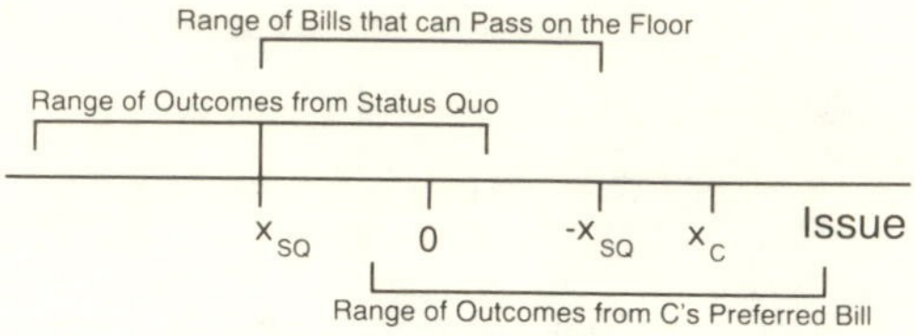

Figure 8.4 What Bills Will Pass on the Floor with an Uninformed Committee

proposes x_C. Figure 8.4 illustrates the second case here. Any bill between x_{SQ} and $-x_{SQ}$ passes the floor. The floor proposes the bill closest to its ideal point, x_C.

> Exercise 8.4: Find the equilibrium under the open rule when the committee does not collect information.
>
> **a)** Find the set of bills the floor prefers to the status quo.
>
> **b)** To what bill y', if any, will F amend y?
>
> **c)** What bill y does C report to F? Does it matter?

What are the consequences of the uninformed committee under the closed rule? The closed rule gives the committee significant proposal power. When the status quo is far from both the floor's and the committee's ideal points ($x_{SQ} \leq -x_C$ or $x_C \leq x_{SQ}$), the committee can achieve its ideal point as the approved bill. When the status quo is close to the floor's and the committee's ideal points ($-x_C < x_{SQ} < x_C$), the committee can block change or shape change to serve its interests at the expense of the floor. The closed rule then provides an advantage to the committee. However, the final outcome will not be its ideal point except in the rare case that $\epsilon = 0$. If $\epsilon < -x_C$ or $\epsilon > 0$ and the floor and the committee knew its true value, both would prefer some other bill to x_C. The final outcome, $x_C + \epsilon$, falls outside the set between their ideal points. Although passing x_C is optimal ex ante facto (when proposed and passed), it may be inefficient ex post facto (after the true value of ϵ is revealed). Both parties' lack of information about the consequences of policy limits their ability to choose the policy that leads to the outcomes they desire.

> Exercise 8.5: Find the outcome under the open rule when the committee is uninformed. Who benefits relative to the closed rule? Find the values of ϵ where both the committee and the floor would prefer to substitute some other bill if they knew the true value of ϵ.

The uninformed case parallels the model of structure-induced equilibrium in Chapter Five. There are no signaling issues because the committee is unin-

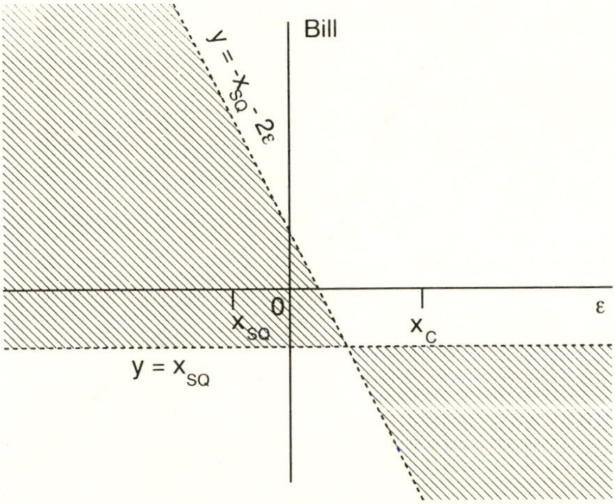

Figure 8.5 What Bills Will Pass on the Floor When an Informed Committee Signals Its Information

formed. But the case where the committee is informed is more difficult. Signaling issues arise because the floor can learn from the bill the committee reports. Start by looking for a separating equilibrium. Such an equilibrium can be supported only if the floor prefers the bill to the status quo and the committee offers a different bill for every value of ϵ. The floor knows ϵ when it must vote in a separating equilibrium. The value of ϵ gives the committee's type. By the definition of a separating equilibrium, the floor can determine the committee's type from the bill the committee proposes. The floor then also knows ϵ when it votes.

Figure 8.5 shows what bills the floor will approve. The horizontal axis gives the value of ϵ, and the vertical axis gives the proposed bill. The floor passes any bill in the shaded area between the two dashed lines in Figure 8.5. The equation of the horizontal line is $y = x_{SQ}$; the floor is indifferent between the status quo and a bill affirming the status quo. The equation of the diagonal line is $y = -x_{SQ} - 2\epsilon$; that bill produces a final outcome of $-x_{SQ} - \epsilon$, which is the opposite of the outcome the status quo produces, $x_{SQ} + \epsilon$.

Given this voting rule for the floor, what bill should the committee report? Figure 8.6 illustrates the logic. The solid diagonal line gives the bill that produces the committee's ideal point given ϵ. The equation of this line is $y = x_C - \epsilon$. The committee would like the final bill to be as close to this line as possible. When $\epsilon < -x_C - x_{SQ}$ or $\epsilon > x_C - x_{SQ}$, F will pass C's preferred bill, so C should propose that bill. When $-x_C - x_{SQ} < \epsilon < x_C - x_{SQ}$, the floor will not pass the committee's preferred bill. C then proposes the closest bill to its preferred bill that will pass the floor. The thick line in Figure 8.6 gives the bill that the committee should propose in this candidate separating equilibrium. F can determine the value of ϵ by working backwards from the reported bill.

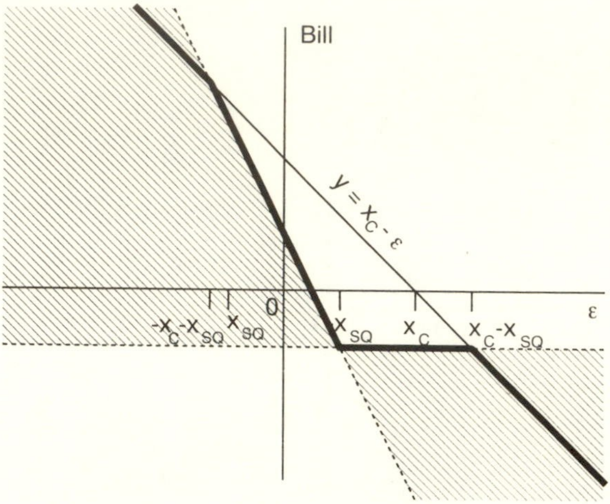

Figure 8.6 What Bills an Informed Committee Would Like to Report to the Floor

But this strategy is not incentive compatible when $-x_C - x_{SQ} \leq \epsilon \leq x_C - x_{SQ}$. The committee prefers sending a different bill than the bill given by this strategy. For example, let $\epsilon = -x_{SQ}$. The strategy proposes bill x_{SQ}, which produces a final outcome of $0 < x_C$. But C is better off proposing $x_C + x_{SQ}$. F infers that $\epsilon = -\frac{1}{2}x_C - x_{SQ}$ after observing that bill if the types separate according to the strategy for proposing bills above. F then accepts $x_C + x_{SQ}$, believing that that bill produces final outcome $\frac{1}{2}x_C$ and the status quo produces $-\frac{1}{2}x_C$. The end result of imitating the type where $\epsilon = -\frac{1}{2}x_C - x_{SQ}$ is x_C. That result is better for the committee than the outcome of 0 that results from the bill the separating strategy suggests. For all $-x_C - x_{SQ} \leq \epsilon \leq x_C - x_{SQ}$, similar bills can be found that produce x_C by tricking the floor about the value of ϵ.

The intuition here is simple. The bill that the committee reports is a credible signal of the exogenous effects on outcomes, ϵ, when those effects are large relative to the differences in preferred outcomes between the floor and committee. When the exogenous effects are large, the floor prefers accepting the committee's ideal outcome to the outcome the status quo policy produces. When the exogenous effects are small relative to their differences in preferred outcomes, the floor cannot trust the reported bill to reflect the exogenous effects accurately. If it does, then the committee can exploit that trust to gain better final outcomes for itself at the expense of the floor.

> Exercise 8.6: Examine the possibilities for a separating equilibrium under the open rule with an informed committee. The open rule differs from the closed rule because the committee's bill can be amended by the floor to anything the latter chooses.

a) What amended bill will the floor pass for a given value of ϵ if the floor knows the true value of ϵ?

b) Consider the incentives of the committee if its proposed bill separates and allows the floor to know the true value of ϵ. Is separation ever incentive compatible for the committee? (You may assume that the committee's bill simply gives the value of ϵ directly.)

A separation of types cannot be supported for $-x_C - x_{SQ} \leq \epsilon \leq x_C - x_{SQ}$. Within this range, there must be a pooling equilibrium. Further, all types of committees in this range offer the same bill, and the floor always rejects that bill. Assume that there is a semiseparating equilibrium such that all types of committees between x_0 and x_1, with $-x_C - x_{SQ} \leq x_0 \leq \epsilon \leq x_1 \leq x_C - x_{SQ}$, report the same bill B, and F approves that bill. The committee of type x_0, the committee of type x_1, and the floor prefer bill B to x_{SQ} as the policy. If committees of types x_0 and greater prefer the bill, its outcome, $B + x_0$, must be less than x_C but greater than $x_{SQ} + x_0$. Otherwise, all types greater than x_0 prefer x_{SQ} to B. But then all types between $-x_C - x_{SQ}$ and x_0 also prefer the bill to the status quo. Then $x_0 = -x_C - x_{SQ}$. If a committee of type x_1 prefers the bill, then $x_C - x_{SQ} - x_0 \geq B + x_0 - x_C$ (the outcome of the bill is closer to the committee's ideal point than the outcome of the status quo policy). The two outcomes, $B + x_0$ and $x_{SQ} + x_0$, must bracket x_C. Otherwise, types greater than x_1 prefer B to x_{SQ}. This inequality implies that

$$B \leq 2x_C - 2x_1 - x_{SQ}.$$

Equality holds when $x_1 < x_C - x_{SQ}$. The floor's expected utility for the bill must be greater than its expected utility for the status quo. It prefers the bill when the midpoint of the possible outcomes of the bill is closer to its ideal point, 0, than the midpoint of the possible outcomes of the status quo.[3] This implies that

$$B + \frac{x_0 + x_1}{2} \leq -x_{SQ} - \frac{x_0 + x_1}{2}.$$

Simplifying this inequality, we obtain

$$B \leq -x_{SQ} - x_0 - x_1.$$

These two inequalities imply that $x_1 = x_C - x_{SQ}$. If $x_1 < x_C - x_{SQ}$, then $B = 2x_C - 2x_1 - x_{SQ}$. Substitute this expression for B in the second inequality to obtain $x_1 - x_0 \geq 2x_C$. But $x_0 = -x_C - x_{SQ}$, so $x_1 \geq x_C - x_{SQ}$. Then all types of committees between $-x_C - x_{SQ}$ and $x_C - x_{SQ}$ pool by reporting the same bill.

The floor rejects any bill presented by the range of committees that pool. If a committee reports such a bill, the floor believes that all values of ϵ between $-x_C - x_{SQ}$ and $x_C - x_{SQ}$ are equally likely. The range of outcomes the floor expects from the status quo after observing a pooling bill is $-x_C$ to x_C. No bill can beat that range of outcomes for the floor given the floor's uncertainty about the true value of ϵ.

I have shown so far that separation is incentive compatible for all types less than $-x_C - x_{SQ}$ or greater than $x_C - x_{SQ}$, and that all types within that range offer the same bill and have their bill rejected by the floor. These two observations create one final problem in finding a complete equilibrium. When types in the pooling range know that their bill will be rejected, they have an incentive to imitate a type in the range $-3x_C - x_{SQ}$ to $-x_C - x_{SQ}$. Consider $\epsilon = -x_{SQ}$ as an example. Under the pooling strategy, a committee of this type expects an outcome of 0. By reporting a bill of $2x_C + x_{SQ}$ instead, the floor will believe that $\epsilon = -x_C - x_{SQ}$ and approve that bill over the status quo (the final outcomes given the false belief are equally distant from 0). But the true final outcome under this deception is $2x_C$, which is as good for the committee as the outcome of the status quo policy.

The floor prevents this deception by refusing to draw the inference the separating equilibrium suggests for any bill between $4x_C + x_{SQ}$ and $2x_C + x_{SQ}$. If it does so, the committee can exploit that inference to its own advantage when ϵ is between $-x_C - x_{SQ}$ and $x_C - x_{SQ}$. Separation and complete communication of the committee's information is possible only when $\epsilon < -3x_C - x_{SQ}$ or $\epsilon > x_C - x_{SQ}$. The full equilibrium is as follows:

> <u>Committee's Bill</u>: If $\epsilon < -3x_C - x_{SQ}$, propose $x_C - \epsilon$. If $-3x_C - x_{SQ} \leq \epsilon < -x_C - x_{SQ}$, propose $4x_C + x_{SQ}$. If $-x_C - x_{SQ} \leq \epsilon < x_C - x_{SQ}$, propose B, with $4x_C + x_{SQ} < B < x_{SQ}$. If $\epsilon \geq x_C - x_{SQ}$, propose $x_C - \epsilon$.
>
> <u>Floor's Beliefs</u>: If $B > 4x_C + x_{SQ}$, $\epsilon = x_C - B$. If $B = 4x_C + x_{SQ}$, ϵ is uniformly distributed on $[-3x_C - x_{SQ}, -x_C - x_{SQ}]$. If $4x_C + x_{SQ} > B > x_{SQ}$, then ϵ is uniformly distributed on $[-x_C - x_{SQ}, x_C - x_{SQ}]$. If $B < x_{SQ}$, $\epsilon = x_C - B$.
>
> <u>Floor's Vote</u>: Accept B if $B \geq 4x_C + x_{SQ}$ or $B < x_{SQ}$. Reject B otherwise.

This equilibrium illustrates how committees can be used to collect information in the floor's interest. It also shows the limits of a committee system, when it works best, and whose interests it serves. The committee fully reveals its information when the results of the status quo policy are far from both the floor and the committee's ideal points. This range is asymmetric; accurate signaling is easier when the committee's private information works against its particular interest (i.e., when $\epsilon > x_C - x_{SQ}$). The committee has an incentive to overstate the effects of ϵ to shift the outcome of policy away from the floor's ideal point and towards its own ideal point. The floor deters such overstatements by ignoring all bills that might be used for deception. Of course, this response hurts both parties by preventing some bills where both parties would be better off with honest revelation (i.e., $-3x_C - x_{SQ} < \epsilon < -x_C - x_{SQ}$). The committee is rewarded for revealing its information when ϵ is large in either direction. It gets to set policy to produce its ideal point, and the closed rule prevents the floor from amending the bill in its own interest. But this protection benefits both parties. The committee would not reveal its information without the reward. The floor is better off with the committee's ideal point than with the outcome of the status quo policy.

The committee system is more effective at communicating information when the committee and floor have similar preferences over the outcomes. The closer to 0 that x_C is, the greater the range of values where the committee reveals its information. The smaller the cost of the reward to the floor, the smaller the incentive for the committee to try to deceive the floor, and the more likely the floor is to grant the reward. All of these incentives reinforce the committee's incentive to reveal information truthfully. This result parallels the preference for biased information discussed in Chapter Six. Signaling is most effective when the sender and receiver have the same preferences. When their preferences differ, the sender has an incentive to try to deceive the receiver. The receiver knows this and consequently discounts the sender's signals.

Informed committees reduce some, but not all, of the inefficiencies that uncertainty introduces. There are many cases where both the committee and the floor could be made better off after the fact when the committee was uninformed. The final outcome is inefficient when it falls outside of 0 and x_C. Inefficiency occurs with an informed committee when $-3x_C - x_{SQ} < \epsilon < -x_C - x_{SQ}$. The final outcome is $4x_C + x_{SQ} + \epsilon > x_C$. In all other cases, the final outcome falls between 0 and x_C, typically falling at x_C.

Exercise 8.7: Exercise 8.6 showed that separation cannot be supported under the open rule. Find a semiseparating equilibrium under the open rule. Divide the range of possible ϵ into intervals between $x_0(= -1), x_1, \ldots, x_n(= 1)$. C signals in which interval that ϵ lies. F believes then that C is uniformly distributed on that interval.

a) Find the bill the floor approves if it believes that ϵ is uniformly distributed on $[x_i, x_{i+1}]$.

b) Find the indifference condition for C when $\epsilon = x_i$. Set C's value for the bill that is approved if it signals that ϵ lies between x_{i-1} and x_i equal to its value for the bill approved if ϵ lies between x_i and x_{i+1}.

We can use the relationship among the x_i's found in part b) to solve for the exact limits of each interval.

Under the open rule, the communication of information from the committee to the floor is not as efficient. The floor always chooses a bill to suit its interests over the committee's. The committee cannot use its informational advantage to shift legislation in its interest, so its incentive to reveal its information is reduced. What information the committee reveals reflects only the broad outlines of the likely outcomes of policy. The information the committee reveals serves the interests of both the floor and the committee. The greater the difference in their interests (i.e., the bigger x_C), the less information transmitted.

This observation suggests another rationale for restrictive amendment rules on the floor. Such rules advance the motivation for a committee to seek information on the consequences of policy in uncertain areas. Such information benefits the floor by avoiding legislation with disastrous consequences. Closed rules provide a benefit to committee members to encourage them to collect and reveal information about the likely consequences of policy. Open rules increase the ability of the floor to discipline the bills that committees report, but at the cost of reducing the committee's incentive to reveal what it knows.

Contrasting this model with the structure-induced–equilibrium model of the committee system in Chapter Five provides a test of these competing hypotheses. In the latter model, rules were a way to enforce distributive bargains among members. Members received committee positions that fit their particular interests and promoted legislation that suited those interests. Closed rules helped protect that legislation from the general interest of the floor. In the informational model, committees also received particular benefits from the closed rule. But the two stories differ about the composition of committees they predict. The structure-induced–equilibrium model suggests that committee members should look different from the general floor. Members seek committee assignments that reflect their particular rather than general interests. The informational model says committee members should not differ from the floor membership. Signaling is most effective when there is little difference between the floor's and committee's preferred outcomes. The critical test here is to see whether the preferred outcomes of committee members regularly differ from those of floor members on the issues that a committee covers.

I am not going to go into the difficulties of conducting such a test here. They are significant; see Snyder 1992 for one problem. My point is that the models helped us understand the consequences of both models and this critical test between them. Both of these views are compelling when described in general terms. Both probably represent some aspect of the reality of congressional politics. But without the models, we would be hard pressed to see the consequences of the strategic logic of each view. There is much evidence used to support one view or the other that does not allow us to separate between the two views. In both models, for example, committees receive preferential treatment of their bills under the closed rule, and that preferential treatment leads to distributional gains for the committee at the expense of the floor. This is how models help us sort out the evidence that might allow us to judge which view matches reality.

Bargaining under Incomplete Information

Bargaining under complete information tends to be quite strange. If an agreement is possible, then the parties must reach it if either party faces a final choice of accepting the last offer or ending bargaining and the other side knows it. If the order of offers and responses is structured into a game with complete and perfect information where each side can make and accept any offer at any move, the sides should reach agreement immediately. The Rubinstein model in Chapter Five has both of these features. Both of these observations differ from how bargaining actually occurs. Most observers of bargaining find cases where the parties fail to reach an agreement, even when an agreement acceptable to both sides exists. Bargaining fails in these cases because one or both sides played too "hard" in the bargaining, leading the other side to stop bargaining in the belief that a bargain was impossible. Moreover, each side tends to resist making concessions in order to help preserve its position and achieve the best possible deal.

The failure of bargaining models under complete information to explain these bargaining behaviors is disturbing and leads us to explore bargaining under incomplete information. The insight underlying these models is simple: the essence of bargaining is communication, and when the players already know everything about the game, there is no need for them to communicate and therefore no bargaining. These models examine how players should bargain when they possess private information about the attractiveness of different bargains. Offers and rejections operate as signals to the other player, influencing its willingness to accept or reject offers.

There are many models of bargaining under incomplete information. Most of them are technically complex, and all of them work on very simple bargaining situations. This field has a long way to go to capture what most of us think of as bargaining. Nevertheless, it is one of the most promising areas in game theory, both in theory and application.

To illustrate these models, I present a simple model of bargaining under incomplete information. I begin with a complete information model. After solving it, I add some uncertainty. There are two players, a buyer (B) and a seller (S). The buyer offers one of two prices, high (7 units) or low (5 units), to the seller. The seller can then accept or reject the offer. If the initial offer is rejected, then the buyer can make a final offer of 7 or 5. The players have a discount

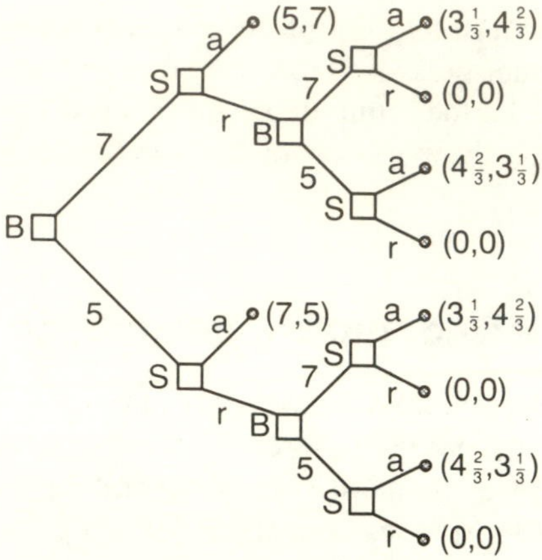

Figure 8.7 A Bargaining Game Where the Buyer Can Make Two Offers

factor of $\frac{2}{3}$ (if they make a trade in the second round, they receive only two-thirds of the value), so they prefer a trade in the first round to the same trade in the final round. The object they are bargaining over has 0 value to the seller and value 12 to the buyer at the end of the game. Figure 8.7 gives the extensive form of this game. The payoff for the buyer is given first, followed by the seller's payoff. The actions are labeled 7 and 5 for the offers and a and r for accept and reject for the seller's reaction to an offer. I have not differentiated all the offers and responses.

> <u>Exercise 8.8</u>: Find the subgame perfect equilibria of the bargaining game in Figure 8.7 under complete information.

Now add some uncertainty to the bargaining. Let there be two possible types of sellers, one that places no value on the object, called soft sellers, and another that places value 6 on the object, called tough sellers. Tough sellers never accept low offers. The tough seller's payoff is its net gain from the game. If a tough seller replaces the soft seller shown in Figure 8.7, the payoffs change as follows: 7 goes to 1, 5 goes to -1, $4\frac{2}{3}$ in the second round (corresponding to an offer of 7) goes to $\frac{2}{3}$, $3\frac{1}{3}$ goes to $-\frac{1}{3}$, and 0 remains as 0. I state the game with incomplete information as the time line below rather than as an extensive form because it is easier to analyze in time line form:

> **1.** Chance determines the seller's payoffs with probability $\frac{1}{4}$ that $r_S = 6$ (the seller is tough) and probability $\frac{3}{4}$ $r_S = 0$ (the seller is soft). The seller (S) is informed of its payoffs.

2. Buyer (B) offers either a high (7) or low (5) price. Call this offer Ω_1.

3. S accepts or rejects Ω_1. If it accepts, the game ends with $u_B = 12 - \Omega_1$ and $u_S = \Omega_1 - r_S$.

4. If S rejects Ω_1, B offers Ω_2 with either a high (7) or low (5) price.

5. S accepts or rejects Ω_2. If it accepts, payoffs are $u_B = \frac{2}{3}(12 - \Omega_2)$ and $u_S = \frac{2}{3}(\Omega_1 - r_S)$. If it rejects the offer, $u_B = 0$ and $u_S = 0$.

The game starts with a chance move, with probability $\frac{1}{4}$ that the seller is tough and probability $\frac{3}{4}$ that the seller is soft. The seller is informed of its value for the object, defining its payoffs. The seller's value becomes its private information. The buyer's initial belief that the seller is tough is $\frac{1}{4}$ as given by the probability of the chance move.

In equilibrium, tough sellers always reject offers of 5 and accept offers of 7. Soft sellers always accept any offer in the final round and always accept 7 in the first round. These moves dominate the alternative moves. To specify an equilibrium, I note the buyer's offers in both rounds, the soft seller's response to an offer of 5 in the first round, and the buyer's belief that the seller is hard in the final round. A perfect Bayesian equilibrium of this model is (5,7;a:1), read as (the buyer's first offer, the buyer's final offer; a soft seller's response if the buyer offers 5 in the first round: the buyer's belief that the seller is tough in the final round).

In this equilibrium, the types of sellers separate in their responses to an initial low offer. I prove it is perfect Bayesian. Begin with the buyer's beliefs after the seller's response to the first offer. According to the equilibrium strategies, tough sellers always reject that offer, and soft sellers always accept it. Only tough sellers should be left after the first round; $\overline{\beta}$ (the buyer's updated beliefs) must equal 1:

$$\begin{aligned}
&p(\text{S tough} \mid \Omega_1 \text{ rejected}) \\
&= \frac{p(\text{S tough})\, p(\Omega_1 \text{ rejected} \mid \text{S tough})}{p(\text{S tough})\, p(\Omega_1 \text{ rejected} \mid \text{S tough}) + p(\text{S soft})\, p(\Omega_1 \text{ rejected} \mid \text{S soft})} \\
&= \frac{(\frac{1}{4})(1)}{(\frac{1}{4})(1) + (\frac{3}{4})(0)} = 1
\end{aligned}$$

Given a belief that the seller is tough, the buyer will always offer high (7) in the final round because tough sellers will not accept a low (5) offer. In the first round, the buyer's expected payoff from offering 5 is $\frac{3}{4}(7) + \frac{1}{4}(3\frac{1}{3}) = \frac{73}{12} = 6\frac{1}{12}$. The buyer's expected payoff from offering 7 in the first round is 5 because all sellers accept such an offer. The buyer prefers an initial low offer in the first round. If the seller is soft, it receives 5 if it accepts the first low offer and $4\frac{2}{3}$—that is, $\frac{2}{3}(7)$—if it waits for the final offer, so it prefers accepting the first offer.

The buyer uses a low bid to separate the two types of sellers, with the soft sellers taking the first offer. The buyer learns from its first offer because only hard sellers are left in the second round. This is how the players communicate tacitly through their bargaining. The effects of such tacit bargaining can be traced in the buyer's beliefs. Notice that bargaining is inefficient here: both the parties lose value when they go to the second offer.

Exercise 8.9:

a) Find a pooling perfect Bayesian equilibrium of this bargaining game when the initial draw gives the probability of a tough seller to be $\frac{2}{3}$. How does this change in the initial beliefs shift the balance of bargaining leverage between the parties?

b) Find the range of initial beliefs for the buyer that can support the pooling equilibrium. (Hint: Find the belief where the buyer is indifferent between a high and low offer in the first round.)

Exercise 8.10: Consider a case where there are two types of buyer and one type of seller. One type of buyer is soft and places value 12 on the object, call them soft. The other type of buyer is tough and places value 6 on the object. (Notice that tough buyers will never offer 7 for the object.) The seller is soft: it always places value 0 on the object. The players share a common discount factor of $\frac{2}{3}$. Let the initial probability of a tough buyer be $\frac{1}{2}$.

a) Write down the game in time line form.

b) Find the perfect Bayesian equilibrium of the game.

Models of bargaining with incomplete information get more complicated from here. I provide some references for further reading at the end of this chapter. For now, I give a brief review of some typical results of these models. One type of these models has one side making offers and the other side accepting or rejecting them. Typically, the first side is uninformed about the second's reservation level. "Walking offers" typically result in these models. The first actor begins with a low offer and increases it each round until the second player accepts it. The second player accepts any offer better than its reservation level. Another set of models vary the Rubinstein model by adding uncertainty about discount factors and produce similar results. Both types of model assume that a deal is always possible. For example, stipulate that the buyer's reservation price is known to be $50 and the seller's reservation price lies between $20 and $40. If the players know that it is possible that there is not a deal that both prefer to no deal, agreement is more difficult. Models where both sides can make offers are more difficult. Multiple equilibria become a major problem in these models because both sides must consider how their offers affect the other side's beliefs about the first side's reservation level. In economics, these bargaining models have been applied to strikes. In political science, they have been used to study prewar bargaining and other international negotiations. Now I move onto a different topic and explore reputations and deterrence.

Deterrence and Out-of-Equilibrium Beliefs

Many scholars argue that reputation is an important motivation behind costly acts in international politics. States may act in international crises not for the intrinsic value of the immediate issue, but rather to deter future challenges to their interests by building a reputation for responding to such challenges. For instance, some argue that it was important for the United States to demonstrate its willingness to use force in the wake of the fall of South Vietnam in 1975. According to this argument, President Ford's use of the Marines to free the Mayaguez, a ship seized by Cambodia, demonstrated U.S. willingness to use force. If the United States used force over such a minor issue, the argument ran, surely it would be perceived as ready to use force against a more important challenge, and thus deter such challenges.

But this argument creates a paradox. Deterrence of important threats requires a reputation for the willingness to suffer the high costs of fighting such threats. If a low-cost use of force always succeeds in creating such a reputation, then all types of deterring powers, regardless of the costs they face, want to engage in the low-cost use of force. The long-run benefits justify the short-run costs. But if deterring powers engage in the demonstrative use of force regardless of the costs they face, the demonstration lacks credibility. Threatening powers are not convinced by the demonstration of the willingness to bear costs precisely because *all* deterring powers carry it out.

There is a further twist on this problem of credibility. Action can also be interpreted as a signal of weakness. Those deterring powers who will pay any cost to block a major threat do not need to prove their willingness to fight. Only those powers whose credibility is in doubt need make such demonstrations. Thus fighting to counter minor threats signals weakness, and even deterring powers who face high costs to repel threats will not wish to fight low-cost threats.

This paradox of credibility is a problem of out-of-equilibrium beliefs. What should other nations infer from non-intervention when they expect the deterring power to always intervene? This paradox will not occur in some cases because some types of deterring powers will fight, others will not, and there are no beliefs off the equilibrium path. But it does occur when the deterring power always or never fights as a demonstration of will. This section presents a simple model, drawn from Nalebuff 1991, that explores this paradox and how different beliefs off the equilibrium path influence behavior on the equilibrium path.

We focus on the actions of a possible deterring power, D. D must choose whether to intervene in an immediate crisis. The stakes of the crisis to D are x; if D intervenes, it gains x immediately. D also pays costs, c, if it intervenes. These costs are private information for D and are drawn from a uniform distribution from 0 to 1. D knows the true value of c, but the threatening power, T, does not.

T's uncertainty creates the possibility of D's developing a reputation by intervening in the immediate crisis. We do not model directly the dynamics of future crises here. Instead, we assume that T's set of beliefs about D's costs for intervention gives D's value for its reputation. If $\bar{c}$ is the mean of T's beliefs about D's costs, $1 - \bar{c}$ is D's reputation, and let $a(1 - \bar{c})$ be D's value for its reputation. The lower the costs that T believes that D faces for intervening, the stronger is D's reputation. Presumably, the lower T believes D's costs to be, the more likely is T to believe that D will intervene in a future crisis, and so the less likely T is to start a crisis in the future. The value to D of future threats relative to the current crisis is given by a, with $a > 0$. The greater a is, the more D values its reputation relative to the current crisis.

If D's reputation did not matter, D would intervene when the benefits of intervention exceeded the costs, $x - c > 0$. Adding reputations complicates the question. D adds the effect of intervention on its reputation to this simple calculation. But we must add both the effect of intervening and the effect of not intervening on D's reputation. If c_i is the mean of D's costs after intervening and c_n is the mean of D's costs after not intervening, then D intervenes when

$$x - c + a(1 - c_i) > a(1 - c_n).$$

Simplifying, we get

$$x + a(c_n - c_i) > c.$$

When the inequality above is changed to an equality, D is indifferent between intervening and not intervening. Call c^* this critical cost. If $c < c^*$, D intervenes; if $c > c^*$, D does not intervene. The greater D's costs, the less likely it intervenes.

If D intervenes for some values of c and not for others, we can calculate D's reputation after intervening and after not intervening. We just update T's beliefs about D's costs, using Bayes's Theorem. The value of c_i is the mean of all the values of c for which D intervenes. This mean is the midpoint of 0 and

c^*, $\frac{c^*}{2}$, because c is uniformly distributed. Similarly, c_n is the midpoint of c^* and 1, $(1 + c^*)/2$. We have three equations in three unknowns, c_i, c_n, and c^* as follows:

$$c^* = x + a(c_n - c_i),$$

$$c_i = \frac{c^*}{2},$$

and

$$c_n = \frac{1 + c^*}{2}.$$

From the two equations for c_i and c_n, we can eliminate c^* and solve for their difference: $c_i - c_n = \frac{1}{2}$. Substitute this value back in the equation for c^* in the last paragraph to get $c^* = x + \frac{1}{2}a$. Substitute c^* back into the equations for c_i and c_n: $c_i = \frac{1}{2}x + \frac{1}{4}a$, $c_n = \frac{1}{2} + \frac{1}{2}x + \frac{1}{4}a$.

So far the model fits some of our intuition about building reputations. First, taking costly actions improves one's reputation for being willing to bear costs. The lower D's costs, the more likely it is to intervene, and its reputation improves if it intervenes. Intervention is a noisy signal about D's costs. T cannot determine exactly what D's costs are if D intervenes. But T has learned that those costs are lower than T originally believed. On the other hand, failure to intervene by D reduces its reputation. Second, the greater the value of the future relative to the current crisis, the more likely D is to intervene now; c^* increases as a increases. Finally, the greater the value of the current crisis relative to costs, the more likely D is to intervene; c^* increases as x increases.

This equilibrium requires D to intervene for some costs and not for others. If D always intervenes (or never intervenes), T's beliefs for nonintervention (or intervention) are off the equilibrium path and cannot be calculated by using Bayes's Theorem. The first equation above still describes the incentives that D must satisfy in the initial crisis. One of the equations for T's beliefs also holds, depending on what all Ds do. I look at the case where no D intervenes and leave the case where all Ds intervene to an exercise. I examine the incentives and beliefs in each of these polar cases to show the effects of beliefs off the equilibrium path on equilibrium behavior.

The case where no D intervenes requires T to infer weakness from intervention. Does the model support such an interpretation? Can we find an equilibrium where no D intervenes? If no D intervenes, then $c^* \leq 0$. We can solve for c_n with the third equation above: $c_n = \frac{1}{2}$. We should expect this answer; if no Ds intervene, T cannot learn about D's costs when it observes nonintervention. But the equation for c_i no longer holds because D never intervenes in this equilibrium and we cannot calculate c_i by using Bayes's Theorem. Instead, we can choose c_i to be any value from 0 to 1 that we like. From the first equation, we have $x + a(\frac{1}{2} - c_i) < 0$ because $c_n = \frac{1}{2}$ and the inequality must be true when $c = 0$. Choose $c_i = 1$, and this inequality becomes $x < \frac{1}{2}a$. These beliefs are extremely optimistic for the threatening power. If T should observe intervention by D, T concludes that D is the weakest type possible. The condition $x < \frac{1}{2}a$ is required for the nonintervention equilibrium. When $x > \frac{1}{2}a$, Ds that face no cost for intervening now (i.e., $c = 0$) prefer intervention now even though such intervention destroys their reputation. They believe that winning the current crisis is more valuable than sustaining their reputation. The smaller x is, the greater the range of beliefs after intervention (c_i) that can sustain the nonintervention equilibrium. For example, $c_i \geq \frac{1}{2}$ supports the nonintervention equilibrium when $x \leq 0$. This case covers situations where no D would intervene in the current crisis if there were no reputational effects. The cost of intervention always exceeds its immediate benefits.

Exercise 8.11: Find a perfect Bayesian equilibrium where all Ds intervene in the current crisis.

a) Find the relationship among x, a, and c_n that must satisfied for all Ds to intervene.

b) Find the relationship necessary for this equilibrium if T draws the more optimistic inference from nonintervention, $c_n = 1$.

c) Are there any values of a and x such that both the nonintervention and the all-intervene equilibria are possible? If so, describe these cases.

Both of the self-fulfilling equilibria are possible. They differ in the nature of the inference that the threatening power draws from behavior that should not occur. Beliefs off the equilibrium path influence what behavior is rational on the equilibrium path. But are all beliefs off the equilibrium path equally valid inferences? The next section discusses what restrictions can plausibly be placed on inferences off the equilibrium path.

An Introduction to Restrictions on Beliefs

The introduction of beliefs alters the idea of backwards induction. Backwards induction directly compares the outcomes that each available move will produce. We compare equilibrium outcomes with possible outcomes off the equilibrium path. But moves can change beliefs, and beliefs affect which moves are optimal. The evaluation of alternative moves is not so simple after adding beliefs. Because we can choose beliefs off the equilibrium path freely, we can choose odd beliefs that lead to odd actions off the equilibrium path. These odd actions then convince other players to choose peculiar actions on the equilibrium path.

Restrictions on beliefs are a way to address this problem. Nash equilibria judge just the optimality of actions along the equilibrium path; actions off the equilibrium path can be chosen freely. Perfect Bayesian equilibria require actions off the equilibrium path to be optimal as well, but we can choose beliefs off the equilibrium path freely. Restrictions on beliefs judge the plausibility of beliefs off the equilibrium path.

Return to the lawsuit signaling game in Figure 8.2. Consider the beliefs that support the equilibrium (B,B;r,a′). This equilibrium is supported by $(p,\frac{1}{2})$ with $p \geq \frac{3}{5}$. But are these beliefs reasonable? They imply that negligent defendants are more likely than nonnegligent ones to defect from the equilibrium by making a small offer. But nonnegligent defendants gain from defection whenever negligent defendants do, and the opposite is not true. We would like to say that these off-the-equilibrium-path beliefs are unreasonable and eliminate them and the equilibrium they support. Recent work in the field has concentrated on the question of what restrictions should be placed on beliefs off the equilibrium path beyond the weak restrictions imposed by perfect Bayesian and sequential equilibrium.

To introduce the ideas behind restrictions on beliefs, I turn to one of the cuter examples in noncooperative game theory, the Beer-Quiche Game (Cho and Kreps 1987). The Game Theory Bar & Grill has only two items on its breakfast menu, beer and quiche. Only two types of people frequent the Game Theory Bar & Grill, surly guys and wimps. Surly guys like beer for breakfast better than quiche; wimps prefer quiche to beer. But both types want to be left in peace to enjoy their breakfast and value that peace more than what they eat.

You, on the other hand, are a troublemaker. You enter the Game Theory Bar & Grill looking for a fight. But you are also a discriminating connoisseur of the sweet science of boxing. Surly guys are tough; wimps are not—that is why they are wimps, after all. You want to fight a wimp but not a surly guy. You enter the bar knowing that more surly guys eat there than wimps do. To be precise, you believe that 90 percent of the patrons of the Game Theory Bar & Grill are surly. But you can observe what a possible target of your aggression has eaten for breakfast. The question is what you can learn about their type from their breakfast.

The extensive-form game in Figure 8.8 specifies this problem. The game begins with a chance move that determines the type of bar patron, surly or wimpy. There is a .9 chance of a surly guy and a .1 chance of a wimp. For ease of presentation, I have labeled this player as S in the upper branch, for Surly

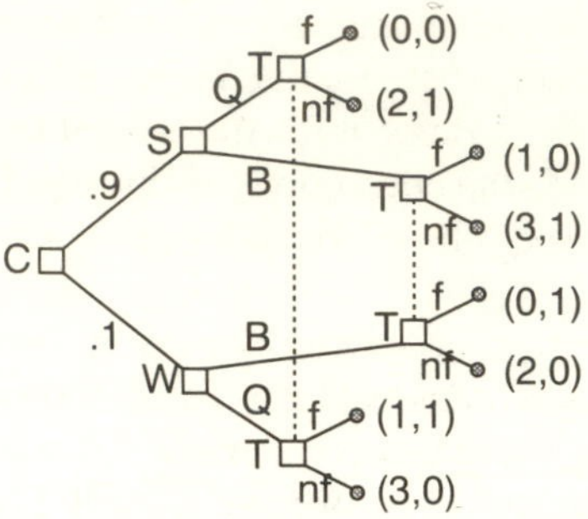

Figure 8.8 The Beer-Quiche Game

Guy, and W in the lower branch, for Wimp. The patron chooses his breakfast, beer or quiche, labeled B or Q. The troublemaker, T, enters the bar and chooses whether to fight the patron (f or nf, for fight or not fight) after observing what the patron ate for breakfast. Payoffs are written (Patron, Troublemaker). The patron receives a payoff of 2 for no fight, compared to 0 for a fight, and an additional 1 for eating his preferred breakfast. For instance, a surly guy who has quiche for breakfast and does not have to fight receives a total payoff of $0 + 2 = 2$. The troublemaker gets 1 for fighting a wimp or not fighting a surly guy and 0 for the opposite outcomes.

One equilibrium of the Beer-Quiche Game is (B,B;f,nf:0,.9) where the equilibrium is read (Surly Guy's breakfast, Wimp's breakfast; Troublemaker's choice after observing quiche, Troublemaker's choice after observing beer: Troublemaker's belief that patron is surly after observing quiche, Troublemaker's belief that patron is surly after observing beer). Wimps imitate surly guys in this equilibrium to avoid a fight. The chance of facing a surly guy is high enough to deter the troublemaker from starting a fight. The wimps are willing to have beer for breakfast because they avoid a fight by doing so. If they eat quiche, they get pounded. Someone eating quiche is off the equilibrium path here. The troublemaker infers that only a wimp would eat quiche when everyone else is having beer for breakfast. The troublemaker, then, prefers fighting anyone eating quiche.

> Exercise 8.12: Demonstrate that (B,B;f,nf:0,.9) is a perfect Bayesian equilibrium of the Beer-Quiche Game.

But there is another perfect Bayesian equilibrium of this game, where surly guys eat quiche: (Q,Q;nf,f:.9,0). The troublemaker is deterred by seeing the patron eat quiche. The chance that the patron is surly is still too high to take the chance on a fight. Here, beer for breakfast is off the equilibrium path. Perfect Bayesian equilibrium allows us freely to choose the troublemaker's beliefs after someone has beer. I choose to let the troublemaker conclude that anyone having beer for breakfast is a wimp. So the troublemaker is happy to fight anyone having beer for breakfast. Everyone has quiche because peace is more important than the preferred breakfast. Wimps do better in the quiche-eating equilibrium than in the beer-for-breakfast one. They get to eat their quiche in peace. Surly guys eat quiche because beer for breakfast convinces the troublemaker that you are a wimp. Maybe real men do eat quiche.

> Exercise 8.13: Demonstrate that (Q,Q;nf,f:.9,0) is a perfect Bayesian equilibrium of the Beer-Quiche Game.

This second equilibrium seems implausible. In the first equilibrium, wimps paid a price by having beer for breakfast in order to avoid a fight. The troublemaker construes quiche for breakfast as a signal that the patron is a wimp. This interpretation of the patron's behavior is a belief off the equilibrium path because no patron eats quiche in the first equilibrium. In the second equilibrium, the troublemaker understands a breakfast of beer as a signal of wimpiness; if you have beer for breakfast, you are a wimp. This interpretation should strike you as odd. A more plausible inference off the equilibrium path here is that beer signals that the patron is surly. Surly guys prefer beer for breakfast while wimps prefer quiche. If either type defects from this equilibrium, it must be a surly guy. Wimps cannot benefit by having beer for breakfast; their equilibrium payoff is 3, and the most they can receive if they have beer is 2. A surly guy can benefit by defecting if that defection convinces the troublemaker to leave him alone. His payoff would rise from 2 to 3. Why would you infer that a defector is a wimp then? The critical idea here is that wimps cannot benefit by defection from the equilibrium whereas surly guys might.

The opposite is true of the first equilibrium. Wimps might benefit by defection because they prefer quiche to beer. Surly guys cannot benefit even if they eat their quiche in peace. In this case, the inference off the equilibrium path that defectors are wimps is plausible. Wimps have an incentive to defect from the equilibrium of beer for breakfast, and surly guys do not.

This idea can be generalized. Beliefs off the equilibrium path should place zero probability on types that cannot ever benefit by defecting from equilibrium behavior. This restriction unravels the equilibrium where all patrons eat quiche. It requires the troublemaker's belief that the patron is a wimp to be 0 if the patron has beer for breakfast in the second equilibrium. Wimps cannot benefit by having beer for breakfast over their equilibrium payoff. But then not fighting rather than fighting is the optimal response for the troublemaker if the patron has beer for breakfast in this equilibrium. If the probability of facing a wimp is 0, the patron is undoubtedly surly, and the troublemaker does not want to fight a surly guy. Finally, surly guys want beer for breakfast over quiche once the troublemaker will not pick a fight with them after seeing them have beer for breakfast. By restricting beliefs off the equilibrium path to place

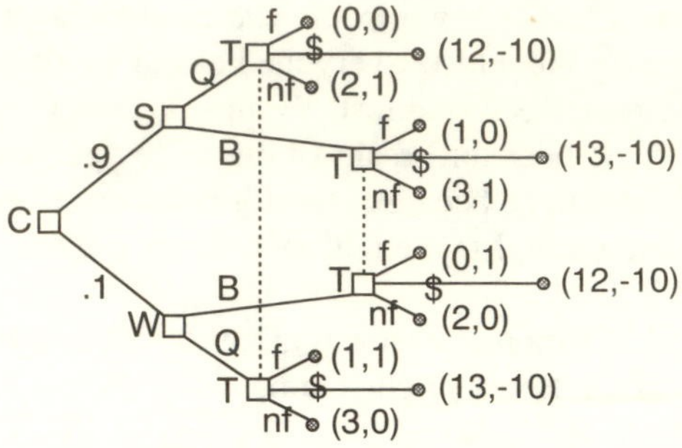

Figure 8.9 The Beer-Quiche Game with Bribes

zero weight on the type that cannot possibly benefit from defecting, we eliminate the (Q,Q;nf,f:.9,0) equilibrium. The threat of fighting patrons who have beer for breakfast is based on an implausible inference about who is likely to defect from this equilibrium.

Although this initial restriction on beliefs is reasonable, there are many equilibria of many games where it provides little ability to eliminate equilibria based on implausible beliefs. It can be strengthened in several ways that I briefly sketch here. My purpose here is not to provide a complete treatment of restrictions on beliefs. The ideas behind these restrictions are intuitive, but the formalisms are not. Further, there is not one commonly accepted set of restrictions on beliefs. An informal treatment of these ideas should help you understand what beliefs off the equilibrium path are eliminated.

First, we broaden this initial criterion for beliefs off the equilibrium path to assess the rationality of both parties in response to a possible defection. As before, consider two types of senders, t and t′. Both types' interest in defecting from an equilibrium depends upon the response of the receiver to that defection. The only responses that could make defection attractive to the sender are out of equilibrium and occur off the equilibrium path. Otherwise, our equilibrium would not be an equilibrium: at least one type of sender would do better by defecting. The second restriction on beliefs assesses the ranges of responses that might provoke defection across types of senders. If type t wants to defect for any response that makes type t′ want to defect, then the receiver's beliefs at the node following that defection cannot increase the probability of type t′ relative to that of type t. The receiver should believe that type t is at least as likely to defect as type t′.

An example may help clarify this idea. Add another response to the Beer-Quiche Game; the troublemaker can give the patron \$10. Figure 8.9 gives the modified game. The dollar sign denotes the move of paying the patron.

This game has the same two equilibria as the Beer-Quiche Game, (B,B;f,nf: 0,.9) and (Q,Q;nf,f:.9,0). Fighting and not fighting dominate paying the patron for the troublemaker regardless of her beliefs at either node. The first restriction on beliefs does not bind on the quiche-eating equilibrium of the modified game. There is now a response by the troublemaker, paying the patron, that makes defection better than the wimp's equilibrium payoff. But any response that makes a wimp defect from the quiche-eating equilibrium also makes a surly guy defect. The wimp prefers beer for breakfast when the troublemaker plays mixed strategy (p nf, q f, $1 - p - q$ \$), with probabilities p and q such that $p + q \leq 1$ and $2p + 0q + 12(1 - p - q) \geq 3$. Adding 1 to each side of the inequality, we get $3p + 1q + 13(1 - p - q) \geq 4 > 2$, which implies that surly guys also prefer beer for breakfast against (p nf, q f, $1 - p - q$ \$). The troublemaker's beliefs off the equilibrium path cannot increase the probability of a wimp from its initial beliefs under the second restriction because surly guys defect whenever wimps defect. The troublemaker must believe that there is at least a .9 chance of a surly guy and so no longer prefers to fight if the patron has beer for breakfast. As before, surly guys then want to have beer for breakfast.

> Exercise 8.14: Show that the (B,B;f,nf:0,.9) equilibrium of the modified game survives after applying the second restriction on beliefs.
>
> **a)** Find the inequality that expresses when surly guys wish to defect from the beer-drinking equilibrium.
>
> **b)** Do wimps also want to defect whenever surly guys do?
>
> **c)** What beliefs are consistent with the restriction?
>
> **d)** What is the troublemaker's optimal strategy given these beliefs, and what beliefs support this equilibrium?
>
> **e)** Why do wimps continue to have beer for breakfast?

The third restriction on beliefs uses the ideas above repeatedly to hone the set of plausible beliefs down. First, ask what range of beliefs meet the second criterion above and update the range of possible beliefs. Second, find the set of optimal responses for the receiver given those beliefs. Third, find which types of senders wish to defect for the responses found in the second set, and apply the second restriction on beliefs again. Repeat these three steps until the set of beliefs and responses does not change.

Return to the modified Beer-Quiche Game and test the plausibility of beliefs in the (B,B;f,nf:0,.9) equilibrium. Let p be the troublemaker's out-of-equilibrium belief that the patron is surly if he has quiche for breakfast. By the second restriction, $p \leq .9$ as shown above. The troublemaker's optimal response is fighting if $p < .5$ and not fighting if $p > .5$ ($p = .5$ produces indifference). If $p > .5$, wimps defect to quiche, but surly guys do not. Updating p produces $p = 0$. This repetition of the restriction on beliefs eliminates all $p > .5$. The only plausible beliefs have $p \leq .5$, then.

Exercise 8.15: Apply these restrictions on beliefs to the self-fulfilling equilibria of the geopolitical deterrence and reputation game discussed earlier in this chapter. Begin with the equilibrium where all deterring powers (Ds) intervene.

a) What type of D is most likely to defect from the equilibrium by not intervening? Recall that D's type is defined by its costs for intervening, with $0 \leq c \leq 1$, and that the response of the threatening power, T, can be summarized by the reputation c_n.
b) What beliefs can T hold after a defection by D from this equilibrium?
c) Given these beliefs off the equilibrium path, when do all Ds prefer intervention to nonintervention? Discuss; what cases does this represent, and does the restriction on beliefs reduce the set of equilibria?

Now turn to the equilibrium where no D intervenes.

d) What type of D is most likely to defect from the equilibrium by intervening?
e) What beliefs can T hold after a defection by D from this equilibrium?
f) Given these beliefs off the equilibrium path, when do all Ds prefer nonintervention to intervention? Discuss; what cases does this represent, and does the restriction on beliefs reduce the set of equilibria?

This section gives you some sense of the basic ideas behind restrictions on beliefs. If you are interested further in this topic, I provide references for further reading at the end of the chapter. The reader should be warned; restrictions on beliefs is a highly technical subject. There are several different ideas of such restrictions, and their differences are subtle and generally expressed technically. I turn now to one final issue in signaling, how costless signals can communicate information.

"Cheap Talk" and Coordination

The examples of signaling games so far use costly signals. The sender's payoffs vary with the signal it sends. Wimps do not like beer for breakfast; acting like a surly guy is costly for them. Costly signals aid separation of types. Some

		Player 2	
		s_1	s_2
Player 1	S_1	(a,1)	(0,0)
	S_2	(0,0)	(1,a)

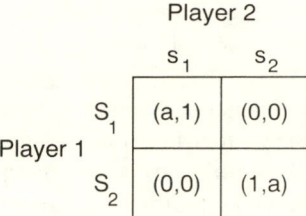

Figure 8.10 General Battle of the Sexes

types bear a cost for attempting to imitate other types, and sometimes those costs outweigh the benefits of imitation. This section covers costless signaling, better known as "cheap talk," from the saying "Talk is cheap." It addresses how communication can help players select among multiple equilibria of games with complete information. Unlike the examples earlier in this chapter, this section does not present a game of limited information.

Cheap talk can be effective in fostering coordination of strategies among players. Players often share an interest in coordinating their strategies for mutual benefit. For example, consider the problem of deciding on which side of the road to drive. If no one owns a car, driving on the right side or the left side of the road are equally attractive. What matters is that we all agree on which side we will drive. Talking among ourselves or coordinating around an external signal should suffice to get us to all drive on the same side of the road. The problem is more complicated if some of us own cars with the steering wheel on the left, while others own cars with the steering wheel on the right. We continue to share an interest in agreeing to drive on the same side of the road, but those with steering wheels on the left prefer an agreement to drive on the right side of the road to an agreement to drive on the left side (and vice versa for those with steering wheels on the right). Can costless signals help us to reach an agreement about the side we will drive on in the face of these divergent preferences?

The Battle of the Sexes game, introduced in Chapter Four, is the simplest representation of this problem. Shown in Figure 8.10, Battle of the Sexes captures a situation where the players wish to coordinate their strategies but disagree on which strategy they prefer to coordinate. We assume that $a > 1$; Player 1 prefers that they play $(S_1; S_1)$, and Player 2 prefers that they play $(S_2; S_2)$. Both prefer coordinating on the other's preferred strategy to not coordinating.

Battle of the Sexes has three equilibria: $(S_1; s_1)$, $(S_2; s_2)$, and

$$\left[\left(\frac{a}{a+1}S_1, \frac{1}{a+1}S_2\right); \left(\frac{1}{a+1}S_1, \frac{a}{a+1}S_2\right)\right],$$

which provide values of (a,1), (1,a), and

$$\left(\frac{a}{a+1}, \frac{a}{a+1}\right)$$

to the players. Battle of the Sexes is a symmetric game because the players are identical. If we believe that symmetric games should have symmetric equilibria, then the mixed strategy equilibrium is chosen equilibrium. The argument here is simple. The pure strategy equilibria require both players to know which strategy to play in advance and have sufficient confidence that the other player will play that same strategy. But from where does such a common conjecture arise? If the players do not have the opportunity to communicate with one another before selecting their strategies, such a common conjecture seems highly unlikely.

Cheap talk can help create shared expectations between players. Assume that players can exchange messages before selecting their strategies. Further, restrict the set of possible messages to the pair "I want to play (S_1;s_1)" and "I want to play (S_2;s_2)." Call these messages $\underline{1}$ and $\underline{2}$ respectively. The addition of these costless messages creates a game with the following time line:

1. The players simultaneously exchange messages from the set ($\underline{1}$,$\underline{2}$). Both messages are revealed.

2. Both players simultaneously choose their moves in the Battle of the Sexes.

3. Moves are revealed, and payoffs received.

An equilibrium of this game requires that the players select optimal moves given the messages they have received and that they select optimal messages given their expectations about what moves will result from those messages. What equilibria does this game have?

The first equilibrium is depressing: the players do not use their messages to coordinate their moves. Player 1 always sends $\underline{1}$, and Player 2 always sends $\underline{2}$ (or vice versa), and both play the mixed strategy equilibrium of Battle of the Sexes for their moves regardless of what message they have sent or received. Each player anticipates that the other will use its mixed strategy to determine its move, so using its own mixed strategy to choose its move is a best reply. The signal sent has no effect on the other player's choice of move, so any signal is optimal. The important feature of this **babbling equilibrium**, as it is called, is that neither player conditions its move on the signals. The signals "babble" about the moves that the sending player intends; they provide no clue about what move that player will select. Neither player can condition its move on the signals.

All games with cheap talk have babbling equilibria. It is always possible to find an equilibrium where the players do not use the signals to coordinate their moves later in the game. It is more interesting to ask if they can use the signals to help them coordinate their moves.

The second equilibrium uses a straightforward interpretation of the signals. If the players' signals agree, they both play that strategy. If their signals disagree, they play the mixed strategy equilibrium of Battle of the Sexes. If both players understand that they will both use this rule in their choices of both signals and moves, what is the equilibrium? Begin with the selection of moves, and focus on Player 1 for convenience (Player 2's choices mirror these calculations, through symmetry). If ($\underline{1}$,$\underline{1}$) are the messages—read this as (Player 1's message, Player 2's message)—then Player 1 should play S_1 because he expects that Player 2 will play s_1. To do otherwise reduces his payoff. Similarly, if ($\underline{2}$,$\underline{2}$) are the messages, then Player 1 should play S_2 because he expects that Player 2 will play s_2. If ($\underline{1}$,$\underline{2}$) or ($\underline{2}$,$\underline{1}$) are the messages, Player 1 expects that Player 2 will play her mixed strategy for Battle of the Sexes. His mixed strategy then is a best reply to her mixed strategy. The strategies then are optimal given the signals.

But what signal should Player 1 send? Let p be the probability that Player 2 sends $\underline{1}$. The probability that she sends $\underline{2}$ is 1 − p. If Player 1 sends $\underline{1}$, there is p probability that Player 2 also sends $\underline{1}$, and they coordinate on (S_1;s_1), which gives Player 1 a payoff of a. There is 1 − p probability that Player 2 sends $\underline{2}$, leading to the mixed strategy equilibrium of Battle of the Sexes. Player 1 receives an expected payoff of a/(a + 1) in that case. If Player 1 sends $\underline{2}$, there is 1 − p probability that Player 2 also sends $\underline{2}$, and they coordinate on (S_2;s_2), which gives Player 1 a payoff of 1. There is p probability that Player 2 sends $\underline{1}$, leading to the mixed strategy equilibrium of Battle of the Sexes and an expected payoff of a/(a + 1) for Player 1. Find p for Player 2 that makes Player 1 indifferent between sending $\underline{1}$ and $\underline{2}$. Calculate his expected utility for sending each signal and set them equal:

$$p(a) + (1 - p)\left(\frac{a}{a+1}\right) = p\left(\frac{a}{a+1}\right) + (1 - p)1$$

$$p = \frac{1}{a^2 + 1}.$$

Player 2's mixed signaling strategy that makes Player 1 indifferent between sending $\underline{1}$ and $\underline{2}$ is

$$\left(\frac{1}{a^2+1}\underline{1}, \frac{a^2}{a^2+1}\underline{2}\right).$$

By symmetry, Player 1's optimal signaling strategy is

$$\left(\frac{a^2}{a^2+1}\underline{1}, \frac{1}{a^2+1}\underline{2}\right).$$

Both players send a signal that they are willing to coordinate on their less preferred strategy pair—which is (S_2;s_2) for Player 1—occasionally because coordination on that pair is preferable to playing the mixed strategy equilibrium.

This cheap talk equilibrium makes both players better off than the mixed strategy equilibrium does. In the mixed strategy equilibrium, there is a probability of

$$\frac{2a}{(a + 1)^2}$$

that the players successfully coordinate their moves. Each player expects $a/(a + 1)$ from the mixed strategy equilibrium. In the cheap talk equilibrium, the players successfully coordinate their moves with a probability of

$$\frac{2a(a^2 + a + 1)}{(a + 1)^2(a^2 + 1)}.$$

This chance is greater than the probability of successful coordination in the mixed strategy equilibrium by a factor of

$$\frac{a^2 + a + 1}{a^2 + 1} > 1.$$

Each player's expected payoff from the cheap talk equilibrium is

$$\frac{a(a^2 + a + 1)}{(a + 1)(a^2 + 1)}.$$

This payoff is greater than its expected payoff from the mixed strategy equilibrium by a factor of

$$\frac{a^2 + a + 1}{a^2 + 1} > 1.$$

Both players are better off because they receive the mixed strategy payoff when their signals do not match and a better payoff when the signals do match. The improvement produced by cheap talk declines as the distributive issue in the underlying Battle of the Sexes increases. The magnitude of a reflects the distributive problem here: the greater a is, the greater risks each player accepts to gain its preferred strategy pair. The greater a is, the smaller the increases in probability of successful coordination and payoff that cheap talk can produce in this equilibrium. Both factors approach 1 as a grows without bound.

Exercise 8.16: We can improve the performance of cheap talk by allowing the players to exchange two rounds of messages. Again restrict the messages to the set 1 and 2, and keep the interpretation of the second-round messages the same. Change the interpretation of the first-round messages to be as follows: If the signals match, play that move and do not send a second signal. If they do not match, send a second signal and follow the cheap talk equilibrium above. Then find Player 1's optimal mixed strategy for his first-round signal. Is the probability of Player 1's sending a signal of 2 higher in the first or second round? (Hint: If the players have to send a second signal, they will follow the cheap talk equilibrium above for those signals. Those with a taste for messy algebra can calculate the probability that the players coordinate their moves and their payoffs, using two rounds of cheap talk.)

Two rounds of cheap talk improves the efficiency of cheap talk. Coordination is more likely, and the players' expected payoffs increase over one round of cheap talk. But there still remains a significant probability that the players will fail to coordinate their moves.

There is another form of cheap talk that achieves complete efficiency by always coordinating the players' moves. Change the interpretation of the signals as follows: If the players' signals match, that is, (1,1) or (2,2), play $(S_1;s_1)$; if they differ, play $(S_2;s_2)$. Given that the players expect each other to follow this rule, it is optimal to play the moves dictated by each pair of signals. If Player 1 believes that Player 2 will play s_2, then he should play S_2. What are the optimal signaling strategies? Let p be the probability that Player 2 sends 1 and choose p to make Player 1 indifferent between sending 1 and 2:

$$a(p) + 1(1 - p) = 1(p) + a(1 - p)$$

$$p = \tfrac{1}{2}.$$

Player 1 should send the signals with equal probability. The players always coordinate their moves in this equilibrium and receive expected payoff $(a + 1)/2$ in it. I call this equilibrium a **matching pennies** equilibrium because the logic of the signals is identical to that of the Matching Pennies game in Chapter Three. Each player wants its preferred equilibrium to be chosen, but both signals together determine which equilibrium they play. My optimal signal is obvious if I know what signal you are sending. Thus you must make your signal unpredictable to protect yourself.

There are other ways to achieve perfect efficiency besides the matching pennies equilibrium. Both of the asymmetric equilibria of Battle of the Sexes also achieve perfect equilibrium. But they create a distributional problem between the players. If the game is repeated several times, the players can agree to alternate between the two equilibria. Alternation does create a distributional problem if the players discount future payoffs. The player who first receives its preferred pair of moves benefits because its large payoff is discounted less than that of the player who receives its big payoff second. The players could also use external events to coordinate their moves. They could flip a coin and play (S_1;s_1) if the coin came up tails and (S_2;s_2) if it came up heads. This agreement makes both players better off than the mixed strategy equilibrium ex ante. All of these agreements require the players to communicate their shared understanding about how they will coordinate their moves.

This example of cheap talk may seem trite and excessively abstract to you. But cheap talk is a way to address a number of very important questions about politics. For example, legislative debate is basically cheap talk.[4] Debate provides a way for legislators with similar underlying preferences to coordinate their votes. Speeches by knowledgeable members serve as cues about how less-informed members should vote on complex legislation. Cheap talk is most effective when the sender and the receiver hold similar preferences over the outcomes. Members are unlikely to take cues from those whose underlying values are greatly different from their own. I provide a brief guide to the literature on debate as cheap talk in the references. Cheap talk also provides a way to think about some issues in negotiations. Battle of the Sexes is a simple representation of a bargaining problem. Both sides wish to reach an agreement, but they differ about the exact form of the agreement. If there is a cost to delaying agreement, then the players can speed an agreement though cheap talk. I have used this idea to explore bargaining under international regimes (Morrow 1994a). Regular rules of bargaining assist the parties in exchanging information that can help them reach mutually beneficial agreements. Nations almost always have incentives to misrepresent their position in negotiations. Common understandings of how disputes will be negotiated can assist in solving those disputes.

Review

This chapter has covered games under limited information, focusing on signaling games. These games provide a way to explore important questions in politics that cannot be addressed by using classical game theory. Limited information creates the possibilities of misperception, deception, and honest communication among the players. Signaling games are now a standard way to analyze questions where all of these issues are central.

A game of limited information is modeled by a set of games, one game for each possible combination of the types of the players. A chance move determines which combination of types will actually be played. Each player knows only its own type. The players' beliefs express the likelihood of the different types of other players in the game. Because a player's type can influence its moves, the other players can infer a player's type from its moves.

The strength of these inferences depends on equilibrium behavior. In a pooling equilibrium, all types of a player take the same action, so other players cannot infer anything new about its type from that action. In a separating equilibrium, each different type of a player takes a distinct action, so the other players can determine its type by observing its action. A separating equilibrium requires incentive compatibility. No type can prefer taking the action of another type to its own action in equilibrium.

Pooling equilibria raise the question of beliefs off the equilibrium path. When all types take the same action, any beliefs after observing any other action are off the equilibrium path. Strange behavior on the equilibrium path can be driven by strange beliefs off the equilibrium path. In some situations, we can judge some beliefs off the equilibrium path as unreasonable. The general principle is that beliefs off the equilibrium path should not increase the probability of types that have less incentive to defect than other types.

Further Reading

Most of the literature here is quite difficult to read. The original approach was presented in Harsanyi 1967–1968. However, this topic only took off with the sequential equilibrium concept and the addition of beliefs.

The signaling game presented here is lifted from Banks and Sobel 1987. Banks 1991 is an excellent technical introduction and survey of how signaling games have been applied to numerous areas of political science.

The informational approach to congressional structure draws on research by Thomas Gilligan and Keith Krehbiel. The model in the text is taken from Gilligan and Krehbiel 1987. My presentation of their model has been helped by the clear presentation in Epstein and O'Halloran 1993. Gilligan and Krehbiel (1989, 1990) advance their work on the informational role of congressional committees. Krehbiel (1991) presents this view informally.

The best beginning source on noncooperative bargaining theory is Kennan and Wilson 1993. I have also found Sutton 1986 and Wilson 1985 useful. Binmore 1992, Fudenberg and Tirole 1991, Kreps 1990a, Myerson 1991, and Rasmusen 1989 all have chapters on bargaining.

The model on deterrence and out-of-equilibrium beliefs is taken directly from Nalebuff 1991. Nalebuff provides a good discussion of the different ideas of beliefs off the equilibrium path and how they apply to his model.

If you wish to read more about restrictions on beliefs, I recommend one of the textbooks. Look for their sections on equilibrium refinements. Chapter Eleven of Fudenberg and Tirole 1991 is the most complete discussion in the textbooks. Original sources for restrictions on beliefs are Banks and Sobel 1987, Cho and Kreps 1987, and Kohlberg and Mertens 1986. Cho and Kreps 1987 is the source of the Beer-Quiche Game.

The term *cheap talk* was coined by Joseph Farrell. His work on cheap talk is central to the topic (Farrell 1987; Farrell and Gibbons 1989). David Austen-Smith has done extensive work applying cheap talk models to legislative debate. See Austen-Smith 1990 and Austen-Smith and Riker 1987, the latter as corrected by Austen-Smith and Riker 1990. Johnson 1993 connects cheap talk in game theory to the idea of free and open debate in critical theory. I apply a cheap talk model to international cooperation in Morrow 1994a.

International Politics

International politics has been a major area for game-theoretic work in political science. Because the number of actors is small, strategic interaction is important in international politics.

Crises and war have been the primary focus of formal models in international politics. O'Neill (1992) provides a comprehensive survey of papers using game theory to analyze issues of war and peace. Models of crisis bargaining draw on the literature on bargaining under incomplete information discussed in this chapter. This literature is now quite large. I recommend that you begin with Kilgour and Zagare 1991; the model in this paper is simple and easy to follow. Morrow 1989 is the first paper in which these models were used to analyze conventional crises. Selection effects in observed crises and how they affect empirical analysis is that paper's central point. Fearon (1994) is clearer about selection effects than Morrow (1989), and he extensively discusses evidence supporting the selection effects hypothesis. Bueno de Mesquita and Lalman (1992) use their crisis model to examine structural theories of international politics, including why democracies do not fight other democracies. Kilgour (1991) also addresses why democracies do not fight one another. Other sources on crisis bargaining are Banks 1990, Langlois 1991, Morrow 1992, and Nalebuff 1991. Banks (1990) proves a general theorem about how success in crises and the probability of war must rise as the challenger's resolve increases. Langlois (1991) provides a general model of punishments that stabilize crises. Morrow (1992) discusses the credibility of linkage as a signal of resolve. Nalebuff 1991 is the source of the model on deterrence and out-of-equilibrium beliefs in this chapter.

Models of nuclear strategy are closely related to models of crisis bargaining. Powell (1990) presents a series of different models of arguments in nuclear crises, including the fear of reciprocal surprise attack, the threat that leaves something to chance, and limited retaliation. Wagner (1991) also discusses the rationality of counterforce strategies.

In the area of security studies, Brams and Kilgour (1988) present a series of models, beginning with their model of a nuclear crisis. Downs and Rocke (1990) investigate how arms control agreements can be enforced in the face of verification difficulties. Wittman (1989) uses a model of limited information to address verification and arms control. Kilgour and Brams (1992) study the stability of arms control agreements. Powell (1993) builds a noncooperative model of arms competition between two nations. Morrow (1994b) models alliance formation for deterrence of a common threat.

In the area of structural theories of international politics, Niou and Ordeshook's (1989, 1990) work on the balance of power is important. Niou and Ordeshook (1989) uses a cooperative game framework to analyze the stability of balance-of-power systems. Niou and Ordeshook (1990) extend their results to a noncooperative game. Wagner (1986) begins to develop a formal model of the balance-of-power theory. Kim and Morrow (1992) address power transition theory by asking when power transitions should lead to war.

In the area of international political economy, Alt, Calvert, and Humes (1988) use a modified Chain Store Paradox (presented in Chapter Nine) to address hegemonic stability theory. Martin 1993 is an informal presentation of a noncooperative model of economic sanctions. Powell 1991 is a simple model of trade and conflict between two nations. Morrow (1994a) uses the notion of "cheap talk" as presented in Chapter Eight to model why the forms of cooperation might vary across issues. Putnam's (1988) informal argument began the formal analysis of the links between domestic politics and foreign policy. Iida 1993 and Morrow 1991 use the framework of the two-level game to address this question. Domestic politics and foreign policy is a central issue in Bueno de Mesquita and Lalman 1992.

Chapter Nine
Repeated Games

Many political relationships persist over time. Politicians face the electorate in elections over time, nations expect to deal with one another in the future, and political leaders in legislatures must organize their followers for each new issue. The anticipation that the players will have to deal with one another in the future can change the strategic logic of games. The actors must consider not only the immediate consequences of their choices, but also the effect of those choices on the long-term relationship. The future benefits from a continued good relationship can outweigh the immediate benefits of taking advantage of other players. Players may be able to use the threat of breaking the long-term relationship in order to discipline short-term exploitation. When are such threats credible, and what outcomes can be achieved with such credible threats?

Repeated games are a way to model such ongoing relations. The players play a game repeatedly. This game is called the **stage game**, and each individual play of that game is called a **stage**, or **round**, of the repeated game. There can be either a fixed, known number of rounds, or the game could be indefinitely repeated. In the latter case, either the players' payoffs must be discounted or else there must be a fixed, known chance of the game's ending after each round. Otherwise, the sum of the players' payoffs across the entire game would be infinite. If the game is infinitely repeated, a player's payoff for the entire game is the discounted sum of its payoffs for each round. If M_i^t is player i's payoff for round t, then its total payoff for the game is

$$\sum_{k=0}^{+\infty} \delta^k M_i^k$$

where the game begins with round 0. If there is a chance that the game ends after each round, let p be this fixed and known probability. A player's expected payoff for all possible future rounds gives its payoff for the game. Player i's expected payoff is

$$\sum_{k=0}^{+\infty} (1-p)^k M_i^k$$

because $1 - p$ is the probability that the game continues after each round. Because both δ and $(1 - p)$ are between 0 and 1, these two forms of a repeated game with an indefinite end are equivalent.

Finite repeated games present a different problem. When there is a fixed, known number of rounds, we may be able to solve the game by backwards induction from the last round. But the results of backwards induction often conflict with both our intuition and experimental results in such games. The issue I examine in finite, repeated games is how uncertainty about the players' payoffs can produce effects similar to those of indefinite iteration. Such uncertainty provides a way to model reputations within a game. A player's beliefs about the other player's payoffs is the second player's reputation. A reputation can deter the first player from taking actions against the second player's interests. We can examine how the players can try to manipulate their reputations to advance their interests. In these games, we may assume that payoffs are discounted from round to round or that the players maximize the sum of their payoffs across all rounds. Finite, repeated games are important models of long-term relations that face an eventual, known end. We can use such models to examine what happens when the end of the relationship looms.

Whether the game is finitely or indefinitely repeated, the strategy set of a repeated game is much more complicated than that of its stage game. For example, compare the strategy set of a two-by-two game to that of the same game repeated twice. Each player possesses only two pure strategies in the two-by-two game played once. Playing that game twice increases each player's strategy set to thirty-two pure strategies. A complete pure strategy specifies a move in the first round and a move in the second round for each of the four combinations of moves that the players could make in the first round. There are two choices in each case, for a total of $2^5 = 32$. Adding a third round of the game increases the number of pure strategies to 2^{21}, or 2,097,142. The strategy set of an indefinitely iterated game is infinite because there is not a fixed number of rounds of the game. We can often summarize strategies of repeated games with an indefinite end because many such strategies can be characterized by simple decision rules. These strategies often form equilibria, and as such are the center of analysis of repeated games.

Repeated games also allow us to analyze situations where the payoffs from current actions lie in future benefits. For example, voters cast their votes on the basis of the policies the candidates will deliver in the future. Their current choices are based on an expectation of candidates' future behavior. Officeholders select policies based in part on the effect of those policies in the next election. A repeated game allows us to analyze this interaction between the voters' choices and the policies candidates adopt in office. The players do not use the repeated nature to police an agreement here. This logic differs from reciprocal punishment. Rather, their payoffs are received in future plays of the game. So their choices are based on their expectations of the future of the interaction.

Both reciprocal punishments and future judgments require the players to hold expectations across an indefinite future. An incumbent must calculate the value of satisfying the electorate at the expense of the policies he or she prefers.

Actors using reciprocal punishments to enforce an agreement need to compare the value of cheating on the agreement to the punishment. Otherwise, the punishment may not be sufficient to deter cheating. The **continuation value** at a particular point in a game for given strategies specifies the players' expected payoffs for playing the game from that point on using those strategies. Continuation values are calculated from an equilibrium; they depend upon the players' strategies as well as the current point in the game.

I used continuation values in calculating the equilibrium in the Rubinstein bargaining model in Chapter Five. That model is a repeated game where one player makes an offer to divide a unit and the other player accepts or rejects the offer. If the first offer is rejected, the second player makes a counteroffer, which the first player then accepts or rejects. The game is repeated if the second offer is rejected. Because each round begins in an identical position, we could assume that the game had the same value for the first player from the start of each round. This value is the continuation value of the game. We could then solve for the continuation value because the first player's offer depends on its continuation value. We calculated the optimal offer given the continuation value of M and set the two equal. In this way, continuation values can be used to solve repeated games.

There are more complicated repeated games that I do not consider in this chapter. For example, the players could face difficulties in ascertaining what one another did in a prior round of the game. "Noise" in monitoring introduces important questions about a long-term relationship. There could be several games that the players could be playing. Their moves in each round determine not only their payoffs in that round, but also the game they will play in the next round. Each of these games is called the **state** of the repeated game. Changes in the state of the game can reflect changes in the players' payoffs or available options from prior plays of the game. The players generally know the current state of the game and the transformation rules from one state to another. In these more general repeated games, the players do not know the current state but each holds some private information about the current state. I do not go into all the complexities of such general repeated games. The easiest way to understand repeated games is to begin with the best-known repeated game, iterated Prisoner's Dilemma.

Thinking about Repetition: Iterated Prisoner's Dilemma

The Prisoner's Dilemma is commonly seen as the simplest model of the problem of the enforcement of long-term relations in the face of incentives to cheat on the agreement. I presented Prisoner's Dilemma and the story behind it in Chapter Four. The general version of Prisoner's Dilemma (often called PD for short) is the two-by-two game in Figure 9.1. The strategies in this general ver-

Player 2

Player 1		c	d
	C	(R,R)	(S,T)
	D	(T,S)	(P,P)

with T > R > P > S

Figure 9.1 General Prisoner's Dilemma

sion are labeled C, for Cooperate, and D, for Defect. The payoffs are T, for temptation, R, for reward, P, for punishment, and S, for sucker. It is also commonly assumed that $R > (S + T)/2$.

Prisoner's Dilemma has a dominant strategy equilibrium (D;d) that is Pareto dominated by (C;c). Individual rationality drives the players to defect when they have a shared, common interest in cooperation. Both would be better off if they both played Cooperate rather than Defect. But both are always better off playing Defect no matter what the other does. Prisoner's Dilemma captures the problem behind enforcing agreements in a simple fashion. Actors often have short-run incentives to take advantage of others with whom they have agreements. Can the long-run benefits of sustained agreement be used to enforce short-run compliance with the agreement?

Many political problems resemble the strategic dilemma of the Prisoner's Dilemma. The regulation of international trade is one such problem. According to classical international trade theory in economics, all nations are better off under free trade than under mutual tariffs. Each nation makes the goods it has a comparative advantage in producing. But if one nation can raise its tariffs while its trading partner retains low tariffs, the first nation can shift the terms of trade in its favor. This shift in the terms of trade can make the first nation better off than it would be under free trade. The rise in price in its goods allows it to buy more of the other nation's production, making it better off. If we think of high tariffs as Defect and low tariffs as Cooperate, the setting of tariffs resembles a Prisoner's Dilemma. High tariffs strictly dominate low tariffs for both nations. But both nations are better off if they both set low tariffs than if they both set high tariffs. The rise in production from the specialization produced by comparative advantage makes both better off. Because (D;d) is the only equilibrium of Prisoner's Dilemma, we expect nations to raise tariff barriers against one another. Each is always better off doing so than holding down its tariffs. But international trade, unlike Prisoner's Dilemma, has a future. Can the nations support low tariffs through the threat of retaliation with high tariffs? The repeated Prisoner's Dilemma addresses this question as, Are there equilibria where the players play (C;c)?

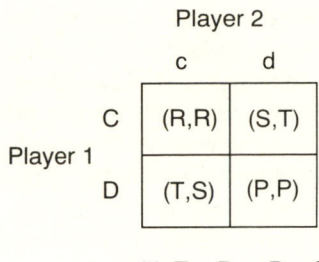

I begin with the depressing result. The strategy where a player always defects, often called All D, forms a Nash equilibrium with itself. If I know you are going to play Defect, then I should play Defect. This equilibrium is the failure of an agreement. If the other side always plays Defect, the best you can do is to respond with Defect yourself. This Nash equilibrium is subgame perfect because all the subgames of iterated Prisoner's Dilemma are iterated Prisoner's Dilemma beginning at any round. All these subgames are strategically identical to the entire game. All D for both players is a Nash equilibrium of these games, so it is subgame perfect. Further, it is also a perfect Bayesian equilibrium.

In iterated Prisoner's Dilemma, both players are better off if they both play Cooperate on every round. But All C, the strategy where a player always plays Cooperate, is not a Nash equilibrium with itself. If you are going to play Cooperate regardless of what I do or have done, then I am better off playing Defect. Both players do better under All C than under All D, but both have the incentive to defect from their strategy.

The strategies All D and All C are independent of the history of the game. My move does not depend upon your or my prior moves. But players can condition their moves in a repeated game on the history of the game. Can they deter each other from playing Defect with the threat of playing Defect after one player defects? I begin with the simplest, and best-known, reciprocal strategy, Tit for Tat. A Tit for Tat player plays Cooperate on the first round of the game and in all later round matches the other player's move in the previous round. It uses immediate reciprocal punishments: if you defect, I will defect in the next round.

When does Tit for Tat form a Nash equilibrium with itself? In that equilibrium, both players play Cooperate on every round. Defection from that equilibrium requires that a player play Defect. There are two extreme types of defection to consider. First, a player could play Defect for one round, and then return to playing Cooperate in the next round to restore the cooperative agreement implicit in Tit for Tat. The other player will play Cooperate in the round the defection occurs and Defect in the next round. The defector's payoff over these two rounds is $T + \delta S$. If the defector stays with Tit for Tat, its payoff would be $R + \delta R$. After these two rounds, the players return to playing Cooperate in all rounds. Both Tit for Tat and the defection produce the same payoff across all rounds after the first two. This first type of defection is deterred when the second payoff exceeds the first:

$$R + \delta R > T + \delta S.$$

Solving for δ shows that this type of defection is deterred whenever the players' discount factor is high enough:

$$\delta > \frac{T - R}{R - S}.$$

Whenever δ satisfies the inequality above, neither player defects for one round from Tit for Tat.

The second type of defection violates the agreement forever. A player could simply play Defect in all future rounds. A player playing Tit for Tat would respond by playing Defect in all rounds after the first round of defection. The payoff from the defection is $T + \delta P + \delta^2 P + \delta^3 P + \ldots = T + \delta P/(1 - \delta)$ (the trick used in summing the infinite series is in Appendix One). The payoff for staying with Tit for Tat is $R + \delta R + \delta^2 R + \delta^3 R + \ldots = R/(1 - \delta)$. This permanent defection from Tit for Tat is deterred when

$$\frac{R}{1 - \delta} > T + \frac{\delta P}{1 - \delta}.$$

Solving for δ again, we get the following condition:

$$\delta > \frac{T - R}{T - P}.$$

If both types of defections are deterred, then any other type of defection is also deterred. Assume that defection both for one period and forever are deterred, that is, that the two equations above are satisfied. Also assume that defection from Tit for Tat for n rounds and then restoring cooperation is preferred to playing Cooperate. The defector's payoff from the n-round defection is greater than its payoff from continuing the cooperative arrangement:

$$T + \delta P + \ldots \delta^{n-1} P + \delta^n S > R + \delta R + \ldots \delta^n R$$

$$T + \frac{\delta(1 - \delta^{n-1})}{1 - \delta} P + \delta^n S > \frac{1 - \delta^{n+1}}{1 - \delta} R$$

$$T - \delta T + \delta P - \delta^n P + \delta^n S - \delta^{n+1} S > R - \delta^{n+1} R.$$

Because playing Defect forever is deterred, $R > T + \delta P - \delta T$. This inequality follows from a rearrangement of the condition that δ must satisfy for permanent defection to be deterred. Subtract the left side of this inequality from the right side of the inequality above and the right side from the left side to get the following inequalities:

$$-\delta^n P + \delta^n S - \delta^{n+1} S > -\delta^{n+1} R,$$

and

$$S + \delta R > P + \delta S.$$

The left side of the inequality above is the payoff for restoring cooperation this round instead of waiting until next round to do so. The defector suffers the S payoff this round and receives δR next round. That quantity exceeds the payoff for continuing to play Defect this round and playing Cooperate in the next round, $P + \delta S$. If infinite defection is deterred but n-round defection is not, then the defector prefers ending its defection one round earlier. But this argument also holds then, so the defector prefers ending its defection two rounds earlier. The argument unzippers all the way back to a one-round defection. If infinite defection is deterred but n-round defection is not, then one-round defection is not deterred. Deterring both one-round and infinite-round defection deters all other possible defections.

Tit for Tat forms a Nash equilibrium with itself when

$$\delta > \max\left(\frac{T - R}{R - S}, \frac{T - R}{T - P}\right).$$

The arrangement to play Cooperate on every round can be enforced by Tit for Tat when the above inequality is true. Cooperation is more likely to be supported as (1) the value the players place on future payoffs increases (i.e., δ increases), (2) the reward from cheating decreases (T decreases), (3) the punishment gets more painful (P decreases), (4) the reward from cooperation increases (R gets bigger), and (5) the cost of restoring cooperation increases (S gets smaller).

The simple, direct reciprocity of Tit for Tat can produce cooperation in many circumstances. But there is another reciprocal strategy that is even more effective for enforcing cooperation. The Grim Trigger answers any play of Defect with Defect for all future rounds of the game. Once the trigger is pulled, the future of (D;d) is, indeed, grim for both players. The Grim Trigger can enforce cooperation in some situations where Tit for Tat cannot because there are no one-round defections against the Grim Trigger—playing Defect once triggers the eternal punishment.[2] The Grim Trigger is a Nash equilibrium with itself when

$$\delta > \frac{T - R}{T - P}.$$

The right side above is less than the condition for Tit for Tat when

$$\frac{T - R}{R - S} > \frac{T - R}{T - P}.$$

The Grim Trigger can support cooperation for some discount values where Tit for Tat cannot. In that sense, the Grim Trigger is a more effective threat than Tit for Tat. It is also subgame perfect; once the trigger is pulled, both players wish to play Defect from then on.

To return to the example of international trade, these strategies suggest that tariff reductions can be supported by the threat of reciprocal punishments. Mutual low tariffs can be enforced when both sides place sufficiently high value on trade in the future relative to the gains from cheating now. The value of long-term trade increases as δ (the shared discount value), T − P (the effect of the punitive tariffs), and R − S, (the reward from free trade) increase. It decreases as T − R (the short-term gains from cheating on the agreement) increases. Nations that cheat by raising their tariffs suffer retaliation from their trading partners. The loss from a trade war may suffice to enforce low tariff barriers.

I have shown that these reciprocal strategies can be used to enforce a cooperative agreement to play (C;c) in the repeated Prisoner's Dilemma.[3] But this result has four important limitations. First, it does not imply that cooperation will occur when the discount factor condition is satisfied. All D is always a subgame-perfect equilibrium of repeated Prisoner's Dilemma for any discount factor. We have no way of knowing which equilibrium the players will choose when they play repeated Prisoner's Dilemma.

Second, this equilibrium selection problem cannot be solved by appealing to Pareto optimality alone. Pareto optimality suggests that the players would play one of the reciprocal strategies that supports (C;c). But the set of outcomes that can be supported with reciprocal strategies can be quite large. For example, alternation between (C;c) and (D;c) can be supported with the Grim Trigger when

$$\delta > \max\left(\frac{P - S}{R - P}, \frac{P - S + \sqrt{(P - S)^2 + 4(T - P)(T - R)}}{2(T - P)}\right).$$

The first term in the right side above covers defection by Player 2 from (D;c); the second term covers defection from (C;c). An infinite number of cooperative agreements can be supported by this reciprocal threat. Some divide the payoff symmetrically between the players; others do not. Many of them are Pareto optimal. For example, playing (C;c) every round does not Pareto dominate alternation between (C;c) and (D;c); Player 1 is better off in the latter than the former. Pareto optimality alone cannot select one equilibrium out of the complete range of possible equilibria.

Third, there is no obvious source of a common conjecture that would allow the players to judge which equilibrium they are playing. Both Tit for Tat and the Grim Trigger produce the same behavior in equilibrium, (C;c) in every period. But the players' responses to any deviation from the equilibrium depend upon a shared conjecture about what punishments are used to enforce cooperation. Imagine a situation where one player expects that they will use the Grim Trigger to enforce cooperation, and the other player believes they are using Tit for Tat. The latter may refuse to play Cooperate in the first round because (C;c) cannot be enforced by Tit for Tat even though it can be enforced under the Grim Trigger. The first player may refuse to play Cooperate once a defection occurs because cooperation can never be restored under the Grim Trigger. Without some common conjecture, the players may not coordinate on what punishments will enforce cooperation.

Fourth, reciprocal punishments may not be credible. Consider the position of the players after the Grim Trigger has been pulled. They must now play (D;d) forever. Both players are better off if they end the eternal punishment and restore cooperation. But doing so may undermine the credibility of the punishment, and thus undermine the players' ability to enforce cooperation. Why should I believe that you will punish me when it is not in your interest to punish me? Tit for Tat also suffers from this credibility problem, although not as severely as the Grim Trigger does. The punishing player benefits when the defector plays Cooperate to end the punishment. But the defector also suffers during that round. When $P + \delta S > S + \delta R$, the defector is better off waiting another round before playing Cooperate to end the punishment. Both players may be better off then if they agree to end the punishment without forcing the defector to accept S for a round. But this argument also undermines the incentive to punish at all. If a defector prefers to continue to play Defect after its initial defection, then the punishing player is better off not punishing the defection when $R + \delta R > P + \delta T$.

Reciprocal punishments face these four limitations. I now turn to discussing how reciprocal punishments can be used in general repeated games. This example looked at Prisoner's Dilemma, which is a very special game. Can reciprocal strategies be used to enforce mutually beneficial outcomes in general?

Folk Theorems

Folk theorems (often collectively referred to as "the folk theorem") generalize how reciprocal threats can be used in repeated games. In this section, I present several folk theorems that explain what outcomes can be supported in repeated games with different types of reciprocal threats. They are called folk theorems because they entered into the folklore of game theory before anyone published a folk theorem with a proof. As this section shows, there are several interesting and important twists and variations on the basic idea. I, for one, am glad that someone eventually published some folk theorems.

For convenience, I assume that the game has only two players and is infinite, with payoffs discounted by a common discount factor, δ. The results generalize to n players and open-ended games with a fixed termination probability after

		Player 2	
		s_1	s_2
Player 1	S_1	(1,3)	(4,2)
	S_2	(0,0)	(-1,5)

Figure 9.2 The Strategic Form of a Stage Game

every round. I begin with the simplest folk theorem, using the Grim Trigger and the worst possible punishments available to the players. Such punishments are the most effective for enforcing cooperative outcomes if we ignore the issue of their credibility. The harshest punishment for eternity is the strongest threat a player can use against another player. If this threat cannot enforce an agreement, nothing will. But what do we mean by the "harshest punishment"? If I am trying to punish you but you still possess control over your own move in each round, I should strive to choose my moves to limit your payoff no matter which move you choose.

Definition: Player i's **minmax payoff** (or **minmax value**), $\underline{v}_i$, is the lowest payoff that the Player j can hold i to:

$$\underline{v}_i = \min_{s_j}\left[\max_{S_i} P_i(S_i;s_j)\right].$$

Player 2's strategy that limits Player 1 to his minmax payoff is her **minmax strategy** $\underline{s}_j$ against Player 1. (There are corresponding definitions for Player 2 and for n players.)

To determine a player's minmax payoff, find the other player's strategy that reduces the first player's payoff to a minimum, assuming that the first player plays its best reply. The first player's payoff from the resulting strategies is its minmax payoff, and the other player's strategy is its minmax strategy.

Example: The minmax values for the stage game in Figure 9.2 are 1 for Player 1 and $2\frac{1}{2}$ for Player 2. Player 1's minmax strategy is $\left(\frac{5}{6}S_1, \frac{1}{6}S_2\right)$, and Player 2's is s_1. S_1 is a dominant strategy for Player 1. Player 2's minmax strategy is chosen to minimize his payoff given that he plays S_1. Player 2's response depends on Player 1's strategy. She plays s_1 if he plays S_1, and s_2 if he plays

		Player 2: s_1	Player 2: s_2
Player 1	S_1	(1,2)	(5,-2)
	S_2	(4,-1)	(3,3)

Figure 9.3 Exercise 9.1a

		Player 2: s_1	Player 2: s_2
Player 1	S_1	(7,5)	(-2,9)
	S_2	(10,-4)	(-5,-5)

Figure 9.4 Exercise 9.1b

S_2. Player 1 uses a mixed strategy to limit Player 2 below what she can obtain against his pure strategies. This mixed strategy is chosen to make Player 2 indifferent between her two pure strategies. Her minmax value is calculated from the mixed minmax strategy. The minmax strategies differ from the Nash equilibrium of the stage game, $(S_1;s_1)$.

Exercise 9.1: Find the minmax values and strategies for both players in the stage games in

a) Figure 9.3.

b) Figure 9.4.

Minmax values and strategies give maximal punishments per round. They place a ceiling on the size of punishments. The other players cannot force a player to accept less than its minmax value for each round the player is punished. When a player plays its minmax strategy against another, it is trying to reduce the other's payoff as much as it can. The harshest penalty combines minmax strategies with the Grim Trigger. Any player who deviates from the prescribed equilibrium strategies is punished with its minmax value for all subsequent periods of the game.

What outcomes we can support with such a relentless punishment depends upon what divisions of the payoff we can create for the players within the game. We can vary the division of the payoff between the players by prescribing that they change the moves they play across rounds. Like the example of alternating between (C;c) and (D;c) in repeated Prisoner's Dilemma, we can create a range of divisions of the possible payoffs. The players' average payoffs across rounds is an easy way to discuss what payoffs can be achieved in a repeated game. Average payoffs eliminate the complexities of dividing discounted payoffs. The discounted sum of payoffs depends on the order of how the players cycle through the pairs of moves in an equilibrium. But the effects of this order are small, and average payoffs can be approached by discounted payoffs of some set of moves.

Example: Continue with the stage game in the previous example. The players can achieve expected payoffs of

$$\left(\frac{4-\delta}{1-\delta^2}, \frac{2+5\delta}{1-\delta^2}\right)$$

by alternating between $(S_1;s_2)$ and $(S_2;s_2)$, beginning with $(S_1;s_2)$. If they begin with $(S_2;s_2)$, they receive

$$\left(\frac{-1+4\delta}{1-\delta^2}, \frac{5+2\delta}{1-\delta^2}\right).$$

When δ is close to 1, it makes little difference who goes first. Each player does better under either alternation than its minmax value discounted and summed across all future rounds, which are

$$\left(\frac{1}{1-\delta}, \frac{5}{2(1-\delta)}\right).$$

The average payoffs of both alternations are $\left(\frac{3}{2}, \frac{7}{2}\right)$. The average payoffs provide an easier way to think about feasible payoffs because they do not depend on the exact value of δ.

Average payoffs can be compared directly to payoffs of the stage game. Any distribution of the payoff that is a combination of the different outcomes possible in the stage game can be achieved in average payoffs. We call a set of payoffs **feasible** if they are a combination of payoffs for different outcomes in the stage game.

Definition: Payoffs (M_1,M_2) are **feasible** iff for $i = 1, 2$,

$$M_i = \sum_{\text{all } S_k, S_l} p_{kl} M_i(S_k;s_l) \text{ for } 0 \leq p_{kl} \leq 1,$$

and

$$\sum_{\text{all } k,l} p_{kl} = 1.$$

Feasible payoffs must be the average sum of payoffs of some combination of the payoffs of the stage game.

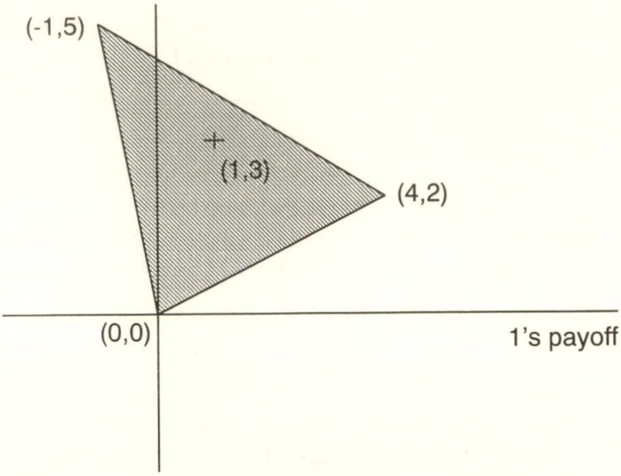

Figure 9.5 The Feasible Set of Payoffs for the Stage Game in Figure 9.2

Example: Continuing with the example above, Figure 9.5 graphs the players' payoffs. The four points in Figure 9.5 are the four pairs of payoffs produced in the stage game. All the payoffs inside the triangle and along its edges can be produced by some combination of these four outcomes. The feasible payoffs are given by the shaded area in the figure. The payoff from (1,3) is inside the triangle. Algebraically, the feasible set of payoffs is all (x,y) with $5x + y \geq 0, x - 2y \geq 0$, and $3x + 5y \leq 22$. These three inequalities define the edges of the triangle. The first inequality gives the line between $(-1,5)$ and (0,0), the second gives the line between (0,0) and (4,2), and the third gives the line between $(-1,5)$ and (4,2).

The feasible payoffs define what division of the payoffs can be achieved through cooperation in a repeated game. But no player will agree to any division where it receives its minmax value or less. By refusing to cooperate, a player can guarantee itself at least its minmax value for all future rounds of the game. Neither player should accept its minmax value or less as its average payoff in a cooperative agreement. The additional amount a player receives above its minimax value gives it an incentive to abide by the cooperative agreement.

Definition: Payoffs (M_1, M_2) are **individually rational** iff for $i = 1,2,\ M_i > \underline{v}_i$.

The first folk theorem can be stated now.

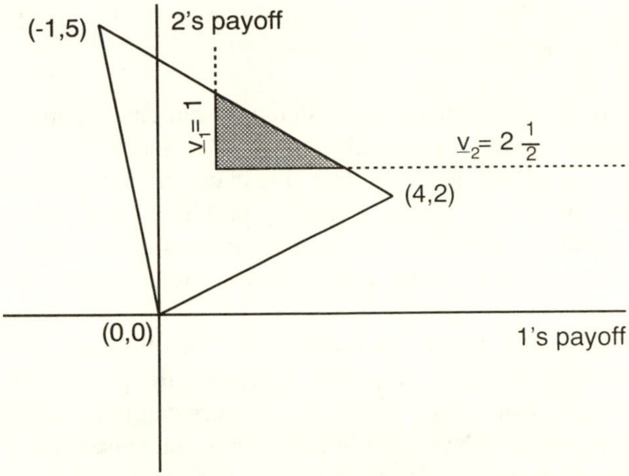

Figure 9.6 Minmax Values and the Individually Rational Payoffs for the Stage Game in Figure 9.2

Theorem (The Minmax Folk Theorem): For any individually rational, feasible payoffs M of repeated game with stage game G and sufficiently large δ, there is a Nash equilibrium that has payoffs M.

This theorem uses the threat of the Grim Trigger of minmax strategies against any player who defects from the equilibrium. The equilibrium strategies produce the combination of outcomes of the stage game that provide payoffs of M over the game. Of course, this combination may be very complicated, but we assume that the combination needed is common knowledge. The equilibrium is enforced by the threat of eternal minmax payoffs for any player who defects. If δ is sufficiently large, this threat always outweighs the attraction of any short-term defection. The minimal δ necessary for the minmax threat to be effective depends on the stage game. Its calculation parallels the calculations used to determine when the Grim Trigger is effective in enforcing cooperation in iterated Prisoner's Dilemma.

Example: Continuing with the example above, Figure 9.6 depicts the set of payoffs that are individually rational and feasible. This set is all (x, y) with $x > 1$, $y > 2\frac{1}{2}$, and $3x + 5y \leq 22$. The first two inequalities give the minmax values for the players. The two dotted lines in Figure 9.6 depict the players' minmax values for the game. The third inequality is the equation for the line through $(-1,5)$ and $(4,2)$ that bounds the set of feasible payoffs. All of the payoffs shaded in Figure 9.6 are feasible, and both players receive more than their minmax value.

Exercise 9.2: Find the set of individually rational, feasible payoffs for both of the stage games in Exercise 9.1.

Players may be reluctant to play minmax strategies against one another however. Minmax strategies not only hurt their target; they are often painful for the punishing player as well. The threat of playing minmax strategies against a defector suffers from a credibility problem. Why would I carry out a threat that is painful to me? If my minmax strategy against you is not part of a Nash equilibrium, then I have an incentive to defect from my punishment strategy.

One solution to this credibility problem changes the punishment. Instead of playing minmax strategies to punish defectors, the players instead play a Nash equilibrium of the stage game. The players can make this punishment effective if they choose a Nash equilibrium that is unpleasant for both players. They play this Nash equilibrium for all future periods if either player deviates from the cooperative strategies. The equilibrium is the cooperative strategies that produce the desired feasible payoffs. Because playing a Nash equilibrium of the stage game every period is a Nash equilibrium of the repeated game, the threat is credible. Both players play the punishment Nash strategy if they anticipate the other player will play its Nash strategy. This observation leads us to the following folk theorem:

Theorem (the Nash-Threats Folk Theorem): For repeated game with stage game G, let $(S_k;s_l)$ be a Nash equilibrium of G with payoffs $N(S_k;s_l)$. For any feasible payoffs M of the repeated game with $M_i > N_i(S_k;s_l)$ for $i = 1,2$ and sufficiently large δ, there is a subgame-perfect equilibrium that has payoffs M.

Each player must do at least as well in the repeated game as it does in the Nash equilibrium used to enforce a feasible payoff. The equilibrium is subgame perfect because the punishment is a Nash equilibrium of the subgame beginning with any defection from the equilibrium.

Example: Return yet again to the previous example. This game has only one Nash equilibrium, $(S_1;s_1)$ with payoffs (1,3). Any feasible payoff where Player 1 receives more than 1 and Player 2 receives more than 3 can be supported under the Nash-Threats Folk Theorem.

Exercise 9.3: Find the set of feasible payoffs that can be supported under the Nash-Threats Folk Theorem for the stage games in Exercise 9.1.

A requirement that the threat be credible reduces the range of agreements that reciprocal threats can enforce. The Nash-Threats Folk Theorem supports a smaller set of payoffs than does the Minmax Folk Theorem. In the example above, payoff distributions where Player 1 receives an average payoff of more than 1 and Player 2 receives an average payoff of between $2\frac{1}{2}$ and 3 can be supported under the Minmax Folk Theorem but not under the Nash-Threats Folk Theorem. A Nash equilibrium cannot produce less payoff for either player than the combination of minmax strategies does. Otherwise, that player could increase its payoff from the "Nash" equilibrium by playing its minmax strategy instead. But then the "Nash" equilibrium would not be a Nash equilibrium because, by definition, players cannot improve their payoffs by unilaterally changing their strategy from a Nash equilibrium. In most repeated games, the set of payoff distributions that can be supported under the Nash-Threats Folk Theorem is smaller than those that can be supported under the Minmax Folk Theorem.

Iterated Prisoner's Dilemma is an important exception to this point. The minmax strategies of Prisoner's Dilemma are the Nash equilibrium of the game. Prisoner's Dilemma has one Nash equilibrium, (Defect; Defect). But this is also both players' minmax strategy. Both folk theorems support the same distributions of payoffs in iterated Prisoner's Dilemma because the punishment is the same. But this property is peculiar to iterated Prisoner's Dilemma, and so we should not think of repeated Prisoner's Dilemma as the general model of cooperation over time.

The Nash-Threats Folk Theorem deals with the credibility problem of minmax threats by substituting a weaker, but credible, threat. There are two other solutions to this credibility problem, the Escalating-Punishments Folk Theorem and the Minmax-Rewards Folk Theorem.

In the Escalating-Punishments solution, the players agree to punish players that fail to carry out costly punishments. We could agree to enforce an agreement with minmax punishments for n rounds. If you fail to punish me for the full n rounds after I have defected, we agree that I should punish you by playing my minmax strategy for n^2 rounds. If I fail to punish you for n^2 rounds, you punish me for n^3 rounds, and so on. These enforcing punishments escalate, with n^k rounds of punishment for a failure to carry out an n^{k-1}–round punishment. This system of escalating punishments makes costly punishment credible because the alternative of a longer counterpunishment is worse. It is better to suffer for n^k rounds than n^{k+1} rounds.

However, these escalating punishments may fail if a player's payoff for playing its minmax strategy against the other player is less than its own minmax value. Punishing you requires me to accept lower payoffs than your worst punishment against me. At some level, such reciprocal threats stop being incredible. For any $\delta < 1$, there is some finite k where punishing you for n^k is worse

		Player 3: *U*		Player 3: *D*	
		Player 2: u	d	Player 2: u	d
Player 1	U	(1,1,1)	(0,0,0)	(0,0,0)	(0,0,0)
	D	(0,0,0)	(0,0,0)	(0,0,0)	(1,1,1)

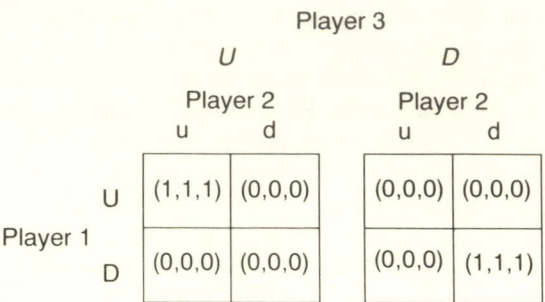

Figure 9.7 A Stage Game where the Players Cannot Be Punished or Rewarded Separately

for me than not punishing you and accepting my minmax value for n^{k+1} rounds instead. When this occurs, the entire structure of reciprocal threats unravels. Each player can anticipate that the k-level punishment is not credible, so the (k − 1)–level punishment cannot be enforced. Then the (k − 2)–level punishment is not credible, and so on. The system of escalating punishments is noncredible when a player carrying out a punishment receives less than its minmax value.

The second solution to the credibility problem of minmax threats, the Minmax-Rewards Folk Theorem, uses rewards to motivate players to carry out costly punishments. If you defect, I punish you by playing my minmax strategy against you for n rounds, where n is large enough to eliminate the benefits of cheating on the agreement. After the punishment, we play a reward segment where I receive a greater payoff than I receive under the original cooperative equilibrium. The reward segment must last long enough for me to be more than compensated for my cost of punishing you. Punishments are credible because players are rewarded for carrying them out.

These rewards require the stage game to have a particular structure of payoffs when there are more than two players. For the rewards to motivate punishment, we must reward the players who carry out punishments without also rewarding the defector who triggered the punishment. There must be a strategy combination in the stage game for each player where that player is not rewarded while the other players are. Otherwise, players who carry out punishments against a defector cannot be rewarded without also rewarding the defector.

The stage game in Figure 9.7 fails to meet this criterion. The minmax strategies against each player have the other two players playing different strategies. For example, (U;d) minmaxes Player 3's payoff to 0. It also reduces the payoffs of Players 1 and 2 to 0. Assume that the punishment reduces all players' payoffs to 0 for n rounds, and then the players receive average payoffs of $v' \leq 1$ afterwards. If Player 3 defects from the initial cooperative strategies, either

Player 1 or Player 2 has an incentive to defect from the punishment against Player 3. If Player 3 plays *U*, Player 2 receives 1 by switching from d to u. This defection is worth 1 to Player 2 in the period she defects, 0 across the n-period punishment of Player 2, and

$$\frac{\delta^{n+1}}{1-\delta}v'$$

for the reward phase after Player 2's punishment, for a total of

$$1+\frac{\delta^{n+1}}{1-\delta}v'$$

Punishing Player 3 is worth 0 for Player 2 across the n-round punishment of Player 3 and

$$\frac{\delta^{n}}{1-\delta}v'$$

for the reward phase after the punishment, for a total of

$$\frac{\delta^{n}}{1-\delta}v'.$$

Defecting from the punishment is better for Player 2 because $1 > \delta^n v'$. The inability of the players to reward those who carry out punishments separately from those who are punished prevents them from providing compensation to players who carry out costly punishments. Reciprocal punishments are not credible in this game because they are too costly to carry out.

In general, then, any feasible division of the payoffs where all players receive more than their minmax value can be supported by an equilibrium in a repeated game. The equilibrium that supports a division uses reciprocal punishments. The players agree to play the strategies that produce the division of the payoff. If any player defects from its strategy, the other players punish it for an agreed number of periods. As long as each player receives more than its minmax payoff, all players have an incentive to comply with a cooperative agreement. The threat of punishment for defection is worse than compliance.

Example: Return to the game used to illustrate the first two folk Theorems. The shaded region in Figure 9.6 gives the set of divisions that can be supported. A division with average payoffs of $(1\frac{1}{2}, 3\frac{1}{2})$ is created by an equilibrium where the players alternate between $(S_1;s_2)$ and $(S_2;s_2)$ from round to round. If either player defects from this arrangement, the other player plays its minmax strategy for an agreed number of rounds. The exact length of the punishment depends upon the discount factor. After the punishment phase is complete, the punishing player is rewarded for an agreed period. Player 1 is rewarded with an average payoff of 4 by playing (S_1;s_2); Player 2 is rewarded with an average payoff of 5 by playing (S_2;s_2). If either player fails to carry out the prescribed punishment, it does not receive the reward. If the player being punished defects during the reward phase, it is punished again.

I do not present formal statements of the Escalating-Punishments Folk Theorem or the Minmax-Rewards Folk Theorem because both require some technical details that are beyond the level of this book. Both theorems produce subgame-perfect equilibria that can support any feasible division of the payoff where both players receive more than their minmax values. I discussed them above to show the limits of what can be accomplished in a repeated game with reciprocal threats. These theorems also show how costly reciprocal threats can be made credible.

The limitations of reciprocal strategies discussed in the section on repeated Prisoner's Dilemma also hold for folk theorems. First, a very wide range of payoffs can be supported under any of the folk theorems. All Nash equilibria of the stage game can be supported by the folk theorems. Payoffs where all players get only small rewards above their minmax values can be supported with the folk theorems. We cannot say, then, that actors will cooperate when the conditions of any folk theorem are met. Nor can we say much about the extent of cooperative agreements between the players. Nor can we say much about shifts in the level of cooperative behavior between the players. Further, many different combinations of strategies can be enforced under the folk theorems. Thus many different behaviors are consistent with the folk theorems, and it is difficult to falsify the assertion that the folk theorem is working.

Second, there is still a credibility problem facing these reciprocal threats. The Escalating-Punishments and Minmax-Rewards folk theorems ensure that players will not defect from punishments unilaterally. But they do not protect against several players' agreeing to defect from a punishment as a group. When punishments are costly to all players, they as a group can all increase their payoffs by ending punishments before the punishment is complete. This joint incentive to defect from punishments can undermine the credibility of reciprocal punishments. If I defect from the original cooperative agreement, I should appeal to you to end my punishment early. We will both be better off. The problem of the players' having an incentive to agree to end punishment prematurely is called **renegotiation**, because the players are renegotiating the punishments that enforce their cooperative agreement. The topic of renegotiation is beyond the scope of this book. I suggest you see Fudenberg and Tirole

		Player 2 s_1	Player 2 s_2
Player 1	S_1	(5,5)	(0,10)
	S_2	(10,0)	(-5,-5)

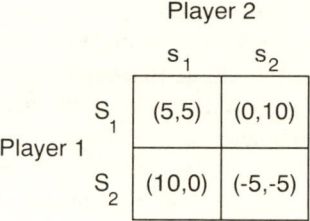

Figure 9.8 Chicken

1991 (174–82) for a further discussion of renegotiation. Work on renegotiation also strives to reduce the set of payoffs that can be supported under a folk theorem.

Finite Repeated Games: The Chain Store Paradox

As just discussed, indefinite iteration offers several ways to make costly threats credible. But these ways of motivating reciprocal threats may not work in repeated games with a known end. Reciprocal threats can support cooperative agreements in stage games with multiple Nash equilibria. The players use the threat of playing a less pleasant Nash equilibrium in the final stages to enforce cooperation in earlier rounds.

> Example: Figure 9.8 gives the strategic form of Chicken. If the players play three rounds of Chicken they can enforce an agreement to play (S_1;s_1) on the first round. If neither player defects in the first round, they play (S_2;s_1) in the second round and (S_1; s_2) in the third round. Their expected payoffs across all three rounds are (15,15). If Player 1 defects in the first round and plays S_2, they agree to play (S_1;s_2) in the second and third rounds. Player 1 receives a total payoff of 10 if he defects, so he cannot profit by defecting from the cooperative agreement.

But this logic cannot work in stage games with a unique Nash equilibrium. Consider repeated Prisoner's Dilemma played for twenty rounds. In the last round, both players should play Defect. Defect is a strongly dominant strategy in Prisoner's Dilemma, and there is no future to enforce moves of Cooperate in the last round. But then the players should also play Defect in the next-to-last round of the game. They should both anticipate that the other will play Defect in the last round. But then there is no incentive not to play Defect in the next-to-last round. The players cannot threaten each other to enforce a deal to play Cooperate in the next-to-last round. Defect strongly dominates Cooperate in the next-to-last move. This logic continues through the entire game. There is only one Nash equilibrium of finite repeated Prisoner's Dilemma: both players play Defect in every round. Imagine that there were a Nash equilibrium such that at least one of the players played Cooperate in at least one round. Let the nth round be the last round where a player plays Cooperate. But then that player can unilaterally improve its payoff by changing its move in the nth round from Cooperate to Defect. Reciprocal strategies do not work because both players know when the game ends and will play Defect in the last round.

This result is disturbing, and it is general to finite repeated games where the stage game has a unique equilibrium. When people play finite repeated Prisoner's Dilemma in experiments, they play Cooperate some of the time. Even when people expect that their relationship will end at a definite time in the future, they should still be able to reach some agreements for their short-term gain. Both players are better off if they can play (C;c) for several rounds of finite repeated Prisoner's Dilemma, even if their agreement breaks down as the end of the game approaches. Further, the problem of cooperative agreements in finite repeated games is general. If the players need reciprocal punishments to enforce a cooperative agreement, the logic of backwards induction destroys the credibility of such punishments in finite repeated games with a unique equilibrium.

The solution to this problem is clever (Kreps et al. 1982). We assume there is a small chance that one of the players is "crazy" and always plays Tit for Tat in repeated Prisoner's Dilemma. Formally, we move to a game of limited information with two types. One type of player has Prisoner's Dilemma payoffs; the other type is fixed to play Tit for Tat. The first type has an incentive to imitate the second type and play Tit for Tat in the early rounds of the finite repeated game. Further, the second player has an incentive to play along with the first type's imitation of the second type. Both players benefit by playing (C;c) in the early rounds of the game.

This clever solution models the idea that a player cannot be certain about the other player's motivations. The logic of backwards induction requires complete information. (D;d) in every round is the only Nash equilibrium of finite repeated Prisoner's Dilemma under complete information. Because both players can anticipate the end of the game and each other's moves before then, they cannot make conditional threats against one another. The backwards induction depends not only on my incentive to play Defect, but also on my anticipation that you will play Defect no matter what I do. But if there is a small chance that you will reciprocate to my plays of Cooperate, the chain of backwards induction is broken. I can no longer anticipate that you will play Defect on all future rounds of the game. The benefit of playing (C;c) for many rounds merits my taking the chance of playing Cooperate in the early rounds of the game.

This solution is a second, general approach to understanding reciprocal threats and promises in repeated games. The first approach stated that indefinite iteration created the possibility of credible reciprocal threats. This second solution states that the players' inability to know one another's payoffs can produce credible threats and promises in finite repeated games. This argument provides a way to model reputations in a game; your reputation is the chance that you are the type that always carries out your promise or threat. When there are many rounds left to play, even a small reputation makes threats and promises effective. Threats are credible because a player cannot be certain that carrying out the threat will be costly to the player making the threat. If I know that making good on your threat will be costly to you, I can anticipate that you will not carry out the threat. But if there is a chance that carrying out your threat will be beneficial to you, I have to consider what risk of punishment I am willing to run. Further, you may want to punish me even when punishment is costly to you because you can deter me in the future by punishing me now.

I present this approach through the classic example of the problem of costly threats, the Chain Store Paradox (Selten 1978; Kreps and Wilson 1982b). Consider the position of a large monopoly faced with the possibility of entrants to its many, separate markets. The best of all worlds occurs when no one ever enters its markets, allowing it to reap monopoly profits in all of them. Should entry occur, the monopoly must decide whether or not to fight the entrant through price competition. A price war would punish the entrant, causing it to lose money compared to not entering the market. But the punishment would also cost the monopoly more than acquiescing in the invasion of one of its markets. The best of all possible worlds for the entrant is entering the market without resistance. Staying out is preferable to entering and facing a price war. The questions are, When should entry occur, and when should it be resisted?

Although the description of the game talks about monopolies and price wars, it is a special case of the general question of when costly threats are credible. One can think of many situations where the question of credibility of threats pops up. To an international relations scholar, the Chain Store Paradox suggests the ideas of containment and appeasement. War is a costly way to prevent aggression, but sometimes one may need to carry out such a threat to maintain credibility. Actors sometimes implement costly threats in order to maintain a reputation for carrying out their threats. Otherwise, their future threats will not be credible. Appeasement may be less costly in the short run, but it may encourage further demands whose total cost exceeds the cost of fighting once.

The Chain Store Paradox also represents part of the relationship between political leaders and their followers (Calvert 1987). Groups benefit from the cooperation of their members to produce collective goods. Collective goods benefit the entire membership, but individual followers pay for their own contribution. Whenever the cost of contributing exceeds the marginal benefit to the contributing actor, followers have an incentive to not contribute. The incentives of a collective dilemma are those of the Prisoner's Dilemma.

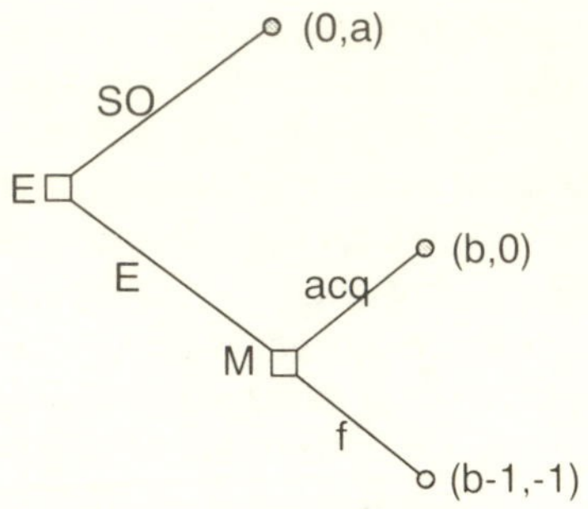

Figure 9.9 The Stage Game of the Chain Store Paradox

Leaders exist, in part, to police this problem. If a follower fails to contribute, the leader can punish the follower. But punishment is often costly in the short run, even if it helps enforce contributions in the long run. The act of punishment has a natural sequence, which matches the Chain Store Paradox. A leader prefers unchallenged cooperation from his or her followers. But followers prefer not contributing if they can avoid punishment afterwards. Leaders punish followers after observing defection by the latter. If punishment is costly, the threat of punishment may not be credible.

The game in Figure 9.9 formalizes this situation. Assume that $a > 1$ and $0 < b < 1$. E stands for Entrant and M for Monopolist. The entrant begins a round of the game by either entering the market or staying out. I abbreviate these moves as E and SO. If the entrant stays out, then the round ends. The monopolist reaps monopoly profits of a in that market, and the entrant receives 0. If the entrant enters the market, the monopolist must decide whether to fight against the entrant with a price war. I abbreviate these moves by f and acq for Fight and Acquiesce. If the monopolist acquiesces to the entry, the entrant receives profits of b, and the monopolist's profits are reduced to 0. If the monopolist fights against the entrant, both sides pay a cost of 1, making both worse off than if the monopolist had acquiesced or if the entrant had stayed out.

We assume further that there are n different entrants, one for each of n different markets. Each entrant considers entering its market in turn, creating n repetitions of the game in Figure 9.9. The monopolist's payoff is just the sum of its payoff for all the stages. The monopolist is willing to suffer the costs of fighting against an entrant if doing so will discourage the next entrant from entry. The cost of fighting is -1 and the benefit of successful deterrence is $a > 1$. Each entrant receives its payoff for the stage it plays.

The stage game here should be familiar. It is the game I used to demonstrate subgame perfection in Chapter Five. It is the simplest game that addresses the credibility of costly threats. The monopolist always has an implicit threat to fight against the entrant. Is that threat credible, that is, will it convince the entrant to stay out of the market? Under complete information, the threat is not credible in a single stage. The entrant knows that fighting is costly to the monopolist and anticipates that the monopolist will acquiesce to entry. The threat of fighting is not subgame perfect in the stage game alone.

But is the threat of fighting credible in the repeated game? (SO;f) is a Nash equilibrium of the stage game. Can the entrant deter entry and enforce this equilibrium in the repeated game played under complete information? No. The repeated game has one and only one perfect equilibrium: the entrant should always enter and the monopolist should always acquiesce.

<u>Exercise 9.4</u>:

a) Demonstrate that in any Nash equilibrium of the Chain Store Paradox, the players must play one of (SO;f) or (E;acq) in every stage.

b) Show that (SO;f) in every stage is not a perfect equilibrium. (Hint: Think about the last stage.)

c) Show that the only perfect equilibrium of the Chain Store Paradox is (E;acq) (i.e., the entrant enters and the monopolist acquiesces) in all stages.

1) Show that for the last stage of the game, (E;acq) is the only perfect equilibrium.

2) Show that if (E;acq) will be played in the last stage of the game, then (E;acq) is the optimal strategy for the next-to-last stage of the game.

We can generalize part 2 to show that if (E;acq) will be played for the remaining k stages of the game, (E;acq) is the optimal strategy for the (n − k)th stage of the game. We can conclude by induction that (E;acq) in all stages is the only perfect equilibrium from subpart 1 and the generalization of subpart 2. (See the section on the idea of a mathematical proof in Appendix One for a brief discussion of proof by induction.)

Here lies the paradox in the Chain Store Paradox. It is never in the interest of the monopolist to fight entry, so entrants should always enter. Because the entrants know that fighting is costly to the monopolist, its threats to fight entry are never credible. The last entrant always enters because the monopolist will not fight. The monopolist cannot deter the last entrant, so there is no benefit to fighting against the next-to-last entrant. This logic unzippers any equilibrium where the monopolist fights entry in any stage. But this equilibrium behavior

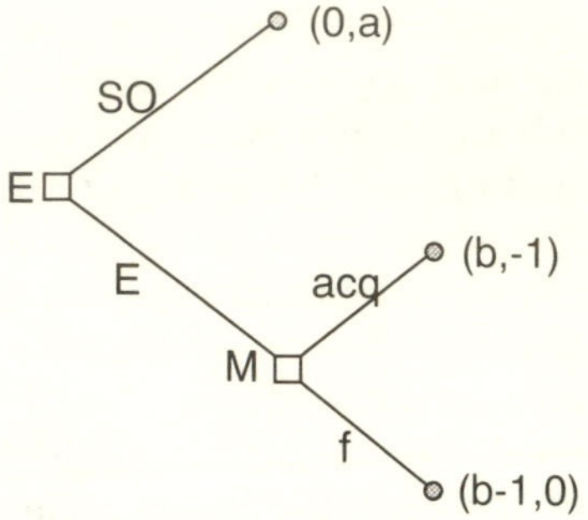

Figure 9.10 The Stage Game of the Chain Store Paradox with a Vengeful Monopolist

violates our intuition and experimental results. Even in finite games, we expect the monopolist to fight entry in early stages of the game to deter entry in later stages of the game. Fighting entry is not rational in this game because the monopolist cannot make the threat of retaliation credible. The entrants know fighting is costly to the monopolist.

But what if the entrants are not certain that fighting is costly to the monopolist? They have to judge whether the monopolist will fight against them when they decide whether to enter. The monopolist also has an incentive to fight entry to convince other possible entrants that it will fight against them in the future. We model this uncertainty by adding a second type of monopolist, the vengeful monopolist, who benefits from fighting against entrants. If the monopolist is vengeful, Figure 9.10 gives the extensive form with $a > 1$ and $0 < b < 1$ as before. In it, the vengeful monopolist benefits by fighting against entrants.

> Exercise 9.5: Find the Nash and subgame-perfect equilibria of the stage game against the vengeful monopolist.

The Chain Store Paradox with uncertainty starts with a random draw with probability ϵ that the monopolist is vengeful and probability $1 - \epsilon$ that it is normal. Fighting is costly for normal monopolists, while a vengeful monopolist suffers costs when it fails to fight against entrants. Only the monopolist sees the outcome of this draw. The entrants do not know the monopolist's type. The beliefs of the initial entrant that the monopolist is vengeful equal ϵ. The strategy space of this game, as with all repeated games, is very complex. We must specify moves for the entrants and each type of monopolist for each round. Fortunately, the assumption of two types of monopolists, their payoffs, and separate entrants in every period simplifies the model.

Rather than directly analyzing the n-round Chain Store Paradox, I solve the two-round model first. I generalize the equilibrium to the n-round model later. The logic is easier to follow in the two-round model than in the full n-round model. In each of the two stages, the entrant must decide whether the monopolist is vengeful or normal. Let $\pi(k)$ be the kth entrant's beliefs that the monopolist is vengeful for $k = 1, 2$, with $\pi(1) = \epsilon$.

Solve the two-round model by working backwards from the monopolist's move in the last stage. Vengeful monopolists always fight, and normal monopolists always acquiesce. For the entrant, calculate the critical belief $\pi(2)$ where the second entrant is indifferent between entering and staying out:

$$0 = \pi(2)(b - 1) + (1 + \pi(2))(b)$$

$$\pi(2) = b.$$

(Recall that $0 < b < 1$.) If $\pi(2) > b$, the second entrant stays out. If $\pi(2) < b$, the second entrant enters.

Working backwards, consider a normal monopolist's position in the first stage of the two-round model. Assume that vengeful monopolists fight entry in any round.[4] They prefer fighting to acquiescing even when fighting produces no long-run benefits. A normal monopolist's choice depends upon whether it can deter the second entrant. If $\pi(1) > b$, it should fight now. When both types of monopolists always fight, $\pi(2) = \pi(1)$. The following Bayesian calculation shows this:

$$\pi(2) = \frac{p(VM)p(1f|VM)}{p(VM)p(1f|VM) + p(NM)p(1f|NM)}$$

$$= \frac{\pi(1)(1)}{\pi(1)(1) + [1 - \pi(1)](1)} = \pi(1),$$

where VM means Vengeful Monopolist, NM means Normal Monopolist, and 1f indicates fighting in the first round. If $\pi(1) > b$ and the normal monopolist fights in the first round, $\pi(2) > b$. The second entrant stays out when $\pi(2) > b$. If the monopolist fights in the first round when $\pi(1) > b$, the benefits of deterrence in the second round cover the costs of fighting.

If $\pi(1) < b$, find a mixed strategy for normal monopolists to make the second entrant indifferent between entering and staying out. The second entrant is indifferent when $\pi(2) = b$. Let p be the probability that normal monopolists fight in the first stage. Calculate p such that $\pi(2) = b$, as follows:

$$b\pi(2) = \frac{p(VM)p(1f|VM)}{p(VM)p(1f|VM) + p(NM)p(1f|NM)}$$

$$= \frac{\pi(1)(1)}{\pi(1)(1) + [1 - \pi(1)](p)}$$

$$p = \frac{(1 - b)\pi(1)}{b[1 - \pi(1)]}.$$

When $\pi(1) < b$ and normal monopolists fight with the probability above, the second entrant is indifferent between entering and staying out. Its indifference allows it to play a mixed strategy in the second round. It needs to find a mixed strategy that makes a normal monopolist indifferent between fighting and acquiescing in the first round. The normal monopolist's mixed strategy in the first round requires indifference between fighting and acquiescing then. Let q be the probability that the second entrant enters. Calculate q to make a normal monopolist indifferent between fighting and acquiescing to entry in the first round:

$$\begin{aligned} u_{NM}(acq) &= u_{NM}(f) \\ 0 + 0 &= -1 + q(a) + (1 - q)(0) \\ q &= \frac{1}{a}. \end{aligned}$$

If the normal monopolist acquiesces in the first round, it receives 0 in that round, the second entrant always enters, and the monopolist never fights the second entry, for a payoff of 0. If it fights, it receives -1 now, 0 if the second entrant enters, and a if the second entrant stays out.

To complete our illumination of the equilibrium, find the first entrant's strategy. When $\pi(1) \geq b$, all monopolists punish, so the first entrant should stay out. Each entrant is separate and has only one opportunity for entry. If $\pi(1) <$ b, calculate the critical belief that makes the first entrant indifferent between entering and staying out, assuming that normal monopolists use their mixed strategy:

$$\begin{aligned} u_E(SO) &= u_E(E) \\ &= u_E(f)[p(VM) + p(NM)p(F|NM)] \\ &\quad + u_E(acq)p(NM)p(acq|NM) \\ 0 &= (b - 1)\left(\pi(1) + [1 - \pi(1)]\left\{\frac{(1 - b)\pi(1)}{b[1 - \pi(1)]}\right\}\right) \\ &\quad + (b)[1 - \pi(1)]\left\{1 - \frac{(1 - b)\pi(1)}{b[1 - \pi(1)]}\right\} \\ \pi(1) &= b^2. \end{aligned}$$

If $\pi(1) > b^2$, stay out; if $\pi(1) < b^2$, enter; and if $\pi(1) = b^2$, mix.

Rather than just pulling together this equilibrium to the two-round Chain Store Paradox, I leap to the equilibrium of the n-round model. The calculations for the backwards induction from a round to the previous round parallel the calculations for the first period of the two-period model.

Proposition: The following belief-strategy pair is a perfect Bayesian equilibrium of the n-round Chain Store Paradox:

Monopolist's strategy: If the monopolist is vengeful, always play f. If the monopolist is normal, play acq in the nth stage. Before the nth stage, play f in the kth stage if $\pi(k) \geq b^{n-k}$; otherwise mix f and acq with probability

$$\frac{(1 - b^{n-k})\pi(k)}{b^{n-k}[1 - \pi(k)]}$$

of playing f. The monopolist's beliefs are irrelevant because all its information sets are singletons.

Entrants' strategy: If $\pi(k) > b^{n-k+1}$, play SO. If $\pi(k) < b^{n-k+1}$, play E. If $\pi(k) = b^{n-k+1}$, mix E and SO, with probability $1/a$ of SO.

Entrants' beliefs: If no entry has ever occurred, $\pi(k) = \epsilon$. If any entry has been acquiesced to, $\pi(k) = 0$. If all entries have been fought, $\pi(k) = \max(b^{n-m}, \epsilon)$ where m is the last stage where entry was fought.

Before demonstrating that the belief-strategy combination above is an equilibrium, let us explore the intuition behind it. The entrants' beliefs, π, reflect the reputation of the monopolist for fighting entry. Their beliefs allow the entrants to gauge the monopolist's likely response to entry. When $\pi = 0$, the monopolist's reputation is shot, the entrants know that fighting is costly for the monopolist, and they always enter. The monopolist's reputation collapses after any acquiescence. Normal monopolists fight entry as long as the future benefits of deterrence outweigh the immediate costs of fighting. As the game progresses, the future benefits of establishing a reputation decrease. The entrants in the later rounds anticipate that normal monopolists are less likely to fight. Successful deterrence requires a stronger reputation as the game progresses.

The entrants stay out until the initial reputation of the monopolist is no longer strong enough to deter them. The critical reputation needed to deter the entrants begins very low, b^n, which is close to 0 for $b < 1$ and n larger then ten. This critical reputation, b^{n-k+1} for the kth round, rises as the game progresses until it exceeds the monopolist's initial reputation, ϵ. Entry then occurs, and a normal monopolist fights that entry often enough to make the next entrant indifferent between staying out and entering. Once any acquiescence occurs, the entrants enter on all future rounds because they know the monopolist is normal, and so will not fight. If an entrant enters prematurely, any monopolist fights entry in order to maintain its reputation.

Now we turn to the details of the equilibrium. The proof proceeds by induction. The optimal strategies for the last round of the game are the same as in the two-round model. We derive the optimal strategies and beliefs for the kth round given those for the (k + 1)th round. We then can use this derivation to work backwards through the game to determine the optimal strategies and beliefs for each round. Assume that the strategies and beliefs above are an equilibrium for the (k + 1)th round. I show that they are also in equilibrium for the kth round.

Vengeful monopolists always fight. If they ever acquiesce, π drops to 0, leading to automatic entry by all future entrants. Then f dominates acq for vengeful monopolists because f is better in the current stage and cannot be worse in future stages.

For the entrants, there are four cases to consider: $\pi(k) \geq b^{n-k}$; $b^{n-k} > \pi(k) > b^{n-k+1}$; $\pi(k) = b^{n-k+1}$; and $\pi(k) < b^{n-k+1}$. For the first case, the monopolist will fight entry (remember the monopolist's strategy is fixed when you check the entrants' strategy), so entrants should stay out.

For the second case, calculate expected utilities for entering and staying out:

$$u_E(SO) = 0$$

and

$$\begin{aligned} u_E(E) &= (b-1)\left(\pi(k) + [1-\pi(k)]\left\{\frac{(1-b^{n-k})\pi(k)}{b^{n-k}[1-\pi(k)]}\right\}\right) \\ &\quad + (b)\,[1-\pi(k)]\left\{1 - \frac{(1-b^{n-k}\pi(k)}{b^{n-k}[1-\pi(k)]}\right\} \\ &= (b-1)\left[\frac{\pi(k)}{b^{n-k}}\right] + (b)\left[1 - \frac{\pi(k)}{b^{n-k}}\right] \\ &= b - \frac{\pi(k)}{b^{n-k}} < b - \frac{b^{n-k+1}}{b^{n-k}} = 0. \end{aligned}$$

Staying out is better than entry in this case.

> Exercise 9.6: Demonstrate that the entrants' strategy is a best reply to the monopolist's strategy in cases 3 and 4 above, when $\pi(k) = b^{n-k+1}$ and $\pi(k) < b^{n-k+1}$.

Turning to the normal monopolist's strategies, we have two cases, $\pi(k) \geq b^{n-k}$ and $\pi(k) < b^{n-k}$. In the former case, compare expected utilities for punishing and acquiescing:

$$u_{NM}(acq) = 0,$$

and

$$u_{NM}(f) = -1 + a + u_{NM}(\text{stages } k + 2 \text{ on}).$$

The utility for acquiescing is 0 in this stage and for all future stages. Acquiescing once makes $\pi(k+1) = 0$, leading to acquiescence to entry in all future stages. If the monopolist fights, the next entrant stays out. The monopolist's utility for rounds after the next one cannot be less than 0 because it can guarantee itself 0 by acquiescing at all future stages.

> Exercise 9.7: Show that the normal monopolist's strategy is indifferent between f and acq for $\pi(k) < b^{n-k}$ (and so its mixed strategy is a best reply then).

I show the beliefs are consistent with the strategies and Bayes's Theorem. According to the strategies, vengeful monopolists never acquiesce. If aqs is ever played, the monopolist must be normal and $\pi = 0$ from then on. If entry does not occur in any stage k, $\pi(k) = \pi(k-1)$ because the entrants have learned nothing from that stage of the game. If entry is fought in stage k, we have the following:

$$\pi(k+1) = \frac{p(VM)\,p(kf|VM)}{p(VM)\,p(kf|VM) + p(NM)\,p(kf|NM)},$$

$$\pi(k+1) = \frac{\pi(k)(1)}{\pi(k)(1) + [1 - \pi(k)]\left\{\dfrac{(1 - b^{n-k}\,\pi(k)}{b^{n-k}[1 - \pi(k)]}\right\}}$$

$$= \frac{\pi(k)\,b^{n-k}}{\pi(k)} = b^{n-k}.$$

If $\pi(k) \geq b^{n-k}$,

$$\pi(k+1) = \frac{\pi(k)(1)}{\pi(k)(1) + [1 - \pi(k)](1)} = \pi(k).$$

where VM is Vengeful Monopolist, NM is Normal Monopolist, and kf indicates fighting in the kth round. If $\pi(k) < b^{n-k}$, The probabilities in the normal monopolist's mixed strategy have been chosen to produce the desired beliefs in the equilibrium.

Finally, the beliefs off the equilibrium path are as follows. If a vengeful monopolist ever acquiesces, $\pi(k) = 0$ from then on. If a monopolist ever fights when $\pi(k) = 0$, $\pi(k+1) = 0$. Both of these are consistent with the strategies. We have assumed that once the monopolist blows its reputation by acquiescing, it can never regain its reputation.

The Chain Store Paradox is an example of the second approach to the credibility of potentially costly threats in repeated games. A small uncertainty in the mind of the entrants allows normal monopolists to make credible threats by mimicking vengeful monopolists. Early on, the benefits of deterrence cover the immediate costs of fighting. The uncertainty in the entrants' minds creates the possibility of effective deterrence. It breaks the backwards induction that made deterrence impossible under complete information. Eventually, an entrant challenges this charade, and continuing the charade is too costly for the monopolist. As the final round approaches, entry is more likely and resistance less likely.

Some may object and say this is too much work for so obvious a payoff. The formalization adds more than just math to a reputational argument; it adds precision to the argument. For example, reputations run out at some point. The shadow of the future eventually stops hanging over the heads of the entrants. An informal argument cannot tell you when that occurs; the model tells you exactly. The question of when potentially costly threats are credible is central to many concerns. This model provides one way to think about how such threats can be made credible.

Uncertainty about the players' payoffs can be used generally to make threats and promises credible in finite repeated games. The Tit for Tat strategy can be supported in finite iterated Prisoner's Dilemma if there is a small chance that one of the players is a type that always plays Tit for Tat. Normal types of that player want to imitate the Tit for Tat type until the late rounds of the game. They gain the benefits of cooperation. The other player plays Cooperate early in the game because the first player will reciprocate its moves.

A similar strategy can be applied to the centipede game discussed in Chapter Five. In the centipede game, the players make sequential decisions to continue or end the game. They both benefit the longer they continue the game. But each player is better off ending the game with its move if the other player is going to end the game in its next move. Backwards induction shows that the first player's ending the game in his first move is the only perfect equilibrium. Adding a small probability that one player always plays Continue creates equilibria where both players continue the game for several moves. This probability can be quite small if there are many moves left in the game. The large benefits of continuing the game for many moves increase both players' interest in playing Continue instead of taking the additional payoff from ending the game.

This approach has been generalized to provide a folk theorem for incomplete information (Fudenberg and Maskin 1986). For any small amount of uncertainty about other players' payoffs and any feasible division of the payoffs above their minmax payoffs, you can find a game of incomplete information with that amount of uncertainty that has a perfect Bayesian equilibrium where the players receive that division. Any division of the payoff that can be achieved in an open-ended repeated game can also be achieved in a finite repeated game with incomplete information. Limited information can be as effective as indefinite iteration in making threats and promises credible. Of course, the same limitations of the folk theorems also hold for the limited information approach. A large range of behavior and divisions of payoffs are in equilibrium according to these results.

This approach to the credibility of threats parallels and differs from the idea behind perfect equilibrium. Both approaches assume that the players cannot absolutely know that the other players will follow their equilibrium strategies. Optimal strategies must be robust against deviations by the other players. The trembles in strategies used in perfect equilibrium are one way to represent the possibility that other players deviate from an equilibrium. Perfect equilibrium eliminated Nash equilibria that were not best replies against such trembles. Trembles can be thought of as hypotheses that account for defections from equilibrium. In perfect equilibrium, defections are treated as random errors; one defection does not imply that the defecting player will defect from equilibrium again later in the game. The approach in this section also allows for small chances that a player may deviate from equilibrium. But a defection in this approach signals other players that future defections are likely to follow. Defection here is not a random error. You defect because defection is optimal given your payoffs.

Stationarity

The folk theorems show that wide ranges of behavior can be in equilibrium when we allow the actors to use conditional punishment strategies. Punishments can be made sufficiently severe to support some very bizarre behavior in equilibrium. Very complex punishment strategies can be designed to enforce equilibria. There are several reasons to believe that such strategies are impractical. As previously covered in the section on the folk theorems, players may lack an incentive to carry out a complex punishment strategy. Some punishment strategies require all players to know that punishment will last for a set number of rounds. How do the players guarantee that they all know the length of punishments? Given the wide range of equilibria possible under the folk theorems, what common conjecture do the players use to determine which equilibrium they are playing?

Often we wish to examine repeated interactions to see what behavior results when we do not allow the actors to use the full range of punishment strategies.

We do not allow the players to condition their strategies on the history of the game. Instead, we limit their strategies to respond only to the current and future rounds of the game. Players should make the same moves when they find themselves in the same strategic situation. We make this idea precise by first defining what "the same strategic situation" means.

> **Definition**: Two rounds of a repeated game are **structurally identical** iff the players have the same moves available in the same sequence with the same consequences, whether those consequences are final outcomes, stage payoffs, or further rounds of the game.

An example may help clarify this definition. Recall the model of bargaining in legislatures in Chapter Five (Baron and Ferejohn 1989). There are three actors in the legislature. Each round begins with an equal chance of each member's being recognized. The recognized member makes a proposal, on which all three vote. If two or more vote yes, the proposal passes, and the game ends. If the proposal fails, a new round begins with a member's being recognized. Payoffs are discounted across rounds by a common discount factor. All rounds of this model are structurally identical. At the beginning of each round, the strategic position of the actors is always the same. Each has a $1/3$ chance of being recognized and making a proposal. The same set of proposals is always available to the recognized member. The consequences of the vote are the same for identical proposals.

Strategies in a stationary equilibrium are not conditioned on the history of the game. Instead, the current strategic environment determines them. Prior moves matter in a stationary equilibrium only if they create the current strategic environment.

> **Definition**: An equilibrium is **stationary** iff all players take the same action (including mixed strategies) in all structurally identical rounds.

The equilibrium of the model of bargaining in legislatures in Chapter Five is stationary. The players' strategies are the same in every round of the game, and every round is structurally identical. That model has many other equilibria if we look for nonstationary equilibria. Any distribution of the unit to be divided can be supported by punishment strategies if the legislature has at least five members and δ is sufficiently high. A recognized member makes the distribution and everyone votes for it. Anyone who deviates at either stage can be punished with 0 payoff if the desired distribution does not pass. Other members carry out the punishment because if they defect, they will be punished in the place of the original defector. The threat of punishment is sufficient to enforce the distribution.

One justification for stationary equilibria is that they are a natural focal point in the set of all equilibria that can be supported by the folk theorems. Different equilibria depend on different punishment strategies. Some require a common conjecture that the players will play the Nash equilibrium used as the punishment for an agreed number of rounds. Given that there is an infinite set of possible equilibria and punishment strategies that support them, how do the players know which equilibria they are playing and what punishment strategies to use? Stationary equilibria depend on the shared expectation that neither player will engage in reciprocal punishments. This is the simplest common conjecture about what punishments will be employed. Only those punishments that can be carried out within one round of the game are permissible.

Stationary equilibria eliminate reciprocal strategies. Repeated games provide a way to study how reciprocal strategies can operate. But repetition produces strategic incentives other than just reciprocity. Stationarity allows us to see how expected rewards from future events can shape current decisions. For example, actors' willingness to reach agreements depends on their expectation of the alternative of further negotiations. Continuation values capture expectations about future play. Equilibrium strategies determine the continuation values. Because the equilibrium strategies also depend upon the continuation values, we solve for the two simultaneously. We can then see how expectations about the future and current choices are interrelated. Because players in a stationary equilibrium always make the same move from structurally identical rounds, the continuation values of a stationary equilibrium are easy to calculate. I now present an example of how stationarity works in a concrete example.

Retrospective Voting and Electoral Control*

The models of electoral behavior that I presented in Chapters Two and Eight are prospective in nature. The voters consider the future performance of the candidates when deciding for whom to vote. They judge that future performance by the positions the candidates espouse during the campaign. But many voters appear to vote retrospectively. They judge the candidates by examining the record of the incumbent in office. Performance in office can be a sign of competence and effort.

This section presents Ferejohn's (1986) model of how voters can use retrospective voting to control elected officials. Voters and officeholders do not agree on all policies. Elected officials can be tempted to pursue the policies they prefer, instead of those that the voter elected them to enact. Reelection is an incentive to officeholders to pursue the ends desired by the voters instead of those they personally prefer. But if voters choose candidates prospectively rather than retrospectively, incumbents' chances of reelection do not depend upon their performance in office. Voters vote retrospectively because

*This section requires differential and integral calculus.

such votes encourage candidates to perform when they hold office. Retrospective voting, then, is a rational response to the problem of how electorates control elected officials.

This model is a principal-agent model, which is used in economics to examine contracts. The principal hires the agent to perform a task for it. But the principal cannot monitor the agent's actions perfectly. The principal's inability to monitor the agent provides an opportunity for the agent to cheat on the contract. One class of principal-agent models studies how employers motivate their employees to prevent shirking on the job. By tying rewards and punishments to performance, employers gain some control over their employees' actions on the job. In the retrospective voting model here, the electorate is the principal, and the politician is the agent. The electorate can only observe the final result of the politician's acts in office. It cannot determine exactly what the politician has done. By rewarding the politician on the basis of the final results, the electorate does gain some control over the politician's acts in office. But that control is not perfect.

The model has two actors, a politician, P, and a voter, V. The idea behind the model is simple. The voter's welfare is determined by a combination of exogenous events and effort by the officeholder. But that effort is costly to the officeholder. When in office, the politician enjoys the benefits of office. He or she wishes to be reelected, then, in order to continue to enjoy these benefits. The politician when in office is willing to make some effort to improve conditions for the voter; otherwise, the voter will vote him or her out of office.

The benefits of office can be thought of in two ways. Typically, they are thought of as the perquisites of high political office. Voters try to prevent incumbents from spending all their time at Camp David or their favorite vacation haunt and get them to devote some time to minding the ship of state. I prefer to think of these benefits as ideological. Executive officials have limited resources that they can expend to change policy. In the United States, for example, it takes effort to shepherd bills through Congress or control executive agencies. The electorate and the president have different priorities. Will the president spend his or her effort on the policies he or she wishes to pursue at the expense of those that the voters prefer?

We assume that the politician can be returned to office in a later election and can be reelected indefinitely.[5] It is simpler to assume that politicians live forever than to delve into the complexities of end-game effects. When officeholders cannot run for reelection, there is no way for voters to discipline them. Voters should understand their inability to control these "lame ducks" and refuse to elect them in their final election. But then they cannot discipline an officeholder in his or her next-to-last term. The remaining backwards logic should be obvious by now. But "lame duck" officeholders do appear to indulge solely their own interests. If you are troubled by the possibility of these end-game effects, think of the politician as a party instead of an individual politician.

Parties do care about their future prospects and can discipline "lame duck" heads of state who ignore their party's long-term interest.

We treat the alternative candidate as simply a clone of the officeholder. Differences between parties and candidates are critical elements of any election. This model simplifies away from ideological and personal differences between candidates to focus on just the dynamics of electoral control. The question here is just how retrospective votes can be used to discipline officeholders. The assumption of identical politicians makes the model symmetric between the two. Their strategies in office are the same because their positions and utility functions are identical. Thus we can solve the model for both politicians by solving for just one. Call this shadow politician P′. P′ is identical to P except that one and only one of the two is in office in a round.

We also simplify the electorate to a single voter. This voter could represent either one member of a homogenous electorate or else the median voter of the electorate. Again, this outrageous simplification allows us to focus solely on the question of retrospective voting. If there are a number of different types of voters, incumbents may try to "buy" one section of the electorate at the expense of the other voters. They may try to assemble a winning block of voters by extracting benefits from the omitted voters. This question is important and interesting, but this model is the place to begin before trying to answer that more difficult question.

The first round begins with player 1, the politician, in office. P observes exogenous conditions, θ, that influence the welfare of player 2, the voter. We can think of θ as the underlying economic or political conditions that are beyond the control of P. Let θ be uniformly distributed on [0,1]. P can take actions that improve the V's welfare. Let $A \geq 0$ be the level of effort that P makes. V's utility for a given round of the game is $u_V(A, \theta) = A\theta$. The more effort P makes, the better off V is. P receives utility W each round he holds office. But the more effort P makes, the worse off P is. P receives benefits B for each round he is in office. These benefits are reduced by the effort P makes during that round. When P is out of office, he receives 0 benefits. Thus $u_P(A) = B - A$ if P is in office and 0 if P is out of office.

The trick is that V cannot observe the underlying exogenous conditions θ or effort A; she can only observe the result, $A\theta$. After P chooses his level of effort, V observes the net effect and then decides whether to retain P in office. If so, a new round of the game begins with P in office. If not, a new round begins with P out of office. P returns to office in the new or later round if and when V chooses to replace the new incumbent. Both players discount future rounds by a common discount factor δ. The time line of a round of the game with P in office is given below:

1. The incumbent, P or P′, observes θ.

2. The incumbent chooses A.

3. V observes $A\theta$.

4. V decides whether to retain the incumbent in office.

5. P receives payoff $B - A$, and V receives payoff $A\theta$. If P is out of office, he receives payoff 0. A new round begins with P the incumbent if P is the incumbent and is retained or if P' is the incumbent and is voted out of office. Otherwise, P' is the new incumbent.

Stationarity plays an important role in solving this model. If we allow the voter to use punishment strategies that extend across several elections, a very wide range of equilibria can be supported. The voter could threaten to throw out nonperforming incumbents and prevent them from ever returning to office. This threat can be used to support distributions of the payoff where the incumbent's continuation value is above B, the one-time payoff for defecting and the voter receives the remaining surplus. Punishment strategies across several elections may be part of real elections. The Democratic party in the United States still loves to remind the voters of Herbert Hoover, and one might think that Jimmy Carter ran for president five times, given how often Ronald Reagan and George Bush mentioned his name in their campaigns. I exclude these multiperiod punishment strategies in this model.

I solve for a stationary equilibrium that produces retrospective votes within the confines of a single round of the game. This game has a stationary equilibrium where the politician never makes any effort and the voter always turns the incumbent out no matter what he has done in office. Given the other's action, neither player has an incentive to change its strategy unilaterally. But I wish to find an equilibrium where retrospective voting occurs.

Because every round is structurally identical, both players must adopt the same strategy in every stage.[6] The voter's strategy is given by a cutoff level, K. If $A\theta \geq K$, V returns the incumbent to office; if not, she turns him out. Given such a cutoff voting strategy, the incumbent either makes the minimal effort needed to secure reelection, K/θ, or makes no effort at all. His choice is driven by the magnitude of θ.

Whether the incumbent makes the effort needed for reelection depends upon that level relative to the benefits of continuing in office. Given P's strategy of no effort or sufficient effort to assure reelection, V selects K to maximize its expected utility from any round. V faces two problems in setting K. First, greater performance is better. A higher K produces greater effort and performance by the incumbent. Second, she must create an incentive for the incumbent to make any effort. A higher K increases the chance that the incumbent will make no effort to be reelected.

Begin with the incumbent's decision as to whether to make the needed effort to secure reelection. Let U^I be the continuation value to P of starting a period of the game as the incumbent and U^O be the continuation value of starting a period out of office. P makes effort K/θ if and only if

$$B - \frac{K}{\theta} + \delta U^I > B + \delta U^O.$$

Solving for θ, we have the following condition for P's making the necessary effort to be reelected:

$$\theta > \frac{K}{\delta(U^I - U^O)}.$$

This condition characterizes the incumbent's strategy. When it is satisfied, he makes K/θ effort; when it is not, he makes 0 effort.

With the incumbent's strategy for fixed K, we can now calculate what K is optimal for the voter. Her utility for the game is the discounted sum across all future periods of the performance that the incumbent produces in each period. That performance is 0 if the incumbent makes 0 effort and K if he makes K/θ effort. Because θ is uniformly distributed on [0,1], the chance that the incumbent makes the necessary effort is $1 - K/[\delta(U^I - U^O)]$. V's utility for the game is

$$\begin{aligned} U_v &= \sum_{t=0}^{+\infty} \delta^t K\left[1 - \frac{K}{\delta(U^I - U^O)}\right] \\ &= \frac{\delta K(U^I - U^O) - K^2}{\delta(1-\delta)(U^I - U^O)}. \end{aligned}$$

Choose K to maximize V's utility by calculating the derivative and setting it equal to 0. The optimal K is

$$K = \frac{\delta(U^I - U^O)}{2}.$$

Substitute this value for K back into P's strategy for choosing when to make the effort needed for reelection; P makes the needed effort only when $\theta > \frac{1}{2}$. The probability that an incumbent is reelected in this model is $\frac{1}{2}$. Substituting K back into V's expected utility, we have the following:

$$U_v = \frac{\delta(U^I - U^O)}{4(1-\delta)}.$$

To complete the model, we need to solve for P's continuation values in and out of office, U^I and U^O. We need those values to solve for both players' value for the game in this equilibrium. The value of holding office, U^I, is the utility the incumbent derives for this period plus his value for holding office in the future. The calculation is as follows:

$$\begin{aligned}U^I &= \int_{\frac{1}{2}}^{1}\left(B - \frac{K}{\theta} + \delta U^I\right)d\theta + \int_{0}^{\frac{1}{2}}(B + \delta U^O)\,d\theta\\ &= B + K\ln\frac{1}{2} + \frac{\delta(U^I + U^O)}{2}\\ &= B + \frac{\delta(U^I - U^O)}{2}\ln\frac{1}{2} + \frac{\delta(U^I + U^O)}{2}.\end{aligned}$$

The first integral gives P's expected utility when θ is greater than the cutoff, so that P makes the effort needed for reelection. The second integral gives P's expected utility when he writes off the election because exogenous conditions are too bad to justify the effort needed for reelection. The value of not holding office, U^O, lies in the chance of getting back into office, calculated as follows:

$$\begin{aligned}U^O &= \int_{\frac{1}{2}}^{1}\delta U^O d\theta + \int_{0}^{\frac{1}{2}}\delta U^I d\theta\\ &= \frac{\delta(U^I + U^O)}{2}.\end{aligned}$$

This calculation assumes that P returns to office whenever he is out of office and P' loses the election. These two equations can be solved simultaneously for the values of U^I and U^O, as follows:

$$\begin{aligned}U^I &= \frac{B(2-\delta)}{(1-\delta)(2-\delta\ln\frac{1}{2})},\\ U^O &= \frac{\delta B}{(1-\delta)(2-\delta\ln\frac{1}{2})}.\end{aligned}$$

With the model completely solved, we can look for its implications. First, the greater the benefits of office, the greater the motivation of the politician to stay in office and to return once voted out. Both U^I and U^O increase with B. Second, the level of performance that the voter receives, K, increases with the benefits of office. U^I increases faster in B than U^O does. K is proportional to $U^I - U^O$; it increases as B increases because this difference increases with B. Third, not only does the voter receive greater performance as the benefits of office rise, her expected utility also rises. The exogenous conditions that are sufficient for the incumbent to make the effort needed to get reelected do not change as B does. The incumbent makes the effort when $\theta > \frac{1}{2}$ regardless of B. Fourth, the incumbent and the voter share in the benefits of the candidate's effort. The voter cannot discipline the incumbent perfectly. The incumbent can use his informational advantage over the voter to lower his effort when times are good. But her retrospective vote does induce some effort on her behalf from the incumbent.

Exercise 9.8:

a) Solve for U^I when P can never return to office once voted out. Do this by assuming that $U^O = 0$. We can think of this case as corresponding to either multiparty competition or the availability of many candidates within the incumbent's party.

b) Does the incumbent or the voter benefit from this change? Does this suggest that voters should try and increase the benefits of holding office for the officeholders themselves or for their parties?

Obviously, this model is a great simplification of the question of how voters can use retrospective voting to discipline politicians. I discuss two lines for developing this model. A heterogeneous electorate is the first possibility (Ferejohn 1986, 20–22). Incumbents have constituencies within the electorate. Performance in office generally means delivering "goodies" to one's constituency. "Goodies" could be desired policies or simply money through government programs. One way to think about heterogeneous voters is to assume that voters care only about the "goodies" they alone receive. If they receive a sufficient amount, like K in the model above, they vote to reelect the incumbent. The incumbent's problem reduces to the production of a pot of "goodies" and division of those "goodies" among the voters. Consider division of the pot first. The incumbent offers sufficient "goodies" to a bare majority of the voters to secure their votes and ignore all other voters. Such a strategy would secure reelection. But all the voters in the minority have an incentive to accept fewer "goodies" than those in the majority set as the price for their votes. The incumbent then can play voters off one another to reduce the level of "goodies" he or she must produce to 0. Any voter who demands more than 0 is left out of the coalition in favor of another voter who demands less. Every voter left out is willing to accept less because it receives nothing otherwise. In the limit, the incumbent can reduce his or her effort to 0.

This observation suggests that there is more to retrospective voting with heterogeneous electorates than just the production and division of "goodies." The second variation on retrospective voting considers the role of campaign promises in retrospective voting. Candidates make promises (implicitly at least) about what they will do in office. Promises are cheap talk; candidates are not bound to carry out what they promise. But candidates can use promises to indicate to voters the amount of effort they will make in office. Voters can use such promises to select between candidates. The promises are credible because voters can compare the performance of incumbents to their promises in the previous election. Candidates have an incentive not to "overpromise" their effort because they will be held to those promises if they win.

Review

This chapter has presented the central approaches and results in repeated games. Repeated games allow us to examine how potentially costly threats can be made credible and how future payoffs affect current actions. A repeated game consists of a stage game that is repeated. It could have a known number of rounds or be indefinitely repeated. Indefinite repetition can be produced by a fixed probability of termination after each round or an infinite number of rounds with discounted payoffs. Continuation values give the players' expectations for continuing to play the game from any point in the game. They depend upon the equilibrium strategies being played.

The folk theorems provide the central result in repeated games with an indefinite endpoint. Reciprocal strategies can support any feasible division of the payoffs where all players receive at least their minmax values. The precise reciprocal strategies used to enforce the agreement to divide the payoff vary with the particular folk theorem. Simple minmax punishments suffer from a credibility problem, so more sophisticated punishment strategies may be necessary. Costly threats then can be credible when the parties anticipate a long-term relationship.

In finite repeated games, reciprocal threats can be used if the stage game has multiple Nash equilibria. If it has only one Nash equilibrium, backwards induction dictates that that equilibrium be played in all rounds. The second way to make potentially costly threats credible is uncertainty about those costs. Small probabilities of a type that always carries out the threat can be sufficient to make the threat credible for all types in early rounds. The Chain Store Paradox is the basic example of how uncertainty can make potentially costly threats credible.

Stationary equilibria eliminate reciprocal strategies. Players play the same moves from structurally identical situations in a stationary equilibrium. Players must still consider their long-term payoffs as captured in their continuation values in stationary equilibria. A stationary equilibrium is a natural focal point among the set of all divisions of the payoff that can be supported in a repeated game.

Further Reading

Repeated games have been a central topic in noncooperative game theory. All of the textbooks have good sections on this topic.

The Chain Store Paradox was originally presented in Selten 1978. The solution presented here is taken from Kreps and Wilson 1982b; the authors also discuss the case where both sides have private information, leading to a process of challenges between the players. Milgrom and Roberts (1982) present a different solution to the Chain Store Paradox by eliminating the common knowledge assumption in the game. The same issue of the *Journal of Economic Theory* also includes an interesting treatment of iterated Prisoner's Dilemma in Kreps et al. 1982.

The folk theorems have attracted a great deal of attention. Most famous is Axelrod (1984), in part for his computer simulation results and use of evolutionary arguments. His formal results about the collective stability of Tit for Tat directly follow from the folk theorem. Taylor's work (1976, 1987) predates Axelrod and is more thorough.

Bianco and Bates (1990) use a folk theorem to discuss leadership within a three-player collective dilemma. Alt, Calvert, and Humes (1988) use a modified Chain Store Paradox game to discuss leadership in the context of hegemonic stability theory from international relations. Relevant to the same topic is Calvert's (1987) article on legislative leadership.

The model of retrospective voting is drawn from Ferejohn 1986. This literature has expanded rapidly, and many good papers are available with models of retrospective voting. Austen-Smith and Banks (1989) present a model where candidates make promises in electoral campaigns that are rendered credible by retrospective voting in future elections. Alesina and Rosenthal (1989) reverse the retrospective voting argument. Morrow (1991) adapts the Ferejohn model to the control of foreign policy.

Administrative Politics

Formal models of administrative politics are not as common as those of legislative politics. Bendor and Hammond 1992 is a place to begin reading. These authors reassess Allison's (1971) three models of decision-making in the light of existing formal models of administration.

Models of administration often use repeated games. Bendor and Mookherjee (1987) show that organizational structures can assist collective action. Bendor (1987) discusses how monitoring noise affects reciprocal strategies used to enforce cooperation. Kreps (1990c) discusses organizational culture as a focal point in the set of all the different ways an organization could function.

Legislative-executive oversight is another important topic addressed by formal models. Limited information is the classic problem that requires oversight. Agencies know more about the area they address and what they are doing than legislators do. They may be able to use their superior information to gain an advantage against the overseers. Banks (1989b), Banks and Weingast (1992), and Bendor, Taylor, and Van Gaalen (1987) all analyze this important issue. It is not always clear that the bureaucrats hold the advantage of information over their overseers.

Chapter Ten
Conclusion: Where Do We Go from Here?

The models used as examples in this book provide the raw material for seeing how game theory can increase our knowledge of politics. This chapter assesses some of the strengths and weaknesses of game theory. I use the weaknesses as an avenue to discuss some of the frontiers of game theory. Finally, I try to explain how to build models, and I exhort readers to explore the literature on their own.

How Do Formal Models Increase Our Knowledge?

In Chapter One, I presented the advantages of formal models. I also discussed four different problems in political science—congressional rules, deterrence, voting in mass elections, and bargaining. I now wish to use the models of the four problems scattered throughout the other eight chapters to illustrate the points I made about the value of models in Chapter One.

First, models force precision of argument. Assumptions, derivations, and conclusions must all be explicit in a model. All are then open to inspection by the reader. Weak logic cannot be hidden. A modeler must clarify his or her assumptions about the subject. For example, consider the models of nuclear deterrence in Chapter Six. The first model captured the logic of the reciprocal fear of surprise attack described by Schelling (1960). That model had an equilibrium where both sides attacked because each feared the other would do so if it had a chance. But that conclusion relied critically on the assumption that the sides could not avoid war by surrendering the stakes of the crisis. Adding the option of surrender stabilized the situation; attacking was never a move in equilibrium after adding the surrender move. The formal models raised the question of quitting that informal arguments had not. Of course, one can try to write down another model where the reciprocal fear of surprise attack does lead to war. We might also conclude that the option to surrender does not exist in the situations in which we are interested. But these formal models improved Schelling's informal argument by exposing its limits.

Second, models show why conclusions follow from assumptions. Derivations of results, whether those results are general theorems or the equilibria of a specific model, provide explicit logic about how the conclusions follow from the assumptions. We can then see the role each of the assumptions plays in the argument. We can ascertain how the conclusions will change if we make different assumptions. For example, the four models of bargaining spread throughout the text make different assumptions about the bargaining process. The Rubenstein bargaining model assumed complete information. The result was that bargaining was perfectly efficient; the two sides always reached an agreement that completely divided the amount available with the first offer. The side making the first offer knew exactly what the other side would accept. It could make the acceptable offer that provided it with the greatest share of the pie. In Chapter Eight, incomplete information was added, and inefficiency was introduced into the bargaining process. In this model, the side making the offers has to judge the risk that a lower offer will be rejected against the benefits of offering the other side less, and so saving more for itself. Because it does not know the receiver's reservation level, bargaining will be inefficient. The explicit logic of these models clarifies the efficiency of bargaining in them.

Third, models often lead to conclusions beyond those we expect when they are designed. The logical structure opens up additional results from the same argument. These added conclusions can lead to empirical tests of the model and underlying theory. Consider the informative committee model of Congress in Chapter Eight as an example of this point. That model has an important, unexpected conclusion; the floor prefers committees that share its preferences. The transmission of information from the committee to the floor is more efficient when they share preferences over outcomes. The floor is certain that the bill reported by the committee will serve the floor's interests as well as the committee's interests. The preference of the median member of a committee, then, should not differ from the preferences of the median member on the floor (Krehbiel 1990). This conclusion contradicts the common wisdom that the preferences of the typical committee member diverge from those of the floor on the jurisdiction of the committee.

Fourth, models help discipline our intuition. Intuition is central to any understanding, even in modeling. But intuition alone is not reliable. Although the results of many models agree with our intuition, not all intuitions can be supported by a model. The results of models differ from intuitive expectations sufficiently often that models do refine the intuition on which they are based. For example, signaling games are a natural way to model tacit communication through actions. Current actions may signal future intentions. But the receiver's existing beliefs about the sender's intentions color its interpretation of the sender's signals. The central insight of signaling games is that separation of types, that is, differences in behavior across types, is essential to the transmission of information. The strength of a signal matters only if strong signals produce greater separation of types. Working with signaling games reinforces this insight. You can see the change in the receiver's beliefs when different types of senders separate. The models tie the sender's motivations into the separation of types. The difficulty of convincing receivers with strong initial beliefs emerges clearly from these models. All of these points about signaling can be understood without a model, but a model makes grasping them easier.

These four strengths of modeling also direct us to two important characteristics of progress through modeling. First, chains of models are necessary for progress in our understanding. Any individual model cannot reflect the complexity of any real situation, and no model should be expected to match reality. But through a succession of models, we can judge the consequences of relaxing assumptions of a simple model or adding additional complications to it. In this way, we advance towards a better understanding of the phenomena, one model at a time. For instance, the analysis of spatial voting models began in Chapter Four with the Median Voter Theorem. In Chapter Five, I presented the application of spatial models to legislatures through a string of examples that built upon one another. Sophisticated voting was the first variation, followed by agenda control. Both of these sections covered the results of chains of models on these topics. Both of these topics are necessary for understanding the structure-induced–equilibrium model of Congress. The results of each section in this chain lead to the questions of the next. Several of the Further Reading sections lay out other chains of models that follow from some of the examples in the text. The simplest, most abstract models can lead to a deep understanding of complex issues.

Second, progress in our understanding requires the existence of contending models of the same phenomena. There is no single correct model of a situation. Many different games are plausible representations of a situation. There are no obvious best representations of the problem of, say, bargaining in international crises. We need to understand how behavior varies with these differences in the specific model. Sometimes the variations in expected behavior are great for small variations in the specification of the game. At other times, behavior appears robust to such variations. Confidence in conclusions is built by exploring their robustness. Writing down a model helps us realize what variations are possible and think about what elements are critical to understanding a situation.

Finally, there is no single rational choice theory of politics. Game theory is a tool for exploring the strategic logic of situations. It does not tell us how to characterize political situations, but it does force us to be specific about the characteristics of situations. Who are the actors? What choices do they have? What are the consequences of their choices, and how do they evaluate those consequences? Political science theory, not game theory, answers those questions. Different models then can capture competing theories of a phenomena.

The specific advantage of game theory in formal modeling is its focus on strategic interaction. Actors choose their actions within political situations. Game theory forces us to confront the endogenity of behavior. It naturally leads us to consider the choices that are not made, those off the equilibrium path. Game theory provides a way to think about the complexity of strategic interaction. How do beliefs, goals, and social structure lead to chosen behavior when actors must consider that the choices of others also affect the outcome?

Game theory also provides a way to begin to think about social structure. When you write down a game, you have specified the choices of the players and their consequences. That specification is a representation of a social structure. If you believe rules for reaching group decisions are structural, the game tree captures those rules. If you believe capabilities to produce outcomes are structural, the outcomes that result from the actors' choices in a game reflect capabilities. If you believe the choices that people see or do not see in a situation are structural, the game tree specifies the choices the actors perceive. We can vary each of these structures by varying the game. Such variations may then help us understand the consequences of social structure.

The Weaknesses of Game Theory

Game theory, like any method, has its limitations. This section considers the limitations of game theory and how game theorists are thinking about them. What problems do the theorists see with their method in the abstract, and how do they propose to address those weaknesses? I discuss some of the frontiers of game theory here. My discussion is broad and general. I provide references for those who wish to do further reading on these topics.

Common Conjectures

Nash equilibria assume that the players hold a common conjecture about what strategies one another will play. The common conjecture ensures that they know their strategies are best replies against one another. In Chapter Four, I discussed several reasons why the players might share a common conjecture and the implications of those conjectures for selecting among multiple equilibria. But this assumption still seems excessively strong; why should one player know what another will do?

If the players do not hold a common conjecture, how will they play the game? Rationalizability, also discussed in Chapter Four, attempted to limit what strategy pairs players without a common conjecture might play. But multiple strategies are rationalizable in most games.

An alternative approach is rational learning in repeated games. In such models, the players begin with prior hypotheses about what strategies the other players will use. They play their best replies given these conjectures and update their conjectures as they observe the other players' actions. The players then learn how the other players play the game. Kreps (1990b, 158–69) discusses some early attempts along this line of argument. Crawford and Haller (1990) show that rational actors can learn how to coordinate their behavior.

Fudenberg and Levine (1993) and Kalai and Lehrer (1993) demonstrate that rational learning in repeated games causes the players to play a Nash equilibrium eventually. Their conjectures converge, at least along the equilibrium path. Off the equilibrium path, the conjectures need not converge because the players do not observe moves off the equilibrium path by definition. Players may then want to experiment with strategies that are not best replies to test other players' reactions. This last argument leads to a rational-learning approach to subgame perfection and restrictions on beliefs off the equilibrium path.

Multiple Equilibria

Many games have multiple equilibria, no matter which equilibrium concept we use. Repeated games typically generate a wide range of possible equilibria. Which equilibrium will the players play (assuming that they play an equilibrium)?

The existence of multiple equilibria does not imply either that any behavior is possible or that such games do not have testable hypotheses. Not all strategy pairs are equilibria. For example, the folk theorem shows that, typically, many divisions of the payoff can be supported by an equilibrium of a repeated game. But it also shows that no player will ever receive less than its minmax payoff. The equilibrium strategies used in the folk theorem also predict patterns of sanctions and rewards.

The refinements of Nash equilibria, such as subgame perfection and restrictions on beliefs, are one approach to selecting among multiple Nash equilibria. Refinements are commonly thought of as additional rationality conditions for playing a game. Those equilibria that fail to satisfy the conditions of a refinement are eliminated from consideration. If an agreed set of refinements eliminated all equilibria but one, the remaining equilibrium would be selected.

Chapter Four considered several ways to select among multiple equilibria, based on what common conjectures are plausible. If the players can communicate before playing, they would not choose a Pareto-dominated equilibrium. Both could be better off if they played a different equilibrium. If the players are playing a symmetric game and cannot communicate, some argue that a symmetric equilibrium should be played. Finally, the players may choose a focal point in the set of equilibria. Symmetric division of the payoff is a focal point. Other focal points can be created by different payoffs or societal distinctions among strategies or outcomes that are not captured within the game. Convention or common experience could also create focal points for the players. Of course, a game could have several focal points.

But a complete theory of equilibrium selection lies outside the range of game theory at this time. There is not a commonly agreed-upon set of refinements for Nash equilibria. It is difficult to know what a theory of focal points would look like beyond a description of what strategies were focal. Even with such a theory, game theory would still play a critical part in the analysis. Equilibrium selection arguments, of which focal points are one, assume that the players hold a common conjecture about how the game will be played. The existence of focal points may be the reason they share a common conjecture. But then equilibrium analysis is still part of solving the game. We would not want to use focal point arguments to select strategy pairs that were not equilibria.

Finally, consider some of the arguments used to select among multiple equilibria in some of the examples. Refinements do help us eliminate some equilibria, especially those with noncredible threats. In the Chain Store Paradox, I rejected the equilibrium where acquiescence signals willingness to fight in the future. The inference is contrary to our intuition. Stationarity was a focal point in the range of equilibria that can be supported in a repeated game. Equilibrium analysis in these cases helped us see what strategy pairs might be thought of as focal points among the multiple equilibria of those games. Selection among equilibria is easier after we understand the logic of each possible equilibrium.

Common Knowledge

Equilibrium analysis assumes that the players hold a great deal of common knowledge. Information is common knowledge when all players know it, all players know that all other players know it, and so on. The game, the fact that the players share a common conjecture about how the game will be played, and even the rationality of both players are common knowledge. Games of limited information introduce some private information, but the players' beliefs about one another's private information are common knowledge. Lack of common knowledge in a game could undermine equilibrium analysis. The players would not know what to expect about one another's behavior. Anticipations about one another's actions in equilibrium might not be in equilibrium. Effective signaling would be impossible if the sender could not anticipate the effect of its signal on the receiver's beliefs.

Common knowledge is convenient because lower levels of knowledge are complex. Information could be mutual knowledge (known to all players), without being common knowledge (they may not know that the other players also know that information). Analysis of information that is less than common knowledge is a difficult frontier of game theory. The formal analysis of information, both common and private, represents an actor's information as a partition across states of the world. We need to think about what players know and what they know about other players' information. Actors draw inferences about other players' information from public pronouncements. Geanakoplos 1992 is an accessible introduction to this difficult topic.

Common knowledge leads to some startling conclusions. The best known of these is that rational actors cannot "agree to disagree." It cannot be common knowledge that two rational actors with the same prior probabilities have different posterior probability estimates of an event. The intuition is that each adjusts its posterior probability in light of the information that the other's posterior probability is different. Consider a trade of stock where we both begin with the same information about the company. If you offer to sell the stock to me, I should suspect that you know something that I do not and so adjust my estimate of the value of the stock downwards. This adjustment process must continue until we have the same estimate if our estimates are common knowledge.

Incomplete information provides a way to loosen some of the requirements of common knowledge in a game. We can interpret the Chain Store Paradox as an exception to the common knowledge that both players are rational. The vengeful monopolist represents a specific form of "irrational" behavior; this player type punishes its opponents (in this case, market entrants) even though such punishment is costly for it. The rationality of the monopolist is no longer common knowledge. Entrants can never be certain that it will not punish them if they enter its market. That breakdown of common knowledge provides a motivation for rational players to imitate the "irrational" vengeful monopolist.

A breakdown of common knowledge of rationality can address the paradox of backwards induction in the centipede game in Chapter Five. It cannot be common knowledge that both players are rational if either player ever continues the centipede game (Reny 1992). Once the rationality of the players is not common knowledge, even rational players can benefit by continuing the game.

Bounded Rationality

The impossibility of "agreeing to disagree" and the advantages of irrationality in the centipede game lead to the question of limits on rationality. Herbert Simon (1955) coined the term *bounded rationality* for goal-direct behavior that is limited in its ability to reason. It may have struck you as strange back in Chapter Two that I did not mention bounded rationality then. Bounded rationality is an attractive concept in the abstract, but then so is rationality. Objections to rational choice arise after we specify what we mean by rational choice carefully. Specifying bounded rationality may lead to objections to those specific definitions. I discuss some of the ways game theorists are trying to think about bounded rationality in games in this section. I try to give you some idea of how bounded rationality might be built into game theory. The best discussions of bounded rationality and game theory are Binmore 1990 (151–231) and Kreps 1990 (150–177).

Let me begin with a simple representation of bounded rationality, the method of fictitious play. Here the players play a game repeatedly. In each round, each player assumes that the other (for simplicity, assume a two-person game) will play each of its pure strategies with the frequency that it has in previous rounds.

		Player 2	
		s_1	s_2
Player 1	S_1	3	1
	S_2	2	4

Figure 10.1 A Two-Person, Zero-Sum Game to Illustrate Fictitious Play

Each player plays its best reply against the mixed strategy given by the other player's frequencies of each strategy so far. The players use a very simple decision rule to arrive at conjectures about the other player's strategies in fictitious play. They do not attempt to assess what strategy the other will play. In contrast to the rational learning model, the players just use each other's prior frequencies for their conjectures.

Figure 10.1 gives the strategic form of the zero-sum game used in Chapter Four to introduce mixed strategies. It has a mixed strategy equilibrium of $[(\frac{1}{2}S_1,\frac{1}{2}S_2); (\frac{3}{4}s_1,\frac{1}{4}s_2)]$. Assume the players play $(S_1;s_1)$ on the first round of fictitious play. In the second round, they play their best replies against the other player's strategy in the first round. Player 2's best reply to S_1 is s_2, and Player 1's best reply to s_1 is S_1. They play $(S_1;s_2)$ in the second round, then. In the third round, Player 1 chooses his best reply against $(\frac{1}{2}s_1,\frac{1}{2}s_2)$, S_2, because Player 2 has played each of her pure strategies once. Player 2 plays s_2, which is her best reply against S_1. In the fourth round, Player 1 chooses his best reply against $(\frac{1}{3}s_1,\frac{2}{3}s_2)$, which is S_2, and Player 2 plays s_1, her best reply against $(\frac{2}{3}S_1,\frac{1}{3}S_2)$. In the long run, the probabilities that each player will play each of its pure strategies converge on the mixed strategy equilibrium of the game.

The rationality in fictitious play is very bounded. The players never attempt to reason about the other player's strategy. Instead, they play mechanically against the other's long-run frequencies. Their projections about each other's future moves are very naive. They do not use the information in the other player's moves efficiently.

Fictitious play does not converge for all games. Binmore (1992, 409–12) describes the classic example of a game where the long-run frequencies of fictitious play do not converge.

A second way to think about bounded rationality is finite automata theory. A finite automaton is an idealized computer with a limited ability to remember earlier moves. Finite automata theory investigates how such machines play repeated games. A finite set of states defines a finite automaton. Each state orders a move to be made when the player is in that state. After each move, the player shifts to another state on the basis of the result of the current moves. For example, the finite automaton that plays Tit for Tat has two states, Cooperate and Defect. It begins in the Cooperate state. It moves after each round to the state that corresponds to the other player's move in that round. If the other player plays Cooperate, it stays in Cooperate (or moves there if it is in the Defect state). If the other player plays Defect, it moves to the Defect state (or stays there if it began the round in the Defect state). The finite set of states represents bounded rationality in finite automata theory. A player cannot remember all possible histories of the game. Strategies that respond to the complete history of the game, like those in fictitious play, are not possible in a finite automaton. Fewer states mean a simpler procedure for choosing and a more bounded rationality.

Finite automata theory pits such machines against one another in a game. Each player picks a finite automaton knowing that the other player must also use a finite automaton to play. Rationality in finite automata theory is bounded, then, during the play of the game but not before the game when the players choose their machines. The definition of the complexity of a strategy implemented by a finite automaton is not clear. The typical definition judges complexity by the number of states of the machine. Banks and Sundaram (1990) show that if complexity is judged by the transitions between states as well as the number of states, then only Nash equilibria of the stage game are equilibria of the repeated game between finite automata.

The third approach to bounded rationality, evolutionary models, limits the rationality of the evaluation and selection of strategies. Imagine that we allow a variety of strategies to compete against one another over many rounds of the game. We then evaluate how each has done so far. An adaptive mechanism selects in favor of those that have done well and against those that have done poorly, and the game continues. Over time, the set of strategies evolves to select those that have done the best. The best-known example of such an evolutionary model is Axelrod's (1984) tournament. He invited a number of social scientists to submit computer programs to play repeated Prisoner's Dilemma. Anatol Rapoport submitted a program that played Tit for Tat, which won both the original tournament and a rematch later. Axelrod then analyzed the properties of Tit for Tat as a strategy in evolutionary settings. Maynard Smith 1982 is the fundamental source on the application of game theory to biological evolution.

Evolution is an attractive model of bounded rationality because the actors do attempt to better themselves, but their ability to evaluate strategies is limited. Players change their strategies through adaptation and imitation. They seek to change when their current strategy is failing, and they imitate those strategies that are successful in the current environment. Innovation can be introduced through a mechanism for mutation in the current set of strategies.

As I see it, evolution also has important limitations as a model of bounded rationality. An evolutionary model must specify the composition of the population of strategies at the beginning, the mechanism of selection, how often selection occurs, and the forms of mutation. The results of a model may depend on any of these factors, and there are not hard-and-fast rules for any of them. Mutation and imitation may not be good models of human innovation. Mutation is a random process, while innovation is conscious and planned. Imitation, while clearly an important factor in the spread of innovation, does not account for its origin. In some sense, human innovation falls between full rationality and bounded rationality. Fully rational actors exploit every opportunity in their environment subject to the costs of those opportunities; actors in evolutionary models innovate only on a regular cycle. Real humans fall in between these two extremes. They innovate at different times in different ways. Failure certainly spurs innovation, but so does success in some settings.

Binmore (1990) distinguishes between eductive and evolutive processes of equilibrium. An eductive process is based on reasoning by the actors. It is logical and involves reflection on what other players will do. An evolutive process uses evolution to reach equilibrium. Equilibrium analysis in game theory is an eductive process. Evolutionary alternatives for selecting strategies are evolutive. The difficulty, it seems to me, is that human rationality falls somewhere between these two poles. (This comment is not meant to suggest that Binmore feels that human rationality is solely one or the other.) It is both eductive and evolutive. Progress towards a complete understanding will require analysis of both poles. At a minimum, then, game theory provides an important step in understanding rationality in strategic settings.

But before bounded-rationality approaches supplant fully rational ones, we need a much clearer idea of what bounded rationality is and what it implies. I have laid out three possible approaches and some of their difficulties. Bounded rationality, like rational choice, is attractive in the abstract. Once we specify what we mean by rational choice, some object to the concept. Will bounded rationality be as attractive once we specify what it means?

In conclusion to this section on the weaknesses of game theory, I would like to point out that current research on all four of these problems appears to converge on some common concerns. Models of rational learning and bounded rationality provide both an explanation of why common conjectures exist and a way to select among multiple equilibria. Both of these models can be expanded to cover situations where critical elements are not common knowledge. However, the results of these models are preliminary. The generality of their conclusions is yet to be seen. Applications of these models may have to wait.

How Does One Build a Model?

Building a model requires many choices. You must design a game tree, assign payoffs to the outcomes, and solve the resulting game. The best models are those clearly attached to an intuitive argument about their subject. Moving from an intuitive grasp of a subject to a formal model is difficult. One of the most important elements in this transition is creativity. Still, some guidelines may help in this creative process. I have found the following rules of thumb useful when I model. This section also addresses the question of how much mathematical sophistication is appropriate in a model.

The single most important principle in modeling is simplify, simplify, simplify. Simple models are easier for you to solve and for the reader to follow than complex models. Begin a model by writing down a sequence of choices. What choices do the actors have, and in what order? What information do they have when they choose? These choices lead to outcomes; next, you consider plausible preferences over these outcomes that the actors might hold. Writing down a game tree forces you to confront these questions. Try to solve the resulting model. Almost always, some choices or wrinkles in your model will add nothing but additional work. Out they go. On average, I work through eight to ten versions of a model before I am happy with it. Each version adds or deletes features of the earlier version. Deletions are more common than additions. In these revisions, try to capture the essence of the problem as simply as possible. Solving early versions of the model helps you understand what is essential to an understanding of the problem.

A second strategy is to vary an existing model. Models not only provide answers; they also raise questions. Do the candidates always converge in the single-dimension spatial voting model? What happens when we change some of the assumptions of that model? A variation of an existing model is often easier to solve than a completely novel model because you can draw on the existing results. Such variations lead to a chain of models, as discussed earlier in this chapter. Such chains typically start with a very simple model.

In line with the admonition to simplify models, there is no reason to rush to the most sophisticated techniques. Actors may be uncertain about something in almost every situation. That observation does not mean that a limited information model is necessarily the best model of every situation. Even if you feel strongly that a limited information model is appropriate for your problem, such models are much easier to solve if you understand the game played under complete information. Solve all of the possible games among the different combinations of types under complete information first. Then you will understand the incentives of each type in a separating equilibrium. You can then determine if separation is incentive compatible. Often, you will find that a complete information model has interesting conclusions on its own, even though it may also lead to some nonsensical conclusions. Many interesting results have been found with backwards induction.

The complexity of the model drives the choice of equilibrium concept. Nash equilibrium is sufficient to solve static games of complete information. In a static game, all players make one choice simultaneously, as in a two-by-two game. Any Nash equilibrium of a static game of complete information is also subgame perfect and a perfect Bayesian equilibrium. Dynamic games require stronger equilibrium techniques than Nash equilibrium. Players have multiple or sequential moves in a dynamic game. Credibility of future moves is critical in a dynamic game. Models of complete and perfect information can be solved by backwards induction. Subgame perfection is sufficient for games of complete but imperfect information. Perfect Bayesian equilibrium is needed for dynamic games of incomplete information. Again, chains of models are central to progress in our understanding, and those chains begin with simple models. You need not rush to the technical frontier to establish interesting arguments.

The discipline of even simple models would be a boon to many informal arguments in political science. As noted earlier, many games are plausible representations of a problem. Informal arguments may obscure what could prove to be important details that differ across these plausible models. Formalization may expose these differences and their consequences. Writing down a model forces us to make choices among the plausible representations. There are not correct choices before the modeling process begins, and there may not be any after you have tried several models of the same problem. But awareness of these choices and their consequences improves our understanding of the original argument.

Finally, this book should have prepared you to begin reading the literature. If you want to understand how political scientists use game theory, read their work. The essays on Further Reading guide you to further readings. Reading this literature may require closer attention than descriptive work in political science. Formal theory rewards careful reading. Work through the analysis on your own to see why the propositions follow from the assumptions. Think about alternative assumptions and further deductions. After reading in the field, you may wish to know more about game theory. Go to the other textbooks then. Formal theory may not be the easiest road available, but I have found it the most rewarding. I hope you do too.

Further Reading

Kreps (1990b) provides an accessible introduction to the issues in this chapter. Fudenberg and Levine (1993) and Kalai and Lehrer (1993) use the rational-learning approach to support Nash equilibria. Crawford and Haller (1990) provide a rational-learning approach to equilibrium selection in coordination games. Kreps (1990c) uses focal points to consider important issues in organization. Geanakoplos 1992 is an accessible introduction to common knowledge and analysis without common knowledge.

Models of bounded rationality have generated much interest among game theorists recently. The sources cited in the text, Binmore 1992 and Kreps

1990b, are useful places to begin. Two good essays on evolutionary game models are Mailath 1992 and Selten 1991. Both are introductory essays to special issues of journals on evolutionary game theory. Maynard Smith 1982 is a fundamental source in evolutionary game theory. Axelrod 1984 is the best-known application of evolutionary models in social science. Sugden (1989) discusses why conventions might arise in an evolutionary way. Young (1993) shows that Nash equilibria will be selected by a bounded rationality procedure that combines elements of all three approaches mentioned in the text. He also shows which Nash equilibrium is stable under evolutionary pressure.

If you are interested in bounded-rationality models in political science, two recent papers, Kollman, Miller, and Page 1992 and Vanberg and Congleton 1992, are good places to start. Kollman, Miller and Page (1992) examine a model of electoral competition where the parties or candidates are boundedly rational. They use different search routines to model different forms of bounded rationality. Their main result is that convergence to the median is robust to several variations in bounded rationality. Vanberg and Congleton (1992) use an evolutionary model, realized in computer simulations. They show that ending relations with actors who cheat can survive in an iterated Prisoner's Dilemma with a number of other finite automata.

Appendix One
Basic Mathematical Knowledge

This appendix covers the mathematical knowledge that is basic for understanding game theory as presented in this book. It begins with algebra, continues with set theory and probability theory, and ends with some calculus. It also includes a discussion of what is a mathematical proof. This appendix is a quick review for those readers whose mathematical skills are but a memory; it is not a course in elementary mathematics. I realize that for some readers, mathematics is a distant and painful memory of the one subject you could not master in high school. I hope that this appendix does not remind those readers of the pain they once felt, but rather helps them summon up the mathematical skills they once had.

For convenience, I use a, b, c for constants, p, q, r for probabilities, and x, y, z for variables.[1]

Algebra

Exponents

Exponents are a shorthand way to write a number multiplied by itself many times.

$$x^1 = x \quad x^2 = x \cdot x \quad x^n = x \cdot x \cdot x \ldots x \text{ (n times)}$$

For x^n, *x* is called the **base** and *n* the **exponent**. We say "*x* to the *n*th power" or "*x* to the *n*." Exponents make multiplication, division, and exponentiation of powers of the base easy.

$$(x^n)(x^m) = x^{n+m} \quad \frac{x^n}{x^m} = x^{n-m} \quad (x^n)^m = x^{nm}$$

By convention, zero exponents give one for any base except 0, negative exponents give division by that power of the number, and fractional exponents give various roots of the number.

$$x^0 = 1 \text{ if } x \neq 0$$

$$x^{-1} = \frac{1}{x} \qquad x^{-n} = \frac{1}{x^n}$$

$$x^{\frac{1}{2}} = \sqrt{x} \qquad x^{\frac{1}{n}} = \sqrt[n]{x}$$

Logarithms

Logarithms, logs for short, are the reverse of exponents. The **logarithm** of a number to a fixed base is the exponent to which the base must be raised to get the number.

$$\log_a x = b \quad \text{means} \quad a^b = x$$

Like exponents, logarithms observe simple rules for multiplication, division, and exponentiation.

$$\log_a(bc) = \log_a b + \log_a c$$

$$\log_a\left(\frac{b}{c}\right) = \log_a b - \log_a c$$

$$\log_a\left(b^c\right) = c\left(\log_a b\right)$$

Two bases are commonly used for exponents, base 10 and base e (≈ 2.71828, say "e"). Logs to the base e are called **natural logarithms** and written ln (say "lin"), rather than $\log_e$.[2]

Summation Notation and Infinite Series

Summation notation is a way to simplify writing large sums. A capital sigma, Σ, denotes a sum. Each term in the summation is indexed, typically by *i* or *k*, and the first and last terms of the summation are given by the bounds of the sum placed below and above the summation sign respectively. The index is used to state the common pattern of the terms being summed. For example:

$$\sum_{i=1}^{4} x^i = x + x^2 + x^3 + x^4$$

Summations observe the following rules:

$$\sum_{i=1}^{n} a = na$$

$$\sum_{i=1}^{n} ax_i = a\sum_{i=1}^{n} x_i$$

$$\sum_{i=1}^{n}(x_i + y_i) = \sum_{i=1}^{n} x_i + \sum_{i=1}^{n} y_i$$

However, the sum of a product is not the product of the sums.

$$\sum_{i=1}^{n} x_i y_i \neq \left(\sum_{i=1}^{n} x_i\right)\left(\sum_{i=1}^{n} y_i\right)$$

Summation notation provides an easy way to write down the sum of infinite series. We replace the upper bound with $+\infty$ to denote an infinite sum. For most infinite series, the sum of the infinite series does not converge to a finite value. One infinite series that does converge and is very useful is the following:

$$\sum_{i=0}^{+\infty} x^i = 1 + x + x^2 + x^3 + \ldots = \frac{1}{1-x} \text{ for } 0 < |x| < 1$$

Solving Linear Equations

A linear equation is of the form $ax + b = 0$, more generally, $ax + b = cx + d$. Linear equations have only first powers (i.e., linear terms) in the variable, here x. Linear equations are solved by collecting the variable on one side and the constant terms on the other.

$$ax + b = cx + d$$
$$(a - c)x = d - b$$
$$x = \frac{d - b}{a - c}$$

Solving Quadratic Equations

A quadratic equation includes squared and linear terms of the variable, but no higher powers of the variable. A general quadratic equation is $ax^2 + bx + c = 0$. Quadratic equations are solved by factoring or the quadratic formula. If an equation can be factored, set each factor equal to 0 in turn to obtain its two solutions.

$$acx^2 + (ad + bc)x + bd = 0$$
$$(ax + b)(cx + d) = 0$$
$$ax + b = 0 \quad \text{or} \quad cx + d = 0$$
$$x = -\frac{b}{a} \quad \text{or} \quad x = -\frac{d}{c}$$

The quadratic formula is a way to solve quadratic equations that do not factor easily. It factors the equation by completing the square.

$$ax^2 + bx + c = 0$$

$$x = \frac{-b \pm \sqrt{b^2 - 4ac}}{2a}$$

Solving Systems of Linear Equations

Systems of equations have more than one equation in more than one unknown. Linear systems of equations generally have a unique solution when the number of equations and number of unknowns are equal. To solve linear systems, solve first for one variable. Eliminate the other variables by adding several of the equations together.

$$\begin{cases} ax + by = c \\ dx + ey = f \end{cases}$$

Multiply the first equation by e and the second by $-b$, and then add the two together to eliminate y. Solve the resulting linear equation in x.

$$\begin{aligned} aex + bey &= ce \\ -bdx - bey &= -bf \\ \hline (ae - bd)x &= ce - bf \\ x &= \frac{ce - bf}{ae - bd} \end{aligned}$$

Substitute the value of x into either original equation, and then solve for y.

$$a\left(\frac{ce - bf}{ae - bd}\right) + by = c$$

$$y = \frac{1}{b}\left[c - a\left(\frac{ce - bf}{ae - bd}\right)\right] = \frac{af - cd}{ae - bd}$$

Set Theory

Set theory is the basis of all mathematics. A **set** is a collection of **elements**. The set of all elements is called the **universal set** and is written U. If an element x belongs to a set S, we say x is a **member** of S and write $x \in S$. A set containing no elements is called the **empty set** (or **null set**) and is written $\varnothing$. If all the members of a set S_1 are also members of set S_2, we say that S_1 is a **subset** of S_2 and that S_2 **contains** S_1, and write $S_2 \supset S_1$. If $S_2 \supset S_1$ and there exists x such that $x \in S_2$ and $x \notin S_1$, we say that S_1 is a **proper subset** of S_2 and write $S_2 \supseteq S_1$. If $S_2 \supset S_1$ and $S_1 \supset S_2$, then S_1 and S_2 must have the same elements, and we write $S_1 = S_2$.

There are three basic operations in set theory. The **union** of two sets S_1 and S_2, written $S_1 \cup S_2$, is the set of all elements that are members of S_1 alone, S_2 alone, or both S_1 and S_2. For any sets S_1 and S_2, the following properties are true:

$$S_1 \cup S_2 = S_2 \cup S_1$$
$$S_1 \cup S_1 = S_1$$
$$S_1 \cup \varnothing = S_1$$
$$S_1 \cup U = U$$

If $S_1 \subseteq S_2$, then $S_1 \cup S_2 = S_2$. The **intersection** of two sets, S_1 and S_2, written $S_1 \cap S_2$, is the set of all elements that are members of both S_1 and S_2. For any sets S_1 and S_2, the following properties are true:

$$S_1 \cap S_2 = S_2 \cap S_1$$
$$S_1 \cap \varnothing = \varnothing$$
$$S_1 \cap S_1 = S_1$$
$$S_1 \cap U = S_1$$

If $S_1 \subseteq S_2$, the $S_1 \cap S_2 = S_1$. The **complement** of a set S_1, written S_1^c, is the set of all elements that are not members of S_1. For any set S_1, the following properties are true:

$$(S_1^c)^c = S_1$$
$$\varnothing^c = U$$
$$U^c = \varnothing$$
$$S_1 \cup S_1^c = U$$
$$S_1 \cap S_1^c = \varnothing$$

Two sets, S_1 and S_2, are **disjoint** if they have no elements in common.

The **integers** are the set of all numbers, ... −2,−1,0,1,2, ... The **rational numbers** are all numbers that can be expressed as fractions of integers. The **real numbers** are the set of all numbers that can be expressed as an infinite decimal, such as .4298581 .... Intervals are an easy way to talk about some subsets of the real numbers. [0,1], called the **closed interval** from 0 to 1, is the set of all real numbers x such that $0 \leq x \leq 1$. (2,3), called the **open interval** from 2 to 3, is the set of all real numbers y such that $2 < y < 3$. We can have half-open intervals, such as (0,1]—the set of all real numbers z such that $0 < z \leq 1$.

Relations and Functions

Relations and functions are ways to express relationships between sets. Typically these sets are numbers, but the sets could be anything. Functions of multiple variables are quite common in this book. An **ordered pair** (x,y) specifies a first member, $x \in X$, and a second member, $y \in Y$, where X and Y are sets. A **relation** is a set of ordered pairs, and we often write xRy if x is related to y. Relations provide an abstract way to analyze relations among members of sets. For example, think of the relation "greater than" among the integers (numbers $\ldots -1, 0, 1, 2 \ldots$). Then 2R1 as $2 > 1$. The **domain** of a relation is the set of all first coordinates of its members; the **range** of a relation is the set of all second coordinates. The **inverse** of a relation is the relation that reverses the original relation; $xR^{-1}y$ if and only if yRx.

A **function** is a relation such that no two distinct second coordinates of the relation share the same first coordinate. In other words, a function maps each element of its domain into only one element of its range. If f is a function from X to Y, write $f : X \rightarrow Y$ and $f(x) = y$ for $x \in X$ and $y \in Y$ that x is mapped into. If $f(x) = y$, y is the **image** of x. A function f maps X **onto** Y if the range of f is Y. A function f is **one-to-one** if distinct points have distinct images—in other words, if the inverse relation of f, $f^{-1}(y)$, is also a function.

Probability Theory

For our purposes, set theory is necessary for probability theory. In probability theory, outcomes are the elements, and sets of those outcomes are **events**. The universal set is called the **sample space**, written S, and is the set of all possible outcomes, where one and only one outcome occurs. The union of two sets of outcomes A and B is the event that A occurs, B occurs, or both A and B occur. The intersection of two sets A and B is the event that both A and B occur. The complement of a set A is the event that A does not occur. Disjoint sets are **mutually exclusive** events; if one occurs, the other cannot occur. A set of n events, $\{A_i\}_{i=1}^n$ (this notation indicates that events A_i are indexed from $i = 1$ to n), is **exhaustive** if one of them must occur (i.e., their union is the sample space, $\cup_{i=1}^n A_i = S$).

We write the probability of an event A as p(A). For all events A, $0 \leq p(A) \leq 1$. Let e_i be the ith outcome from the set of n possible outcomes, $S = \{e_i\}_{i=1}^n$, and $p(e_i)$ be the probability of outcome e_i. Then for event A,

$$p(A) = \sum_{e_i \in A} p(e_i).$$

The set of outcomes is exhaustive and mutually exclusive. One outcome must occur, so $p(S) = 1$ and $p(\varnothing) = 0$.

For any events A and B, the probability that A or B occurs equals the probability that A occurs plus the probability that B occurs minus the probability that both occur (this subtraction eliminates double counting of outcomes in both A and B); $p(A \cap B) = p(A) + p(B) - p(A \cup B)$. If A and B are mutually exclusive, $A \cup B = \emptyset$, so $p(A \cap B) = p(A) + p(B)$. The probability that an event A does not occur is 1 minus the probability that it does occur, $p(A^c) = 1 - p(A)$.

A **random variable** takes on one of a number of values, with a given probability for each value. Let *X* be a random variable with possible values $\{x_i\}_{i=1}^{n}$. The **expectation** of *X*, written E(X), is the sum of the possible values of the variable multiplied by the probability that each occurs:

$$E(X) = \sum_{i=1}^{n} x_i[p(x_i)].$$

The **conditional probability** that event A occurs given that event B has occurred, written $p(A|B)$, is the probability that both events occur divided by the probability that event B occurs:

$$p(A|B) = \frac{p(A \cap B)}{p(B)}.$$

Conditional probabilities allow us to discuss how the occurrence of some events affects the likelihood of other events. We can then discuss how the knowledge that B has occurred affects the likelihood of A's occurring.

Combinations and the Binomial Theorem

The Binomial Theorem is useful for finding the probabilities of events with only two possible outcomes that are repeated many times. The **factorial** of a positive integer *x*, written x!, is the product of all the positive integers less than or equal to *x*. Thus $x! = (1)(2)\ldots(x)$. The **combinations of n things taken k at a time** with $k < n$, written

$$\binom{n}{k},$$

equals

$$\frac{n!}{k!(n-k)!}$$

and gives the number of different ways *k* objects can be selected from a set of *n* objects. Combinations are useful in binomial calculations because they count the number of separate orders that events could occur.

Binomial trials have only two possible outcomes, often called success and failure. The Binomial Theorem calculates the probability of a number of successes in a given number of independent trials with the same probability of success. If p is the probability of success, then the probability of k successes in n trials with $k < n$ is

$$\binom{n}{k} p^k (1 - p)^{n-k}.$$

Continuous Probability Distributions

We typically assume that the sample space is a finite set of outcomes. Infinite sample spaces can be represented by sets of real numbers. For example, all the numbers between 0 and 1 inclusive define a sample space. Probabilities on such sample spaces are given by a function, called the **probability density function**, or **pdf**. A pdf specifies the probability that the outcome will fall within any range of values of the sample space. The probability that the outcome will fall between two values in the sample space is the area under the pdf between those two values. A pdf $p(x)$ must satisfy two requirements:

$$p(x) \geq 0 \text{ for all x and}$$

$$\int_{-\infty}^{+\infty} p(x)\,dx = 1$$

(If the second expression is utterly foreign to you, see the section on integral calculus in this appendix.) Subject to these constraints, pdf's, often called continuous probability distributions, obey all the laws of probability as laid out above. The expectation of a random variable with a continuous probability distribution is given by the following integral:

$$\int_{-\infty}^{+\infty} x p(x)\,dx$$

Limits

Limits allows us to discuss how a function behaves close to a particular point even if it is not defined at that point. Limits are necessary for derivatives, integrals, and perfect equilibria of games. A function f approaches a **limit** L at a point z if we can make $f(y)$ as close to L as we like for all y by choosing y to be close to z. Figure A1.1 illustrates the idea. The function f is graphed in Figure A1.1, and the open circle at $f(z)$ indicates that f has no value at z. The value of f at z is irrelevant to the limit of f at z because the limit depends on behavior of f near, but not at, z.

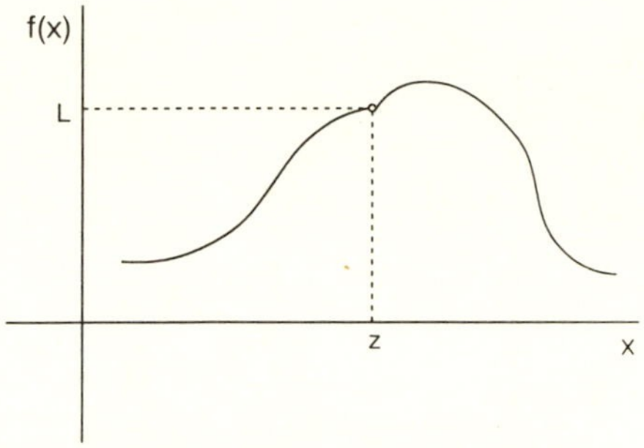

Figure A1.1 A Function Undefined at Point z and Its Limit There

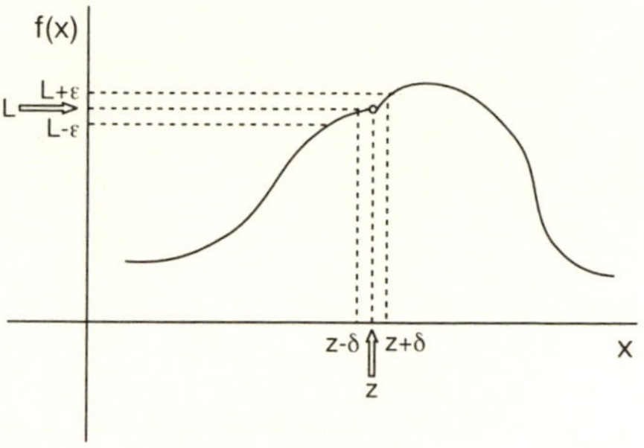

Figure A1.2 The Limit of f at z, in Terms of δ and ε

We choose a degree of accuracy, $\epsilon > 0$, around L. For this ϵ, we find another degree of accuracy, $\delta > 0$, around z such that all y within δ of z have f(y) within ϵ of L. Figure A1.2 shows this idea for a particular ϵ and δ. For all y with $z - \delta < y < z + k$, we have $L - \epsilon < f(y) < L + \epsilon$. The limit exists if we can choose a δ for each possible $\epsilon > 0$. Then we can get f(y) as close to L as we want by choosing y close to z.

Limits observe the following results:

$$\lim_{x \to a} mx + b = ma + b$$

$$\lim_{x \to a}[f(x) + g(x)] = \lim_{x \to a} f(x) + \lim_{x \to a} g(x)$$

$$\lim_{x \to a}[f(x)g(x)] = [\lim_{x \to a} f(x)][\lim_{x \to a} g(x)]$$

Differential Calculus

Differential calculus allows us to determine the instantaneous rate of change of a function. The average rate of change of a function between two points x and x + h is given by

$$\Delta f|_x^{x+h} = \frac{f(x + h) - f(x)}{x + h - x} = \frac{f(x + h) - f(x)}{h}$$

and illustrated in Figure A1.3.

To get the instantaneous rate of change, let x + h approach x, that is, let h go to 0. Figure A1.4 illustrates that as h gets smaller in moving from h to h′, the average rate of change approaches the slope of the curve at x. To find the instantaneous rate of change, we look at the limit of the average rate of change

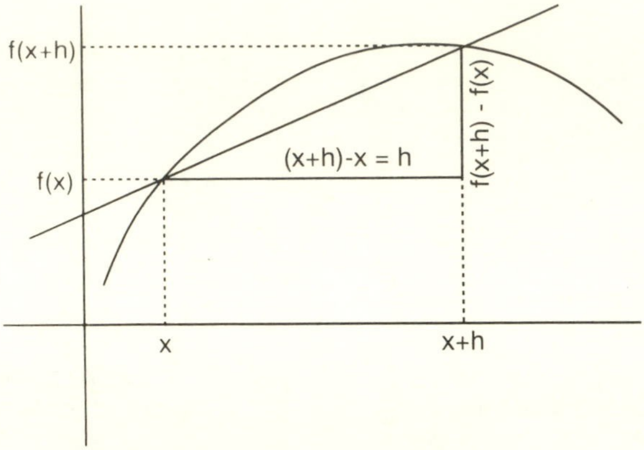

Figure A1.3 The Average Rate of Change between x and x+h

as the interval over which the rate of change is measured, *h*, goes to 0. The **derivative** of a function *f* at a point *x* is

$$f'(x) = \lim_{h \to 0} \frac{f(x + h) - f(x)}{h}.$$

Derivatives are often written with primes as above and occasionally the derivative of *f* is called f', f-prime. Other notations used for the derivative of *f* with respect to *x* include

$$\frac{df}{dx} \text{ or } \frac{dy}{dx}$$

and $D_x f$.

There are simple formulas for finding the derivatives of many common functions. Some of these are given below.

$$(c)' = 0$$

$$(x^n)' = nx^{n-1} \text{ for all real n}$$

$$(e^x)' = e^x \quad (a^x)' = \ln(a)a^x$$

$$[\ln(x)]' = \frac{1}{x} = x^{-1}$$

To calculate the derivative of the sum, product, and division of two functions, *f* and *g*, use the following rules:

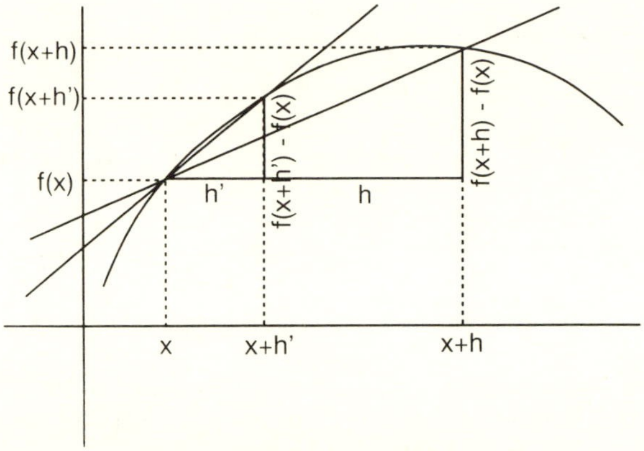

Figure A1.4 How the Average Rate of Change Approaches the Instantaneous Rate of Change as h Decreases to h′

$$[f(x) + g(x)]' = f'(x) + g'(x)$$

$$[f(x)g(x)]' = f'(x)g(x) + f(x)g'(x)$$

$$\left[\frac{f(x)}{g(x)}\right]' = \frac{f'(x)g(x) - f(x)g'(x)}{g(x)^2}$$

For the composition of two functions, f[g(x)], use the chain rule:

$$\{f[g(x)]\}' = g'(x)f'(g(x))$$

I present these rules as a summary to help remind you how to take derivatives. I suggest you seek the assistance of a good calculus text if the application of the above rules is mysterious.

Derivatives of functions can be used to find the maximum and minimum points of a function. As we are interested in maximizing utility, derivatives are extremely useful in decision problems. To find candidate points to be maximum and minimum points of a function, calculate the derivative of the function, set it equal to 0, and solve. The insight behind this result is that a function "levels off" at a maximum or minimum. In Figure A1.5, f(x) has a maximum at x, and the derivative as given by the slope of the line tangent to the function at x is 0. Thus the derivative must be 0 at that point.

We call points where the derivative of a function is 0 the **critical points** of the function. However, not all critical points are minima or maxima of the function. This procedure finds the **local maxima** and **local minima** of a function, points where the value of the function is greater than (for the maxima) or less than (for the minima) the value of the function for all points around that point. We can distinguish maxima from minima by two tests. The first-derivative

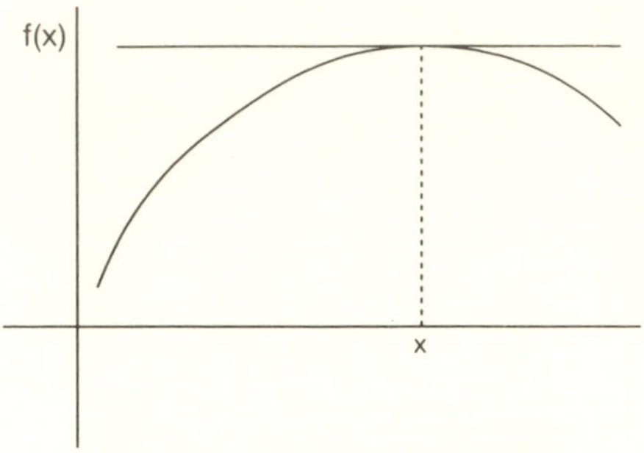

Figure A1.5 The Derivative of a Function Is Zero at a Maximum

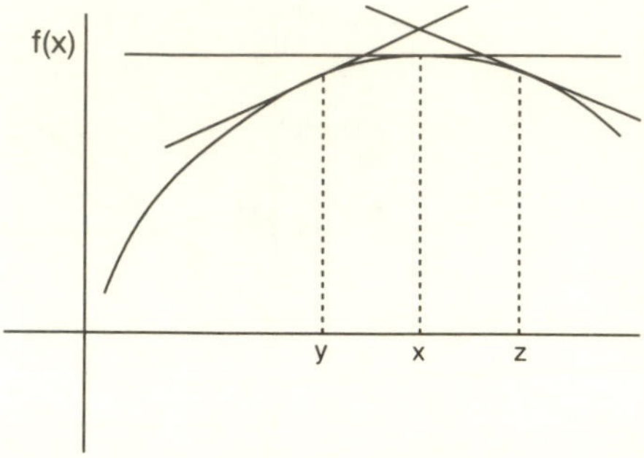

Figure A1.6 The First-Derivative Test for a Maximum

test examines the sign of the derivative for points less than and greater than the critical point. If $f'(y) > 0$ for all y slightly less than critical point x and $f'(z) < 0$ for all z slightly greater than x, then x is a local maximum. (The reverse holds for local minima.) Figure A1.6 illustrates the intuition behind the first-derivative test. At y less than critical point x, the slope of the tangent line is upward, so the derivative is positive. At z greater than critical point x, the slope of the tangent line is downward, so the derivative is negative.

The second-derivative test looks at the sign of the derivative of the derivative, called the second derivative and written $f''(x)$, at the critical point. At a maximum, the first derivative is decreasing; it is positive for numbers smaller than the critical point and negative for numbers larger than the critical point. The second derivative is negative at a local maximum, then. Similarly, the second derivative is positive at a local minimum.

Local maxima or minima are the largest or smallest values of the function compared to values around them. A **global maximum** and **global minimum** are the greatest and smallest values that a function takes on for the range of the function. Calculate the value of the function for each local maximum and any endpoints of the range of the function to find the global maximum of the function; it will be the greatest of these values.

Derivatives can also be used to calculate the limit of the quotient of two functions if the limit of the quotient is indeterminant, such as 0/0. L'Hôpital's rule states that if

$$\lim_{x \to a} f(x) = 0$$

$$\lim_{x \to a} g(x) = 0$$

and

$$\lim_{x \to a} \frac{f'(x)}{g'(x)} = L,$$

then

$$\lim_{x\to a} \frac{f(x)}{g(x)} = L.$$

In words, differentiate both the numerator and denominator, and take the limit of their quotient. If it exists, it equals the limit of the quotient of the original functions. Other versions of L'Hôpital's rule exist for other indeterminant forms, such as ∞/∞.

Partial Derivatives and Lagrange Multipliers

Partial derivatives are used to calculate rates of change of functions of multiple variables. They are particularly useful in performing comparative statics analyses. The idea is simple: we fix all the other variables, and then see how the value of the function changes as one variable changes. Practically, we assume that all other variables are constants and calculate the derivative of the function with respect to one variable. To distinguish partial derivatives from derivatives of a function of a single variable, we write the former as

$$\frac{\partial f}{\partial x}$$

rather than

$$\frac{df}{dx}.$$

Other notations for this partial derivative are $D_x f$ and f_x. Higher-order partial derivatives also exist. The partial derivative with respect to *y* of the partial of *f* with respect to *x* is written

$$\frac{\partial^2 f}{\partial y \partial x}$$

(or $D_{xy}f$ or f_{xy}) and called a **mixed partial derivative**.

To find the minima and maxima of a function of multiple variables, calculate all the first partial derivatives and set them equal to 0. Any point where all the first partials are 0 is a **critical point**. To determine if a critical point is a maximum or a minimum, either a first-derivative test or a second-derivative test can be conducted. The first-derivative test is the same as for a function of a single variable except that it must produce the same result, maximum or minimum, for all variables. Otherwise, the critical point is a local maximum for one variable and a local minimum for another and is called a **saddle point**.

The second-derivative test for functions of several variables is more complex. I give the version for functions of two variables; see a calculus text for the test with more variables. Calculate

$$\left(\frac{\partial^2 f}{\partial x^2}\right)\left(\frac{\partial^2 f}{\partial y^2}\right) - \left(\frac{\partial^2 f}{\partial x \partial y}\right)^2$$

at the critical point and compare it to 0. If

$$\left(\frac{\partial^2 f}{\partial x^2}\right)\left(\frac{\partial^2 f}{\partial y^2}\right) - \left(\frac{\partial^2 f}{\partial x \partial y}\right)^2 < 0,$$

the critical point is neither a maximum nor a minimum; it is a saddle point. If

$$\left(\frac{\partial^2 f}{\partial x^2}\right)\left(\frac{\partial^2 f}{\partial y^2}\right) - \left(\frac{\partial^2 f}{\partial x \partial y}\right)^2 > 0,$$

check the sign of

$$\frac{\partial^2 f}{\partial x^2}.$$

If

$$\frac{\partial^2 f}{\partial x^2} > 0,$$

the critical point is a minimum; if

$$\frac{\partial^2 f}{\partial x^2} < 0,$$

the critical point is a maximum; the test is inconclusive if the second partial equals 0.

Constrained optimization problems are solved by the method of Lagrange multipliers. Constrained optimization finds the maximum or minimum of a function within a set of points, rather than across the entire range of the function. We define the constraint by using a function, g, to define all the points that satisfy the constraint. To optimize $f(x, y)$ subject to the constraint that $g(x, y) = 0$, construct a new function $F(x, y, \lambda) = f(x, y) - \lambda g(x, y)$ and find its optima as in the previous paragraph. The Lagrange multiplier is written λ and has an important interpretation in some constrained optimization problems. If there are multiple constraints, use a Lagrange multiplier for each constraint and enter all the constraints into one new function.

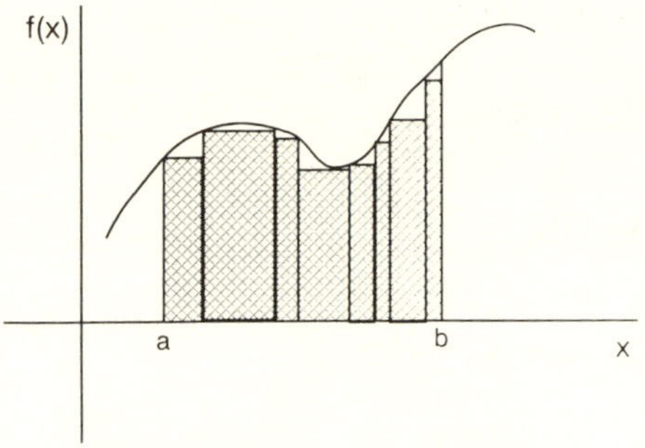

Figure A1.7 Estimating the Area under a Curve with Rectangles

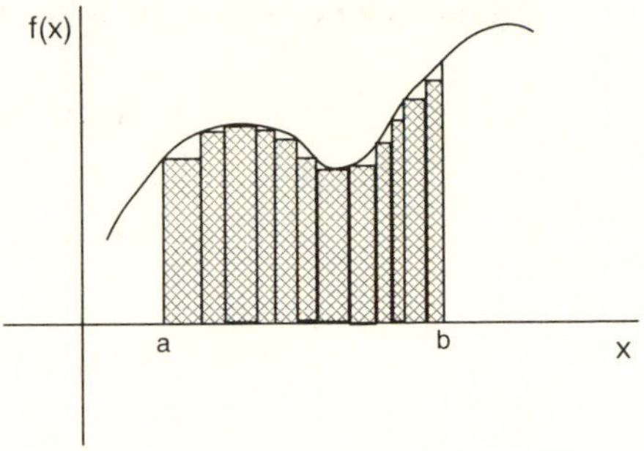

Figure A1.8 The Estimate of the Area under a Curve Improves as the Length of the Longest Base Decreases

Integral Calculus

Integration allows us to find the areas under curves and average values of functions. We find the area under a curve by stuffing rectangles with increasingly shorter bases under the curve. As the longest base of any of the rectangles goes to 0, the area of all the rectangles approaches the area under the curve. Figure A1.7 illustrates the idea of measuring the area under a curve with rectangles. The shaded area is the sum of the area of all the rectangles that fit under the curve. The white area above those rectangles and below the curve is the error.

As the longest base of any of the rectangles gets smaller, the approximation to the area under the curve becomes better. In Figure A1.8, dividing the three rectangles with the longest bases in Figure A1.7 improves the approximation to the area under the curve.

To find the area under a curve, we let the longest base of any of those rectangles go to 0. The limit of that sum is the **definite integral** of f(x) from a to b:

$$\int_a^b f(x)\,dx = \lim_{\Delta \to 0} \left[\sum_{i=1}^{n} f(\xi_i)(x_{i+1} - x_i) \right]$$

$$\text{where } \Delta = \max(x_{i+1} - x_i) \text{ and } f(\xi_i) = \min f(x) \text{ for } x_i \leq x \leq x_{i+1}$$

The definite integral of a function from a, called the **lower limit**, to b, the **upper limit**, gives the area under f(x) between a and b. The "dx" in an integral just reminds us which variable we are integrating over, *x* in this case, and where the integral ends. For some functions, this limit does not converge, and the integral does not exist. If this limit exists, the function is **integrable** between a and b. For ease of exposition, I assume that all integrals in this section do exist.

Definite integrals have the following basic properties:

$$\int_a^a f(x)\,dx = 0 \text{ if } f(a) \text{ exists}$$

$$\int_a^b kf(x)\,dx = k\int_a^b f(x)\,dx$$

$$\int_a^b (f(x) + g(x))\,dx = \int_a^b f(x)\,dx + \int_a^b g(x)\,dx$$

$$\int_a^b f(x)\,dx = \int_a^c f(x)\,dx + \int_c^b f(x)\,dx$$

The Fundamental Theorem of Calculus shows how to calculate definite integrals and unifies the two branches of calculus, differentiation and integration.

Theorem (the Fundamental Theorem of Calculus): Let $g'(x) = f(x)$ for all $a \leq x \leq b$. Then

$$\int_a^b f(t)\,dt = g(x)|_a^b = g(b) - g(a).$$

Integration is the reverse of differentiation. We call this operation **indefinite integration** (or antidifferentiation). Indefinite integrals are denoted by the integral sign without the bounds. By convention, a constant of integration, C, is added to all indefinite integrals. The definite integral of a function is its indefinite integral evaluated at the upper bound minus its value at the lower bound. The constant of integration drops out, then, when we calculate a definite integral.

To evaluate a definite integral of a function from a to b, calculate its indefinite integral, evaluate the indefinite integral at the two limits, and subtract the value at the lower limit from the upper limit. Indefinite integrals can be calculated with the following results:

$$\int k\,dx = kx + C$$

$$\int x^n\,dx = \frac{1}{n+1}x^{n+1} + C$$

$$\int [g(x)^n]g'(x)\,dx = \frac{1}{n+1}g(x)^{n+1} + C$$

The last equation is the Chain Rule for integration. The calculation of integrals can be quite elaborate, and some definite integrals cannot be represented by simple functions. I have tried to keep the integrals in the text simple. If you have difficulties calculating an integral, I suggest you refer to a calculus text.

The main use of integration in this book is to calculate the expected values and utilities of continuous probability distributions. Integration is the parallel of summation when we move from a discrete to a continuous probability distribution.

The Idea of a Mathematical Proof

Many people believe that mathematics is about numbers. It is not; it is about the careful use of words. Numbers are just a careful way to discuss quantities. Think how difficult it would be to think about quantities if the only words we had to describe them were "none," "few," and "many." What is the difference between "more than a few" and "somewhat less than many?" Mathematicians are obsessed with defining exactly what words mean and what exactly can be deduced from those definitions. Arguments are required to demonstrate what follows from a set of assumptions and definitions. A mathematical proof is a formal argument. Only the statements that logically follow from the assumptions of the proposition are allowed in a mathematical proof of that proposition.

Most of us encounter mathematical proofs in high school geometry. In this section, I strive to give a simple introduction to the idea of a mathematical proof. I also explain the different types of mathematical proofs. I draw on examples from high school geometry and algebra to illustrate my points. I have refrained from giving mathematical proofs in this book, choosing instead to sketch the ideas behind major theorems. Those sketches do not provide proof of those theorems. If you wish to go further in game theory, you need a better understanding of logic and mathematical proof than I provide here. Mathematics courses are the best way to gain such an understanding.

Mathematical systems consist of undefined terms, axioms, definitions, and propositions. Some terms are undefined in any logical structure. Otherwise, we have no starting point. In geometry, "point," "line," and "plane" are undefined terms. The undefined terms are used to define the other concepts. Angles, triangles, and circles can all be defined with points, lines, and planes. Axioms are the basic assumptions of a mathematical system and characterize that system. Systems change if you change the axioms. For example, it is an axiom of Euclidean geometry that one and only one line parallel to a given line can be drawn through a point not on that line. If we change this axiom, we get a non-Euclidean geometry. If no parallel lines can be drawn through a point, spherical geometry results. Spherical geometry is the geometry where spheres replace planes and great circles on spheres replace lines.[3] If more than one parallel line can be drawn through a point, we get hyperbolic (or Riemannian) geometry. We use the definitions and axioms to deduce propositions.

Mathematical propositions are conditional, not absolute. They make assumptions and assert what conclusions follow if those assumptions are true. Conditional statements are composed of antecedents and conclusions, joined as in "If antecedent, then conclusion." Conditional statements are true if the conclusion is true whenever the antecedent is true. The assumptions of a proposition are the antecedent. Propositions that appear to be absolute are properly stated as conditional statements. For example, the angles opposite the equal sides of an isosceles triangles are always congruent (i.e., equal). This proposition can be restated as "If a triangle is isosceles, then the angles opposite the equal sides of that triangle are congruent." When the assumptions of a proposition are not true, the conclusion still follows but is not necessarily true.

The proof of a proposition demonstrates logically that the conclusion of the proposition must be true if the assumptions are true. Proofs use definitions, axioms, and other propositions to show that the conclusion must be true if the assumptions are true. You may recall this from highly formalized proofs from high school geometry. The first line of such a proof is one of the assumptions. Each succeeding line is a statement about a geometric relationship that follows directly from the previous line according to some axiom or previously proved proposition. Proofs do not need to be stated in this formal fashion, but all proofs must show that the conclusion must be true if the antecedent is true.

There are three different forms of proofs: constructive proofs, proof by contradiction (or indirect proof), and proof by induction. Constructive proofs derive the conclusion from the antecedent directly. Proof by contradiction begins by assuming that the conclusion is incorrect. The proof shows that a contradiction results if the antecedent is true and the conclusion is false. Proof by induction is used for propositions where the conclusion holds across a set that can be indexed by the counting numbers (1,2,3, . . .). For example, the Binomial Theorem holds for any number of trials. The number of trials indexes the set where the Binomial Theorem holds. To prove it for each number separately would be impossible. Proof by induction begins by proving the proposition is true for the first case. You then show that if the proposition is true for the ith case, it must also be true for the (i+1)th case. The proposition must then be true for all cases; the second case can be deduced from the first case by using the induction principle.

Propositions are often called by other names. A **theorem** is a major proposition and is generally reserved for the most important and general results. Very important theorems are given names as well. A **lemma** is an intermediate result in the proof of a proposition that is of interest by itself. A **corollary** is a proposition that follows directly from a theorem.

Appendix Two
Answers to Selected Problems

This appendix gives the answers to selected problems in the exercises accompanying the text. Answers to exercises that call on the reader to show a result stated in the problem or to discuss or recast a model are not included. Readers should be aware that the value of doing problems comes from finding the answers on your own. Those who look at the answers before they try to solve the problems will lose this value. Sometimes, working backwards from the solution can help to understand why the solution is correct. I have not provided explanation or detail for most of these answers for lack of space.

Chapter 2

2.2: a) $EU(A_3) = .7 + .3x$. b) $u(C_4) < -1\frac{1}{3}$.

2.3: ($.452\ C_1$, $.288\ C_2$, $.26\ C_3$).

2.4: a) $u(C_1) = 1$, $u(C_2) = .65$, $u(C_3) = .4$, $u(C_4) = 0$ (or any linear transformation of it). b) L_1PL_2.

2.6: For u_1, $L_1IL_2PL_3$, risk-neutral; for u_2, $L_3PL_1PL_2$, risk-acceptant; for u_3, $L_2PL_1PL_3$, risk-averse.

2.7: a) 11.11 guilders. b) $[100(1 - \delta)]/\delta$ guilders.

Chapter 3

3.1: See Figure A2.1.

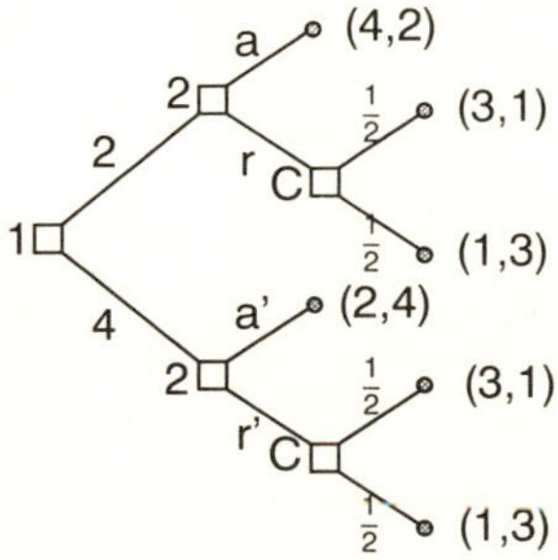

Figure A2.1 Exercise 3.1

3.2: Three players bargain sequentially over three units (or dollars if you prefer). Each has an opportunity to end the bargaining by playing U for Player 1, d for Player 2, or *U* for Player 3. Any player ending the game receives 0 units, the next player to move receives 2 units, and the third 1 unit. If they play D, u, *D* in sequence, each player receives 1 unit.

3.3: Figure A2.2 gives the fragment of the game tree where M is the middle box, C is the corner box, and MS is the middle of a side for Player 1. For Player 2, c is the corner box, s is the side box, m is the middle box, oc is the opposite corner, nc is the near corner, fc is the far corner, os is the opposite side, ns is the near side, and fs is the far side.

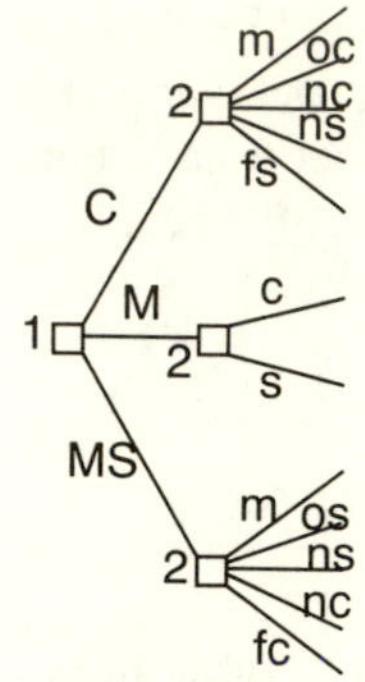

Figure A2.2 Exercise 3.3

3.4: a) See Figure A2.3.

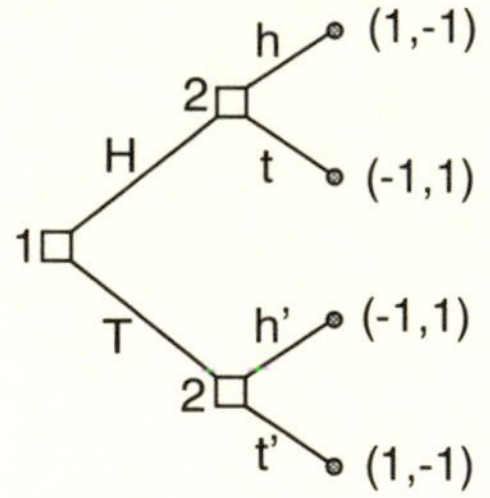

Figure A2.3 Exercise 3.4a

b) See Figure A2.4.

		Player 2			
		h,h'	h,t'	t,h'	t,t'
Player 1	H	(1,-1)	(1,-1)	(-1,1)	(-1,1)
	T	(-1,1)	(1,-1)	(-1,1)	(1,-1)

Figure A2.4 Exercise 3.4b

3.5: a) See Figure A2.5.

Player 2

Player 1		a,a'	a,r'	r,a'	r,r'
	2	(4,2)	(4,2)	(2,2)	(2,2)
	4	(2,4)	(2,2)	(2,4)	(2,2)

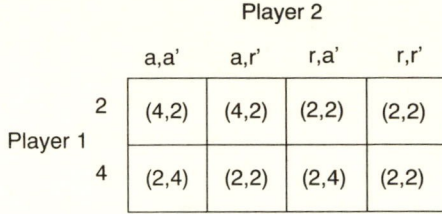

Figure A2.5 Exercise 3.5a

b) See Figure A2.6.

Player 3

		U: Player 2 u	*U*: Player 2 d	*D*: Player 2 u	*D*: Player 2 d
Player 1	U	(0,2,1)	(0,2,1)	(0,2,1)	(0,2,1)
	D	(2,1,0)	(1,0,2)	(1,1,1)	(1,0,2)

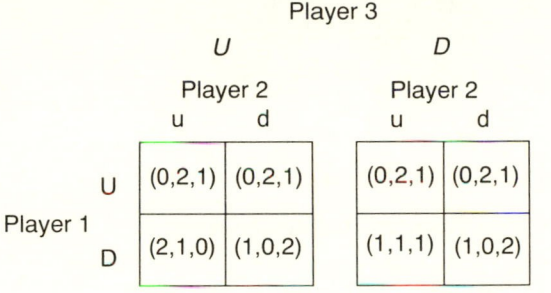

Figure A2.6 Exercise 3.5b

Chapter 4

4.1: a) S_2 strongly dominated by S_1 and s_2 strongly dominated by s_1, $(S_1;s_1)$. b) S_2 weakly dominated by S_1 and s_2 strongly dominated by s_1, no dominant strategy equilibrium. c) S_1 and S_2 weakly dominated by S_3, s_2 strongly dominated by s_1, no dominant strategy equilibrium.

4.2: a) $(S_2;s_2)$. b) $(S_2;s_1)$. c) $(S_1;s_1)$ and $(S_2;s_1)$. d) $(S_1;s_1)$, $(S_3;s_1)$, and $(S_2;s_3)$. e) $(S_2;s_1)$ and $(S_1;s_2)$.

4.3: a) $(S_1;s_2)$. b) $(S_1;s_1)$. c) $(S_1;s_2)$. d) $(S_2;s_1)$. e) $(S_1;s_1)$, $(S_1;s_3)$, $(S_2;s_1)$, $(S_2;s_3)$.

4.4: $(\frac{3}{4}s_1, \frac{1}{4}s_2)$, $v_1 = 2\frac{1}{2}$.

4.5: a) $\left[(\frac{3}{10}S_1, \frac{7}{10}S_2); (\frac{1}{2}s_1, \frac{1}{2}s_2)\right], v_1 = -\frac{1}{2}, v_2 = \frac{1}{2}$.
b) $\left[(\frac{5}{9}S_1, \frac{4}{9}S_2); (\frac{2}{3}s_1, \frac{1}{3}s_2)\right], v_1 = -\frac{5}{3}, v_2 = \frac{5}{3}$.
c) $\left[(\frac{1}{10}S_1, \frac{9}{10}S_2); (\frac{3}{5}s_1, \frac{2}{5}s_2)\right], v_1 = \frac{7}{5}, v_2 = -\frac{7}{5}$.

4.6: a) $\left[\left(\frac{7}{11}S_1, \frac{4}{11}S_2\right); \left(\frac{1}{2}s_1, \frac{1}{2}s_2\right)\right], v_1 = -\frac{1}{2}, v_2 = 3\frac{1}{11}$.
b) $\left[\left(\frac{8}{11}S_1, \frac{3}{11}S_2\right); \left(\frac{3}{5}s_1, \frac{2}{5}s_2\right)\right], v_1 = \frac{3}{5}, v_2 = 1\frac{6}{11}$.

4.7: $[(\frac{2}{3}S_1, \frac{1}{3}S_2); (\frac{1}{3}s_1, \frac{2}{3}s_2)], v = (\frac{2}{3}, \frac{2}{3})$.

4.8: a) $(S_1;s_2)$ and $(S_2;s_1)$. b) Yes, $[(\frac{1}{2}S_1, \frac{1}{2}S_2); (\frac{1}{2}s_1, \frac{1}{2}s_2)]$, $v = (2\frac{1}{2}, 2\frac{1}{2})$.

4.9: a) See Figure A2.7.

Player 2

Player 1		s_1,s'_1	s_1,s'_2	s_2,s'_1	s_2,s'_2
	S_1	(5,5)	(5,5)	(0,10)	(0,10)
	S_2	(10,0)	(-5,-5)	(10,0)	(-5,-5)

Figure A2.7 Exercise 4.9a

b) $(S_2;s_1,s'_1)$, $(S_2;s_2,s'_1)$, and $(S_1;s_2,s'_2)$.

4.10: Yes, the game is dominance solvable; the result is $(S_2;s_5)$.

4.11: a) $M = \left(\#\text{ of voters with ideal points} < \frac{x_1 + x_2}{2}\right) - \left(\#\text{ of voters with ideal points} > \frac{x_1 + x_2}{2}\right)$. Candidate 1's majority over Candidate 2 consists of all the voters who vote for Candidate 1 minus all the voters who vote for Candidate 2. The midpoint between the two candidates' positions, $\left(\frac{x_1 + x_2}{2}\right)$, separates the voters who vote for each candidate. b) If $i < n$, choose x such that $x_2 \leq x < 2y_{i+1} - x_2$. If $i > n$; choose x with $2y_i - x_2 < x \leq x_2$. If $i = n$, choose $x = y_n$. In words, voter n is the median voter. Position Candidate 1 to attract the voter between the median voter and Candidate 2's position that is closest to Candidate 2's position. c) Both candidates choose the ideal point of the median voter, y_n.

4.12: a) A best reply does not exist in general when there is a continuous distribution of voters. If Candidate 2 does not adopt the ideal point of the median voter, Candidate 1 should position itself between the median voter's ideal point and 2's position as close as possible to 2's position. Because there is no such "closest" point to 2's position, no such best reply exists. b) Both candidates' adopting the position of the median voter is an equilibrium.

4.13: a) $\frac{1}{2}$. You should expect this answer because both players' utility functions are linear. They can be transformed then so the players have the same utility function. By assumption, they must receive equal shares of the surplus. b) $\frac{\sqrt{5}}{5} \approx .447$.

Chapter 5

5.1: a) (U,R;u,r). b) (S,S,S;s,s,s). c) (D,R;d,l;*D*).

5.2: a) (U;u,l), (U;d,l), (D;u,r), and (D;d,r); (D;u,r) and (D;d,r) are subgame perfect. b) (U;u) and (D;d); (U;u) and (D;d) are subgame perfect. c) (U;d,l), (D;u,r), and (D;d,r); (D;d,r) is subgame perfect. d) (U,L;d), (U,R;d), and (D,R;u); (U,L;d) and (D,R;u) are subgame perfect. e) (U;u;*U*;*u*), (U;u;*D*;*d*), (D;d;*U*;*u*), (D;d;*D*;*d*), (D;u; $(\frac{1}{3}U, \frac{2}{3}D)$; $(\frac{2}{3}u, \frac{1}{3}d)$), (U;u;$(pU, 1-pD)$; $(qu, 1-q\,d)$) and (D;d;$(pU, 1-pD)$; $(qu, 1-q\,d)$) with $p + q - 2pq < \frac{1}{2}$; (D;d;*U*;*u*), (D;d;*D*;*d*), and (D;u;$(\frac{1}{3}U, \frac{2}{3}D)$; $(\frac{2}{3}u, \frac{1}{3}d)$) are subgame perfect.

5.5: (Y,Z;y,w;*X*,*W*). There are other possibilities here. I have assumed that the players vote sincerely in the vote between z and w. Once y defeats x in the first pairwise comparison, the outcome of the second between z and w cannot affect the outcome. (Y,W;y,z;*X*,*Z*) is also a sophisticated voting equilibrium then.

5.7: a) $4 \le x \le 7$ is stable. If $x > 5$, any proposed bill will be amended to the floor leader's position, 5. The committee chair will block any bill when $5 < x_{SQ} < 7$. If $5 > x > 4$, the committee median and floor leader want 5, but the floor median wants 4, so the committee will not report a bill. If $x < 4$, any bill will be amended to the smaller of $8 - x$ or 5, and then passed. b) For $x \le 3$ or $x > 7$, the floor leader's position, 5, is the final outcome. For $3 < x < 4$, the position closest to the floor leader for which the floor median will vote, $8 - x$, is the final outcome.

5.8: a) On Issue 1, $x_{SQ} < x < 8 - x_{SQ}$ if $x_{SQ} < 4$ (the floor median), and $8 - x_{SQ} < x < x_{SQ}$ if $x_{SQ} > 4$. On Issue 2, $y_{SQ} < y < 8 - y_{SQ}$ if $y_{SQ} < 4$ (the floor median), and $8 - y_{SQ} < y < y_{SQ}$ if $y_{SQ} > 4$. b) On Issue 1, $x_{SQ} < x < 8 - x_{SQ}$ if $x_{SQ} < 4$; $10 - x_{SQ} < x < x_{SQ}$ if $x_{SQ} > 5$, and if $4 < x_{SQ} < 5$, the committee will not report a bill (i.e., it prefers the status quo to any bill that can pass on the floor). On Issue 2, $y_{SQ} < y < 8 - y_{SQ}$ if $y_{SQ} < 4$; $10 - y_{SQ} < y < y_{SQ}$ if $y_{SQ} > 5$, and if $4 < y_{SQ} < 5$, the committee will not report a bill. c) On Issue 1, $x = \min(5, 8 - x_{SQ})$ if $x_{SQ} < 4$, $x = 5$ (the committee chair's position) if $x_{SQ} > 5$, and no bill if $4 \le x_{SQ} \le 5$. On Issue 2, $\min(6, 8 - y_{SQ})$ if $y_{SQ} < 4$, 6 (the committee chair's position) if $x_{SQ} > 6$, and no bill if $4 \le y_{SQ} \le 6$.

5.9: a) On Issue 1, $4 \leq x \leq 6$. On Issue 2, $2 \leq y \leq 6$. b) On Issue 1, $4 \leq x \leq 8$. On Issue 2, $0 \leq y \leq 8$.

5.12: In the first round, M_1 proposes that it receive $1 - \frac{\delta n}{2n + 1}$ and n other members receive $\frac{\delta}{2n + 1}$. M_1 and other members who receive positive benefits vote for the proposal, and it passes. In the second round, M_2 proposes that it receive 1 and the other members receive 0. All members vote for the proposal, and it passes.

5.13: a) In the first and second rounds, M_i for $i = 1,2$ proposes that it receive $1 - \frac{1}{3}\delta$ and another member receive $\frac{1}{3}\delta$. M_i and the other member vote for the proposal, and it passes. In the last round, M_3 proposes that it receive 1 and the other members receive 0. All three members vote for the proposal, and it passes. b) In all rounds i before the last, M_i proposes that it receive $1 - \frac{1}{3}\delta$ and another member receive $\frac{1}{3}\delta$. M_i and the other member vote for the proposal, and it passes. In the last round, M_m proposes that it receive 1 and the other members receive 0. All three members vote for the proposal, and it passes. c) In all rounds i, M_i proposes that it receive $1 - \frac{1}{3}\delta$ and another member receives $\frac{1}{3}\delta$. M_1 and the other member vote for the proposal, and it passes.

Chapter 6

6.1: a) .0034. b) .0546. c) .7690.

6.6: a) (D;u,r) and (D;d,r), beliefs not needed. b) (U;u:1) and (D;d:0). c) (D;d,r), beliefs not needed. d) (D,R;u:1) and (U,L;d:p) with $p < \frac{1}{6}$. e) (D;d;*U*;*u*:p) with $p > \frac{1}{3}$, (D;d;*D*;*d*:q) with $q < \frac{1}{3}$, and [D;u;($\frac{1}{3}$*U*, $\frac{2}{3}$*D*); ($\frac{2}{3}$*u*, $\frac{1}{3}$*d*): $\frac{1}{3}$]. Beliefs are for the upper node in each information set with multiple nodes.

6.7: a) (U;u:1). Beliefs are for Player 2's upper node if her information set is reached. (A;d) is a Nash equilibrium that is not perfect Bayesian. b) (Y,Y′;n,y′;*Y*,*N*′). c) (A;a:1;1), (D;d:$\frac{1}{2}$;$\frac{1}{2}$), and [($\frac{2}{3}$A, $\frac{1}{3}$D); ($\frac{2}{3}$a, $\frac{1}{3}$d): $\frac{3}{4}$; $\frac{3}{4}$], where the beliefs are the probability that side is moving first if its information set is reached (i.e., Player 1's upper node and Player 2's lower node).

Chapter 7

7.1: (A;d) and (L;u). Yes, L is weakly dominated by R, so (L;u) would be eliminated.

7.2: a) Figure A2.8 gives one extensive form. Others are possible. I have called the moves in Battle of the Sexes Up and Down.

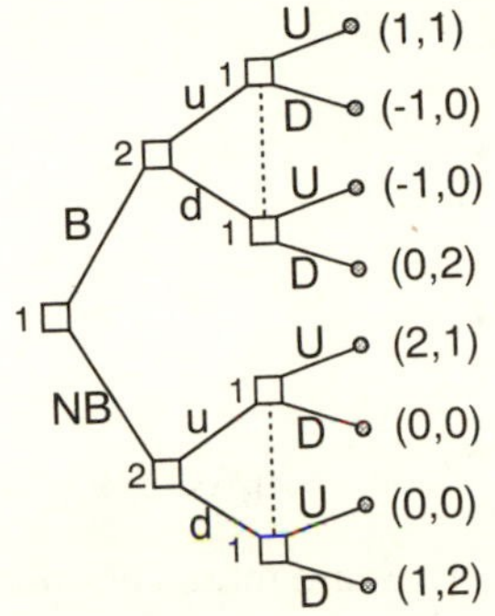

Figure A2.8 Exercise 7.2a

b) Figure A2.9 gives the strategic form. I call Player 1's strategy (Burn or Not Burn, Move in Battle of the Sexes) and Player 2's strategy (Move If Player 1 Plays Burn, Move If Player 1 Plays Not Burn).

Player 1 \ Player 2	u,u	u,d	d,u	d,d
B,U	(1,1)	(1,1)	(-1,0)	(-1,0)
B,D	(-1,0)	(-1,0)	(0,2)	(0,2)
NB,U	(2,1)	(0,0)	(2,1)	(0,0)
NB,D	(0,0)	(1,2)	(0,0)	(1,2)

Figure A2.9 Exercise 7.2b

c) (NB,U;u,u), (NB,U:d,u), (NB,D;u,d), (NB,D;d,d), and (B,U;u,d).
d) The only strategy pair left is (NB,U;u,u) with payoff (2,1). Player 1 always gets his preferred outcome of Battle of the Sexes without burning money.

7.4: a) (D;u,r) and (D;d,r). b) (U;u). c) (D;d,r).
d) (U,L;d). e) (D;d;U;u), (D;d;D;d), and [D;u;($\frac{1}{3}U$, $\frac{2}{3}D$); ($\frac{2}{3}u$, $\frac{1}{3}d$)].

7.5: (R,D;u) is subgame perfect and perfect, (L,D;d) is subgame perfect but not perfect, and (L,U;d) is neither.

7.6: (R,D;u:1) where Player 1's belief is for the upper node.

7.7: (C,P;nr).

7.8: a) P regardless of $\overline{\gamma}$. b) r for resolute D, nr for irresolute D.
c) $\gamma_{crit} = \dfrac{1 - u_{CH}(SQ)}{1 - u_{CH}(W)}$.

7.9: a) $p(\text{crisis}) = \dfrac{1 - u_{CH}(SQ)}{1 - u_{CH}(W)}$;

$p(\text{nr}|\text{crisis}) = \dfrac{1}{2} + \dfrac{u_{CH}(SQ) - u_{CH}(W)}{2(1 - u_{CH}(W))}$;

$p(\text{war}|\text{crisis}) = \dfrac{1}{2} - \dfrac{u_{CH}(SQ) - u_{CH}(W)}{2(1 - u_{CH}(W))}$. b) Assuming that γ is fixed across the two sets of equilibria, crises are more common in the exercise.

$$\frac{u_{CH}(W^*)(1 - u_{CH}(SQ))}{u_{CH}(W^*) - u_{CH}(W)} < 1 - u_{CH}(SQ) < \frac{1 - u_{CH}(SQ)}{1 - u_{CH}(W)}.$$

The challenger is more likely to secure concessions short of war in the text.

$$\frac{1 + u_{CH}(SQ)}{2} = \frac{1}{2} + \frac{u_{CH}(SQ)}{2} = \frac{1}{2} + \frac{u_{CH}(SQ)(1 - u_{CH}(W))}{2(1 - u_{CH}(W))}$$

$$> \frac{1}{2} + \frac{u_{CH}(SQ) - u_{CH}(W)}{2(1 - u_{CH}(W))}$$

It is not clear in which equilibria war is more likely given a crisis. One could make war more likely in either equilibrium by choosing values for $u_{CH}(W^*)$ and $u_{CH}(W)$ in both the text and the exercise. There are values of each consistent with the assumptions that make war more likely in either of these equilibria. If the chance of escalation were higher in the exercise, the probability of a crisis might be lower in the exercise than the text. The higher probability of war would act as a partial deterrent on starting crises.[1]

7.10: $C_i = \dfrac{1}{2}\begin{pmatrix} C_i n - 1 \\ \frac{C_i n}{2} - 1 \end{pmatrix}\left(\dfrac{1}{2}\right)^{C_i n - 1} = \left[\left(\dfrac{1}{2}\right)^{C_i n}\right]\dfrac{(C_i n - 1)!}{\left(\frac{C_i n}{2} - 1\right)!\left(\frac{C_i n}{2}\right)!}$.

7.11: $\dfrac{C_i}{B} = \dfrac{1}{2}\begin{pmatrix} C_i n - 1 \\ \frac{C_i n}{2} - 1 \end{pmatrix}\left(\dfrac{1}{2}\right)^{C_i n - 1} = \left[\left(\dfrac{1}{2}\right)^{C_i n}\right]\dfrac{(C_i n - 1)!}{\left(\frac{C_i n - 1}{2}\right)!\left(\frac{C_i n + 1}{2}\right)!}$.

Turnout does increase as B increases. The left-hand side decreases as B increases. An increase in C_i restores the equality by increasing the left-hand side and decreasing the right-hand side.

Chapter 8

8.1: (B,B;r,a′) and (S,S;a,r′).

8.2: For (B,B;r,a′), (p, $\frac{1}{2}$) for p ≥ $\frac{3}{5}$; for (S,S;a,r′), ($\frac{1}{2}$, 1).

8.3: a) If both types make small offers, the plaintiff's belief that the defendant is negligent after receiving a small offer is $\frac{3}{4}$. The defendant will reject a small offer with these beliefs.
b) [S,($\frac{1}{2}$S,$\frac{1}{2}$B);($\frac{3}{4}$a,$\frac{1}{4}$r),a′:$\frac{3}{5}$,1].

8.4: a) Any bill y with $|y| < |x_{SQ}|$. b) F always amends the bill to 0, F's ideal point. c) The bill reported does not matter. F always amends it to 0.

8.5: Outcome: ϵ. Both prefer another bill when $\epsilon < 0$ or $\epsilon > x_C$.

8.6: a) $-\epsilon$. b) No, separation is never incentive compatible for the committee. C prefers reporting a bill that leads F to think that $\epsilon = -(x_C - \epsilon)$. F adopts a bill of $x_C - \epsilon$ as its bill if it believes that $\epsilon = -(x_C - \epsilon)$, producing x_C as the final outcome.

8.7: a) $-\dfrac{x_i + x_{i+1}}{2}$. b) $4x_C = 2x_i - x_{i-1} - x_{i+1}$.

8.8: (5,5,5;a,a,a,a,a,a).

8.9: a) (7,7;a:p), with $p > \frac{2}{7}$. b) $\frac{6}{11} \leq \beta \leq 1$.

8.10: a)
1. Chance determines the buyer's payoffs with probability $\frac{1}{2}$ that $r_B = 6$ (the buyer is tough) and probability $r_B = 12$ (the seller is soft). Buyer (B) is informed of its payoffs.
2. B offers either a high (7) or low (5) price. Call this offer Ω_1.
3. Seller (S) updates its beliefs on B's type.
4. S accepts or rejects Ω_1. If accepted, game ends with $u_B = r_B - \Omega_1$ and $u_S = \Omega_1$.
5. If S rejects Ω_1, B offers Ω_2 with either a high (7) or low (5) price.
6. S accepts or rejects Ω_2. If accepted, payoffs are $u_B = \frac{3}{4}(r_B - \Omega_2)$ and $u_S = \frac{3}{4}\Omega_2$. If rejected, $u_B = 0$ and $u_S = 0$.

b) By dominance, S always accepts any high offer and any offer in the second round. Tough buyers always offer 5, and soft buyers offer 5 in the second round. You need specify just the soft buyer's offer in the first round, the seller's reaction to a low offer in the first round, and the seller's beliefs after receiving the first offer. With that specification, (5;a:$\frac{1}{2}$) is the perfect Bayesian equilibrium.

8.11: a) $x + a(c_n - \frac{1}{2}) > 1$. b) $x + \frac{1}{2}a > 1$. c) $a \geq 1$ and $\frac{1}{2}a \geq x \geq 1 - \frac{1}{2}a$. Reputation must have a high value; greater than the costs of intervening now for all Ds and at least twice as great as the value of the current crisis.

8.14: a) $2p + 0q + 12(1 - p - q) \geq 3$ for mixed strategy (p nf, q f, $1 - p - q$ \$). b) Yes. c) $p \leq .9$ d) f if $p < .5$, nf if $p > .5$; $p \leq .5$ e) If they eat quiche, T's belief that the patron is surly is 0, and so T always fights.

8.15: a) $c = 1$. b) $c_n = 1$. c) When $a \geq 1$ and $\frac{1}{2}a \geq x \geq 1 - \frac{1}{2}a$. These conditions are the same as those without the restrictions on beliefs. d) $c = 0$. e) $c_n = 0$. f) When $x < -\frac{1}{2}a$. The restriction on beliefs eliminates the nonintervention equilibrium when $-\frac{1}{2}a < x < \frac{1}{2}a$. The nonintervention equilibrium requires extraordinarily high costs for intervening in the initial crisis.

8.16: $\left(\frac{a^4}{a^4+1}\underline{1}, \frac{1}{a^4+1}\underline{2}\right)$ The probability that Player 1 sends $\underline{2}$ in the first round is lower than that in the second round by a factor of $\frac{a^2+1}{a^4+1} < 1$.

Chapter 9

9.1: a) $(\frac{2}{5}s_1, \frac{3}{5}s_2)$ produces $\underline{v}_1 = 3\frac{2}{5}$, $(\frac{1}{2}S_1, \frac{1}{2}S_2)$ produces $\underline{v}_2 = \frac{1}{2}$. b) s_2 produces $\underline{v}_1 = -2$, S_2 produces $\underline{v}_2 = -4$.

9.2: a) (x,y) such that $x > -2, y > -4, 4x + 9y \leq 73$, and $9x + 3y \leq 78$. b) (x,y) such that $x > 3\frac{2}{5}, y > \frac{1}{2}$, and $5x + 2y \leq 21$.

9.3: a) The stage game has three Nash equilibria, $(S_2; s_1)$, $(S_1; s_2)$, and $[(\frac{1}{5}S_1, \frac{4}{5}S_2); (\frac{1}{2}S_1, \frac{1}{2}S_2)]$. The two pure strategy equilibrium can only support themselves played every round. The mixed strategy Nash equilibrium can support any (x,y) such that $x > 2\frac{1}{2}, y > -2\frac{1}{5}$, $4x + 9y \leq 73$, and $9x + 3y \leq 78$. b) The stage game has one Nash equilibrium, $[(\frac{1}{2}S_1, \frac{1}{2}S_2); (\frac{2}{5}s_1, \frac{3}{5}s_2)]$. This Nash equilibrium can support any (x,y) such that $x > 3\frac{2}{5}, y > \frac{1}{2}$, and $5x + 2y \leq 21$.

9.5: (SO;f) is the only Nash equilibrium and the only perfect equilibrium.

9.8: a) $U^I = \dfrac{2B}{2 - \delta(1 + \ln\frac{1}{2})}$. b) The voter is better off. Benefits of office should be extended to individual officeholders rather than parties. Individual officeholders will work harder to retain office, which benefits the voter.

NOTES

Chapter Two

1. You have to keep the Bernoullis straight; as all the Kennedys seem to go into politics, all the Bernoullis were mathematicians.

2. The relation R is sometimes subscripted to identify which actor's preferences are represented. The greater-than-or-equal-to sign, $\geq$, is used occasionally in the place of R.

3. One of my friends in graduate school, a liberal Democrat, posed this choice to another friend, a conservative Republican. The latter friend preferred meat to anything from a plant and despised pears most of all. My first friend saw this choice as a way to find out how intensely my second friend hated the prospect of Teddy Kennedy's being elected president during the 1980 election. This choice was no simple matter for my second friend.

4. David Lalman of the University of Maryland thought up this example. This presentation is my version of his example.

5. You might want to kick the machine after hearing your friend's story. That action produces a different outcome, which may be satisfying in and of itself, but does not produce the desired drink.

6. For now, ignore the problems in mathematics in defining what an "infinite" quantity means. "Infinity" is a more subtle idea than it appears at first sight.

7. I choose world peace as the archetype of bliss because so many cars where I live in California bear the bumper sticker "Visualize World Peace." Others would disagree; some cars display the bumper sticker "Visualize Whirled Peas."

8. Comparative statics analysis commonly uses partial derivatives from multivariate calculus. See Appendix One for a brief explanation of partial derivatives.

9. Yes, Daniel Ellsberg of Pentagon Papers fame invented this paradox during his days at the Rand Corporation.

Chapter Three

1. Tic-tac-toe is a children's game played on a three-by-three matrix of cells. The players mark the cells alternately, one player using *X*s, the other, *O*s. Once one player marks a cell, that cell cannot be marked again. The first player who marks three cells in a row wins the game. If neither player marks three cells in a row before all the cells are marked, the game is a draw.

Chapter Four

1. Around the turn of the century there was a football play that was a pure strategy equilibrium for all situations, the flying wedge. The flying wedge consisted of a ball carrier surrounded by all his teammates. The teammates linked arms, and the mass attempted to bull its way through the defense. The optimal defensive response crowded all the defenders around the wedge and tried to bring the entire mass down. The result was an extremely violent game. The rules of football were changed to ban blockers from locking arms and to make forward passing feasible. The result of these changes was an extremely violent *strategic* game.

2. I am indebted to John Setear of the UCLA Law School for the suggestion to name the players Chris and Pat.

3. To be precise, the symmetric version of Battle of the Sexes has the players trying to coordinate on $(S_2;s_1)$ or $(S_1;s_2)$, with each player preferring coordination when it plays the first strategy.

4. Rationalizability is more complex in games with more than two players. See Fudenberg and Tirole 1991, 50–53.

5. See Geddes (1991) for the evidence supporting her hypotheses.

6. Does this sound familiar?

7. My cynicism about politics tells me it is safe to assume that Congress and the president will be negotiating over the deficit as long as this book is in print.

Chapter Five

1. Economists refer to this as "a cake of 100 units." Why do economists divide "cake" while political scientists wonder about how the "pie" will be split up?

2. Actually, the trick is not that simple if you are careful. A game with an infinite number of rounds is not well defined. There are ways to be careful about this, but we will charge in blindly where economists fear to tread. The basic idea here is correct.

3. The members could choose to divide less than the whole unit. But it is easy to show that the members will not leave any "pork" on the table because any proposal that does is dominated by a proposal that divides the entire unit.

4. If members always vote against proposals when they are indifferent between the current proposal and continuing the game, there is no equilibrium to the game. If a member i expects x_i from both the current proposal and continuing the game, it will vote for any proposal y with $y_i > x_i$. Because there is no smallest y_i here, there is no equilibrium. The proposer needs to give the indifferent voter a small concession to get him to vote for the proposal, and the smaller the concession, the better for the proposer. But there is no smallest concession possible, and so there is no equilibrium if indifferent voters vote against proposals. There are technical ways to fix this problem, but the assumption in the text is easier.

5. I say "an equilibrium" here to be careful. Any distribution can be supported in equilibrium in the open-ended game if we allow the members to use punishment strategies and the discount factors are large enough. Any member who fails to propose or vote for the chosen outcome is then stripped of benefits in the next and all future proposals. For more on the topic of what outcomes can be supported in equilibrium in open-ended iterated games, see Chapter Nine.

6. I believe the name *centipede game* comes from the 100-level version of the game. The resulting game tree does resemble a centipede.

Chapter Six

1. He proposed some other solutions, too, but I focus on the reciprocal fear of surprise attack.

Chapter Seven

1. There is a more careful way of solving the problem of correlated trembles by examining ϵ-perfect equilibria in the agent-strategic form of a game. The former requires ϵ-sized deviations from best replies, and the latter decomposes a game so that a different agent plays each information set for the moving player. See Fudenberg and Tirole 1991 (351–56) for the full story.

2. There is a technical way to say "almost all," which I avoid here. See Fudenberg and Tirole 1991 (355) for a technical statement of the relationship between sequential and perfect equilibrium.

3. Or when the challenger backs down against an irresolute defender. Misperception can cause peace as well as war.

4. This conclusion assumes that the benefits of determining the winning candidate exceed the costs of voting. Obviously, no one's voting is an equilibrium if the costs of voting exceed the benefits of determining the winning candidate for all voters.

5. It is extremely unlikely that $C_i n$ is an integer. Alternatively, round up $C_i n$ to the nearest integer. The case where $C_i n$ (or the next-greatest integer) is even is presented as an exercise.

6. John Ledyard (1984) reports that the 1983 election for the Board of Trustees of Pasadena Community College was tied after a recount. The law dictated that the trustee be selected by lot in case of a tie. Both candidates objected that drawing lots was undemocratic.

Chapter Eight

1. Of course, that does not mean they do not think they are experts on all issues.

2. Formally, compare the expected utility of y and x_{SQ}:

$$EU_F(y) = -\int_{-1}^{1} (y+\epsilon)^2\, d\epsilon = -(y+\epsilon)|_{-1}^{1}$$

$$= -(y+1)^3 + (y-1)^3 = -6y^2 - 2,$$

$$EU_F(x_{SQ}) = -\int_{-1}^{1} (x_{SQ}+\epsilon)^2\, d\epsilon = -6x_{SQ}^2 - 2.$$

F prefers y over x_{SQ} if $|y| < |x_{SQ}|$.

3. This statement is true because ϵ is uniformly distributed and distance from F's ideal point gives its preferences. Then all $x_0 \le \epsilon \le x_1$ are equally likely.

4. One can argue that challengers use incumbents' speeches against them in future election campaigns, creating a cost for speeches on the floor. Although some legislative speeches fall under this argument, many do not. I think this argument cannot explain all debate, so some falls into the area of cheap talk.

Chapter Nine

1. I capitalize these moves because I want to differentiate them from the general idea of defection and cooperation. By defection with a small d, I mean a player's deviating from its equilibrium strategy. By cooperation with a small c, I mean a relationship between the players that is mutually advantageous. Of course, Defect could be defection from an equilibrium, and Cooperate is generally part of a cooperative agreement. But confusing the moves with these more general ideas of cooperation and defection is sloppy. I also capitalize strategies of the repeated game (for example, Tit for Tat) for convenience.

2. I avoid the obvious religious parallels to the Grim Trigger.

3. Another solution to the Prisoner's Dilemma was suggested by Jung Joon, a formal theorist, after reading Axelrod (1984) on the repeated Prisoner's Dilemma—"If you take no prisoners, there is no dilemma." It should be kept in mind that not every situation that resembles a Prisoner's Dilemma actually is one.

4. There is another perfect Bayesian equilibrium in the Chain Store Paradox where punishing entry in the first round leads the second entrant to enter. Both sides acquiesce to entry to deter entry in the second round. This equilibrium parallels the quiche-eating equilibrium of the Beer-Quiche Game in Chapter Eight. Restrictions on beliefs off the equilibrium path also eliminate this equilibrium.

5. Of course, no politician lives forever; it only seems that way.

6. To be careful here, I note that it does not matter which politician is the incumbent because the two are identical. You could say that the rounds separate into two structurally identical classes, depending on which politician is the incumbent. The symmetry of the game dictates that they follow the same strategy when in office.

Appendix One

1. One wag has noted that in political science, the constants aren't and the variables don't.

2. Even if the idea of e seems completely unnatural to you, this notation does make sense.

3. Non-Euclidean geometries have propositions that strike one trained in Euclidean geometry as very strange. The sum of the angles in a triangle is 180 degrees in Euclidean geometry. In spherical geometry, the sum is always greater than 180 degrees. You can have a triangle in spherical geometry that has three right angles.

Appendix Two

1. The conclusions of this part of the exercise would be more persuasive if the change in resolve could be traced within one equilibrium of one model.

GLOSSARY OF TERMS IN GAME THEORY

This glossary provides informal statements of important terms in noncooperative game theory and utility theory. Please see the text for formal definitions and complete discussions of these terms.

Action: A possible choice within a game. *See also* BRANCH and MOVE.

Babbling equilibrium: An equilibrium of a cheap talk game where the signals convey no meaning.

Backwards induction: The process of solving a game of complete and perfect information by beginning with choice nodes that lead only to terminal nodes, and then working backwards through the tree to preceding nodes.

Bayes's Theorem: Theorem used for updating conditional probabilities after receiving new information. *See also* POSTERIOR BELIEFS; PRIOR BELIEFS.

Beliefs: A set of conditional probabilities on the nodes of a player's information set with multiple nodes. Beliefs summarize a player's judgment about what has probably happened up to that point in the game.

Best reply: The strategy that is always at least as good as any other for a player against a particular strategy of the other player. A **strict best reply** is a strategy that is always better than any other for the player.

Branch: An action that a player can take from one of its choice nodes. Branches connect nodes in a game tree, and represent moves in a game.

Chance (or Nature): Chance is considered a player that makes random moves in a game tree with known probabilities.

Cheap talk: A cost-free signal.

Common conjecture: The assumption that in equilibrium, the players correctly anticipate one another's strategies.

Common knowledge: Something is common knowledge if all actors know it, all know that all others know it, and so on ad infinitum.

Complete information: A game is played under complete information if all the players' payoffs are common knowledge. *See also* INCOMPLETE INFORMATION.

Completely mixed strategies: A set of strategies is completely mixed if all players have a nonzero probability of playing all actions at every information set.

Consequence: A possible final result of the actors' decisions. *See also* OUTCOME.

Consistent: A pair of beliefs and strategies is consistent if the beliefs are the limit of some sequence of the beliefs generated by a sequence of completely mixed strategies that converges to the strategies in the pair.

Continuation value: The players' expected payoffs for playing a game from a specified point on with given strategies.

Cooperative game: A game in which players can make binding agreements before and during the play of the game and communication between the players is allowed.

Discount factor: How much a decider prefers rewards now over rewards later. Typically written δ, with $0 < \delta < 1$.

Dominance solvable: A game is dominance solvable if each player has only one strategy left at the conclusion of an iterated dominance elimination procedure.
Dominant strategy: A player's strategy that strongly dominates all of its other strategies.
Dominant-strategy equilibrium: A set of strategies such that all players' strategies are dominant.
Equilibrium: *See specific types.*
Equilibrium path: *See* OFF THE EQUILIBRIUM PATH; ON THE EQUILIBRIUM PATH.
Equivalent strategies: Two strategies of a player are equivalent if they lead to the same outcomes for all pure strategies of the other players.
Event: A subset of the set of possible states of the world.
Expected utility: The sum across all possible outcomes of a decider's utility for each possible outcome times the probability of that outcome's occurring if a given action is chosen.
Extensive form: A formal description of a game with a finite set of moves. An extensive form requires a game tree, a partition of the players over the choice nodes of the tree, an assignment of outcomes to the terminal nodes, probability distributions for all chance moves, and utility functions for the players over the outcomes.
Feasible: A set of payoffs of a repeated game that is an average sum of the payoffs of a combination of outcomes in the stage game.
Game tree: A formal representation of the choices that players have in a game. A game tree consists of nodes connected by branches.
History (of a game up to that point): The complete sequence of moves that precedes a node.
Incentive compatibility: In a game of incomplete information, incentive compatibility exists when each type of player prefers sending the signal specified in an equilibrium over the signal sent by any other type.
Incomplete information: A game is played under incomplete information if some player's payoff is its private information. *See also* COMPLETE INFORMATION.
Indifference: An actor is indifferent between two outcomes if each outcome is at least as good as the other.
Individually rational: A set of payoffs of a repeated game where all players receive more than their minmax payoffs.
Information set: An information set connects nodes of one player and represents that player's inability to verify which node it is at when it must move from that information set.
Initial beliefs: *See* PRIOR BELIEFS.
Iterated dominance elimination procedure: A procedure that eliminates all strongly dominated strategies for both players, and then continues to eliminate any strategy that has become strongly dominated on the smaller set of remaining strategies. *See also* DOMINANCE SOLVABLE; RATIONALIZABLE; STRONGLY DOMINATES.
Iterated game: *See* REPEATED GAME.
Lottery: A matched set of probabilities and prizes where the probability of each prize specifies the chance of receiving that prize in the lottery. Lotteries represent choices formally.
Minmax payoff (or **minmax value**): The lowest payoff for a player that the other players can hold it to. *See also* MINMAX STRATEGY.

Minmax strategy: The strategy for other players that limits a player to its minmax payoff. *See also* MINMAX PAYOFF.

Mixed strategy: A probability distribution on the set of a player's pure strategies. *See also* PURE STRATEGY.

Move: An action that a player can take in a game. Moves are represented by branches in a game tree.

Mutual knowledge: Something is mutual knowledge if all players know it. *See also* COMMON KNOWLEDGE.

Nash equilibrium: A pair of strategies that are best replies to each other on the equilibrium path.

Node: A point where a move is made or an endpoint in a game. Moves are called **choice nodes** (or choice points), and endpoints are **terminal nodes**. Each choice node is assigned to one and only one player, including Chance as a player.

Noncooperative game: A game in which players cannot make binding agreements, although communication may or may not be allowed.

Off the equilibrium path: Choices that would not be made or nodes in the tree that would not be reached in an equilibrium are off the equilibrium path. *See also* ON THE EQUILIBRIUM PATH.

On the equilibrium path (or **along the equilibrium path**): Choices made or nodes in the tree reached in an equilibrium are on, or along, the equilibrium path. *See also* OFF THE EQUILIBRIUM PATH.

Ordinal preferences: *See* PREFERENCE ORDERING.

Outcome: A possible final result of the actors' decisions; *See also* CONSEQUENCE.

Pareto dominance: An outcome **Pareto dominates** another outcome if all players are at least as well off in the former outcome as in the latter and at least one player is better off. An outcome **strictly Pareto dominates** another outcome if all players are better off in the former than in the latter.

Payoff: A player's utility for an outcome of a game.

Perfect Bayesian equilibrium: A belief-strategy pair such that the strategies are sequentially rational given the beliefs and the beliefs are calculated from the equilibrium strategies by means of Bayes's Theorem whenever possible.

Perfect equilibrium: A set of strategies that are trembling-hand perfect when trembles are independent across the players' moves.

Perfect information: A game is played under perfect information if all information sets are singletons.

Perfect recall: The assumption that the players remember their prior moves and any information that they knew at an earlier node.

Pooling equilibrium: An equilibrium of a game of incomplete information where all player types play the same strategy. *See also* SEPARATING EQUILIBRIUM.

Posterior beliefs (or **posterior probabilities**): Subjective probabilities of each possible state of the world after including new information by means of Bayes's Theorem. *See also* PRIOR BELIEFS; UPDATING.

Predecessor (or **preceding node**): A node is a predecessor of another node if the former occurs before the latter in a game tree. A node is an **immediate predecessor** of another node if a branch leads from the former directly to the latter.

Preference ordering: Actors are assumed to hold a preference ordering over the outcomes of a game. Preference orderings are **complete** and **transitive**. Completeness requires that all outcomes can be compared; transitivity requires that if one outcome is preferred to a second and the second is preferred to a third, the first must be preferred to the third. A preference ordering leads to **ordinal preferences**.

Prior beliefs (or **prior probabilities;** also called **initial beliefs** or **initial probabilities**): Subjective probabilities of each possible state of the world before consideration of new information. *See also* POSTERIOR BELIEFS; UPDATING.

Private information: Any piece of information known to a player that is not common knowledge. *See also* TYPE.

Proper subgame: A part of a game beginning at one node and including all succeeding nodes that forms a game by itself.

Pure strategy: A strategy that does not include any probabilistic moves. *See also* MIXED STRATEGY.

Rationalizable: Any strategy that is left at the conclusion of an iterated dominance elimination procedure is rationalizable.

Repeated game (or **iterated game**): A game where the players play a game, called the stage game, repeatedly.

Security level: The minimum payoff a player can obtain from a strategy if it declares in advance that it will play that strategy.

Semiseparating equilibrium: An equilibrium of a game of incomplete information where the types neither pool nor separate. *See also* POOLING EQUILIBRIUM; SEPARATING EQUILIBRIUM.

Separating equilibrium: An equilibrium of a game of incomplete information where each type plays a different strategy. The receiver can tell what type of sender it is facing after observing a move. *See also* POOLING EQUILIBRIUM.

Sequential equilibrium: A set of beliefs and strategies that is both sequentially rational and consistent.

Sequential rationality: The condition that for a pair of beliefs and strategies, from every information set, the moving player maximizes its expected utility for the remainder of the game, using all players' strategies and beliefs. A belief-strategy pair is **sequentially rational** if it satisfies this condition.

Signal: A move in a game of incomplete information that may transmit information about the moving player's type.

Singleton: An information set containing only one node.

Stage (or **round**): One play of the stage game of a repeated game.

Stage game: Game played during each round of a repeated game.

State of the world (or **state**): In decision theory, the state of the world and the chosen action determine the outcome. A state of the world encompasses all relevant factors in the situation that are beyond the control of the decider.

Stationary equilibrium: An equilibrium where all players take the same action (including mixed strategies) in all structurally identical rounds.

Strategic form: An array of all the players' pure strategies, with each cell of the array filled with the players' utilities for the outcome that results from that combination of strategies.

Strategy: A complete plan to play the game for a player. A strategy must specify a move for each of the player's choice nodes in a game tree.

Strong preference relation: An actor strongly prefers one outcome to another if the first is better than the second. *See also* WEAK PREFERENCE RELATION

Strongly dominates (or **strictly dominates**): One strategy for a player strongly dominates another strategy if the former is always better for the player than the latter, no matter what the other players do. The latter strategy is **strongly dominated**. *See also* WEAKLY DOMINATES.

Structurally identical: Two rounds of a repeated game are structurally identical if the players have the same moves available in the same sequence with the same consequences, whether those consequences are final outcomes, stage payoffs, or further rounds of the game.

Subgame: *See* PROPER SUBGAME.

Subgame perfect: A set of strategies is subgame perfect if for every proper subgame, those strategies restricted to the subgame form a Nash equilibrium of that subgame.

Successor (or **succeeding node**): A node is a successor of another node if the former occurs after the latter in a game tree. A node is an **immediate successor** of another node if a branch leads from the latter directly to the former.

Symmetric game: A game is symmetric if it does not change when we relabel the players.

Time line form: A formal description of a game with an infinite, but well-specified, set of moves.

Trembling-hand perfect: A set of equilibrium strategies is trembling-hand perfect if it is robust against small chances of deviation from those strategies.

Type: A player's type in a game of incomplete information summarizes its private information.

Updating: Including new information to change prior beliefs into posterior beliefs, using Bayes's Theorem.

Utility function: A function that assigns a number to each possible outcome in order to represent an individual's preferences over the set of possible outcomes.

Value: A player's expected utility for playing a game, measured before the game begins.

Von Neumann–Morgenstern utility function: A utility function that represents a decider's willingness to take risks over the outcomes.

Weak preference relation: An actor weakly prefers one outcome to another if the first is at least as good as the second. *See also* STRONG PREFERENCE RELATION.

Weakly dominates: One strategy for a player weakly dominates another if the former is always at least as good as and sometimes better than the latter for the player, no matter what the other players do. The latter strategy is **weakly dominated**. *See also* STRONGLY DOMINATES.

Zero-sum game: Everything won by one player must be lost by another player in a zero-sum game.

BIBLIOGRAPHY

The asterisks after each listing provide ratings of the mathematical complexity of each cited work. Works with no asterisks are relatively simple and demand at most algebra to be understood. Those followed by one asterisk require either higher mathematics or else greater attention to the formal argument. Those followed by two asterisks are highly formal and require deliberate reading.

Ainsworth, Scott, and Itai Sened. 1993. "The Role of Lobbyists: Entrepreneurs with Two Audiences." *American Journal of Political Science* 37:834–66.*

Aldrich, John H. 1993. "Rational Choice and Turnout." *American Journal of Political Science* 37:246–78.

Alesina, Alberto, and Howard Rosenthal. 1989. "Partisan Cycles in Congressional Elections and the Macroeconomy." *American Political Science Review* 83:373–98.*

Allison, Graham. 1971. *Essence of Decision.* Boston: Little, Brown.

Alt, James E., Randall L. Calvert, and Brian Humes. 1988. "Reputation and Hegemonic Stability: A Game-Theoretic Analysis." *American Political Science Review* 82:445–66.*

Aumann, Robert and Adam Brandenburger. 1991. "Epistemic Conditions for Nash Equilibrium." Working Paper 91-042, Harvard Business School.

Austen-Smith, David. 1990. "Information Transmission in Debate." *American Journal of Political Science* 34:124–52.**

———. 1992. "Explaining the Vote: Constituency Constraints on Sophisticated Voting." *American Journal of Political Science* 36:68–95.**

———. 1993. "Information and Influence: Lobbying for Agendas and Votes." *American Journal of Political Science* 37:799–833.**

Austen-Smith, David, and Jeffrey Banks. 1988. "Elections, Coalitions, and Legislative Outcomes." *American Political Science Review* 82:405–22.**

———. 1989. "Electoral Accountability and Incumbency." In *Models of Strategic Choice in Politics,* ed. Peter C. Ordeshook. Ann Arbor: University of Michigan Press.**

———. 1990. "Stable Governments and the Allocation of Policy Portfolios." *American Political Science Review* 84:891–906.**

Austen-Smith, David, and William H. Riker. 1987. "Asymmetric Information and the Coherence of Legislation." *American Political Science Review* 81:897–918.**

———. 1990. "Asymmetric Information and the Coherence of Legislation: A Correction." *American Political Science Review* 84:243–45.*

Axelrod, Robert. 1984. *The Evolution of Cooperation.* New York: Basic Books.

Banks, Jeffrey S. 1989a. "Equilibrium Outcomes in Two-Stage Amendment Procedures." *American Journal of Political Science* 33:25–43.*

———. 1989b. "Agency Budgets, Cost Information, and Auditing." *American Journal of Political Science* 33:670–99.**

———. 1990. "Equilibrium Behavior in Crisis Bargaining Games." *American Journal of Political Science* 34:599–614.*

———. 1991. *Signaling Games in Political Science.* New York: Gordon Breach.*

Banks, Jeffrey S., and Joel Sobel. 1987. "Equilibrium Selection in Signaling Games." *Econometrica* 55:647–62.**

Banks, Jeffrey S., and Rangarajan Sundaram. 1990. "Repeated Games, Finite Automata, and Complexity." *Games and Economic Behavior* 2:97–117.**

Banks, Jeffrey S., and Barry R. Weingast. 1992. "The Political Control of Bureaucracies under Asymmetric Information." *American Journal of Political Science* 36:509–24.**

Baron, David P. 1989a. "A Noncooperative Theory of Legislative Coalitions." *American Journal of Political Science* 33:1048–84.**

———. 1989b. "Service-Induced Campaign Contributions, Incumbent Shirking, and Reelection Opportunities." In *Models of Strategic Choice in Politics*, ed. Peter C. Ordeshook. Ann Arbor: University of Michigan Press.**

———. 1991a. "A Spatial Bargaining Theory of Government Formation in Parliamentary Systems." *American Political Science Review* 85:137–64.**

———. 1991b. "Majoritarian Incentives, Pork Barrel Programs, and Procedural Control." *American Journal of Political Science* 35:57–90.**

———. 1993. "Government Formation and Endogenous Parties." *American Political Science Review* 87:34–47.*

Baron, David P., and John Ferejohn. 1989. "Bargaining in Legislatures." *American Political Science Review* 83:1181–1206.**

Bates, Robert H., and Da-Hsiang Donald Lien. 1985. "A Note on Taxation, Development, and Representative Government." *Politics and Society* 14:53–70.*

Bendor, Jonathan. 1987. "In Good Times and Bad: Reciprocity in an Uncertain World." *American Journal of Political Science* 31:531–58.*

Bendor, Jonathan, and Thomas H. Hammond. 1992. "Rethinking Allison's Models." *American Political Science Review* 86:301–22.

Bendor, Jonathan, and Dilip Mookherjee. 1987. "Institutional Structure and the Logic of Ongoing Collective Action." *American Political Science Review* 81:129–54.*

Bendor, Jonathan, Serge Taylor, and Roland Van Gaalen. 1987. "Politicians, Bureaucrats, and Asymmetric Information." *American Journal of Political Science* 31:796–828.*

Bianco, William T., and Robert H. Bates. 1990. "Cooperation By Design: Leadership Structure and Collective Dilemmas." *American Political Science Review* 84:133–47.*

Binmore, Ken. 1990. *Essays on the Foundations of Game Theory.* Cambridge, Mass.: Basil Blackwell.*

———. 1992. *Fun and Games: A Text on Game Theory.* Lexington, Mass.: D.C. Heath.*

Black, Duncan. 1958. *The Theory of Committees and Elections.* Cambridge: Cambridge University Press.

Brams, Steven J., and D. Marc Kilgour. 1988. *Game Theory and National Security.* New York: Basil Blackwell.*

Brandenburger, Adam. 1992. "Knowledge and Equilibrium in Games." *Journal of Economic Perspectives* 6:83–101.

Bueno de Mesquita, Bruce, and David Lalman. 1992. *War and Reason: Domestic and International Imperatives.* New Haven: Yale University Press.*

Calvert, Randall C. 1985. "The Value of Biased Information: A Rational Choice Model of Political Advice." *Journal of Politics* 47:530–55.*

——. 1987. "Reputation and Legislative Leadership." Public Choice 55:81–119.*
Cho, In-Koo, and David M. Kreps. 1987. "Signaling Games and Stable Equilibria." *Quarterly Journal of Economics* 102:179–222.**
Coughlin, Peter J. 1990. "Majority Rule and Election Models." *Journal of Economic Surveys* 3:157–88.
Cox, Gary W. 1990. "Centripetal and Centrifugal Incentives in Electoral Systems." *American Journal of Political Science* 34:903–35.*
Crawford, Vincent P., and Hans Haller. 1990. "Learning How to Cooperate: Optimal Play in Repeated Coordination Games." *Econometrica* 58:571–95.**
Davis, Morton D. 1983. *Game Theory: A Non-Technical Introduction.* New York: Basic Books.
DeGroot, Morris H. 1970. *Optimal Statistical Decisions.* New York: McGraw Hill.**
Dixit, Avinash, and Barry Nalebuff. 1991. *Thinking Strategically: The Competitive Edge in Business, Politics, and Everyday Life.* New York: Norton.
Downs, Anthony. 1957. *An Economic Theory of Democracy.* New York: Harper and Row.
Downs, George W., and David M. Rocke. 1990. *Tacit Bargaining, Arms Races, and Arms Control.* Ann Arbor: University of Michigan Press.*
Eatwell, John, Murray Milgate, and Peter Newman, eds. 1989. *The New Palgrave*: Vol. 8, *Game Theory.* New York: Norton.
——, eds. 1990. *The New Palgrave:* Vol. 9, *Utility and Probability.* New York: Norton.
Ellsberg, Daniel. 1960. "The Crude Analysis of Strategic Choices." RAND Monograph P-2183, The RAND Corporation.
Enelow, James M., and Melvin J. Hinich. 1984. *The Spatial Theory of Voting: An Introduction.* New York: Cambridge University Press.*
——, eds. 1990. *Advances in the Spatial Theory of Voting.* Cambridge: Cambridge University Press.**
Epstein, David, and Sharyn O'Halloran. 1993. "Interest Group Oversight, Information, and the Design of Administrative Procedures." Presented at the annual meeting of the American Political Science Association, Washington, D.C.*
Farquharson, Robin. 1969. *Theory of Voting.* New Haven: Yale University Press.*
Farrell, Joseph. 1987. "Cheap Talk, Coordination, and Entry." *Rand Journal of Economics* 19:34–39.*
Farrell, Joseph, and Robert Gibbons. 1989. "Cheap Talk Can Matter in Bargaining." *Journal of Economic Theory* 48:221–37.**
Fearon, James. 1994. "Signaling versus the Balance of Power and Interests." *Journal of Conflict Resolution,* 38:236–69.
Ferejohn, John. 1986. "Incumbent Performance and Electoral Control." *Public Choice* 50:5–25.**
Friedman, James W. 1990. *Game Theory with Applications to Economics.* 2d ed. New York: Oxford University Press.**
Fudenberg, Drew, and David K. Levine. 1993. "Steady State Learning and Nash Equilibrium." *Econometrica* 61:547–73.**
Fudenberg, Drew, and Eric Maskin. 1986. "The Folk Theorem in Repeated Games with Discounting or with Incomplete Information." *Econometrica* 54:533–54.**
Fudenberg, Drew, and Jean Tirole. 1991. *Game Theory.* Cambridge: MIT Press.**

Geanakoplos, John. 1992. "Common Knowledge." *Journal of Economic Perspectives* 6,4:53–82.

Geddes, Barbara. 1991. "A Game Theoretic Model of Reform in Latin American Democracies." *American Political Science Review* 85:371–92.

Gibbons, Robert. 1992. *Game Theory for Applied Economists.* Princeton: Princeton University Press.*

Gilligan, Thomas W., and Keith Krehbiel. 1987. "Collective Decision-Making and Standing Committees: An Informational Rationale for Restrictive Amendment Procedures." *Journal of Law, Economics, and Organization* 3:287–335.*

———. 1989. "Asymmetric Information and Legislative Rules with a Heterogenous Committee." *American Journal of Political Science* 33:459–90.**

———. 1990. "Organization of Informative Committees by a Rational Legislature." *American Journal of Political Science* 34:531–64.**

Greenberg, Joseph. 1989. *The Theory of Social Situations: An Alternative Game-Theoretic Approach.* New York: Cambridge University Press.**

Greenberg, Joseph, and Kenneth Shepsle. 1987. "The Effect of Electoral Rewards in Multiparty Competition with Entry." *American Political Science Review* 81:525–37.**

Hammond, Thomas H., and Gary J. Miller. 1987. "The Core of the Constitution." *American Political Science Review* 81:1155–74.*

Harsanyi, John C. 1967–1968. "Games with Incomplete Information Played by Bayesian Players," Parts 1–3. *Management Science* 14:159–82, 320–34, 486–502.**

———. 1977. *Rational Behavior and Bargaining Equilibrium in Games and Social Situations.* New York: Cambridge University Press.**

Harsanyi, John C., and Reinhart Selten. 1988. *A General Theory of Equilibrium Selection.* Cambridge: MIT Press.**

Huber, John D. 1992. "Restrictive Legislative Procedures in France and the United States." *American Political Science Review* 86:675–87.

Iida, Keisuke. 1993. "When and How Do Domestic Constraints Matter? Two-Level Games with Uncertainty." *Journal of Conflict Resolution* 37:403–26.*

Jackman, Robert. 1993. "Rationality and Political Participation." *American Journal of Political Science* 37:279–90.

Johnson, James. 1993. "Is Talk Really Cheap? Prompting Conversation between Critical Theory and Rational Choice." *American Political Science Review* 87:74–86.

Kahneman, Daniel, and Amos Tversky. 1979. "Prospect Theory: An Analysis of Decision Under Risk." *Econometrica* 47:263–91.*

Kalai, Ehud, and Ehud Lehrer. 1993. "Rational Learning Leads to Nash Equilibrium." *Econometrica* 61:1019–45.**

Kennan, John, and Robert Wilson. 1993. "Bargaining with Private Information." *Journal of Economic Literature* 31:45–104.*

Kilgour, D. Marc. 1991. "Domestic Political Structure and War: A Game-Theoretic Approach." *Journal of Conflict Resolution* 35:266–84.*

Kilgour, D. Marc, and Steven J. Brams. 1992. "Putting the Other Side 'On Notice' Can Induce Compliance in Arms Control." *Journal of Conflict Resolution* 36:395–414.*

Kilgour, D. Marc, and Frank C. Zagare. 1991. "Credibility, Uncertainty, and Deterrence." *American Journal of Political Science* 35:305–34.*

Kim, Woosang, and James D. Morrow. 1992. "When Do Power Shifts Lead to War?" *American Journal of Political Science* 36:896–922.*

Kohlberg, Elon, and Jean-Francois Mertens. 1986. "On the Strategic Stability of Equilibria." *Econometrica* 54:1003–37.*

Kollman, Ken, John H. Miller, and Scott E. Page. 1992. "Adaptive Parties in Spatial Elections." *American Political Science Review* 86:929–37.

Krehbiel, Keith. 1988. "Models of Legislative Choice." *Legislative Studies Quarterly* 13:259–319.*

———. 1990. "Are Congressional Committees Composed of Preference Outliers?" *American Political Science Review* 84:149–64.

———. 1991. *Information and Legislative Organization.* Ann Arbor: University of Michigan Press.

Kreps, David M. 1990a. *A Course in Microeconomic Theory.* Princeton: Princeton University Press.*

———. 1990b. *Game Theory and Economic Modelling.* New York: Oxford University Press.

———. 1990c. "Corporate Culture and Economic Theory." In *Perspectives on Positive Political Economy,* ed. James E. Alt and Kenneth A. Shepsle. New York: Cambridge University Press.

Kreps, David M., Paul Milgrom, John Roberts, and Robert Wilson. 1982. "Rational Cooperation in the Finitely Repeated Prisoners' Dilemma." *Journal of Economic Theory* 27:245–53.*

Kreps, David M., and Robert Wilson. 1982a. "Sequential Equilibria." *Econometrica* 50:863–94.**

———. 1982b. "Reputation and Imperfect Information." *Journal of Economic Theory* 27: 253–79.**

Kuran, Timur. 1991. "Now Out of Never: The Element of Surprise in the East European Revolution of 1989." *World Politics* 44:7–48.

Langlois, Jean-Pierre P. 1991. "Rational Deterrence and Crisis Stability." *American Journal of Political Science* 35:801–32.**

Laver, Michael, and Norman Schofield. 1990. *Multiparty Government: The Politics of Coalitions in Europe.* New York: Oxford University Press.

Laver, Michael, and Kenneth A. Shepsle. 1990. "Coalitions and Cabinet Government." *American Political Science Review* 84:873–90.*

Lebow, Richard Ned. 1981. *Between Peace and War: The Nature of International Crises.* Baltimore: Johns Hopkins University Press.

Ledyard, John O. 1984. "The Pure Theory of Large Two-Candidate Elections." *Public Choice* 44:7–41.**

Lohmann, Suzanne. 1993. "A Signaling Model of Informative and Manipulative Political Action." *American Political Science Review* 87: 319–33.**

Luce, R. Duncan, and Howard Raiffa. 1957. *Games and Decisions.* New York: John Wiley.*

Lupia, Arthur. 1992. "Busy Voters, Agenda Control, and the Power of Information." *American Political Science Review* 86:390-403.*

Machina, Mark J. 1987. "Choice Under Uncertainty: Problems Solved and Unsolved." *Journal of Economic Perspectives* 1:121–54.

——. 1989. "Dynamic Consistency and Non-Expected Utility Model of Choice under Uncertainty." *Journal of Economic Literature* 27:1622–68.*

Mailath, George J. 1992. "Introduction: Symposium on Evolutionary Game Theory." *Journal of Economic Theory* 57:259–77.*

Martin, Lisa L. 1993. "Credibility, Costs, and Institutions: Cooperation on Economic Sanctions." *World Politics* 45:406–32.

Maynard Smith, John. 1982. *Evolution and the Theory of Games*. Cambridge: Cambridge University Press.*

McKelvey, Richard D. 1976. "Intransitivities in Multidimensional Voting Models and Some Implications for Agenda Control." *Journal of Economic Theory* 12:472–82.**

McKelvey, Richard D., and Peter C. Ordeshook. 1985. "Elections with Limited Information: A Fulfilled Expectations Model using Contemporaneous Poll and Endorsement Data as Information Sources." *Journal of Economic Theory* 36:55–85.**

McKelvey, Richard D., and Raymond Riezman. 1992. "Seniority in Legislatures." *American Political Science Review* 86:951-65.**

Milgrom, Paul, and John Roberts. 1982. "Predation, Reputation, and Entry Deterrence." *Journal of Economic Theory* 27:280–312.**

Morrow, James D. 1989. "Capabilities, Uncertainty, and Resolve: A Limited Information Model of Crisis Bargaining." *American Journal of Political Science* 33:941–72.*

——. "Electoral and Congressional Incentives and Arms Control." *Journal of Conflict Resolution* 35:245–65.*

——. 1992. "Signaling Difficulties with Linkage in Crisis Bargaining." *International Studies Quarterly* 36:153–72.*

——. 1994a. "Modelling the Forms of International Cooperation: Distribution Versus Information." *International Organization,* 48:387–423.*

——. 1994b. "Alliances, Credibility, and Peacetime Costs." *Journal of Conflict Resolution,* 38:270–97.*

Myerson, Roger B. 1991. *Game Theory: Analysis of Conflict*. Cambridge: Harvard University Press.**

Myerson, Roger B., and Robert J. Weber. 1993. "A Theory of Voting Equilibria." *American Political Science Review* 87:102–14.*

Nalebuff, Barry. 1991. "Rational Deterrence in an Imperfect World." *World Politics* 43:313–35.*

Niou, Emerson M. S., and Peter C. Ordeshook. 1990. "Stability in Anarchic International Systems." *American Political Science Review* 84:1207–34.**

Niou, Emerson M. S., Peter C. Ordeshook, and Gregory F. Rose. 1989. *The Balance of Power: Stability in International Systems*. New York: Cambridge University Press.*

O'Neill, Barry. 1992. "A Survey of Game Theory Models of Peace and War." In *Handbook of Game Theory,* Vol. 2, ed. Robert Aumann and Sergiu Hart. New York: Springer-Verlag.

Ordeshook, Peter C. 1986. *Game Theory and Political Theory*. New York: Cambridge University Press.*

——. 1992. *A Political Theory Primer*. New York: Routledge.*

Ordeshook, Peter C., and Thomas R. Palfrey. 1988. "Agendas, Strategic Voting, and Signaling with Incomplete Information." *American Journal of Political Science* 32:441–66.**

Ordeshook, Peter C., and Thomas Schwartz. 1987. "Agendas and the Control of Political Outcomes." *American Political Science Review* 81:179–99.**

Owen, Guillermo. 1982. *Game Theory.* 2d ed. New York: Academic Press.**

Palfrey, Thomas R. 1989. "A Mathematical Proof of Duverger's Law." In *Models of Strategic Choice,* ed. Peter C. Ordeshook. Ann Arbor: University of Michigan Press.**

Palfrey, Thomas R., and Howard Rosenthal. 1985. "Voter Participation and Strategic Uncertainty." *American Political Science Review* 79:62–78.**

Pool, Jonathan. 1991. "The Official Language Problem." *American Political Science Review* 85:495–514.*

Powell, Robert. 1990. *Nuclear Deterrence Theory: The Search for Credibility.* New York: Cambridge University Press.**

———. 1991. "Absolute and Relative Gains in International Relations Theory." *American Political Science Review* 85:1303–20.

———. 1993. "Guns, Butter, and Anarchy." *American Political Science Review* 87:115–32.**

Putnam, Robert D. 1988. "Diplomacy and Domestic Politics: The Logic of Two-level Games." *International Organization* 42:427–60.

Quattrone, George A., and Amos Tversky. 1988. "Contrasting Rational and Psychological Analyses of Political Choice." *American Political Science Review* 82: 719–36.

Rasmusen, Eric. 1989. *Games and Information: An Introduction to Game Theory.* Cambridge, Mass.: Basil Blackwell.*

Reny, Philip J. 1992. "Rationality in Extensive-Form Games." *Journal of Economic Perspectives* 6:103–18.

Riker, William H. 1990. "Political Science and Rational Choice." In *Perspectives on Positive Political Economy,* ed. James E. Alt and Kenneth A. Shepsle. New York: Cambridge University Press.

Riker, William H., and Peter C. Ordeshook. 1968. "The Calculus of Voting." *American Political Science Review* 62:25–42.

———. 1973. *An Introduction to Positive Political Theory.* Englewood Cliffs, N.J.: Prentice-Hall.

Rubinstein, Ariel. 1982. "Perfect Equilibrium in a Bargaining Model." *Econometrica* 50:97–109.**

Savage, Leonard J. 1972. *The Foundations of Statistics.* 2d ed. New York: Dover.**

Schelling, Thomas C. 1960. *The Strategy of Conflict.* New York: Oxford University Press.

Schofield, Norman. 1976. "Instability of Simple Dynamic Games." *Review of Economic Studies* 45:575–94.**

Selten, Reinhart. 1975. "Reexamination of the Perfectness Concept for Equilibrium Points in Extensive Games." *International Journal of Game Theory* 4:25–55.**

———. 1978. "The Chain-Store Paradox." *Theory and Decision* 9:127–159.*

———. 1991. "Evolution, Learning, and Economic Behavior." *Games and Economic Behavior* 3:3–24.

Shepsle, Kenneth A. 1979. "Institutional Arrangements and Equilibrium in Multidimensional Voting Models." *American Journal of Political Science* 23: 27–59.*

Shepsle, Kenneth A., and Barry R. Weingast. 1984. "Uncovered Sets and Sophisticated Voting Outcomes with Implications for Agenda Institutions." *American Journal of Political Science* 28:49–74.**

———. 1987. "The Institutional Foundations of Committee Power." *American Political Science Review* 81:85–104.*

———. 1994. "Positive Theories of Congressional Institutions." *Legislative Studies Quarterly,* forthcoming.

Shubik, Martin. 1982. *Game Theory in the Social Sciences.* 2 vols. Cambridge: MIT Press.**

Simon, Herbert A. 1955. "A Behavioral Model of Rational Choice." *Quarterly Journal of Economics* 69:99–118.

Snyder, James M. 1990. "Resource Allocation in Multiparty Elections." *American Journal of Political Science* 34:59–73.**

———. 1992. "Artificial Extremism in Interest Group Ratings." *Legislative Studies Quarterly* 17:319–45.

Sugden, Robert. 1989. "Spontaneous Order." *Journal of Economic Perspectives* 3,4:85–97.

Sullivan, Terry. 1990. "Bargaining with the President: A Simple Game and New Evidence." *American Political Science Review* 84:1167–95.

Sutton, John. 1986. "Non-Cooperative Bargaining Theory: An Introduction." *Review of Economic Studies* 53:709–24.

Taylor, Michael. 1976. *Anarchy and Cooperation.* New York: John Wiley.

———. 1987. *The Possibility of Cooperation.* Cambridge: Cambridge University Press.

Tirole, Jean. 1988. *The Theory of Industrial Organization.* Cambridge: MIT Press.**

Tsebelis, George. 1990. *Nested Games.* Berkeley: University of California Press.

Tversky, Amos, and Daniel Kahneman. 1981. "The Framing of Decisions and the Psychology of Choice." *Science* 211:453–58.

Vanberg, Victor J., and Roger D. Congleton. 1992. "Rationality, Morality, and Exit." *American Political Science Review* 86:418–31.

Von Neumann, John, and Oskar Morgenstern. [1943] 1953. *Theory of Games and Economic Behavior.* 3d ed. New York: John Wiley.**

Wagner, R. Harrison. 1983. "The Theory of Games and the Problem of International Cooperation." *American Political Science Review* 77:330–46.

———. 1986. "The Theory of Games and the Balance of Power." *World Politics* 38:546–76.

———. 1989. "Uncertainty, Rational Learning, and Bargaining in the Cuban Missile Crisis." In *Models of Strategic Choice in Politics,* ed. Peter C. Ordeshook. Ann Arbor: University of Michigan Press.

———. 1991. "Nuclear Deterrence, Counterforce Strategies, and the Incentive to Strike First." *American Political Science Review* 85:727–50.*

Wallerstein, Michael. 1989. "Union Organization in Advanced Industrial Democracies." *American Political Science Review* 83:481–501.*

———. 1990. "Centralized Bargaining and Wage Restraint." *American Journal of Political Science* 34:982–1004.**

Weingast, Barry R. 1989. "Floor Behavior in the U.S. Congress: Committee Power under the Open Rule." *American Political Science Review* 83:795–815.*

Wilson, Robert. 1985. "Reputations in Games and Markets." In *Game Theoretic Models of Bargaining,* ed. Alvin E. Roth. New York: Cambridge University Press.*

Wittman, Donald. 1989. "Arms Control Verification and Other Games Involving Imperfect Detection." *American Political Science Review* 83:923–48.*

Young, H. Peyton. 1993. "The Evolution of Conventions." *Econometrica* 61:57–84.**

Zagare, Frank C. 1990. "Rationality and Deterrence." *World Politics* 42:238–60.

Zermelo, E. 1913. "Über eine Anwendung der Mengenlehre auf die theorie des Schachspiels." *Proceedings of the Fifth International Congress of Mathematicians* 2:501–4.

INDEX

Numbers in boldface indicate the page where the definition of the indexed term or the statement of the indexed theorem is given.